the illustrated
NEW CONCISE
JEWISH ENCYCLOPEDIA

the illustrated
NEW CONCISE
JEWISH ENCYCLOPEDIA

by
ABRAHAM BURSTEIN

revised edition edited by
ROBERT MILCH

picture editor

JANET SCHARFSTEIN

KTAV PUBLISHING HOUSE INC.

Library of Congress Cataloging in Publication Data

Burstein, Abraham, 1893-1966 ed.
   The illustrated new concise Jewish encyclopedia.

   Published in 1962 under title: A new concise Jewish
encyclopedia.
   1. Jews—Dictionaries and encyclopedias. I. Milch,
Robert. II. Title.
DS102.8.B8   1978   909′.04′924   78-8334
ISBN 0-87068-635-6

AARON

Elder brother of Moses; ancestor of the *Cohanim* (priests), Moses' spokesman before Pharaoh. After the revelation at Mount Sinai, Aaron was chosen the first High Priest of Israel. He was succeeded by his son Eleazar.

Traditional tomb of Aaron.

AARON OF LINCOLN

(1123-1185)—Probably the richest Englishman of his day, Aaron had financial dealings with many of the leading nobles and churchmen; a number of abbeys and cathedrals were built with money lent by him. A special branch of the *t*reasury was created to deal with the large fortune which fell to the Crown upon his death.

ABBA AREKHA

One of the most important Babylonian scholars (about 175-247 C.E.), given the honorary title of Rav (master, teacher), founder of the academy of Sura. He and his colleague and friend, Mar Samuel, helped develop the Babylonian Talmud *(Gemara)* and established Babylonia as an important center of Jewish life. As a youth Rav studied in Palestine with Judah Hanasi at the time when Judah was finishing the Mishnah. Rav made brilliant contributions to the Babylonian Gemara. He composed many prayers, among them the *Alenu* and the Rosh Hodesh blessings. Abba Arekha means Abba the Tall.

See also Mar Samuel.

ABBA SIKRA (or Sakkara)

Nephew of Rabbi Johanan ben Zakkai, Abba Sikra was a leader of the *Sicarii,* a group of dagger-bearing terrorists, during the revolt against Rome in 69-70 C.E. When the Rabbi wished to escape from besieged Jerusalem in order to found an Academy in Jabneh, he had Abba Sikra escort him, hidden in a coffin, through the city gates.

ABBAYE

(278-38)—Babylonian Amora, dean of the Pumpadita Academy. A wine dealer by profession, he would turn to popular custom when rendering a decision on doubtful cases. The development of Talmudic argument and reasoning reached its peak in his discussions with Rava. The Midrash, too, was enriched by his alert intellect which emphasized the importance of peace, the love of God and the study of the Torah.

See also Amora

ABDON

Of the tribe of Ephraim; one of the Judges of Israel. He judged for eight years.

ABDULLAH

(1882-1951)—King of Transjordan until his assassination, Abdullah was the most moderate of the Arab leaders with regard to Zionism and Israel. Despite his apparent willingness to negotiate with Chaim Weizmann in 1922, he invaded Israel in 1948. He was assassinated in Jerusalem at the instigation of those Arabs who favored a more uncompromising policy towards the Jews.

ABEL

Younger son of Adam and Eve. He was killed by Cain, his angry brother.

ABIJAH

Also called Abijam, second king of Judah (about 920-917 B.C.E.), son of Rehoboam. Abijah took the territory of Benjamin from the Kingdom of Israel and made it part of the Kingdom of Judah.

ABIMELECH

Son of Gideon (Jerubbaal) the Judge. He tried unsuccessfully to establish a monarchy when he proclaimed himself king of Israel and selected Shechem as his capital. The tyrannical Abimelech killed 70 of his brothers; only the youngest escaped. He ruled only three years and died ingloriously when, in his siege of Thebez, a millstone shattered his skull.

ABOAB, ISAAC DE FONSECA

(d. 1693)—First rabbi in the Western Hemisphere. He was born in Portugal, a Marrano, and taken to Holland when still a child. He entered the service of the Amsterdam community at 21. In 1642 he went to Recife in Brazil, as a rabbi. When Recife was recaptured from the Dutch by the Portuguese in 1654, the Jews fled, Aboab among them. Returning to Amsterdam, he was appointed *Haham* (Rabbi) and served as head of the religious academy. He was a member of the tribunal which excommunicated Spinoza in 1656. He became famous for his preaching and was instrumental in helping to persuade the wealthy members of the community to build the Amsterdam Great Synagogue.

Brass plate with scene of Abraham sacrificing Isaac.

ABRAHAM

Son of Terah; first of the Patriarchs, father of the Jewish people, the first man to believe in the One God and His sovereignty over the whole world. After God made the first covenant with Abraham, he and his wife, Sarah, went to Canaan, the land God had promised him. They had one son, Isaac. Hagar bore Abraham's other son, Ishmael. Abraham, who was born in Ur of the Chaldees, was buried in the Cave of Machpelah.

ABRAHAM, KARL

(1877-1925)—German pioneer in the science of psychoanalysis. Abraham served as president of the International Psychoanalytic Association.

ABRAHAMS, ISRAEL

(1858-1925)—British Hebraic scholar. Abrahams was a leader of Liberal Judaism in England, and founded, with Claude Montefiore, the *Jewish Quarterly Review* in 1888. In 1902 he was appointed reader in Talmudic and Rabbinic Literature at Cambridge University. Among his works are *Jewish Life in the Middle Ages*, and *Hebrew Ethical Wills*, which he edited.

ABRAM

Name of Abraham before God made His covenant with him.

See also Abraham.

ABRAVANEL, DON ISAAC

(1437-1508)—The scholar and statesman who attempted to prevent the expulsion of the Jews from Spain in 1492. He was prepared to ransom them all, but the fanatical Torquemada, chief inquisitor, prevailed upon Ferdinand and Isabella to carry out their decree. Abravanel, born in Portugal, was appointed royal treasurer by Alfonso V. He used his position and wealth to ransom Jews captured by the Moors; perhaps this forced him to flee Portugal after Alfonso died. In Spain he became a tax collector for Queen Isabella of Castile. Though he received assurances that the order of expulsion would not apply to his family, Abravanel and his sons migrated to Naples, where he was also pressed into the king's service. He finally settled in Venice. Despite all hardships and wanderings, he found time to write many scholarly works. Because of the difficult times through which he and his people were passing, Abravanel kept reckoning the date when the Messiah would appear. Three of his books treat confidently of the coming saving of Israel and of all mankind.

ABRAVANEL, JUDAH

(about 1460-1521)—Italian humanist philosopher, known variously as Leone Ebreo (Italian) and Leo Hebraeus (Latin). The son of Don Isaac Abravanel, Judah was a doctor by profession and also wrote poetry. He was the author of one of the first books of philosophy to be written in the Italian language, *Dialoghi d'Amore* ("Dialogues on Love"). Though rarely read by Jews, this book had great influence on 16th century European thought and literature.

ABSALOM

Son of King David; famed for his beauty and abundant hair. He tried to overthrow his father, but his revolt failed. He was caught when his hair became entangled in the branches of a tree. Absalom was killed by David's general, Joab, despite David's orders to deal gently with him.

ABULAFIA, ABRAHAM BEN SAMUEL

(1241-c. 1291) — Spanish Kabbalist who attempted to convert Pope Nicholas III to Judaism and was saved from the stake only by the Pope's death. He announced himself the herald of the coming Messiah, but was forced to stop "prophesying" by the community in Palermo, which was aroused by the letters of Rabbi Solomon ben Abraham Adret. The Kabbalistic school which he founded strove to attain spiritual contact with God through the mystical values of letter (Gematria).

See also Gematria.

ABYSSINIA (Ethiopia)

Country in northeast Africa, whose royal house claims descent from King Solomon and the Queen of Sheba. Many Jewish elements are found in the ritual of the Abyssinian Church.

See also Falashas.

ACADEMIES, BABYLONIAN

The great schools where the Babylonian Talmud

was compiled. The three most important were located at Nehardea, Sura and Pumpadita.

See *also* Babylonia.

ACADEMIES, PALESTINIAN

The great schools in Palestine where the Mishnah was evolved and the Palestinian Talmud was compiled. The most important were located at Javneh, Bet-Shearim, Lydda, Tiberias, Sepphoris, Usha and Caesarea.

ACCENTS

(Heb., *te'amin, neginot*)—Notation system in Hebrew Bible indicating both punctuation and musical symbols. Accents denote divisions of sentences and indicate stress. Divided into *melakhim* (disjunctive accents) which indicate different degrees of pause, and *mesharetim* (conjunctive signs), indicating absence of pause. As musical notations, accents signify a certain grouping of notes. The kind of chant produced is called cantillation. Historians attribute both vocalization and accentuation to Ezra. The written signs date from the second half of the first millennium C.E. There are three systems of vocalization—Babylonian, Palestinian and Tiberian—each having its corresponding systems of accents. Today, the system generally adhered to is the Tiberian, having both disjunctive and conjunctive accents.

See *also* Tropp.

ACHRON, JOSEPH

(1886-1943)—Musician. Achron, first a violin virtuoso, later devoted himself to composing. Many of his works have Jewish motifs, such as "Dance of the Tsaddikim" and "Salome," which was produced at the Metropolitan Opera House in New York (1925.

ACOSTA, URIEL

(1585-1640)—Though born a Jew, Acosta was brought up and educated in the Catholic faith. His doubts concerning Christianity led him to flee to Amsterdam in 1615 where he declared his belief in Judaism. He conceived of Judaism, however, in an abstract and rationalistic sense which differed sharply with traditional teachings. This brought him into conflict with the Jewish community, finally culminating in his excommunication. In 1640 he submitted to the community's demands and formally accepted the traditional teachings but the public ceremony so humiliated him that he committed suicide immediately afterward. In many respects Acosta was a precursor of Spinoza.

ACRE

Israel city on northern tip of Haifa Bay. It was never conquered in the original conquest of Palestine by Joshua nor could the Hasmoneans take it. Till medieval times it was an important port and at one time was the Crusader capital of the country. The Arab population of 12,000 fled the city at the beginning of the Israel War of Independence (1948) and though some returned, Acre is a Jewish city today.

A view of the Crusader wall in Acre.

ADAM AND EVE

As related in the Book of Genesis, the first man and woman created by God; parents of Cain, Abel and Seth. After eating the forbidden fruit of the tree of knowledge of good and evil, they were driven from the Garden of Eden and were forced to toil for their daily bread.

ADAMS, FRANKLIN PIERCE

("F.P.A.") (1881-1960)—American journalist. Wrote a famous newspaper column, *The Conning Tower*, which was known for its humor and wit, as was his *Diary of Our Own Samuel Pepys*. In 1938, he became a panelist on the "Information Please" radio program.

ADAR

Twelfth month in the Jewish calendar.

See *also* Calendar, Jewish; Months, Jewish.

ADAR SHENI

The month that is added to the Jewish calendar in leap years. It contains 29 days and is inserted after the month of Adar, before the month of Nisan. It is also called Veadar.

See *also* Calendar, Jewish; Months, Jewish.

ADLER, CYRUS

(1863-1940)—Scholar and leader of Conservative Judaism in United States; served as president of American Jewish Historical Society, Librarian of the

Smithsonian Institute, president of Dropsie College and of the Jewish Theological Seminary of America. Adler was a great influence in Jewish communal and cultural activities.

ADLER, JULIUS OCHS

(1892-1955)—Newspaperman. Upon graduation from Princeton in 1914, he joined the staff of the *New York Times,* whose general manager he became in 1935. In 1954 he became first vice-president of the paper. Adler was also president and publisher of the *Chattanooga Times* from 1935 until his death. He had a distinguished military record, and was appointed major general in 1948.

ADLER, LARRY

(1914-   )—Great American harmonica artist. Though a popular musician, he has maintained extremely high artistic standards, and noted composers have written for him.

ADLER, YANKEL

(1895-1949)—Painter. Adler was born in Lodz, Poland, but finally settled in England. His paintings, many of which deal with Jewish subjects, hang in museums and galleries in many countries.

An adloyada parade in Israel.

ADLOYADA

Today in Israel, the Adloyada Purim Carnival has been revived. The name itself stems from a Talmudic saying that one should drink on Purim until one is unable to know the difference *(ad d'lo yada)* between *"barukh Mordecai"* ("blessed be Mordecai") and *"arur Haman"* ("cursed be Haman"). The annual Adloyada Purim Carnival in Tel Aviv is a festive affair, made gay and colorful with floats, costumes, balloons and other symbols of joyous celebration.

ADMAH

One of the Cities of the Plain.

See also Cities of the Plain.

ADRET, SOLOMON BEN ABRAHAM (Rashba)

(1235-1310)—Considered leading Rabbi of Spain in his time. He was known for his logical, clear thinking which was exhibited in many commentaries and responsa. Adret defended Judaism from the attacks of Christian and Mohammedan theologians from without and from the influence of Kabbalists and Philosophers from within.

AFGHANISTAN

Country in Central Asia, of which some of the inhabitants believe themselves to be descendants of the Ten Lost Tribes. The Jews of Afghanistan, at present numbering 800, follow the religious practices of Turkish Jewry, and in all probability came to Afghanistan from Persia during the 5th century. Though 40,000 Jews are believed to have inhabited the country a century ago, legal discrimination and severe oppression reduced the population to its present state.

AFIKOMEN

The piece of matzah hidden during the Passover meal and eaten at its completion. The children, who search for the Afikomen, are rewarded for its return.

See also Passover.

AGGADAH

Aramaic form of the Hebrew word *Haggadah* (story or narrative). Aggadah is the part of the Talmud which consists of stories and parables illustrating the meaning of a Biblical passage, in contrast to Halachah which deals with questions of law and religious practice. It was said that, in hard times, "Aggadah refreshes the heart of the people like wine."

See also Haggadah; Halachah.

AGNON, SAMUEL JOSEPH

(1888-1970)—Hebrew novelist and story writer. Agnon, whose family name was Czaczkes, was born in Galicia, spent the war years in Germany, and settled permanently in Palestine in 1923. Agnon's work deals with life in Galicia and Palestine. His style, which relies heavily on Midrashic elements, is original, and his stories are often symbolic and imaginative. Many consider him the greatest Hebrew novelist, and rank him with the leading writers of the world. *T'mol Shilshom (Yesterday and the Day Before),* the story of a young Galician settler's life in Palestine, *Haknasat Kallah (The Briday Canopy), Oreach Natah Lalun (A Guest for the Night),* and *Yamim Noraim (Days of Awe)* are among his most important books.

Samuel Joseph Agnon.

Agnon was awarded the Nobel Prize for Literature in 1966, and also twice received the Bialik Prize, Israel's highest literary honor.

AGRICULTURE

The Bible portrays the early Patriarchs, Abraham, Isaac, and Jacob, as owners of livestock and farmers. Upon Israel's entrance into Canaan following the exodus from Egypt, the Jews became terrace-farmers, due to the hilly country they cultivated. Barley was planted in the valleys, and vines, figs, and olives upon the hillsides. During the period of the Second Temple Palestine exported wine, olive oil, and corn. The Jewish exiles in Babylonia formed large estates, and a Jewish peasant class arose. The Arab countries placed no restrictions on Jews engaging in agriculture until the 15th century, but most Christian states, with the exclusion of Poland, outlawed Jewish farming by the end of the 10th century (Poland followed suit in the 17th). Though most countries had relaxed these restrictions by the 19th century, Jews have not returned to agriculture in large numbers. In Russia, the number of Jews once engaged in farming had reached 250,000, but it is now down to approximately 100,000; Jewish farmers in the U.S., too, number less than 100,000. The Jewish agricultural settlement in Argentina is prosperous, but has hardly fulfilled the expectations of Baron Maurice de Hirsch who, in the 1890's, made an attempt to settle vast numbers of Jews on the Argentine pampas. The modern agricultural settlement in Palestine, begun in 1855 by the efforts of Sir Moses Montefiore, has been much more successful than its counterparts in the diaspora. Some 356,000 Israelis lived on the soil in 1956, having settled either in a *Kibbutz, Kevutzah, Moshav*, or privately owned farms, and of the 875 towns and villages in Israel in 1965, more than 750 were primarily farming communities. The total acreage cultivated by Jewish farmers in Israel amounted to 4,224,000 dunams (1,056,000 acres) in 1968. Citrus fruits and other agricultural produce comprise an important part of Israel's exports. Other important farm products include grapes, grains, sugar beets, vegetables and potatoes, dairy products, and eggs.

AGRON, GERSHON

(1893-1959)—Israeli newspaperman and politician. In 1932 Agron, an immigrant to Palestine from Russia, via the U.S., founded the *Palestine Post* (which became the *Jerusalem Post* in 1950). He edited the newspaper until 1955, when he was elected mayor of Jerusalem.

AGUDAT ISRAEL

(Hebrew, "Union of Israel")—A world organization of Orthodox Jews. It was founded in 1912, at Kattowitz, Poland (then Prussia). Its aim is to solve all social, communal, and political problems, in the spirit of Torah. Until the establishment of the State of Israel, *Agudat Israel* was opposed to Zionism, but it has since been reconciled to it. It runs a network of schools in Israel (*Chinuch Atzmai* — "Independent Education"), and publishes the daily *Ha-modiah* in Jerusalem. It draws its strength mainly from Hasidic elements both in and outside Israel. Agudat Israel has a labor affiliate called *Poale Agudat Israel* ("Workers of A. I.").

AHAB

Seventh king of the northern Kingdom of Israel (about 875-853 B.C.E.), husband of Jezebel, son of Omri. He and Jezebel worshipped the idol Baal. They were cruel rulers who robbed and mistreated the people and persecuted the prophets. The prophet Elijah warned Ahab to return to God but he was not heeded. Ahab died in the battle for the city of Ramoth-gilead.

AHAD HA-AM

See Ginzburg, Asher.

AHASUERUS

Powerful king of Persia, husband of Queen Esther. He consented to Haman's evil plot to destroy the Jews of Persia, but Esther succeeded in turning his mind against Haman's plans. Ahasuerus is probably Xerxes who reigned in the 5th century B.C.E. The holiday of Purim celebrates the escape of the Jews of Persia from destruction.

See also Esther; Haman; Purim.

AHAZ

Twelfth king of Judah, son of Jotham and father of Hezekiah, ruled at the time of Isaiah when Assyria destroyed the northern Kingdom of Israel. Under Ahaz' idolatrous rule (about 735-720 B.C.E.), Judah became Assyria's tribute-paying vassal.

AHAZIAH

1. Eighth king of the northern Kingdom of Israel, ruled from about 853 to 852 B.C.E. The early death of Ahaziah, who was as idolatrous as his father Ahab, was prophesied by Elijah.

2. Sixth king of Judah, son of Jehoram and Athaliah, grandson of Ahab and Jezebel, worshipper of Baal. While on a visit to his relatives, the idolatrous house of Ahab of Israel, he was slain in Jehu's revolt. Ahaziah ruled from about 843 to 842 B.C.E.

AKDAMUT

A poem recited in the synagogue on Shavuot which extols the greatness of God and the wisdom of Torah.

AKEDAH

(Binding, sacrifice) the Biblical passage read on Rosh Hashanah which relates the story of God's test of Abraham's faith when he was asked to sacrifice his son and only heir, Isaac.

AKIBA BEN JOSEPH

(40-135)—One of the greatest of rabbis. Though he did not begin learning until he was forty, he soon became the leading scholar in Israel. During the twelve years he was away at the academy, his wife Beruriah waited patiently. Akiba is honored by all Jewish scholars for his immense service to Jewish learning, then and thereafter, for it was he who demanded that every student be permitted to discuss the law instead of its being laid down by some outstanding scholar. Since then the idea that the majority should rule in the academy has always prevailed among talmudic teachers. Akiba organized the material known as the Mishnah, which is the basis of the Talmud. He showed his disciples how to interpret the words and text of the Bible. When Akiba was dying under Roman torture after aiding the Bar Kochba Rebellion, he accepted his fate without complaint, saying that now he was able to prove that he had loved the Lord with all his soul, with all his might and with all his life.

ALBO, JOSEPH

(15th cent.)—Spanish philosopher and theologian noted for his participation in the Disputation of Tortosa (1413-14), a public debate in which he and other rabbis defended Judaism against the attacks of Christian critics. Albo's *Sefer Ikkarim* ("Book of Principles") is one of the most important medieval Jewish philosophical works. In it he delineated the three fundamental principles of Judaism: the existence of God divine revelation, and divine retribution (rewards and punishments).

ALBRIGHT, WILLIAM F.

(1889-1971)—American archaeologist. Albright was a pioneer in the archaeological investigation of Palestine. In 1929 he became professor of Semitic languages at Johns Hopkins University, and he was director of the American School of Oriental Research in Jerusalem from 1920 to 1929 and from 1933 to 1936. Albright conducted excavations at Tell Beit Mirsim, Gibeath-Shaul, Beth-El, Petra, and many other sites. In addition to his many scholarly works, he wrote *From the Stone Age to Christianity* and *The Archaeology of Palestine* for the general reading public.

ALECHEM HA-SHALOM

Traditional response to the greeting Shalom Alechem. It means "unto you be peace."

See also Shalom Alechem.

ALEPH

First letter of the Hebrew alphabet, has the numerical value of 1.

See also Aleph Bet.

ALEPH BET

The Hebrew alphabet, consists of twenty-two consonants (two of them silent) and five final letters. There are ten vowels in the Hebrew language which are indicated by seven vowel signs.

ALEXANDER JANNAEUS

(Jonathan) Hasmonean king and high priest of Judea (about 126-76 B.C.E.), successor to his brother, Aristobulus I.

ALEXANDER THE GREAT

King of Macedonia, great conqueror, founder of Hellenism, carried Greek culture throughout the ancient world. After he'had defeated the Persians at Issus in 333 B.C.E., in his Syrian and Egyptian campaign, he conquered Judea. Jewish history and legend describe him as a friend of the Jews.

ALEXANDRIA

Egyptian city which was founded in 332 B.C.E. by Alexander the Great, and which became the leading metropolis of the Diaspora during the Hellenistic age. At one time, some 500,000 Jews lived in Alexandria and the community was legally autonomous. They reached the highest offices in the city, and their economic and cultural activities were on the highest level. The success of the Jews aroused considerable anti-Semitism, and massacres occured; in 115-117 C.E. the Great Synagogue of Alexandria, a magnificent building, was burned down by the mobs. The Jewish population amounted to 15,000 until 1956, when many left for Israel.

ALFASI, ISAAC BEN JACOB

(1013-1103)—Talmudic scholar (known as "Rif"). His name stems from Fez, North Africa, where he lived and taught ("Al-Fasi," Man of Fez). He was forced by malicious slander to escape to Spain at the age of 75. His disciples in both countries, Africa and Spain, were many. His *Sefer ha-Halachot* (Book of Legal Decisions)—usually called *Alfas*—is the main collection of its kind prior to that of Maimonides. During the time of the suppression of the Talmud, Alfasi's work was employed to great advantage.

ALIYAH

1. ("Going up") the term for the honor extended a worshipper who is called up to the reading of the Torah.

2. In modern times the term is also used to describe Jewish immigration to Israel.

Rabbi Judah Alkalai.

ALKALAI, JUDAH SOLOMON HAI

(1798-1878)—Rabbi and early Zionist. After the Damascus Blood Libel of 1840, Alkalai became an active advocate of the resettlement of Palestine. In his writings he stresses the point that the Jewish nation must initiate its own redemption by returning to its homeland, and that this natural redemption will be followed by the supernatural one. His message, which preceded the rise of organized political Zionism by almost a century, was not well received in Europe, and in 1874, at the age of seventy-six, Alkalai settled in Jerusalem. Upon his death, his followers bought land on which was later built Petah Tikvah, the first modern Jewish agricultural settlement in Palestine.

ALLENBY, EDMUND H. H., VISCOUNT

(1861-1936)—British military commander. In the first World War he defeated the Turkish forces in Palestine, and victoriously entered Jerusalem on Dec. 11, 1917. Thereafter, he headed the country's Military Administration until 1919. One of Tel Aviv's main streets is named after Viscount Allenby.

ALLIANCE ISRAELITE UNIVERSELLE

International organization founded in 1860 by French Jews to guard the interests of Jews in backward lands, and to provide them with educational opportunities.

The *Alliance* has been of great help to Jews suffering from pogroms, widespread catastrophes, discrimination, and wars. Its educational work has been carried out mainly in the Moslem lands of Asia and northern Africa; it founded the first agricultural school in Palestine, *Mikveh Israel,* in 1870. All told, some 50,000 students attend *Alliance* educational institutions.

Yigal Allon.

ALLON, YIGAL

(1918-   )—Israeli politician. Born in the village of Kfar Tavor, Allon as a youth intended to become a farmer like his father. During the Arab Revolt of 1936, however, he joined the Haganah. In 1945 he was appointed commander of the Palmach. During the Israeli War of Independence Allon, holding the rank of general, planned and directed victorious campaigns on the northern, central, and southern fronts. He resigned from the army in 1949 and soon after entered politics, becoming head of the Achdut Ha'avoda-Poalei Zion party, and winning election to the Knesset in 1954. Allon was minister of labor from 1961 to 1968, became minister of education and culture in 1969, and in 1974 was appointed foreign minister by Prime Minister Yitzhak Rabin. In this capacity he played a key role in the delicate step-by-step negotiations with Egypt, through the intermediary of Henry Kissinger, which led to the Israeli-Egyptian disengagement agreements in the Sinai.

ALPHABET

See Aleph Bet.

AMALEK

A fierce nomadic people living south of Palestine who attacked the Israelites during their forty-year travels in the desert, and prevented them from entering the Promised Land. Amalek continued fighting the Jews up to the time of David. Haman, because of his name "Agagi," is considered a descendant of the Amalekite king, Agag. Amalek represents the permanent enemy of Jews and Judaism, and was doomed by the Bible as a nation with whom "God will have war . . . from generation to generation . . . Thou shalt blot out the remembrance of Amalek from under heaven."

AMAZIAH

Ninth king of Judah (796-767 B.C.E.), conquered Edom and captured its capital, Sela. Amaziah warred against Israel and was conquered. He was slain at Lachish and was succeeded by his 16-year-old son, Uzziah.

AMEN

("So be it") the response upon hearing a blessing or prayer in which the name of God is mentioned.

AMERICAN JEWISH COMMITTEE

Founded in the United States in 1906 to prevent the infringement of the social and religious rights of Jews in any part of the world, to secure for Jews equality of opportunity, and to aid those suffering persecution. The organization's first notable act was its success in persuading the U.S. government to abrogate in 1911 its treaty with Russia, because of discrimination against American Jewish citizens travelling in Russia. It sent a delegation to the Paris Peace Conference, fought for liberal immigration policies, and exposed anti-Semitic propaganda. The AJC's most important publications are the *American Jewish Yearbook,* an annual, and *Commentary,* a monthly magazine. As of 1961, the Committee had 27,000 members.

AMERICAN JEWISH CONGRESS

Organization founded in 1917 to defend Jewish rights wherever they are threatened, and to further the development of Palestine. The Congress was organized by American Zionists against the wishes of many American Jews, who held that since such institutions as the American Jewish Committee already existed, no further organization was necessary. Nevertheless, the Congress was organized, and sent a delegation to the Paris Peace Conference. It fought Nazi propaganda, and aided in the organization of the World Jewish Congress in 1936.

AMERICAN JEWISH HISTORICAL SOCIETY

The Society was organized in 1892 by Cyrus Adler, Oscar Straus, and Sabato Morais to collect and preserve material important for the study of the history of the Jewish community in America. It publishes its proceedings in the *Publications of the American Jewish Historical Society,* a quarterly.

AMICHAI, YEHUDA

(1924-   )—Israeli writer and poet. Born in Wurzberg, Germany, Amichai came to Palestine in 1936. He served in the British Army during World War II and afterwards in the Haganah. One of the first Israeli poets to introduce the idiom of modern technology into Hebrew poetry, he has published several collections of verse as well as short stories and plays. His novel *Not of This Time, Not of This Place,* a powerful and evocative treatment of postwar Jewish-German relations, is perhaps his best-known work.

AMIDAH

Another term for the Eighteen Benedictions *(Shemoneh Esreh),* recited while standing. Amidah means "standing."

See also Eighteen Blessings.

AMMONITES

A Semitic people who lived in the land east of the Jordan. Under Joab, the army of David conquered the Ammonites and annexed their land to Israel.

AMNON OF MAYENCE

Legendary martyr of the time of the Crusades. Amnon, a pious and learned Jew of Mayence, Germany, was asked repeatedly by the bishop to become a Christian. Finally, Amnon requested from the bishop three days in which to come to a decision. He immediately regretted his request, which seemed to show a wavering in his faith, and did not appear before the bishop at the end of the three-day period. The offended bishop ordered that Amnon's hands and feet be cut off as a punishment. All this took place just before the New Year, and on that day Amnon had himself carried to the synagogue, and recited the prayer *U-netanne Tokef* ("We will celebrate the mighty holiness of the day") before the *Kedushah* of the *Musaf* service. Upon reaching the words, "And our name Thou hast linked with Thine own," Amnon died. Ever since, Jews have recited this prayer, which legend says was composed by Amnon himself, during the High Holy Day service.

AMON

Idolatrous fifteenth king of Judah (about 641-639 B.C.E.), son of Manasseh; father of Josiah. He was murdered after reigning but two years.

AMORA

(Hebrew and Aramaic for speaker or interpreter.) The teachers and interpreters of Jewish law in Palestine and Babylonia from the time of the completion of the *Mishnah* (beginning of the 3rd century B.C.E.) until the completion of the Babylonian Talmud (around 500). The Amoraim explained the *Mishnah* and showed how it could be applied to new situations. The names of more than three thousand Amoraim are known; among the more famous are Rabina and Rav Ashi, who began the editing of the Talmud. The Amoraim also concerned themselves with Aggadah and Midrash, and used to give popular sermons before the people.

AMORITES

A warlike tribe of northern Canaan. They were defeated by Joshua and retreated into the mountains. At the time of King Solomon the Amorites paid tribute to Israel.

AMOS

Third of the Books of the Twelve (Minor) Prophets of the Bible. Amos, a shepherd from Tekoa, lived during the reign of Jeroboam II: He criticized the northern Kingdom of Israel for its frivolity and the great differences between its rich and poor. All men, all nations, Amos insisted, were children of the One God. He warned the Kingdom against the Assyrians and foretold its doom.

AMRAM

Husband of Jochebed, father of Moses, Aaron and Miriam, of the tribe of Levi.

AMSTERDAM

Commercial capital of the Netherlands, which since the 17th century has been a leading Jewish city. The first Jewish community was founded by Marranos in 1598, and the city soon possessed many distinguished Jews. Manasseh ben Israel set up the first printing press in 1621, and the Jews of Amsterdam produced many Hebrew grammarians, artists, poets, and authors. The rabbis possessed great power—Uriel Acosta and Baruch Spinoza were both excommunicated in Amsterdam. The Jews had a strong influence on the economic progress of the city, especially in the roles of diamond setters and merchants, and because of their industry helped to develop the Dutch colonies. The Jewish community, severely persecuted by the Nazis, numbers 12,000 at present.
See also Netherlands.

ANAN BEN DAVID

(8th cent. C.E.)—Founder of the Karaite sect. A member of a prominent Babylonian Jewish family claiming descent from King David, Anan was resentful when his younger brother, instead of himself, was elected exilarch in succession to their father. He began to advocate opposition to the Oral law and the rabbinical tradition, calling for abandonment of the Talmud and a return to the Bible as the sole source of knowledge of divine law. Anan explained his views in his Sefer ha-Mitzvot ("Book of Precepts"). The anti-rabbinical sect he founded, at first called the Ananites, eventually came to be known as the Karaites.

ANGEL

Messenger of God, not necessarily in human form, who conveys God's will to man. The Hebrew word for angel is Malach ("messenger").

ANILEWICZ, MORDECAI

(1919-1943)—Leader of the revolt of the Warsaw Ghetto (April-May 1943) against the Nazis. Anilewicz was a member of Hashomer Hatzair, and as head of the Jewish Fighters' Organization led the uprising in the Warsaw Ghetto.

ANOINTING

Pouring of oil on the head, a religious ceremony that took place when high priests and kings were chosen to assume their new responsibilities. This rite ended with the destruction of the Second Temple. Objects were also anointed, giving them a sacred character.

AN-SKI, S.

(Pen-name of Solomon S. Rappaport; 1863-1920)—Yiddish author and dramatist. Until 1917 An-ski lived in Russia, but his last three years were spent in Vilna and Warsaw. He wrote Die Shvue ("The Oath"), the hymn of the Bund movement, and a historical study, The Destruction of the Jews of Poland, Galicia, and Bukovina. An-ski created what is probably the greatest Yiddish play, The Dybbuk, which has been produced in many countries and in many languages.

ANTI-DEFAMATION LEAGUE

An agency of B'nai B'rith which fights anti-Semitism and other types of prejudice in the United States. Founded in 1913, the Anti-Defamation League has combatted the bigotry of the Ku Klux Klan as well as the acceptance of Nazi racist ideology by some Americans. It has conducted studies of the workings of prejudice in conjunction with various universities, and strives to educate the public about the evils of prejudice and discrimination.
See also B'nai B'rith.

ANTIGONUS

(Mattathiah) last Hasmonean king of Judea (about 40-37 B.C.E.). He fought unsuccessfully against the supremacy of Herod, the Idumean, whom the Romans appointed king of Judea. At Herod's instigation, the unfortunate Antigonus was executed by the Romans in Antioch, so ending the rule of the Hasmoneans.
See also Hasmoneans.

ANTIOCHUS IV (EPIPHANES)

The cruel despotic king of Syria. He tried to destroy the Jewish religion and replace it with the Greek gods. He was a cruel ruler to Judea and desecrated the Temple. The Maccabees led the successful revolt against him (165 B.C.E.).
See also Maccabees.

ANTIPATER

Governor of Idumea under the last of the Hasmonean

kings. Antipater cleverly managed to become governor of all Judea for the Romans. His son, Herod, became king of Judea.

See also Herodian Dynasty.

ANTI-SEMITISM

The belief that Jews are an inferior people and should occupy a lower position in society. The lies and the bigotry spread by anti-Semites have been exposed and condemned by the civilized world.

APOCRYPHA

In Hebrew called *Ketubim Aharonim (Latter Writings)*, books similar to those of the Bible but excluded from it. The Books of the Apocrypha are: I and II Esdras, Tobit, Judith, Additions to Esther, Wisdom of Solomon, Sirach (Ecclesiasticus), Baruch (including the Epistle of Jeremiah), three Additions to Daniel, the Prayer of Manasseh, and I and II Maccabees.

See also Pseudopigrapha.

APPLES AND HONEY

Apples dipped in honey are traditionally eaten on Rosh Hashanah as an expression of hope that the coming new year will be sweet and fruitful.

ARABIA

Peninsula in southwestern part of Asia. First definite knowledge about Jews in Arabia dates from the 1st century C.E. although traditions seem somewhat suggestive of Jewish influence as early as Biblical times. As more and more Arabs converted to Judaism, the number of Jews in Arabia increased. In the 6th and early 7th centuries, Jewish population was considerable in Hejaz, especially in Medina and vicinity. After the rise of Islam, Jews were tolerated and allowed to survive only if they paid special taxes. In spite of this, most of the Jews in Hejaz were banished or killed. Jews living in Northern Arabia at the time had become assimilated in every way and even their poetry could scarcely be differentiated from that of the Arabs. The overwhelming majority of Arabian Jews have now emigrated to Israel.

ARAM

1. Grandson of Noah; son of Shem; ancestor of the Aramaeans.
2. Country of the ancient Aramaeans, included Syria and Mesopotamia. The Aramaic city of Damascus was conquered by David but lost by Solomon. Aram, often the enemy of the northern Kingdom of Israel, was invaded by the Israelite kings Ahab and Jeroboam II. It was conquered by Assyria (about 735 B.C.E.) and called Syria henceforth.

See also Syria.

ARAMAIC

Ancient Semitic language, closely related to Hebrew. Aramaic dialects were spoken by peoples from east of the Jordan to the borders of Assyria and Babylonia. In Babylonian Exile the Jews adopted Aramaic; as a result, parts of the Bible and Talmudic writings and the entire Zohar were written in Aramaic. Aramaic translations of the Bible are called Targum. Many important prayers are said in Aramaic, such as the Kaddish and the Kol Nidre.

ARARAT

The great mountain on which Noah's ark came to rest after the flood. Ararat is a mountain range in Turkey, near Iran.

ARAVAH

(Willow) one of the four plants used in the celebration of Sukkot.

See also Hoshanot; Sukkot, Four Plants of

Arba Kanfot.

ARBA KANFOT

("Four corners") a rectangular piece of cloth, with an opening for the head and with fringes at each of its four corners; sometimes referred to as *Tzitzit*. It is worn under a man's regular garments to remind him of God's commandments.

A copy of the carving on the Arch of Titus, showing the menorah and other furniture of the Temple being carried in triumph through the streets of Rome.

ARCH OF TITUS

The triumphal arch erected at Rome in honor of Titus Flavius Vespasian's victory over the Jews and then his destruction of the Temple (70 C.E.). The arch depicts Jewish captives in the triumphal procession, and custom frowns on Jews passing under it.

ARCHAEOLOGY

The science of the study of a civilization through an investigation of its material remains, such as its buildings, pottery, and art. Archaeology was first brought to Palestine in 1838. Then, as now, the most important branch of Palestinian archaeology dealt with the identification of Biblical sites. Early scientists investigated the tombs of the kings of Jerusalem (F. de Saulcy in 1850-51), while more recent excavators have dug at Gezer, Hazor, Lachish, Shechem, and Jericho. Diggings at the *tel* (in ancient times, city was built atop city, and the mound which resulted was called a *tel* in Hebrew) of Megiddo have revealed the chariot-stables of King Solomon, and the palaces of Omri and Ahab have been uncovered in Samaria. Excavations at Massada have uncovered the extensive fortifications of this Zealot fortress against the Romans, while other investigations of the Negev region have proved that the area was once well populated. King Solomon's port city of Ezion-geber was unearthed near Eilath. Perhaps the most spectacular find of recent years was the discovery of the Dead Sea Scrolls, dating from the Second Temple, in a cave near the Dead Sea. Important archaeological work has also been done since 1967 in the area of the Temple Mount in the Old City of Jerusalem. One of today's most noted archaeologists is Yigael Yadin, former Chief of staff of the Israeli army. Another noted modern archaeologist was Nelson Glueck.

ARGENTINA

Marranos who arrived in this South American country during the 16th century were absorbed by the surrounding population, and the history of the present community begins with the Jewish immigration of 1852, which founded the Jewish community of Buenos Aires in 1862. Baron de Hirsch's plan (1891) to settle vast numbers of Jews in Argentina as farmers was unsuccessful, and most of the Jews who arrived from Eastern Europe lived in the cities. Today, Argentina has the largest Jewish population of all Latin American states (nearly 500,000), with only 8,000 Jews engaged in agriculture. The community is quite well organized; there are many Jewish schools, and two Yiddish dailies and a Yiddish theatre are maintained. The D.A.I.A. (Delegacion de Associaiones Israelitas Argentinas) represents all Jews in political affairs.

ARISTOBULUS I

(Judah) Hasmonean king and high priest of Judea (about 104-103 B.C.E.), son and successor of John Hyrcanus. Aristobulus was the first Hasmonean who assumed the title of king.

ARISTOBULUS II

Hasmonean prince who seized the throne (about 67 B.C.E.) and the high priesthood from his brother, Hyrcanus II. Pompey, the Roman, dethroned Aristobulus and sent him to Rome as a captive.

The Ark in the Land of the Philistines. **Copy from the fresco in the synagogue at Dura-Europos, 3rd century, C. E.**
Yale University Art Gallery

ARK OF THE COVENANT

Built by Moses at God's command to house the Tablets of the Law; constructed by the artisan Bezalel. It was placed in the Holy of Holies of the Tabernacle in the wilderness. After the Israelites settled in Canaan, the Ark was taken to the sanctuary at Shiloh. At the time of Eli it was captured by the Philistines who later abandoned it. For a century it was guarded by faithful priests at Kiriath-jearim, until King David brought it to Jerusalem. Later it was deposited in Solomon's Temple. The eventual fate of the Ark is unknown.

See also Aron Hakodesh.

ARMENIA

Armenia is considered the site of the Biblical Mt. Ararat, and legend has it that Jews arrived in the region after the destruction of the First Temple. This Jewish population exercised a strong influence on Armenian culture and literature. Armenia is now partitioned between the U.S.S.R., Turkey and Iran, and the Jewish settlement is fairly small.

ARMY OF ISRAEL

Tzvah Haganah Le'Yisrael (Hebrew for "Defense Army of Israel"), abbreviated as *Tzahal*, is a vital force in the lives of the citizens of the state. As the guardian of its borders and the deterrent to any possible Arab attack, its role is of crucial importance. The Israeli army emerged from the underground Haganah in 1948, when it successfully repulsed the invasion of the new-born state by five Arab armies. It displayed its prowess again in 1956, with a lightning conquest of the Sinai Peninsula which ended Egyptian infiltration into Israeli territory; during the Six-Day War of 1967, when Israel defeated the forces of Egypt, Syria, and Jordan and conquered the Sinai Peninsula, the Golan Heights, and the West Bank of the Jordan; and the Yom Kippur War of 1973, when, though caught by surprise, it threw back an unexpected attack by Egypt and Syria, turning a near defeat into a major military victory. Both men and women are drafted into the service; the men for a 2½ year period, the women for 2 years. Both sexes serve in the reserves for extended periods after completing their active duty, and the main strength of *Tzahal* rests in its reserves, which can be mobilized on very short notice. In the 1970s Israel's defense forces, when fully mobilized, reportedly numbered more than 300,000, most in the army. The tanks, planes, missile boats, and other equipment used by the Israeli forces are among the most up-to-date in the world. Although much of the equipment is imported, mainly from the United States, Israel is building up its own defense industry. The great cost of maintaining such a powerful military establishment, necessitated by the continued hostility of the Arab states and the constant threat of enemy attack, has resulted in Israelis being among the most highly taxed peoples in the world.

See also Haganah, War of Independence, Sinai Campaign, Six-Day War, Yom Kippur War.

ARON HAB'RIT

Hebrew name for Ark of the Covenant.

See also Ark of the Covenant.

ARON HAKODESH

The holy ark which houses the Torah. Because it encloses the most precious spiritual possession of the Jew, the ark is considered holy. It is often the most beautifully decorated part of the synagogue.

ARTAXERXES I

King of Persia, about 465-425 B.C.E. He was sympathetic and helpful to the Jews returning to their homeland from Babylonian Exile. He appointed Nehemiah, his cup-bearer governor of Judea and granted money for the rebuilding of the Temple.

ASA

Third king of Judah (about 915-875 B.C.E.), son of Abijah. Asa rid Judah of idol worship and upheld the religion of the One God.

ASARAH BETEVET

(The Fast of the Tenth of Tevet) a fast day commemorating the beginning of the siege against Jerusalem by the Babylonians in 586 B.C.E.

ASCH, SHOLEM

(1880-1957)—Yiddish novelist and dramatist. He was born in the village of Kutno, Poland, where he spent his youth and received a traditional Jewish education. His first masterpiece was the novel *Dos Stetl* ("The Town"), published in 1904. He has written many stories and novels which use Jewish and Russo-Jewish history as their background, and several plays. Among his most important books are *Three Cities, Salvation,* and *Mottke the Thief.* Asch's writings show a great power of observation and the gift of vivid description. Some of his more recent writings dealt with New Testament figures, such as *The Nazarene,* and aroused much unfavorable comment.

ASENATH

Egyptian wife of Joseph, mother of Ephraim and Manasseh.

ASHER

Eighth son of Jacob; second son of Zilpah, ancestor of the tribe of Asher.

ASHER, TRIBE OF

One of the Israelite tribes. Its territory extended from Mount Carmel and the lower Kishon plain to the Phoenician plain. The tribe conducted a profitable trade with the Phoenicians. Asher eventually became part of the Kingdom of Israel. Asher's banner was pearl; its emblem was a woman and an olive tree. The stone representing the tribe of Asher in the High Priest's breastplate was probably a beryl.

ASHI

Outstanding Babylonian scholar (about 354-427 C.E.), noted collector, codifier and editor of the Babylonian Talmud, with his brilliant assistant and successor, Rabina. Ashi, of a wealthy and scholarly family, was beloved for his purity, charity and learning. He was called Rabbana, a title usually bestowed upon the Exilarchs.

See also Rabina Bar Huna

ASHKENAZIM

Originally Jews from Germany (and France), as distinguished from Sephardim (Jews from Spain and Portugal). During the times of medieval oppressions, Ashkenazim migrated to the eastern countries of Europe, and later to other parts of the world. Today Ashkenazim no longer primarily refers to a geographical division of Jewry. Ashkenazic rituals and pronunciation of Hebrew differ somewhat from the Sephardic. The majority of Jews are Ashkenazim.

ASHTORETH (or Astarte)

Canaanite and Phoenician fertility goddess. Her worship attracted the Israelites as well, particularly between the reigns of Solomon and Josiah.

ASSAF, SIMCHAH

(1889-1953)—Israeli rabbinic scholar. From 1925 Assaf taught at the Hebrew University, where he became professor in 1936. He wrote many books on Jewish law, specializing in the history and literature of the Gaonic period. In 1948, he was appointed to the Israel Supreme Court.

ASSYRIA

Ancient empire of mighty warriors, artists and builders. From its capital Nineveh, on the upper Tigris, Assyria ruled the Middle East (about 2000-600 B.C.E.). It made Judah a vassal state and destroyed Israel (about 722 B.C.E.). The Assyrians were eventually overrun and defeated by the Babylonians (Chaldeans).

ATHALIAH

Queen of Judah (about 842-836 B.C.E.), daughter of Ahab and Jezebel, wife of King Jehoram of Judah. After the death of her son, King Ahaziah, she seized the throne and had the entire house of Jehoram killed. Prince Joash, an infant, alone escaped her—he was saved by the wife of the priest Jehoiada who later headed the revolt against Athaliah that led to her death. She was the seventh ruler of Judah.

AUER, LEOPOLD

(1845-1930)—Hungarian concert violinist and teacher. Tchaikovsky dedicated his famous violin concerto to Auer, who was a pupil of Joachim and who taught at St. Petersburg. In 1918 Auer came to the U.S., where he lived till his death.

AUSTRALIA

Jews were among the earliest settlers of Australia (they were in Sydney before 1817), and contributed in great measure to the economic and political life of the country. Anti-Semitism was never an important factor and Jews have reached high office: Sir Isaac Isaacs (1855-1948) was Governor General and Chief Justice of the country. Sir John Monash (1865-1931) commanded the Australian army in World War I. There are now 72,000 Jews in Australia, living mainly in the large cities.

AUSTRIA

The first mention of Jews in Austria is found in the customs laws of Raffelstatten (905), which give Jewish merchants equal rights with Christians. For many centuries Jewish life and property were protected, but in 1420 all Jews were driven from the country, only to reappear again; this pattern repeated itself a number of times. The Revolution of 1848 eventually brought the Jews of Austria equality, and they became prominent in commerce and culture. During World War II, 100,000 Austrian Jews were killed; there are now 9,000 Jews in the country.

Public execution by the Inquisition.

AUTO-DA-FÈ

(Portuguese for "act of faith") Great public spectacles of the Inquisition (1480-1825). Those condemned by the Inquisition would be led through the streets of the city to the public square by hooded monks. Once at the square, their sentences would be publicly carried out. Some 2,000 auto-da-fès took place in Spain and Portugal, and about 30,000 people were put to death by the Inquisition.

AV

Fifth month in the Jewish calendar.

See also Calendar, Jewish; Months, Jewish.

AV BET DIN

("Father of the Court") one of the two presiding officials of the Great Sanhedrin.

See also Sanhedrin; Zugot.

AVODAH

(Heb. lit., "service")—Though primarily referring to the sacrificial service at the Temple, and with the Temple's destruction, to those portions of the *Musaf* service on the Day of Atonement which describe the Temple ritual, this term also refers to prayer in general. According to Simeon the Righteous (Ethics of the Fathers, 1, 2), it is one of the three foundations of the world.

AYIN

The sixteenth letter of the Hebrew alphabet, has the numerical value of 70.

See also Aleph Bet.

AZULAI, CHAIM DAVID

(1724-1806)—Talmudic scholar, author, and bibliographer. Azulai, known by his initials as "Chidah," was born in Jerusalem, where he received an education in Talmud and Kabbalah. The community of Jerusalem sent him to Europe, to collect money for the poor congregations of the Holy Land. Azulai travelled all over Europe, where he visited public and private libraries and collected much material for his most famous work, *Shem Hagdolim* ("Names of the Great"), which contains the biographies of some 1,500 scholars and lists 2,200 books written since Talmudic times. His travel journals and letters are valuable documents in Jewish history.

BAAL

Idol, often represented as half steer, half human, worshipped by the ancient Canaanites and Phoenicians. Elijah and other prophets warned the Israelites against the worship of Baal. Baal means "lord, master."

BAAL KORE

("Master-reader") the man who reads and chants from the Torah. In some synagogues he is a paid functionary.

BAAL SHEM TOV

Meaning "Master of the Good Name," this is the title given Israel ben Eliezer, who founded the Jewish movement called Hasidism. This saintly leader was born in the Ukraine in 1700; he lived until 1760. As an orphan he was cared for by his community. During his idle moments Israel roved through the forests, thinking about nature and God and man. For his livelihood he engaged successively in teaching, claydigging and innkeeping. Then he had a divine vision which impelled him to become a religious teacher. Soon he was widely known and honored. He taught the many poor people around him that God was everywhere; that He must be served in joy and not through mere self-denial; and that even the most unlearned Jew whose prayers were truly devout might reach closer to God than one who possessed great learning. Many legends have been told of his miracles, his conversations with God and his understanding of heavenly mysteries.

See also Hasidim.

BAAL TOKEA

("Master-blower") an expert in the blowing of the Shofar on Rosh Hashanah and Yom Kippur.

See also Shofar.

BAASHA

Third king of the northern Kingdom of Israel (about 914-890 B.C.E.).

Baal Shem Tov.

BABEL, ISAAC

(1894-1941)—Russian-Jewish author. Until 1923 Babel was a political officer in the Soviet army. After this date he dedicated himself to literature, winning fame for his realistic stories about the Russian revolution, the ghetto, and assimilated Jewish life in Odessa. Among his more famous works are *Odessa Tales*, *Benia Krik*, and *Red Cavalry*. In 1938 he lost favor with the Soviet authorities and dropped out of sight completely. He probably perished in a concentration camp.

BABYLONIA

One of the great ancient centers of civilization, played an important role in Jewish history. Jews had lived there willingly or in exile. Psalm 137 mourns: "By the rivers of Babylon, there we sat down; yea, we wept, when we remembered Zion." Babylonia was conquered

Blowing the Shofar.

18

A painting of the main thoroughfare of Babylon showing the famous Ishtar Gates.

Yellow badge compulsory on outer garment of Jews, Rhineland, end of 16th century.

by Assyria, another of the great empires of antiquity, in 732, and by King Cyrus of Persia in 539 B.C.E. Babylonian armies had taken most of the Jews as captives to Babylonia in 586; Cyrus permitted the Jews to return to their homeland after seventy years of exile. Many Jews migrated to Babylonia after Bar Kochba's disastrous uprising against the Romans in the second century. For about a thousand years Jews lived there unmolested. Because of their liberty and opportunities, they were able to establish great academies of Jewish learning which shaped the future life of Jews everywhere. Not only did this community produce leaders in scholarship but also political leaders, known as *Resh Galuta*, Chief of the Exile.

See also Chaldeans.

BACHYA BEN JOSEPH IBN PAKUDA

(2nd half of 11th century.) The most popular Jewish religious philosopher of the Middle Ages. Bachya's *Torat Chobot Ha-Levavot*, which analyzes the religious-ethical duties of the Jew, was widely studied and was a major influence in the education of many pious Jews. He argues eloquently and lucidly for a life of devotion to God.

BADGE

Means of identification, usually yellow, which Jews were compelled to wear in order to distinguish them from non-Jews. This anti-Semitic custom was established by the Moslems of the 9th century and was subsequently adopted by England (1217), France (1219), Spain (1392), Italy (1350), and Germany (15th century). Often Jews were compelled to wear oddly shaped hats and Jewish women were forced to wear green veils; the Marranos were obliged for a time to wear green clothing with red crosses. The wearing of the badge or other forms of distinctive clothing fell into disuse in the 18th century and was formally abolished at the time of the French Revolution. The badge was re-adopted by Nazi Germany, which forced Jews to sew yellow shields of David enclosing the letter J on their clothing.

BADHAN

(From the Aramaic "to make laugh, to cheer up".) A professional clown who entertained guests at weddings from the Middle Ages on. Many *Badhanim* were poets or rhymesters who composed their rhymes on the spur of the moment at the wedding. One of the last great *Badhanim* was Eliakum Zunser (1836-1913), whose songs were very popular among Polish and Russian Jews. *Badhanim* were called "merry Jews" in Prague, and "Marshalliks" in eastern Europe.

BAECK, LEO

(1873-1956)—German theologian and communal leader. One of the outstanding Jewish theologians of his generation, Baeck wrote such notable works as *The Essence of Judaism* and *This People Israel*. During the 1930s, voluntarily staying with his congregation in Berlin even though he could have escaped, he was a great source of inspiration and spiritual strength for the persecuted Jews of Germany. He was later sent to a concentration camp and after World War II became chairman of the World Union for Progressive Judaism.

BALAAM

Soothsayer asked by King Balak of Moab to curse the Israelites whom he feared. On his way, Balaam's ass spoke to him and reminded him of the will of God. Balaam blessed the Israelites instead of cursing them.

BALAK

Moabite king who sought to destroy the Israelites when they were passing around Moab, on their way to Canaan, by asking Balaam, the soothsayer, to curse them.

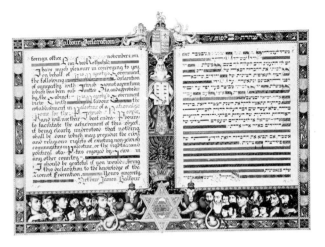

An illustrated version of the Balfour Declaration by the artist Arthur Szyk.

BALFOUR, LORD ARTHUR JAMES

(1848-1930)—A leader of England's Conservative party. He is particularly remembered by Jews as the author of the famous Balfour Declaration. During his tenure as foreign minister, he wrote to Baron Rothschild on November 2, 1917, that "His Majesty's Government view with favour the establishment in Palestine of a national home for the Jewish people, and will use their best endeavours to facilitate the achievement of this object." He promised that Britain would exert every effort to gain that end, under the condition that nothing be done to injure the rights of non-Jews in Palestine or of Jews in other lands. The Balfour Declaration was endorsed by France, Italy, Japan and the United States. It later became part of the document that gave Great Britain its mandate over Palestine. Although some British opposition to the intent of the Declaration developed later, it is considered a great stepping-stone to the establishment of the independent state of Israel.

BALTIMORE HEBREW COLLEGE AND
TEACHERS' TRAINING SCHOOL

The school was founded in 1919. It offers a complete Hebrew teachers' training course, an afternoon high-school program, and adult education classes. It was a pioneer institution in the field of Hebrew teachers' training.

BAMBERGER, SELIGMANN B.

(Isaac Dov; 1807-1878)—German rabbi and Orthodox leader. Bamberger was one of the last of the great Talmudists of the old tradition in Germany. In 1840 he was appointed rabbi in Wurzburg and, in addition to fulfilling his rabbinic duties, founded a noted yeshiva in the city. Bamberger opposed Samson Raphael Hirsch's view that Orthodox Jews secede from official communal organizations in certain circumstances.

BAR GIORA, SIMON

(1st century)—A leader of the Jewish revolt against Rome, 66-70. He was a democrat who believed in the equality of all men and fought for the liberation of slaves. Bar Giora was one of the leaders of the defense of Jerusalem against Titus and when Jerusalem fell he was captured by the Romans and executed.

BAR-ILAN, MEIR

(Formerly Berlin: 1881-1949)—Rabbi and religious Zionist leader. The son of Naphtali Zevi Yehuda Berlin (*Neziv*), he organized the Mizrachi movement in the United States (1914), founded and edited the Tel Aviv daily *Ha-Zofeh* (1937), and initiated the Talmudic Encyclopedia (1947). His autobiography is *From Volozin to Jerusalem*.

BAR-ILAN UNIVERSITY

Israel university, founded in 1955 at Ramat Gan by the Mizrachi organization of America in memory of Meir Bar-Ilan. It gives both religious and secular instruction.

Bar Kokhba coins.

BAR KOCHBA

(died 135)—The leader of the last Jewish rebellion against the Romans. He was a man of great strength; it was said he could uproot trees with his bare hands. So impressed was Rabbi Akiba with this soldier that he even spoke of him as the coming Messiah. Although defeated and killed at Bethar, Bar Kochba was a highly skilled general, who won his victories by surprise attacks. The Jews had for years been preparing their uprising against Rome, for the conquerors had been threatening to take Jerusalem from the Jews and make it a Roman city. They attempted to prohibit the most sacred religious customs. The army under Bar Kochba defeated the Roman forces and recaptured Jerusalem. The Romans sent for their greatest general, Severus, then in England. Severus fought only small engagements, capturing Jewish posts one after the other until only the great fortress at Bethar was left. Almost a million Jewish civilians and soldiers died in the war. Thousands of the remaining Jews were sold into slavery. This defeat of Bar Kochba was considered by Rome one of the greatest triumphs in its history.

BAR MITZVAH

"Son of the Commandment," which is the Hebrew way of saying "responsible for observing God's commandments." A Jewish boy becomes Bar Mitzvah on his thirteenth birthday because, according to Jewish traditions, at that age he is mature enough to understand the meaning of the commandments of his faith. Before he becomes Bar Mitzvah, the boy prepares himself by studying the principles and practices of Judaism, the Bible and Jewish history. The term Bar Mitzvah and the ceremony as we know it today seems to have developed in the thirteenth century. The Bar Mitzvah is held on the Sabbath after the boy's thirteenth birthday. To prove his adulthood, the boy is called up to the reading desk to read the day's selection from the Haftarah (the Prophets) and sometimes to read a portion of the Torah. After the reading the boy often addresses the congregation briefly before the rabbi delivers a special Bar Mitzvah sermon. After the services the family of the Bar Mitzvah usually give him a party, at the Synagogue hall or in their home. After Bar Mitzvah the boy has all the privileges of the adult member of the Congregation. He can be counted as one of the ten men (minyan) who must be present to conduct a service. He can be called upon for the reading of the Torah. He accepts the duties, the customs and ethical commandments of his faith. In some Conservative congregations a new ceremony called "Bat Mitzvah" ("Daughter of the Commandment"), for young girls who have reached the age of 13, has been introduced.

BARAK

The general whom Deborah inspired to a great victory over the Canaanite King Jabin, and his general, Sisera, near Mount Tabor. His victory is described in the Song of Deborah.

BARNATO, BARNETT ISAACS

(1852-1897)—Born in London, he emigrated to South Africa in 1873 and earned his living as a magician (Barnato was his stage name). Ultimately he entered the diamond industry, in which he became a multimillionaire; together with Cecil Rhodes he formed the De Beers Consolidated Diamond Mines. He acquired another fortune in the gold mining industry. His suicide at sea was probably caused by his later financial losses through speculation.

BARON, SALO W.

(1895-   )—American historian. Born in Galicia, Baron came to the U.S. in 1926, and, since 1930, has been professor of Jewish history at Columbia University. His greatest work is the multi-volume *Social and Religious History of the Jews*, which is marked by vast knowledge and insight. He has also written *Modern Nationalism and Religion*, the 3-volume *The Jewish Community*, *A Documentary History of American Jews*, and other works, and is the editor of *Jewish Social Studies*.

BARON DE HIRSCH FUND

Foundation founded in New York State in 1891 to aid Jewish immigrants. It provided work, temporary aid, agricultural training, and general education. An agricultural college was founded in Woodbine, New Jersey, in 1894—the first school in the United States to provide secondary education in agriculture. Many refugees were aided by the Fund during World War II as well.

BARUCH, BERNARD

(1870-1965)—U.S. financier and government official. Baruch is famous as the "advisor to presidents," particularly to President Franklin D. Roosevelt. In 1946 he presented the "Baruch Plan" for the control of atomic weapons to the United Nations Atomic Energy Commission on behalf of the United States.

BARUCH, BOOK OF

Book of the Apocrypha, contains sermons, prayers and prophecies of Baruch, disciple of Jeremiah.

BARUCH HASHEM

("Blessed be His Name"; "thank God"). Many Jews say this in response to the question, "How are you?" and when reporting happy news.

BAT MITZVAH

See Bar Mitzvah.

BATH-SHEBA

Favorite wife of King David, the widow of the warrior Uriah. She was the mother of King Solomon.

BATHS; BATHING

Both physical and ritual cleanliness are important to Jews. Immersion in a ritual bath (*Mikveh*) the running waters of which cover the entire body, provides ritual cleanliness. In Biblical times the *Mikveh* was used upon recovery from leprosy, discharge of semen, menstruation, or contact with a corpse to restore the purity demanded by the presence of the temple. Now it is chiefly used by women, after menstruation or childbirth. Various Kabbalists and Hasidic sects emphasized the importance of the spiritual purification given by the *Mikveh*.

BEAME, ABRAHAM

(1906-   )—American politician. The son of Jewish immigrants from Poland, Beame was born in London and was brought to New York City at the age of three months. He was educated at City College and began his career as a certified public accountant, working concurrently as a high school accounting teacher. Entering local politics in Brooklyn around 1928, Beame rose rapidly in the Democratic party, and in 1961 was appointed budget director by Mayor Vincent Impellitteri. In 1962 Beame was elected controller, the second highest office in New York's municipal government. He ran unsuccessfully for mayor in 1965, was elected controller again in 1969, and in 1973 won a landslide victory, becoming New York City's first Jewish mayor. Beame's mayoral administration was marked by grave financial problems that had been developing for at least a decade before he took office.

BEDIKAT HAMETZ

(The searching for leaven) a symbolic ceremony that takes place the night before the eve of Passover. After all leaven is removed from the home, pieces of bread are placed about the house, and then searched for and collected with the aid of a wooden spoon, a candle and a feather.

BEERSHEBA

An ancient city in southern Israel that had seven wells, a grazing area and watering place used by all the Patriarchs. It was the southern most city of Israel (hence the well-known expression, "From Dan to Beersheba"). The modern town of Beersheba dates from around 1900. It was settled by many new immigrants in 1949. The population of Beersheba in 1972 was 80,000. In addition to being the capital of Israel's southern district, Beersheba is a communications and industrial center.
See also Negev.

Menahem Begin.

BEGIN, MENAHEM

(1913-   )—Israeli political leader. Born in Poland, where he headed the Betar movement, Begin came to Palestine in 1942. Before the rise of the state, he led the *Irgun Zvi Leumi* in its underground fight against the British. In 1948, Begin founded the Herut ("Liberty") party. He has been a member of the Knesset since 1948, and in 1965 played a key role in forming the Gahal political coalition. From 1967 to 1970 he was a cabinet minister without portfolio. An outstanding orator, and a leading right-wing spokesman in Israeli politics, Begin, as head of the Likud bloc, became Prime Minister in 1977.

BEILIS AFFAIR

Mendel Beilis was charged with the ritual murder of a boy in Kiev, and was tried in 1913. The trial, which finally ended in Beilis' acquittal, aroused much anti-Semitic sentiment, which was encouraged by the Russian authorities.

Mendel Beilis on trial.

BELASCO, DAVID

(1853-1931)—American actor and dramatist who won fame as a producer and discoverer of talent. He opened the Belasco theater in 1907.

BELGIUM

Although a few Jews had settled in Belgium in the 13-14th centuries, the first large Jewish immigration into Belgium occurred in 1492, when a number of Spanish and Portuguese Marranos settled in Antwerp. Others followed, but the Jewish population was harassed by frequent anti-Semitic outbreaks. When Belgium gained her independence in 1830, religious equality was granted and the Jews were free to organize their own communal life. Antwerp boasted the largest Jewish community because of its important diamond industry. Belgian Jewry was heavily persecuted by the Nazis; 40,500 Jews, in comparison with the prewar population of 110,000, now live in Belgium.

BELKIN, SAMUEL

(1911-1976)—American rabbi and educator. Born in Poland, Belkin was brought to the United States in 1929. He joined the faculty of Yeshiva University in 1935, and in 1943 became its president. During his administration, which continued until his retirement in 1975, he led Yeshiva through an unparalleled period of growth and expansion. Belkin has also been active as a scholar, concentrating on Jewish life and thought in the Hellenistic period. His works on Philo are especially noteworthy.

Samuel Belkin.

BELLOW, SAUL

(1915-   )—American writer. Born in Montreal, Bellow has lived for most of his life in the United States. He is the author of many best-selling novels, including *The Adventures of Augie March*, *Henderson the Rain King*, and *Herzog*.

BELSHAZZAR

Last king of Babylonia. Daniel interpreted for him the famous "writing on the wall," the Mene Tekel, which predicted the terrible end of his kingdom.

BEN AZZAI, SIMEON

(Early 2nd century C.E.)—Tanna, he lived in Tiberias. Ben Azzai was a companion of R. Akiba and showed great love for the study of the Torah, even remaining unmarried so as to devote all his time to study. His diligence was proverbial, as was his piety and brilliance of mind. Mystical studies interested him also and according to tradition he lost his life because of his presumptuous inquiry into these fields.

David Ben Gurion, the first Premier of Israel.

BEN-GURION, DAVID

(1886-1973)—The first prime minister of the State of Israel. He was born in Poland in 1886; studied law at the University of Constantinople; and moved to Palestine in 1906. In Poland he helped found the Poale Zion, the socialist labor group which has now become Mapai, Israel's leading party. As a fiery editor and unrestrained fighter on behalf of his people, Ben-Gurion was expelled from Palestine by the then Turkish rulers in 1915. For several years he lived in the United States and later went to London. He served in the Jewish Legion from 1918 to 1920. As secretary general of the Histadrut from 1921 to 1933, Ben-Gurion was one of the founders of Mapai in 1930, and became its head. From 1935 to 1948 he also served as chairman of the Jewish Agency executive. As a loyal Israeli, and leader of the nation's largest political party, he was appointed prime minister of the new state in 1948. He led the successful fight against the Arab invaders and helped Israel attain world recognition. Under Ben-Gurion's leadership the State of Israel was consolidated and organized, absorbed vast numbers of immigrants, and experienced great growth in all spheres. Ben-Gurion retired from his high post in 1953 to become a simple farmer once again, in the Negev (southern Israel). In 1955 he returned to governmental service to become defense minister under his successor, Moshe Sharett, and then resumed his premiership, leading Israel during the Sinai campaign and afterwards. He retired again 1963, staged an abortive political comeback in 1965 through the Rafi party, and devoted the remainder of his life, on his beloved kibbutz, Sedeh Boker, to study and to writing his memoirs and histories of Israel and the Zionist movement. He was regarded and loved as the "grand old man" of Israeli politics and the father of the State, and his death was mourned by the entire nation.

and help his adopted land. As a loyal Israeli, and leader of a large political group, he was appointed prime minister of the new state in 1948. He led the successful fight against the Arab invaders and helped Israel attain world recognition. He retired from his high post to become a simple farmer once again, in the Negev (southern Israel). After several years he returned to governmental service to become defense minister under his successor, Moshe Sharett, and then resumed his premiership.

BEN SIRAH, JOSHUA

(2nd century B.C.E.)—Author of the book of proverbs known as "The Wisdom of Ben Sirah," or "Ecclesiasticus," which was incorporated into the Apocrypha. Though modeled after the Biblical Proverbs, the Rabbis detected in it some affinities to Epicureanism and forbade it for general reading.

BEN-YEHUDA, ELIEZER

(1858-1922)—Born in 1858 in Vilna, he was a leading champion of the restoration of Hebrew as a spoken language. He changed his name (originally, Perlman) when he moved to Jerusalem in 1881, where he wrote articles in which he set forth his reasons for the revival of Hebrew as a spoken language. There were many Palestinian Jews who opposed making the holy tongue one of everyday use, but the influence of Zionists throughout the world eventually overcame their objections. Ben-Yehuda did far more than make Biblical Hebrew fashionable and conversational. Aware that the language had to be modernized, that there were thousands of new facts and discoveries which could not be described in the limited vocabulary of ancient times, he devised words which would fill the empty spaces in the Hebrew dictionary. He planned and worked on a complete Hebrew dictionary until his death in 1922. It was to have French and German translations of every word. His family, using his material, completed his undertaking after he died, and today the Ben-Yehuda work consists of sixteen volumes. Eliezer Ben-Yehuda achieved his goal: the revival of the Hebrew language as a living tongue.

BEN-ZVI, YITZHAK

(1884-1963)—Second President of Israel. Born in the Ukraine, Ben-Zvi was a pioneer settler of Palestine in 1907. He studied law in Constantinople (1912-14) and spent some years in the United States during World War I. Ben-Zvi was among the founders of the Histadrut (Israel Labor Federation) in 1920, and of the Mapai party in 1929. Until the founding of the State in 1948, he was president of the Vaad Leumi (National Committee); upon its establishment he was elected a Mapai representative to the Knesset. When President Chaim Weizmann died in 1952, Ben-Zvi was elected to succeed him as Israel's highest official,

serving in this office until his death. Ben-Zvi did important scholarly research on Oriental Jewish communities (some of which is recounted in his book *The Exiled and the Redeemed*), and founded the Ben-Zvi Institute to further this work.

BENAMOZEGH, ELIJAH

(1822-1900)—Italian rabbi and philosopher. As professor of theology and director of the rabbinical seminary at Leghorn (Livorno) for many years, Benamozegh was the chief spokesman for Judaism in the Italy of his day. Within the Jewish community he also defended religious orthodoxy and opposed the development of Liberal (Reform) Judaism. Benamozegh wrote extensively on Judaism in several languages, concentrating mainly on ethical and moral questions.

BENE ISRAEL

The name given themselves by a group of Jews who resemble the Hindus among whom they live. They are descendants of Jews who had fled from ancient Israel and were wrecked in the Indian Ocean at least 2,200 years ago. From the islands on which they landed they made their way to the mainland. Today thousands of Bene Israel live in Bombay and other large Indian and Pakistani cities. They speak a Hindu tongue but observe most of the talmudic laws. They deny that their appearance is due to intermarriage with the native population. Maimonides and many before him knew of these people and commented on their customs. Their observance of the holidays was a strange mixture of Jewish and Mohammedan customs, with some elements taken from Christianity. In the eighteenth century, under the guidance of a learned traveler, David Ezekiel Rahabi, they returned to traditional Judaism. Under British rule many of them became soldiers and many held governmental positions. They have their own synagogues and schools and after long conflict have been admitted as part of the general Jewish community of India and Pakistan. In ancient times the Bene Israel were oilpressers but now the majority of them are artisans and skilled craftsmen and there are a large number of professional people among them. Many of their women work in the nursing profession.

See also India.

BENJAMIN

Twelfth and youngest son of Jacob; son of Rachel, only full brother of Joseph. He was the ancestor of the tribe of Benjamin.

See also Benjamin, Tribe of

BENJAMIN, JUDAH P.

(1811-1884)—One of the outstanding men of the American South when the southern states broke from the North in the Civil War. When very young he came to America from the West Indies. He attended Yale University, studied law and soon became an authority on the courts of Louisiana. He was a state legislator, yet so varied were his interests that he is known as a great agriculturist and railroad lawyer as well as a distinguished public official. Though at first opposed to slavery, he served the South as Secretary of War and Secretary of State. His final post was that of Premier of the Confederacy. Escaping to England after the war at the age of 54, he rose to become one of that country's most praised and capable lawyers. He died in France. Benjamin's life is a true picture of the wandering Jew, ever loyal to the country in which he was living.

BENJAMIN, TRIBE OF

One of the Israelite tribes. Its territory, in central Canaan, between Judah and Ephraim, included Jericho, Ramah, Bethel, Kiriath-jearim and, on its border, Jerusalem (after David's conquest of the Jebusite fortress). Benjamin became part of the southern Kingdom of Judah. Benjamin and Judah are the two surviving tribes. Benjamin's banner was of many colors: its emblem was a wolf. The stone representing Benjamin in the breastplate of the High Priest was probably a jasper.

BENJAMIN OF TUDELA

(12th century)—Traveller, often called the "Jewish Marco Polo." In the course of his business he travelled over most of the world known at that time. He started from Saragossa, Spain, and covered Europe, Asia, and northern Africa, visiting over 300 cities. His diary, called *Massaot shel Rabbi Benjamin* ("Travels of Rabbi Benjamin"), was written in Hebrew, but has been translated into many languages. In this book he gives detailed descriptions of the Jewish settlements he visits, and tells of their religious, political, and social life. The "Travels" is a unique source for the Jewish history and geography of the Middle Ages.

BER (Dov Ber)

(1710-1772)—One of the greatest Hasidic teachers, he was the chosen pupil and successor of Israel Baal Shem Tov. Called the "Maggid of Meseritz," after the town in which he taught, he inspired his students (approx. 300) to spread the Hasidic doctrines and his teachings. His activities incited Elijah, Gaon of Vilna, to issue his famout ban against Hasidism in 1792. Ber left no written teachings but his maxims were taken down by his pupils and later published.

BERDITCHEVSKY, MICHAH JOSEPH

(1865-1921)—Hebrew author. Berditchevsky studied at the Yeshiva of Volozin and the University of Berlin. In his essays, he is critical of religion and tradition, and calls for a Jewish national culture free of these elements. Berditchevsky, who wrote under the penname of Bin-Gorion, authored stories of ghetto life in Hebrew and Yiddish, and collected Jewish fables and legends. He had a great influence over the youth of his time.

BERGSON, HENRI

(1859-1941)—French philosopher. His view opposes the rule of the intellect and favors mystical, intuitive thought. His works have been very influential, the most famous being "Creative Evolution." He received the Nobel Prize for Literature in 1927.

BERNSTEIN, LEONARD

(1918-   )—U.S. conductor and composer, Bernstein was the first American-born musician to be music director and permanent conductor of the New York Philharmonic Orchestra. He has written scores for Broadway musicals (*Wonderful Town*, *West Side Story*), as well as the oratorio *Kaddish*, the *Jeremiah Symphony*, and other works.

BERTINORO, OBADIAH OF

(c. 1450-1510)—Italian rabbi and commentator on the Mishnah. Around 1485 Obadiah settled in Jerusalem, where he founded a yeshivah. He was soon recognized as the foremost halakhic authority in Palestine and Egypt. He is best known for his clear, lucid commentary on the Mishnah, designed as an aid for those who study the Mishnah without the Gemara. Now regarded as the standard work of its kind, it is printed in most editions of the Mishnah. He also wrote an interesting account of his journey from Italy to Jerusalem, describing his adventures and the Jewish communities he passed through. It is an important source for medieval Jewish history.

BET

The second letter of the Hebrew alphabet, has the numerical value of 2.

See also Aleph Bet.

BET ALPHA SYNAGOGUE

Sixth century (C.E.) synagogue unearthed on the site of Bet Alpha, Israel communal settlement founded in 1922 in the Valley of Jezreel. The mosaic floor of the ancient synagogue bears a design depicting the sun-carriage, the wheel of the zodiac, the sacrifice of Isaac, ritual symbols and other significant aspects of the era, including inscriptions in Hebrew, Aramaic and Greek.

BET DIN

("Court of Justice") in ancient times a court that had the power to decide on matters of criminal and civil law. In the United States the Bet Din makes decisions only on religious matters, and acts as a court of arbitration.

Bratislava: Entrance
to the Beth Din.

BET HAKNESET

("House of Assembly") one of several terms for a synagogue.

See also Synagogue.

BET HAMIDRASH

("House of Study") a building for study and prayer for members of the community. In modern times, the Bet Hamidrash usually adjoins the synagogue. It is often equipped with a library and other facilities for study. Prayer is also held in the Bet Hamidrash.

BET HAMIKDASH

("The Holy Temple") refers to the First and Second Temples in Jerusalem.

See also Temple.

BET HATEFILAH

("House of Prayer") another term for a synagogue.

See also Synagogue.

BET HILLEL AND BET SHAMMAI

(Heb., lit., "School of H." and "School of S.")—Two schools of Tannaim which flourished during the 1st century C.E. They differed in many decisions, Bet Shammai usually taking the more stringent view, Bet Hillel the more lenient. The doctrines of Bet Hillel were accepted in most cases, legend telling that a *Bat Kol* (divine voice) made a proclamation to that effect.

BETH-EL

("House of God") ancient place of worship, town between Jerusalem and Shechem where Abraham and Jacob built altars. Jacob erected an altar in commemoration of the dream he had there.

BETHLEHEM

Town in a fertile district of Judea, near Jerusalem. Bethlehem was the home of the family of David—Boaz, Ruth and Jesse—and David's birthplace. Rachel's grave is near Bethlehem.

BET-SHEARIM

City in Galilee, seat of Jewish learning at the time of the Tannaim (2nd century C.E.). The Sanhedrin, under Judah Hanasi, met there for a period of time.

See also Javneh.

BEZALEL

Gifted craftsman and builder of the Tabernacle and the Ark of the Covenant, appointed to this holy task by God through Moses. Bezalel also fashioned all the vessels and instruments of the sanctuary, including the high priest's *Ephod* and his breastplate with the *Urim* and *Tummim*. Bezalel was aided by Oholiab.

BEZALEL SCHOOL OF ARTS AND CRAFTS

The Bezalel School was founded in Jerusalem in 1906 by Boris Schatz. At first it concentrated on silverwork and embroidery of sacred objects, but it has since broadened its scope. The National Museum, also called "Bezalel," was founded in association with the school, but in 1925 became an independent institution. The museum has exhibits of Jewish art, both traditional and secular, and also possesses an art library.

Chaim Nachman Bialik.

BIALIK, CHAIM NACHMAN

(1873-1934)—Known as the Jewish national poet, he is honored today as the greatest Hebrew poet of modern times. Only six when his father died, he was reared by a learned, pious grandfather who possessed an excellent library of ancient and medieval Jewish writings. The boy read works of Maimonides, Judah Halevi and modern Hebraists. In the academy of Volozin he learned Russian and also read the new Hebrew poetry. He began writing essays and verses for Hebrew periodicals. In Odessa, after having worked as teacher, editor and merchant, he helped establish a Hebrew publishing house. Before long he became known as the finest Hebrew poet of his day. After the Russian Revolution, he had to escape to western Europe. In 1924 he settled in Tel Aviv. Bialik made a triumphal tour of the United States in 1926. Those who did not know Hebrew read his poetry in translation. One of his poems praises the Jewish student who spends long hours over his Talmud; others bitterly describe the Russian pogroms. In addition to his poetry Bialik is known for his short stories, essays and translations; he also collected Jewish folklore and medieval Hebrew verse.

BIBLE, LOST BOOKS OF

Works cited by the Bible which have been lost. Such are two poetical books entitled "Book of the Wars of the Lord" (Num. 21:14) and "Book of Jashar" (Josh. 10:13). Also mentioned are "Chronicles of the Kings of Judah" and "Chronicles of the Kings of Israel," "Words of Samuel the Prophet," "Words of Nathan the Prophet" and others.

BIKKUR-HOLIM

(Heb., lit., "Visiting the Sick") The *Mitzvah* of visiting the sick to cheer them during illness. In many communities there exists a society by this name, whose members make it a practice of visiting those confined to the house by sickness; many Jewish hospitals have adopted the name as well.

BILHAH

Handmaid of Rachel and concubine of Jacob. She was the mother of Dan and Naphtali, ancestors of tribes of Israel.

BILU

Group of Russian Jewish students who settled in Palestine after the pogroms of 1881 in Russia. These pioneers, the first organized *Halutzim* of modern Zionism, took their name from the initials of the Biblical "Bet Ya'akov Lechu Venailchah—House of Jacob, come, let us go (Isaiah 2:5)." Their program called for the establishment of an agricultural colony, and looked forward to the "national spiritual revival of the Jewish people in Palestine." The group was made up of twenty members, and most of them took part in the founding of Rishon le-Zion and Gederah. They serve as stirring examples to Israeli youth today.

BIRNBAUM, NATHAN

(1864-1937)—Philosopher and politician. He was the first to use the term "Zionism" in its modern meaning and he was among the founders of the nationalistic students' union, "Kadimah," in 1883. Many of his writings foreshadowed the Zionist ideology later developed by Herzl. From about 1897, however, he sided with Ahad Ha'am in opposing Herzl's "political Zionism." After the 3rd Zionist Congress (1899) he broke with the movement and associated himself with the furtherance of Jewish cultural autonomy in eastern Europe and the development of Yiddish as the national language. About the year 1912 another change overtook him, this time of a religious nature and he turned to Orthodoxy, becoming chief secretary of the "Agudat Israel" movement.

BIROBIDJAN

Area of 10 million acres in eastern Siberia set aside in 1928 by the Soviet government for Jewish agricultural settlement, with a view to creating a Jewish home within the Soviet Union. Yiddish was recognized as an official language, and a Yiddish newspaper and theatre were established. 20,000 Jews came to settle the area, but 11,000 had left by 1934. By 1954, there were some 100,000 Jews in Birobidjan, but the plan of making the area an autonomous Jewish state has been abandoned. The Yiddish theatre shut down in the early 1950's, and most of the inhabitants now speak Russian.

BIUR HAMETZ

The traditional "burning of the leaven." On the morning preceding the first Seder on Passover Eve, the last leaven remaining in the house is burned.

BLESSING OF THE CHILDREN

In the Bible, the blessing of children by the father before his death was of great prophetic significance; one of the most beloved Bible stories is the tale of Jacob's disguising himself as Esau so as to receive his father's blessing. Other famous blessings are those of Jacob (Gen. 49) and Moses (Deut. 33). The customary formula for today's blessing, bestowed upon returning from the synagogue Friday evening is, for boys, "God make thee as Ephraim and Manasseh" (Gen. 48:20), and for girls, "God make thee as Sarah, Rebekah, Rachel and Leah."

BLOCH, ERNEST

(1880-1959)—Composer. A specific "Hebrew character" is present in much of his music, though he did not utilize folk themes. His works include the "Israel" symphony; "Shelomo," a rhapsody for cello and orchestra; "Avo-dat ha-Kodesh," a setting for the Sabbath service, and much chamber music.

BLOOD LIBEL

The accusation that Jews use the blood of Christians for ritual purposes, particularly in the preparation of Passover *Matzot* or in the *Seder* rite. Although mentioned by Josephus in his *Against Apion*, the first in-

A medieval anti-Semitic drawing, depicting Jews taking blood from Christian children for their "mystic ceremonies."

stance of such a charge was at Norwich, England, in 1144. Though many Christians, including some Popes, fought the charges, the masses were incited by them to mass slaughters of and pogroms against the Jews; the Kishinev massacre (1903) followed the spreading of such an accusation. The Nazis tried to revive the accusation during their rule.

BLUM, LEON

(1872-1950)—French statesman. Blum, born in Paris, led the Socialist Party from 1919, when he was first elected to Parliament. He became Prime Minister in 1936-7, and again in 1938. After the German conquest of France, he was deported to Buchenwald, but he was freed in 1945. Soon after his release, he headed the post-war French government (1946-7). Blum was active in Jewish affairs, serving on the council of the Jewish Agency, and devoting himself to the Jewish labor movement.

B'NAI B'RITH

(Hebrew for "Sons of the Covenant") B'nai B'rith was founded in New York in 1843, as a movement with social, educational, and charitable aims. Its total membership in the United States (1962) was 350,000; some 80,000 members are found throughout the world. Its youth organizations (Hillel, B'nai B'rith Youth Organization) have some 32,000 members. The organization fights anti-Semitism, supports Israel, and does much educational and cultural work.

See also Anti-Defamation League.

BNAI ZION

(Hebrew, "Sons of Zion") A fraternal society which supports projects in Israel, and which founded the American branch of the Magen David Adom, the Israeli equivalent of the Red Cross. Founded in 1910, Bnai Zion is the oldest active Zionist fraternal society in America, and has a membership of about 16,000, for whom it provides cultural and social activities.

BOARD OF DEPUTIES OF BRITISH JEWS

The representative body of English Jews, established to watch over Jewish interests in England. First organized in 1760, the members of the Board (about 450) are elected by synagogues and other Jewish institutions in the British Empire. It now reflects popular Jewish opinion in English Jewish life and is strongly Zionistic.

BOAS, FRANZ

(1858-1942)—Pioneer in the science of anthropology. Boas came to the U.S. in 1886, and taught at Columbia University, New York, from 1896-1937. His researches established him as the founder of American anthropology. Boas energetically opposed German "racial" theories, holding that environment was more influential than "purity of blood."

BOAZ

Wealthy farmer of Bethlehem. He helped Ruth when she was a stranger who gleaned the grain from his field, and later married her. They were ancestors of King David.

BOKHARA

Territory in Central Asia, which is one of the Union of Socialist Soviet Republics. Benjamin of Tudela reports that at the end of the 12th century there was a Jewish community in Samarkand of 50,000; later persecutions sent even more Jews to the region. However, expulsion of many Jews took place beginning in 1899 and the community dwindled to its present 50,000. There is a small settlement of Bokharan Jews in Jerusalem.

BOLIVIA

Jewish immigration to Bolivia began, for all practical purposes, in the 1920s, although some Marranos had settled there in the 16th century. The Jewish population of 2,000 is mainly Polish and German in origin, and is involved primarily in business and industry.

BONDI, AUGUST

(1833-1907)—American abolitionist. Bondi was born in Austria, and came to the U.S. after the unsuccessful Austrian Revolution of 1848. Once here, he joined John Brown's small military group in Kansas, and fought with him against the pro-slavery forces at Black Jack and Osawatomie in 1856. After the Civil War, in which he fought on the Union side, Bondi held public office in Kansas.

BOOKPLATES

Bookplates using Jewish themes and motifs became widely used among Jews in the 19th and 20th centuries, though the earliest Jewish bookplates were executed by Benjamin Levi in the mid-eighteenth century. At certain periods, they were almost the only bearers of Jewish artistic expression. An exhibition held in Jerusalem in 1955 displayed over 800 such bookplates.

BOROCHOV, DOV BER

(1881-1917)—Labor Zionist leader and author. Borochov combined Zionism and Marxism by declaring that only in Palestine could the Jewish workingman be victorious. He founded the *Poale Zion* (Workers of Zion) in Russia, and was secretary of its world union. He came to the United States in 1914, and was active here in the Labor Zionist movement, winning many labor leaders over to the Zionist cause. After the Russian Revolution of 1917 he returned to that country, where he died. His most important writings were published in 1937 under the title, *Nationalism and the Class Struggle*.

BRAININ, REUBEN

(1862-1939)—Hebrew author and journalist. Until 1909, when he came to the U.S., the Russian-born Brainin lived in Vienna and Berlin. He demanded that Hebrew literature deal with universal, "human" matters, as well as with specifically Jewish subjects. In literary criticism, too, he introduced Western standards. Brainin was the author of a biography of Herzl, and wrote many volumes of short stories; he also edited Hebrew and Yiddish journals in both Europe and America.

BRANDEIS, LOUIS DEMBITZ

(1856-1941)—Born in Kentucky, Louis Dembitz Brandeis became one of America's greatest jurists. But when President Wilson nominated him for the Supreme Court in 1916, it was necessary to overcome protests on the grounds that he was a Jew and a fighter for popular rights. Brandeis was brilliant in all he undertook. At preparatory school in Dresden and at Harvard College and Law School he stood at the head of his classes. While practicing law in Boston he formed a strong friendship with Oliver Wendell Holmes, who preceded him to the Supreme Court and who joined with him in many notable decisions. Brandeis was known as the "people's attorney," for his legal battles helped change insurance law to provide better protection for policy holders and to curb the unlimited powers of utility companies as against consumers. He was determined to make the law accord with the needs and changes of the times rather than with ancient legal precedents. Every brief he wrote was marked by

BRANDEIS UNIVERSITY

Founded in 1948 as a contribution of American Jewry to American higher education, and named after Justice Louis Brandeis. A coeducational liberal arts college, it is situated in Waltham, Mass., near Boston.

The Graduate School of Arts and Sciences, which offers Master of Arts, Master of Fine Arts, and Doctor of Philosophy degrees, was opened in 1953. In 1970 Brandeis had an enrollment of 2,800 students.

Aerial view of Brandeis University.

BRAZIL

In 1503, the alleged Marrano Fernando de Noronha obtained from King Manuel of Portugal exclusive colonization and trading rights in Brazil, which he used to settle his fellow-Jews in the country. Later immigrants from Portugal, driven to Brazil by the zeal of the Inquisition, brought with them sugar cane and established a flourishing export trade to Europe, especially during the period of Dutch rule, which began in 1631. In 1654, when Portugal reconquered the country, the Inquisition was introduced into Brazil; some Jews left for Holland, while others established the Jewish community at New Amsterdam (later New York). Since 1822, when Brazil attained independence, Jewish immigration to the country has been heavy, and at present there are 150,000 Jews in this South American republic; the largest Jewish communities are in Rio de Janeiro (50,000), Sao Paulo, and Porto Alegre.

BREASTPLATE

1. (*Hoshen Mishpat*—"Breastplate of Judgment") specifically the high priest's breastplate worn over his robe and attached to the *Ephod*. It was a finely made square shield of gold on which were set twelve precious stones in four rows (*Turim*). Each tribe of Israel was represented by its own stone engraved with its name. Under the breastplate were, some believe, the *Urim* and *Tummim*, two small sacred objects, possibly lots. The high priest wore the Breastplate of Judgment over his heart when he stood before God in prayer and in search for advice and judgment, especially on the High Holy Days.

2. (*Tas*—"plate") decorative shield suspended by silver chains over the Torah, resembling the breastplate worn by the high priests.

B'RIT

(Covenant) the holy bond God made with Abraham and renewed through Moses with the whole people of Israel by giving the Tables of the Covenant (*Luchot HaB'rit*) on which were written the Ten Commandments.

See also Covenant

Page from 18th-century illustrated prayer book showing the Brith Milah Ceremony.

B'RIT MILAH

The rite of circumcision performed when a boy is eight days old. The ceremony signifies the parents' agreement to raise their son as a member of the Jewish community.

See also Covenant.

Martin Buber.

BUBER, MARTIN

(1878-1965)—A noted philosopher and author of books on Judaism, Buber was born in Vienna. He is best known as a collector of Hasidic tales and as one who tried to bring back the spirit of the Hasidim, mystics who believe in serving God with gladness and joy. His desire for Jewish learning was stimulated by his distinguished grandfather, Solomon Buber (1827-1906), who spent most of his life gathering and editing medieval and ancient legends and explanations of Bible stories and teachings, generally known as Midrash, Martin Buber studied and taught in European universities, and then worked with the oppressed Jewish community of Germany after Hitler came to power. In 1938 he went to Palestine, where he became a professor at the Hebrew University. Buber developed the thought that the Bible is a record of God's conversation with Israel and that Judaism cannot exist unless Jews look upon God as being very close to them. His philosophical ideas have been very influential in both Jewish and Christian circles. He wrote and edited many volumes of legends and discourses, and books on history and philosophy. Many of his philosophical writings have appeared in English, including *Israel and the World, I and Thou, Between Man and Man,* and *Two Types of Faith,* a comparison of Judaism and Christianity. His widely read *Tales of the Hasidim* recounts the history of the movement through the personalities of its leaders.

BUND

The Jewish socialist organization of Poland, Lithuania and Russia, founded in 1897 at Vilna. It fought for better working conditions and higher wages and was outlawed by the Czarist movement. The Bund denied the unity of the Jewish people throughout the world and was strongly anti-Zionist. The executive of the Bund of non-Communist countries has been situated in New York since 1947 but the movement has little influence on the Jewish scene.

BUSTANAI BEN HANINAI

(620-675)—The first Babylonian exilarch (*Rosh Golah*) after the Arab conquest; ancestor of all later Babylonian exilarchs. The Calif Omar gave him the captive daughter of the Persian King Chosroes II, Izdundad, as a wife, and the disputes concerning the inheritance rights of the children born of this marriage continued into the middle of the 8th century. According to tradition Bustanai was a descendant of King David.

BYZANTINE EMPIRE

The Eastern Roman Empire; it included Greece, Syria, Palestine, Asia Minor and Egypt, lands which contained the majority of the world's Jewish population during the first part of the Empire's existence. The Byzantine Emperors, from Justinian (527-65) on, opposed Jewish religious life and some (Leo, 723; Basil I, 873) forbade the practice of Judaism. Nevertheless, Jewish communities survived, though no distinguished intellectual life flourished. Karaism was always active in the Empire.

CABALA

See Kabbalah

CAESAREA

Port city on the Mediterranean built by Herod. It was a center of Jewish revolt against Rome during the time of Bar Kochba. Rabbi Akiba and other martyrs were executed there. In the 3rd and 4th centuries, a Talmudic academy flourished in Caesarea, whose Amoraim made great contributions to the Palestinian Talmud.

CAHAN, ABRAHAM

1860-1951)—American Yiddish journalist. Forced to leave his native Russia on account of revolutionary, socialistic activities, Cahan settled in the U.S. in 1882. Here he continued his work on behalf of the socialist cause, his greatest achievement being the founding and editing of the *Jewish Daily Forward* in New York. This newspaper, which first appeared in 1897, became the most widely-read Jewish newspaper in the country, with great influence on the American labor movement. His English novel, *The Rise of David Levinsky*, is a most vivid and realistic portrayal of Jewish immigrant life in New York.

CAIN

Son of Adam and Eve. He killed his younger brother Abel in a fit of anger. Thereafter he was a restless fugitive and vagabond, and his forehead bore the "mark of Cain."

CALEB

One of the 12 scouts sent with Joshua to survey Canaan. He and Joshua encouraged the people with reports that Israel was strong enough to occupy it. Joshua and Caleb were the only Israelites who left Egypt and survived to settle in the Holy Land.

Before the invention of printing, the preparation of a calendar was a laborious undertaking. This calendar or *luah* of the Hebrew year 5036 (1276 C.E.), was found in a Bible manuscript.

CALENDAR, JEWISH

Consists of 12 months in regular years and 13 months in leap years, based on the revolutions of the moon, the lunar system (the secular calendar is based on the solar system). Leap year occurs 7 times in every 19 years. The numbering of the years is based on the calculation that the Creation took place in 3761 B.C.E. The calendar took its present form in the 13th century and was based on the formulations made by Hillel II in the 4th century.

See also Months, Jewish.

CANAAN

Early name for the land of Israel; the territory between the Jordan and the Mediterranean, also called the Promised Land, the Holy Land and Palestine.

CANAANITES

The inhabitants of Canaan. They were conquered by the invading Israelites under Joshua. At the time of the Judges, Deborah and Barak defeated the Canaanites in the battle at Mount Tabor, when the Canaanites' iron chariots sank in the mud of the swelling River Kishon.

CANADA

The Jewish community of Canada dates from the British conquest in 1760. Jews received the right to vote in 1832. The present Canadian Jewish community numbers 305,000, the majority of whom live in Montreal, Toronto, Winnipeg, and Vancouver. An excellent system of education has been established, and the community maintains important religious and cultural institutions, a strong Zionist movement, and a Jewish press. Jews have made significant contributions to the economic life of the country as merchants and manufacturers, and have also been active in its cultural life. Mordecai Richler, the author of *The Apprenticeship of Duddy Kravitz*, is a noted Canadian Jewish novelist.

CANTONISTS

Children taken into the army in Czarist Russia, often with the intent of converting them to Christianity. Children were drafted as young as ten years of age and their term of service lasted 25 years, reckoned after the age of 18. The Jewish communities were forced to fulfill a quota of soldiers and usually the sons of the poorer families were substituted for those of the wealthy families who had bought out their children. Professional kidnappers were often resorted to, thus arousing deep resentment.

CANTOR

(*Hazan*) in modern times the official of the synagogue who assists the rabbi in leading the congregation in prayer. He sings many of the prayers and often

CANTOR, EDDIE

(1892-1964)—American comedian. Cantor, whose real name was Israel Itzkowitz, was a prominent entertainer on stage, radio, television, and movies. He often aided Jewish communal efforts such as the United Jewish Appeal.

Benjamin Nathan Cardozo.

CARDOZO, BENJAMIN NATHAN

(1870-1938)—The second Jew to be appointed an associate justice of the United States Supreme Court. He was a descendant of the first Jews to arrive in the United States two centuries ago. In 1913 he was elected a justice of the New York Supreme Court; in 1914 he became a member of the Court of Appeals, highest in the state, being elevated to chief judge in 1927. The federal appointment was made by President Hoover in 1932. Justice Cardozo achieved fame as one whose written judgments were so clear and brilliant as to become models for all jurists; and for his insistence that the law is of interest not alone to lawyers but to all men as helping to adjust their lives to society. He believed that a judge must know more than the law; that he should understand and use every available detail of how men live. So honored and beloved was this faithful Jew that all the country joined in mourning his passing.

CARIGAL, RAPHAEL HAYIM ISAAC

(1733-1777)—Palestinian rabbi and preacher, born at Hebron. Carigal travelled over the world as an emissary of Palestinian Jewry, visiting Constantinople, the West Indies, London, and North America. In America he became the friend and teacher of Ezra Stiles, later to become president of Yale University. Carigal died in Barbados.

CARMEL, MOUNT

The beautiful mountain on the Mediterranean whose eastern ridge is watered by the River Kishon. At Mount Carmel, Elijah defeated the prophets of Baal.

CARO, JOSEPH

(1488-1575)—The author of the great code of Jewish law, the *Shulchan Aruch*, which to this day governs the lives of all observant Jews. Caro was born in Spain, lived in Turkey and then settled in Safed, Palestine. All his earlier years were devoted to study that prepared him for his great work. Strangely, he came to believe that miracles would occur in his day to bring the Messiah and recover Israel's past glories. He was even certain that he possessed a "familiar spirit," another self that conversed with him and controlled his life. But these ideas in no way affected his legal judgments. His ambition to be recognized as the world's greatest authority on Jewish law was realized in his lifetime. Caro began summarizing the decisions of thirty-two outstanding authorities in the year 1522; in 1542 the work was completed. From every part of the Jewish world scholars sent him their queries. Out of his original work, called *Bet Yoseph* ("House of Joseph"), the *Shulchan Aruch* ("Prepared Table") was abridged and popularized. No other code of any kind has persisted so long and been observed by so many people.

CENTRAL AMERICA

The number of Jews in Central America has always been small; 2,000 live in Panama, 1,900 in Guatemala, 300 in El Salvador, 1,500 in Costa Rica, and 200 in Nicaragua. The majority of these Jews are European immigrants and engage in trade.

CENTRAL CONFERENCE OF AMERICAN RABBIS

Reform rabbinical organization, founded in 1889, with a membership of over seven hundred reform rabbis. Though once anti-Zionist, the organization's position has shifted, and it now considers Israel a center of Jewish spiritual and cultural strength. The Conference has brought out the Union Prayer Book, the standard prayerbook of Reform synagogues.

CHAD GADYA

The popular song which concludes the Seder service. Many scholars trace its origin to a popular ballad of the later Middle Ages. It must not be interpreted, however, as a mere nursery rhyme, for it is a graphic illustration of the theme that divine justice governs the universe. According to some interpretations it is symbolical of the whole course of Jewish history, in which God purchased the Jewish people by means of the Two Tablets of Stone (Two *Zuzim*) and will ultimately redeem Israel from all oppressors.

CHAGALL, MARC

(1887-   )—One of the most important artists of modern times, Chagall was born in Russia and has lived since the 1920s in France. His surrealist paintings,

Synagogue painting by Marc Chagall.

noted for their bright colors and sense of fantasy, often derive their themes and inspiration from his memories of Jewish *shtetl* life in Eastern Europe. Chagall's famous series of stained-glass windows, representing the symbols of the Twelve Tribes of Israel, are to be found in the synagogue of the Hadassah Medical Center in Jerusalem.

CHAIN, ERNST B.

(1906-   )—Biochemist and Nobel Prize winner. In 1933 the German-born Chain was invited to lecture in chemical pathology at Oxford. The Nobel Prize Committee awarded him its prize for medicine and physiology in 1945 for his work on penicillin. Since 1949 he has lived in Italy, serving as director of the International Research Center for Chemical Microbiology.

CHALDEANS

People of Chaldea in southern Babylonia at the time of Abraham; the land between the Tigris and Euphrates. The later Babylonians were also called the Chaldeans. They, with the help of the Medes, overthrew Assyria (about 612 B.C.E.). The Babylonian king, Nebuchadnezzar, was a Chaldean. Abraham was born in Ur of the Chaldees.

See also Babylonia.

CHARITY

In Hebrew the word for charity is the same as that for righteousness—*tzedakah*. Judaism believes that helping one's fellowman is not an act of "charity" alone but of simple propriety and justice. The Torah knew that no matter what progress might be made in social life, there would always be some who, through disabilities or misfortunes, would need the assistance of their neighbors. The poor might glean the corners and left-overs of the fields and none could halt or reproach them. Certain tithes, taxes, had to go to the poor. In every Jewish community there have been societies for helping Jewish travelers, burying the needy, clothing the poorly clad, feeding the hungry, assisting the moneyless bride and redeeming enslaved captives. Education, immigration, and a hundred other needs were taken care of by the community. The Jews who first came to America promised to take care of their own poor always. They have never failed to do so.

CHICAGO

Jews first arrived in Chicago in the 1830s, but it was not until the Russian immigration of the 1880s that a large community was established in the city. During the Civil War the community, numbering only 1,000, recruited a Jewish company which fought at Gettysburg. Chicago boasts 89 synagogues (1961), a number of publications, and cultural and philanthropical societies, as well as the College of Jewish Studies and the Hebrew Theological College. In 1971 its Jewish population was 269,000 — the 4th largest American Jewish community.

A Chinese Jew and his son.

CHINA

The settlement of Jews in China dates from approximately 950 C.E., when Persian or Indian Jews emigrated there. This community, at Kai Feng Fu, survived despite hardship and persecution into the 18th century, when it disappeared. Persian Jews came to the land once again in the 19th century, and established themselves in Shanghai. This Shanghai community proved a haven for many refugees from wartorn Europe between the two World Wars; during World War II the Jewish population reached 26,000. Communist persecution drove Chinese Jews to emigrate to Israel and America, and only a few hundred Jews remain in China now.

CHOFETZ CHAIM

(1837-1933)—Talmudic scholar and Orthodox leader. Rabbi Israel Meir Hacohen of Zhitil, Poland, took the name *Chofetz Chaim* (Hebrew for "desirous of life") from the Biblical verse, "Who is the man that desireth life . . . ? . . . Keep thy tongue from evil . . ." (Psalms 34:13-14), which inspired his first book, a treatise against slander. He founded a *yeshiva* at Radin which ranked among the greatest in the world. The *Chofetz Chaim* was considered the dean of judges and his six-volume commentary to *Orach Chaim* is one of the most authoritative works on the subject.

CHOIR

The use of choirs at religious services dates back to the time when the Levites sang in the First Temple. Later, there were periods of opposition to their use in the synagogue. Today many synagogues have well-trained choirs.

CHONI HA-MEAGGEL

(lit., Choni the Circle-Drawer; 1st century)—One of the most pious men of his time, Choni once drew a circle about himself and refused to leave it till his prayer for rain would be answered. Josephus relates that he was put to death by Hyrcanus when he refused to pray for his success in battle against Aristobulus.

CHOSEN PEOPLE

This phrase comes from the Biblical idea that Israel is the possessor of a peculiar treasure. The words oblige the Jew to act in accord with the will of God and be witness of God's rule and goodness among the nations. In the early years of Christianity it was preached that Israel had been rejected in favor of the new religion and its leader. For this reason the rabbis often stressed the chosen-ness of Israel, thus keeping their followers loyal and proud despite the efforts to convert them. The chosen people concept continues to proclaim the need of every Jew to accept the ethical teachings of the Torah and to dedicate his life to serving God and God's children.

CHRONICLES, I AND II

(*Divre Hayamim*) the last two books of historical writings in the 3rd division (*Ketubim*) of the Bible. Chronicles retells the history of Israel up to the return of the Jews to Judea from Babylonian Exile.

CITIES OF REFUGE

Six sacred cities of refuge for men who had unintentionally killed. No refuge from prosecution, however, was extended to a willful murderer. These cities —Bezer, Ramoth-gilead, Golan, Kedesh, Shechem and Hebron—existed as refuges until the destruction of the Second Temple.

CITIES OF THE PLAIN

The cities of Sodom, Gomorrah, Admah, Zeboiim and Zoar. These wicked, inhospitable cities, in the fruitful valley of the Jordan, with the exception of Zoar, were destroyed by fire and brimstone. Their ruins lie on the bottom of the Dead Sea. Zoar was saved for Lot's sake.

CODES OF JEWISH LAW

Systematic explanations of the laws governing Judaism. The Torah is the foundation of all Jewish law upon which all later codes are based. The Talmud, the greatest post-Biblical collection of Jewish law, elaborates and explains the laws of the Torah. The most famous post-Talmudic codes are: Maimonides' *Mishneh Torah* (12th century), Jacob ben Asher's *Turim* (14th century), Joseph Caro's *Shulchan Aruch* and its Ashkenazic addition, Moses Isserles' *Mappah* (both 16th century).

See also Halachah; Noahide Laws.

COHEN

Perhaps the oldest and most common of Jewish names. It comes from the Hebrew word meaning priest and is applied to descendants of Aaron, the first High Priest. Because certain honors and duties fell to the lot of every such descendant (the "kohen" was the first to read the Torah, the redeemer of the first-born, and restricted as to marriage in accord with Biblical teaching), families were proud to add to each male the family name, "Ha-Kohen"—"the priest." Later, the prefix meaning *the* was dropped. There are numerous simple variations of the name in English and all other languages used by Jews—such as Cohn, Kahn, Kahane, Cohon. There are also a number of translations into other languages. Most usual of these variations is from the Hebrew words, *kohen tzedek,* which mean "priest of righteousness" or "righteous priest"; from the two initial letters has been formed the name Katz, which therefore has no connection—as sometimes supposed—with the German word for cat. Some of the family names stemming from priestly connection bear such well-known cognomens as Kaplan, Kraushar, Mandelbaum and Zangwill.

COHEN, GERSON DAVID

(1924-   )—American rabbi and educator. The author of important works on the Kabbalah and messianism, Cohen taught at the Jewish Theological Seminary and at Columbia University, where in 1968 he became head of the Center for Israeli and Jewish Studies. In 1973 he became chancellor of the Jewish Theological Seminary.

COHEN, HERMANN

(1842-1918)—German philosopher who founded the Marburg school of Neo-Kantianism. Cohen was not religious as a young man but turned to Judaism in middle life. In his mature thought, as elaborated in his main work on the subject, *Religion of Reason from the Sources of Judaism*, he stressed the differences between Judaism and Christianity, particularly the fact that Judaism has no concept of original sin and does not require a mediator between man and God. He saw Judaism as a religion of ethical reason based on a universal morality, and stressed the "correlation" between man and God, divine love, and messianic humanism in which man's urge to perfection would eventually triumph.

COHEN, MORRIS RAPHAEL

(1880-1947)—American philosopher and professor. Cohen emigrated to the U.S. from his native Russia in 1892. He received his Ph.D. from Harvard, and was a popular professor of philosophy at City College, New York, for some twenty-six years (1912-1938). His main books are in the fields of logic and the philosophy of law. Late in his life he grew active in Jewish affairs, founding and leading the Conference on Jewish Relations, and serving as an editor of *Jewish Social Studies*.

COHN, EDWIN J.

(1892-1953)—American biological chemist. Cohn's most important work was his investigation of the composition of blood, which made possible the later discovery of gamma globulin. His research also greatly broadened the use of life-giving blood plasma. In 1922 he was appointed to the faculty of Harvard University.

COLLEGE OF JEWISH STUDIES

Institution founded in 1924 by the Chicago Board of Jewish Education. It offers courses in general Jewish studies, Jewish education techniques, and cantillation. In 1970 the student body numbered 370.

COLOMBIA

Although small groups of Marranos came to this South American republic in the 16th century, Jews first arrived in sizeable numbers after World War I. This immigration was halted in 1939 and the present Jewish community numbers 10,000.

COLUMBUS, CHRISTOPHER

(1446-1506)—The famed discoverer of America claimed to be descended from the House of King David, as did his son. It is possible that he was of Marrano blood. One biographer claims that he was a Spanish Jew, and another has found a Marrano family with names resembling those of Columbus' relations and parents. He was a correspondent of Marrano Jews in Spain, and there were Jews in his crew.

CONFIRMATION

Exercises held in some synagogues on the first day of Shavuot for young people (usually 15 or 16 years old) who have completed a course of Jewish studies. This ceremony is of recent origin.

CONSERVATIVE JUDAISM

See Schechter, Solomon.

CORDOVA

Spanish city which played an important role in the history of the Jews in Spain. They had settled there by 711; the first Talmudical college was established there in 972; Cordova was the birthplace of Maimonides (1135). Many Marranos always lived in Cordova and it was there that the wave of massacres of the Marranos began in 1473. The Jews were expelled from Cordova in 1483.

CORDOVERO, MOSES

(1522-1570)—A noted kabbalist, Cordovero was a disciple of Joseph Karo and the teacher of Isaac Luria. A highly systematic thinker, Cordovero, in such works as *Tomer Devorah* ("Deborah's Palm Tree") and *Pardes Rimmonim* ("Pomegrante Orchard") fully discussed the mystical theology of the Kabbalah and attempted to synthesize the many different trends of kabbalistic interpretation.

COSTUME

We may assume that the dress of the Hebrews in Biblical times was similar to that of their neighbors. Except for certain exceptions, Jewish dress has usually followed the custom of the country in which the Jews lived; the distinctive "Jewish Badge" was often imposed to distinguish between Jew and Gentile. Jewish dress, however, tended to be conservative. In Eastern Europe the fur-trimmed hat (*Streimel*), long kaftan and buckled shoes became the traditional garb; once they were the dress of the Polish nobility. The Torah commands that men affix *Tzitzit* to their four-cornered garments, which led to the wearing of the *Tallit-Katan*. Jewish law also stipulates that Gentile dress should not be slavishly imitated.

COVENANT

(*B'rit*) the holy bond between God and man and specifically between God and Israel. The first covenant was made with Abraham. At Mount Sinai, God made the covenant with the whole people of Israel, through the Tablets of the Covenant (*Luchot HaB'rit*). Circumcision (*B'rit Milah*) is a symbol of the great Covenant. *See also* B'rit.

CREATION

The Bible relates that the world was created by God

in six successive days. Some men have accepted this story as fact; others have interpreted it as an allegory. But, remarkably enough, the order of the several steps of creation as described in Genesis is almost exactly like the sequence presented by modern geologists and by believers of the theory of evolution. In every case God "saw that it was good"—scientifically good, too, as it turned out. There is far more literature in Jewish lore on Genesis than on any other part of the Bible. The Midrash wishes to prove that God's glory was existent before heaven and earth were formed. After consulting with the angels God decided to make man a being combining the attributes of heaven and earth. Man came into being at the very end of creation, so that if a person waxed too proud he might be reminded that the tiniest insect has a longer ancestry than himself. Thousands of similar wise comments are to be found in the Midrash.

Isaac
Adolphe
Cremieux.

CRÉMIEUX, ISAAC ADOLPHE

(1796-1880)—The brilliant French diplomat who founded the Alliance Israélite Universelle. To this day the Alliance provides schools in North Africa and other backward lands for the religious and technical training of Jewish children. Crémiuex was born in the south of France, where he was famed as a lawyer and orator before settling in Paris in 1830. He helped abolish the "Jewish oath" in French courts, fought the false ritual murder charge in Damascus and worked with Montefiore to help Jews everywhere. In 1842 Crémieux was elected to the Chamber of Deputies. In 1848, as minister of justice, he abolished capital punishment. Later he became public defender of persons brought to trial by the government of Louis Napoleon. He lived through the Franco-Prussian War, helped save the republic and offered most of his fortune toward the indemnity demanded by the Prussians. Yet this patriot was assailed by Jews and non-Jews alike when he declared that Jews throughout the world were kinfolk. So honorable a man was Crémieux that when in 1832 he discovered that his father had gone bankrupt in 1796—the year of his own birth—he gathered the living creditors together and paid off not only the original principal but all the interest for thirty-six years.

CRESCAS, HASDAI

(1340-1410)—Philosopher, rabbi and statesman. Though Chief Rabbi of the Jews of Aragon, Spain, his fame rests on his philosophical works. His main work, the *Or Adonai* ("The Light of God"), is an attack upon the influence of Aristotelianism on Jewish philosophy and particularly on Maimonides. He claims that the ultimate meaning of life, according to the Torah, is not to be found in intellectual achievement but in the love of God. His criticism of Aristotelian philosophy is brilliant and telling and had a great influence on Spinoza.

Declaration of privileges granted to the Jews of Altona in 1641 by the King of Denmark, Christian IV.

CROMWELL, OLIVER

(1599-1658)—Lord Protector of England (1653-8) who was largely responsible for the readmission of Jews into his country. A Puritan, he was sympathetic to the Jewish religion.

CRUSADES

These holy wars waged by Christians in the Middle Ages to recapture Palestine from the Moslems were responsible for the murder of tens of thousands of Jews and for the destruction of many Jewish communities. Many crusaders were hired mercenaries, whose main interest was booty and adventure. The First Crusade (1096-9) resulted in destruction of the Jewish communities of Metz, Speyer, Mayence, Treves and other towns in the Rhineland under the direction of Count Emicho. When Jerusalem was captured in 1099, Jews and Karaites were burned alive. The later Crusaders were usually better disciplined and caused less harm to the Jews. On the whole, the Crusades began the period of persecution of medieval Jewry.

CUBA

16th century immigrants to Cuba were prevented from openly practicing of Judaism by the Inquisition, and the next immigration to Cuba took place at the end of the 19th century, when Jews from the United States came to the island. The First World War also provided an impetus to Jewish immigration from European countries to Cuba. The Jewish population in 1957 was 11,000, with 80% living in Havana. After Fidel Castro came to power in 1959, a small number emigrated to Israel, and many others fled to the United States. The present Jewish population of Cuba numbers about 1,500.

CYPRUS

Large island in the Mediterranean Sea, the inhabitants of which are called "Kittim" in the Bible (Isa. 23:1). Small Jewish settlements existed on Cyprus in the Middle Ages, and Joseph Nasi aided in the conquest of the island by the Turks in 1571. The end of the 19th century saw several unsuccessful attempts to settle Jews on Cyprus. Cyprus became the main detention center for Jews caught attempting "illegal immigration" to Palestine in 1945-49. There are now about 25 Jews on Cyprus.

Tomb of King Cyrus.

CYRUS THE GREAT

Founder of the Persian empire, conquered Babylonia at the time of the Exile. In 538 B.C.E., he permitted and helped the Jews, led by Zerubbabel, to return to their own land and to rebuild the Temple in Jerusalem.

CZECHOSLOVAKIA

Jews have lived in the region known as Czechoslovakia since the 10th century, and Prague was at one time a center of European Jewry. Jews long ago enjoyed complete equality in the country, and the Jewish population amounted to 357,000 before the Second World War. The Nazi regime annihilated most of the Jews who had not fled the country, and at the end of the war there were only 42,000 Jews left, half of whom emigrated to Israel. The present Communist government has limited communal activities, and in the 1950s was actively anti-Semitic. In 1971 the Jewish population of Czechoslovakia was about 14,000.

DALET

The fourth letter of the Hebrew alphabet, has the numerical value of 4.

See also Aleph Bet.

DAMASCUS

Ancient city and trade center in Syria; capital of a city-state whose kings often waged war against Israel. Damascus was conquered by David but was lost during the reign of Solomon.

DAMROSCH, LEOPOLD

(1832-1885)—Composer, conductor and violinist of distinction. Composed "Shulamith," an opera with a Jewish theme. Father of Frank Damrosch and Walter Damrosch.

DAN

Fifth son of Jacob; oldest son of Bilhah, ancestor of the tribe of Dan.

DAN, TRIBE OF

One of the tribes of Israel, originally occupied a small section of central Canaan. Under Philistine pressure, the tribe moved to the most northerly part of the land. The city Dan marked the northern boundary of Israel (hence the expression "from Dan to Beer-sheba"). Dan's banner was deep-blue; its emblem was a serpent and scales. The stone representing Dan in the High Priest's breastplate was probably a ligure (emerald).

DANIEL

The story of Daniel and his prophetic visions is told in the Book of Daniel. His adventures took place in Babylonia when the Jews were in exile there. Daniel and three companions (best known by their Babylonian names—Shadrach, Meshach, and Abed-nego) were deported to that land in 597 B.C.E. and made servants to the king. They all refused to eat non-kosher foods. When they would not bow down to an idol, Daniel's companions were thrown into a furnace but were not burned. Daniel was famous for interpreting dreams and signs. At a banquet given by Belshazzar, last king of Babylon, during which the king used the sacred wanting; that he would fall very soon—an event which occurred that very night. The final story told about Daniel concerns his refusal to obey a decree of the king forbidding anyone to pray to God. Daniel was thrown into a den of lions but he was not touched by the beasts.

DANIEL, BOOK OF

First book of historical writings in the 3rd division (*Ketubim*) of the Bible. It records the events of the life and time of Daniel and describes his visions.

See also Ketubim.

DANIEL, THREE ADDITIONS TO

Books of the Apocrypha consisting of: The Prayer of Azariah and the Song of the Three Children, the Story of Susannah and the Elders, and the Story of Bel and the Dragon.

DARIUS I, THE GREAT

King of Persia, ruled 522-486 B.C.E. He aided and encouraged the Jews to finish the building of the Second Temple, after their return to Jerusalem from Babylonian Exile.

DAVID

The son of Jesse of Bethlehem, succeeding King Saul. David's descendants ruled for almost 500 years (until the second half of the 6th century B.C.E.). David means "beloved" and he is indeed one of the most brilliant and fascinating figures in the Bible. As a young shepherd he was summoned to soothe King Saul's great melancholy with his beautiful gift of song. While still a boy David helped win a great battle from the Philistines by slaying the giant Goliath with only a slingshot. He became King Saul's armor bearer and his friendship with Saul's son Jonathan is one of the celebrated friendships of history. The melancholic king envied the popular young hero David. He feared for his throne and banished David repeatedly. But when Saul and Jonathan were slain in the battle of Gilboa David mourned deeply for them both. When David became king he fortified and united his country. He fought many successful wars against the Philistines, the Edomites, Ammonites, Aramites and Moabites. He conquered Jerusalem, which until that time had not been a Jewish city. David made it a great political and spiritual center for his people. In the forty years of his reign he created a powerful state. He united the various opposing elements of the people and built a religious, cultural center. In his old age, David suffered the intrigues of his sons who wished to succeed him. His final successor was his son Solomon the Wise. Many of our most beautiful Psalms are ascribed to David. It is said of him that he is the most complete expression of the spirit of Israel. It has been

the house of David.

DAVID, CITY OF

Another name for Jerusalem, also called Zion. David, conqueror of the Jebusite stronghold, Jerusalem, made it his capital and the religious and political center of Israel. He brought the Ark to Mount Zion. With the loyal high priest, Zadok, he instituted the first organized services and sacred music. The City of David refers specifically to the part of Jerusalem which is adjacent to Mount Zion.

See also Jerusalem.

DAVID, HOUSE OF

The dynasty of kings descended from David. David and Solomon ruled over all of Israel. After the division of the kingdom into Israel and Judah, the House of David ruled only over Judah, until the Babylonian Exile. Zedekiah was the last king of the House of David. It ruled from 1010-586 B.C.E.

DAYAN

A rabbi who is a judge in a rabbinical court of the Jewish community. The dayan judges legal and civil disputes as well as religious and ceremonial matters.

DAYAN, MOSHE

(1915-   )—Israeli political leader and military hero. Born in Degania, Dayan joined Haganah as a youth, participating in actions against Arab raiders in the 1930s, in the Allied invasion of Syria in 1941 (during which he lost an eye), and in the resistance against the British during the postwar period. He led the Israeli forces that captured Lod and Ramle during the War of Independence, and after the war

Moshe Dayan.

38

headed the Southern and Northern Commands, then became chief of staff in 1953, leading Israel's army to victory in the Sinai Campaign (1956). After leaving the army in 1958, Dayan entered politics. He was minister of agriculture from 1959 to 1964. As minister of defense from 1967 to 1974, Dayan was praised for the very liberal military-government policies he implemented in the occupied West Bank territories, but later on was also criticized for having contributed to the mood of overconfidence that affected Israeli preparedness just before the Yom Kippur War. In 1977 he became foreign minister in the Beigin cabinet.

DAYS OF AWE

(Yamim Noraim) refers to Rosh Hashanah and Yom Kippur.

DEAD SEA

Also called Salt Sea, or Sea of the Plain, 1,292 feet below sea level, lowest lake in the world. On its bottom lie the ruins of Sodom and Gomorrah, the evil Cities of the Plain. The important Dead Sea Scrolls, which have recently been discovered, were found near it.

DEAD SEA SCROLLS

The first group of these ancient manuscripts was found at Khirbet Kumran, 7½ miles from Jericho, and made known to the world in 1947. Coins discovered there simultaneously set the date of habitation of the site at approximately from the time of John Hyrcanus.

One of the Dead Sea Scrolls.

There was apparent evidence of destruction by earthquake in 31 B.C.E. and later reconstruction. The archeological discoveries and the scrolls' contents show that the people belonged to a Jewish sect. The most widely accepted identification of the sect is the one suggesting that it was a group similar to the Essenes. It is believed this group influenced the beginnings of Christianity. Some of the scrolls came into the possession of the Hebrew University through E. L. Sukenik, while others went to the United States where they were published by Burrows, Brownlee and others, and were later purchased for the government of Israel. Still others are in the possession of the Department of Antiquities of the government of Jordan.

DEBORAH

A judge and prophetess who led the Israelites in the bitter war against the Canaanites and brought about the unity of the northern and the southern tribes. In the battle on the plain of Jezreel, Deborah guided General Barak to the great victory over General Sisera. This was the battle that ended the war. In the Book of Judges, the power and glory of Deborah are fully described. The Song of Deborah, which follows this account in Judges, is one of the oldest poems in Hebrew literature. It describes the conditions of Deborah's times and the details of Barak's battle. It tells how a storm bogged down the Canaanite chariots and helped the outnumbered Israelites and how the enemy general Sisera fled to the tent of Jael, who killed him. The central theme of the poem is the glory and praise of God and illustrates how He protects those who follow Him. Deborah is considered one of the great women of her people and is often called "a mother in Israel."

DECALOGUE

See Ten Commandments.

DELILAH

Samson's betrothed. She betrayed Samson to her people, the Philistines.

DENMARK

The Jewish community of Denmark began in the 17th century. In 1943, while Denmark was occupied by the Nazis, the Danish Christian population successfully helped nearly all their Jewish countrymen to escape to Sweden. The Danish Jews returned after World War II and in 1969 were joined by a sizable number of Jews who had been expelled from Poland in the outbreak of anti-Semitism following the Six-Day War. The present Danish Jewish community numbers 6,000, nearly all of whom live in Copenhagen.

DEUTERONOMY

The Greek word meaning repetition of the Law, it is the fifth book of Moses, Devarim (also known as Mishneh Torah). In this book Moses again expounds the

Law to his people in several vivid orations, including a recital of the blessings and curses that would come according to the extent to which the people observed God's precepts. Moses made clear that there is one God and no other, and that Israel, which has a special relationship to God, who brought them out of the land of Egypt, was specially commanded to observe the Torah's teachings. Though there is no systematic presentation of the laws in Deuteronomy, they cover roughly the religious life of the nation and its Sanctuary, those who administer the religious and secular law, crime and war, and such personal matters as inheritance, divorce, loans and penalties for wrongdoing. Many of the decrees of Moses are found only in Deuteronomy. It limits the rights of the king, who is bound like all his subjects by common law; provides for punishment of false prophets; attempts to civilize and ease the rules of warfare; and includes a number of humanitarian enactments. Parts of Deuteronomy, notably the *Shema*, have been incorporated in the prayerbook.

DIASPORA

A Greek word meaning "scattering," which refers to the dispersion of the Jews after the Exile from the Holy Land. Settlements outside Palestine were called the Diaspora even during the time of the Kings. The ten northern tribes were exiled in 722 B.C.E. and the southern tribes living in Judah were exiled in 586. Jewish settlements appeared thereafter not only in Babylonia but in Egypt (Alexandria, Elephantini), Armenia and many other countries. Jews returned under Cyrus in 517, ending the "Babylonian Exile." After 323, when Alexander the Great died, Jews, buffeted by warring neighbors, migrated to many parts of Europe, Asia and Africa. During the days of the Roman Empire upward of four and a half million Jews were living outside Palestine. They all looked upon Jerusalem as their spiritual center. The practice of calling the dispersal *Galut* ("Exile") grew when various governments began to harass their Jewish subjects. Persecution was responsible for many migrations of Jews—to other parts of Europe, to the Far East and later to America, South Africa, Australia and virtually every country in the world.

DIETARY LAWS

The traditional laws that define which foods Jews are permitted to eat and which foods are forbidden to them, as well as the laws governing the preparation of various foods for eating. These laws can be classified into five categories:

1. Laws defining permitted *(kosher)* and forbidden *(terefah)* animals.

2. Laws governing ritual slaughter.

3. Laws specifying portions of animals that are forbidden to eat.

4. Laws prohibiting the eating of dairy dishes and meat dishes together.

5. Laws governing the preparation of various foods for eating.

See also Fleishig; Kosher; Milchig; Shehitah

DINAH

Daughter of Jacob and Leah.

DISPUTATIONS

Discussions between adherents of different religions; usually debates in which Jews were forced to defend their religion, in the presence of secular authorities, against Christians. Often the Jew got the better of the argument, infuriating his opponent. In many of the arguments the church was represented by apostates. The most important of these are the disputation of Paris (1240), in which the Talmud was defended against the charge of blasphemy, though it was subsequently burned publicly; the disputation of Nachmanides with Pablo Christiani (1263); and the disputation of Tortosa (1413).

Theological disputation between Jews and Christians.

DISRAELI, BENJAMIN

(1804-1881)— Famous English statesman and writer who became one of Britain's greatest prime ministers. He first came to public notice through his brilliant novels and satires. Some of his work is derived from a journey he made to Jerusalem and his interest in byways of Jewish history. Entering politics in 1832, he was elected to Parliament in 1837. Though he was laughed at during his first speech, he determined that he would be heard—and so he was, for the rest of his days. Marriage with an established widow helped further his career, which included cabinet posts and two terms as premier. Disraeli's father, after a quarrel with his synagogue officials, had all of his children converted to Christianity, but Benjamin's career amply

Benjamin Disraeli

illustrates that his relationship to Jews and Judaism remained close. In 1876 Queen Victoria made him Earl of Beaconsfield. Disraeli is remembered for having extended the power of his native land to its greatest extent. Through him Victoria became Empress of India. He was responsible for British control of the Suez Canal.

DIZENGOFF, MEIR

(1861-1936)—First mayor of Tel Aviv. He was a leader in the city's establishment, and laid the cornerstone of the future metropolis in 1909. From 1921 until his death (except from 1925-8) he was mayor of Tel Aviv and played a dominant role in its development.

DJADID UL-ISLAM

Persian Jews who were forced in 1838 to adopt Islam and were called "New Moslems." They kept all the laws of Islam in public but secretly observed Jewish customs; they prayed in underground synagogues, observed dietary laws, circumcision and festivals. Some of these Jews have left Persia and have founded communities all over the world, the colony in Jerusalem being the strongest (app. 500).

DOMINICAN REPUBLIC

Jews first immigrated into the Dominican Republic in the second half of the 19th century. At the Evian Conference of 1938, which President Roosevelt called in order to consider the refugee problem, only the Dominican Republic offered to accept Jewish refugees in large numbers, expressing a willingness to admit 100,000 Jews. Only about 1,000 did enter, however, and the present Jewish community numbers only 600. Most of the Jews live in Santo Domingo and Sosua, each of which has a synagogue.

DREYDEL

A four-sided top used in a game played during Hanukkah. Each of the four sides of the dreydel bears one of the following Hebrew letters: *Nun, Gimel, Hay, Shin.* Each person takes a turn spinning the dreydel. If it comes to *Nun*, the player gets nothing; *Gimel*, he takes all; *Hay*, he takes half; *Shin*, he puts in. These four letters refer to the Hebrew words, *Nes Gadol Hayah Sham* ("A great miracle happened there").

DREYFUS, ALFRED

The Dreyfus affair, a trial for high treason, was one of the outstanding cases of modern anti-Semitism. In 1894, Dreyfus, a captain in the French intelligence service, was accused of selling military secrets to the Germans. He, the only Jew in the department, was sacrificed to protect the real criminals. He was sentenced for life to the penal colony on Devil's Island. Despite renewed petitions, the army refused to reopen the case, although the German ambassador declared Dreyfus had not been involved in the sale of documents. It became known that the documents used to convict Dreyfus had been forged by Colonel Esterhazy. In 1897 Esterhazy faced a sham military trial and, despite overwhelming evidence against him, was acquitted. Several great, liberal Frenchmen protested against the injustice of the case but public sentiment was against Dreyfus. But courageous men kept on fighting to clear him. Among them were Clemenceau, who later became Premier; Emile Zola, the great writer; and Colonel Picquart, then the new chief of the espionage division. The sensational confession of Lt. Colonel Henri, that he had collaborated with Esterhazy in espionage and the forging of letters accusing

The degradation of Captain Dreyfus.

Dreyfus, gave the case a new turn. The case was reopened in 1906 and the old courtmartial verdict was finally set aside. Dreyfus was proved innocent, recalled from Devil's Island and restored to his old rank. Theodor Herzl, who had witnessed the Dreyfus trial as a young newspaper correspondent, was much influenced by the affair. It was one of the factors that brought about Herzl's development into a great Zionist leader.

DROPSIE UNIVERSITY

Dropsie University, formerly named Dropsie College for Hebrew and Cognate Learning, is situated in Philadelphia, and was founded in 1908 with a bequest left by Moses Aaron Dropsie (1821-1905), a Philadelphia lawyer and philanthropist who had converted to Judaism, the religion of his father but not his mother. Dropsie University is the only nonsectarian, nontheological graduate institution in America completely dedicated to Hebrew, Jewish, Biblical, and Middle Eastern studies. It regularly publishes the *Jewish Quarterly Review*.

DRUZE

A scattered mountaineer people with a number of villages in the heart of Israel and in other nearby countries. They believe in one God who periodically appears on earth in the form of a prophet. Unlike the Mohammedans among whom they live, they do not practice circumcision and they eat pork and drink wine. There are no multiple marriages among them but their marriages are often of short duration. Their women enjoy considerable freedom and do not veil their faces. When the Arab nations attacked the new State of Israel in 1948, the Druzes aided the beleaguered Jews. Persons visiting Israel today find the Druze most hospitable, as well as enterprising salesmen of the basketry and metal goods they manufacture. Nevertheless, these people have in the past proved intolerant both toward pious Mohammedans and to neighboring Christian sects. Their massacre of Christian Maronites in 1860 led to European intervention in the internal affairs of the Turks, who then ruled Palestine.

DUBINSKY, DAVID

(1892-   )—American labor leader. Polish-born Dubinsky came to the U.S. in 1911, and became active in the International Ladies' Garment Workers' Union (ILGWU), whose president he became in 1932. He was elected vice-president of the American Federation of Labor in 1934-6, and again in 1945. Dubinsky is a prime example of the modern, intelligent, progressive, labor leader. His union is noted for its honesty and fair play. Jewish causes have also interested Dubinsky, who is a co-founder of the Jewish Labor Committee.

David Dubinsky.

DUBNOW, SIMON

(1860-1941)—Russian-Jewish historian. Dubnow developed his own theory of Jewish nationalism, which states that the Jewish nation is a "spiritual nation" and needs no national territory or state. An opponent of Zionism, he believed in the creative powers of autonomous and self-governing Jewish centers in the Diaspora, living in the territories of other national states. His *History of the Jews of Russia and Poland* was the first scientific work published on the subject, and his many-volumed *History of the Jewish People* (1901) was the most important general Jewish history written since Graetz. The demand for Jewish minority rights in Eastern Europe at the Paris Peace Conference (1918-19) was made on the basis of his theories.

DUCHAN

Heb., lit., platform) — Temple platform where the blessing of the people by the priests, as described in Num. 6:22, took place. In Israel this blessing is given by *Cohanim* daily; in Diaspora it is given on Festivals.

DURAN

Famous medieval family. Profiat Duran (d. c. 1414) was a leading philosopher, scholar, and physician in Spain. He wrote a grammar of the Hebrew language and several polemics against Christianity. Simeon ben Tzemach Duran (1361-1444), known as the Rashbatz, was an outstanding philosopher, scientist, and rabbincal authority in North Africa. He wrote many important responsa, as well as the *Magen Avot* ("Shield of the Patriarchs"), a major philosophical commentary on *Pirke Avot*. His son, Solomon ben Simeon Duran (c. 1400-1467), known as the Rasbash, was also a philosopher and rabbinical authority in North Africa. His *Milhemet Mitzvah* refuted many gentile criticisms of the Talmud.

EBAN, ABBA S.

(1915-   )—Israeli diplomat and statesman. Eban was born in Capetown, South Africa, and educated in England. Upon his graduation with honors from Cambridge, he was appointed to the faculty of that university as an authority on Hebrew, Arabic, and Persian literature. During World War II Eban served with the British forces in Palestine, and at the close of the war, remained in the country. He was a member of the Jewish Agency delegation to the U.N. during the 1947 debates on the establishment of Israel, and was appointed Israel's permanent representative to that body in 1948, a post which he filled with great skill. From 1950 to 1959 he served concurrently as Israel's ambassador to the United States. Eban was Israel's education minister from 1960 to 1963, and from 1966 to 1974 served as his country's foreign minister, gaining widespread admiration for the calm, yet eloquent, oratory with which he presented the Israeli viewpoint to the world.

ECCLESIASTES

The English name of the Biblical Book, *Kohelet* (Preacher). It is ascribed to King Solomon, who wrote it, according to tradition, in his old age when he began to express doubt of the world's worth. It contains twelve chapters consisting of views, poems and sayings, all pessimistic in tone. It begins with the famous saying, "Vanity of vanities, all is vanity." It expresses the attitudes and moods of a very wise and sad old man. The style of the Book is so varied that some scholars have looked upon it as a conversation among men of widely differing characters and temperaments. One scholar divided the verses into nine different authorships. But today it is generally agreed that one man alone was the author and that it remains one of the finest expressions of eastern wisdom.

EDOM

The nation of the Edomites is identified in Jewish lore with Rome. Edom extended south of Judah, from the Dead Sea to the now well known harbor of Elath. In the Bible, Edom is another name for Esau. There was frequent conflict between the two countries through the period of the Kings. Later the Edomites were defeated by Judah Maccabee; and in 126 B.C.E. they were forced to become Jews by King John Hyrcanus. King Herod was of partial Idumean (from the later name of the country) descent. Just before Jerusalem was taken and laid waste by the Romans, bands of Edomites combined with the *Hasideans*, or Zealots, in fighting the civil war which proved largely responsible for the city's fall.

EDUCATION

In Judaism, study (specifically, study of the Law) is equivalent to all other virtues. According to the Bible, the purpose of education is to give the child a knowledge of good and evil so that he may choose the good, for it was felt that learning and righteousness were indivisible. In ancient times every home was a school in which the parents were the teachers. At home the child studied his tradition as well as how to care for cattle and manufacture needed articles. Only later did a formal teaching profession arise. The priests, the Levites, the prophets and the scribes were all essentially teachers. By relating all learning to religion and ethics, the Jews were able to create steadfast souls, not

easily corrupted. When the synagogue was established it was so consistently used for teaching that to this day the word for synagogue is "shul," from the German word for school. After Biblical times, young Jews were taught, in addition to Hebrew, Talmud and related subjects, foreign languages, science and other non-religious courses. The new type of yeshivah for the young, which combines the best in Jewish and general learning, is patterned after this tradition.

EFROS, ISRAEL

(1891-   )—Hebrew poet. Efros arrived in the United States from Poland in 1906, and remained till 1954. Much of his poetry draws on American life and history, as, for example, *Wigwamim Shotekin* ("Silent Wigwams"). He has also done noteworthy translations into Hebrew, including Shakespeare's *Hamlet* and *Timon of Athens*, and he translated Bialik's poetry into English. In 1954 Efros emigrated to Israel, accepting the invitation to be rector of Tel Aviv University and dean of the department of humanities. In 1959 he became the university's honorary president.

EGYPT

(Heb., *Mitzraim*) The periods in which Egypt did not figure in Jewish history were rare. Egyptian cultural influences upon Biblical Palestine were second only to those of Babylon; of the three patriarchs, Abraham and Jacob visited Egypt. Throughout the period of the First Temple, the Jews had constant relations with Egypt. During the Hellenistic Age, the number of Jews in Egypt is said to have reached 1,000,000 and Alexandria was a great center. The Jewish community dwindled considerably after the Hellenistic Age, but was revitalized after the Moslem conquest (640), so that both Saadia and Maimonides made their homes in Egypt. During the Middle Ages, Egyptian Jewry offered a fruitful field for mysticism, and supported Shabbetai Zevi. Since the establishment of the State of Israel, the position of Egypt's Jews has been very difficult, and at present there are only about 30,000 Jews left in Egypt, many having fled to Israel.

EHRLICH, PAUL

(1854-1915)—Considered by many the world's greatest chemotherapist, or developer of drugs to cure diseases. In 1908 he was awarded the Nobel Prize for medicine. Before the wonder drugs were discovered, Ehrlich created Salvarsan, which he called "606" for the number of experiments required to produce it; Neo-Salvarsan, a better form of the drug, was called "914." This drug cured many fevers and skin ailments. Ehrlich's work in chemotherapy opened the way to thousands of later medical researchers. He served as head physician, director or professor at a number of German institutions. Among his many achievements was a method of staining white blood cells so that the physician might better understand his patient's condition; a blue dye whose progress through the body could be recorded; and vastly increased knowledge of the immunity created in the human body by antitoxins. He also advanced understanding of tuberculosis, diphtheria and many other diseases. Ehrlich, though not close to his people in his lifetime, always remembered his origin; his grave is marked with a Shield of David and a Hebrew inscription.

EHUD

Of the tribe of Benjamin; second of the Judges of Israel, a resourceful, left-handed hero who freed Israel from Moab's oppression.

EIGHTEEN BLESSINGS

Most important in each Jewish service is the *Shemoneh Esreh*, meaning eighteen. This was the original number of blessings in the daily prayers. One was later added, making nineteen, but the name persisted, even for Sabbath and festival services, which have only seven. Each benediction ends with "Blessed be Thou, O Lord, Who . . ."—summing up with one of the characteristics of God. The *Shemoneh Esreh* is recited quietly by each worshipper. In most services the cantor then chants the benedictions aloud, with congregational responses. All declarations are in the plural, and the blessings cover national as well as personal petitions. The nineteen benedictions may in brief be described as prayers for (1) the patriarchs; (2) God's power and resurrection of the dead; (3) sanctification of God's name; (4) wisdom and knowledge; (5) repentance; (6) forgiveness; (7) redemption; (8) healing; (9) a good year; (10) gathering dispersed Israel; (11) justice; (12) action against wicked heretics; (13) for the righteous; (14) for Jerusalem; (15) for Messiah of the house of David; (16) for God's hearkening to prayer; (17) for God's acceptance of prayer; (18) for thanks to God; and (19) for peace. In recent times some of the prayers have been modified by Conservative and Reform congregations.

See also Amidah; Shemoneh Esreh.

EINHORN, DAVID

(1809-1879)—American Reform rabbi. Born in Bavaria, Einhorn led a congregation in Budapest, Hungry, until 1855, when he came to the United States. In this country he was spiritual leader of congregations in Baltimore, Philadelphia, and New York City. An exponent of the most extreme version of Reform, Einhorn frequently came into conflict with the more moderate Isaac M. Wise. Einhorn denied the authority of the Talmud, held that the ceremonial laws of the Torah were only symbolic and the biblical miracles allegorical, and introduced Sabbath services on Sunday, with congregants praying bare-headed to the accompaniment of organ music. A scholar and orator of note,

David Einhorn.

Einhorn was an outspoken opponent of slavery in the period before the Civil War.

EINSTEIN, ALBERT

(1879-1955)—Albert Einstein may well be the greatest scientist of all the ages. Thousands of volumes have been based on a short essay on the structure of the universe which he wrote when still a young man. Born in Germany, Einstein studied there and in Switzerland. Until 1908 he was a patent examiner and university lecturer in Berne. It was in 1905 that he published the first papers that brought him enduring fame, on the theory of relativity. In 1909 Einstein was teaching at the University of Zurich; thereafter he taught at Prague and Leyden and was appointed head of the Kaiser Wilhelm Science Academy. This last position he was compelled to resign in 1933 when Hitler rose to power. Einstein came to America and citizenship was bestowed upon him in 1940. He became a professor at the Institute for Advanced Study at Princeton University. He had received the Nobel Prize in 1921. His

Albert Einstein.

44

discoveries had altered almost every previous idea of the universe and were to prove the starting point for the atom bomb. Einstein was a Zionist, beginning in 1920, and aided many Jewish causes. In his later essays he fought totalitarianism, defended his people and expressed the scientist's belief in the works of God. The Albert Einstein School of Medicine of Yeshiva University has been named in his honor.

ELATH

Port city at the southern tip of Israel, on the Gulf of Elath. The site was first settled by the Judean king Amaziah, and was important until its destruction by Crusaders in 1116. An Israeli force took the area in March 1949, and a modern town was built up. The expansion of Elath has been accelerated by the opening of the Gulf of Elath to Israeli shipping after the Sinai Campaign of 1956. The Elath-Ashkelon oil pipeline was completed in 1970. The city, an important center for tourism, is noted for its beautiful scenic situation on the Red Sea, and for its heat and difficult working conditions. Its population (1971) is 15,900.

ELDAD HA-DANI

(late 9th century)—Traveler who claimed to be of the tribe of Dan, which, he said, together with the lost tribes of Asher, Gad and Naphtali, formed a wealthy state in Ethiopia. His travels in Spain (883) aroused great interest. Many of the laws which he described as being followed by the Lost Tribes differ from Rabbinical tradition and there are varying opinions concerning his reliability.

"ELDERS OF ZION, PROTOCOLS OF"

An anti-Semitic forgery written in the late 1800's and published in Russia. The book purports to be a record of the plans made by the World Zionist Congress of 1897 to conquer the world. Anti-Semites of all countries seized on it at once, and it was translated into almost all European and Asiatic languages. The *Protocols* were circulated widely till the defeat of Nazism in 1945.

ELEAZAR

1. Aaron's son and successor, second high priest of Israel.
2. Son of Mattathias, brave brother of Judah Maccabee. He died in battle, crushed by an elephant whom he had killed, thinking that it bore the tyrant, King Antiochus.

ELEAZAR BEN AZARIAH

(1st-2nd century C.E.)—An outstanding *Tanna*, Eleazar was highly respected for his wide knowledge and illustrious ancestors (he was a descendant of Ezra the Scribe). He was appointed temporary successor to Gamliel II as head of the Academy of Javneh, and

was member of a Jewish delegation to Rome. A famed teacher of the Bible, he was usually guided by the plain sense of the text.

ELI

Judge and high priest in Shiloh, teacher and mentor of Samuel. Eli's sons, Hophni and Phinehas, were evil and corrupt. They died in the battle when the victorious Philistines captured the Ark. Eli died of grief. Samuel became his successor.

ELIEZER

1. Steward of Abraham's household, usually identified with the servant of Abraham who was sent to select a wife for Isaac, and who encountered Rebekal at the well.
2. Second son of Moses and Zipporah, ancestor of a group of Levites.

ELIJAH

No other prophet has so romantic a history and legendry as Elijah the Tishbite, who is said to have been transported to heaven in a chariot of fire. Living in the kingdom of Israel under Ahab and Ahaziah (875-853 B.C.E.), he fearlessly denounced the evil in the royal house, the priesthood and among the people at large. Unlike most of the prophets in the Bible he was not privileged to have his words recorded. Nonetheless, he is considered the first of the great prophets of Israel. He first appeared before King Ahab, who, prompted by Queen Jezebel, had the peasant Naboth put to death in order to appropriate his vineyard. Denouncing the king, Elijah had to flee into hiding. He would appear at public gatherings to preach to the people against injustice and idolatry. A number of miracles are ascribed to him. Elijah is often mentioned in the prayers. In the grace after meals there is a plea that the prophet come to life to bring ease to his people. On the Passover seder night a special cup is filled for him as he makes his world rounds. There are many stories of his return to the earth in disguise to give help to people in need. It is said he will return to Israel just before the Messiah appears.

ELIJAH BAHUR

(1468-1549)—Grammarian and author. Born Elijah Levita in Neustadt, Germany, he settled in Italy, where he wrote his Hebrew grammar, called *Ha-Bahur*. He taught Hebrew and the Bible to many Christian scholars, and gave impetus to the study of the language. Some of his works were translated into Latin, while he himself was among the first to translate Hebrew books into Yiddish.

ELIJAH OF VILNA

He was born in 1720 near the Lithuanian capital

and died there in 1797. Known as the Gaon of Vilna; "gaon" means excellence, and the term was applied to Elijah because of his genius, learning and leadership. As a boy of six the Gaon delivered his first learned discourse in the synagogue. It is reported that he could read a book once and recall every word. He not only mastered all Jewish learning but possessed enormous knowledge of such studies as mathematics and science. He composed works on Biblical, Talmudic and rabbinical lore and many others on algebra, geometry and astronomy. Unfortunately, many of his writings have been lost. As he grew to manhood, scholars wrote to him to decide problems in Jewish life and observance. He could solve in a moment difficulties that had troubled other scholars for weeks. He demanded that Jews possess both good character and a high degree of learning. The Gaon of Vilna was modest, simple and pious, an outstanding Jewish saint and scholar of modern times.

ELISHA

The successor to the prophet Elijah, who threw his mantle over Elisha as a sign that he was to succeed him. Many of the deeds and miracles ascribed to him resemble those of Elijah. Elisha accompanied his mentor everywhere and learned much from him. After Elijah's death Elisha continued denouncing the king and queen and their subjects who were faithless to God. Other prophets accepted him as their leader. About 842 B.C.E. he became associated with Jonadab ben Rechab who, having successfully fought idolatry in the southern kingdom of Judah, had come to Israel in the north to continue his efforts. Their chief purpose was to overthrow King Ahab and his wife, Jezebel, and establish Jehu, a general, on the throne. The general slew Ahab and all his male descendants. To wipe out the idol worship in Israel, Jehu pretended to be a Baal-worshipper and invited the priests and others who had accepted Jezebel's religion to meet at a celebration. Most of the important statesmen and leaders of Israel were slain. Elisha had attained a religious reformation in a costly but successful manner. His reputation as a prophet and worker of miracles went beyond the borders of Israel but he never achieved the popularity of his predecessor.

ELISHA BEN ABUYAH

(approximately 80-150 C.E.)—Famed teacher of the Law who became a heretic. Born of a well-to-do Jerusalem family and well-educated in both Jewish and secular branches of learning, Elisha was a friend and colleague of Rabbi Akiba, and a teacher of Rabbi Meir. The study of Greek philosophy, as well as metaphysical and mystical speculation, brought him to a denial of Jewish tradition. In the Talmud he is called, therefore, "Acher—The Other, The One Standing Outside." Nevertheless, Rabbi Meir remained his pupil, explaining, "I found a pomegranate (ben Abuyah); I

ate the fruit (his wisdom) and discarded the rind (his heretical views)."

ELKANAH

Husband of Hannah, father of the judge and prophet Samuel.

EL MALE RACHAMIM

(Heb., lit., "O God, who are full of compassion") Prayer recited in memory of a deceased, either at a funeral, *Yahrzeit*, or days when *Yizkor* is said; usually accompanied by donations to charity.

ELMAN, MISCHA

(1891-1967)—American violinist. The Russian-born Elman was a child prodigy, giving his first concert at the tender age of five. In 1908 he emigrated to the United States. A beloved concert violinist. Elman made many recordings. In addition to his skill as a performer, he composed various pieces for the violin.

ELON

Of the tribe of Zebulun, one of the Judges of Israel. He judged for ten years.

EL SALVADOR

The Jewish population of this tiny Central American country numbers 300, nearly all of them living in San Salvador, the capital city. The Jewish community is represented by the Comunidad Israelita, and there are Zionist groups as well.

ELUL

Sixth month in the Jewish calendar.

See also Calendar, Jewish; Months, Jewish.

EMDEN, JACOB ISRAEL

(1697-1776)—Rabbi of Emden, Prussia, from which he took his name. His quarrels with both secular and religious leaders of the community led him to retire from the rabbinate to the town of Altona, where he opened a printing press and engaged in business. Emden was a leader of the attacks on R. Jonathan Eibeschutz, whom he accused of being an adherent of Shabbetai Zevi.

EMEK JEZREEL

A valley in Israel stretching from the sea at Haifa to the Jordan Valley, bounded on the north by the Mountains of Galilee and on the south by Mount Carmel and the Mountains of Samaria. Its total area is 156 square miles. Many important Biblical battles took place here; Deborah, Gideon and Saul all fought here. The modern Zionist colonization of Palestine drained the swamps which had overflown the valley, and restored its fertility.

ENGLAND

The earliest Jewish settlers came to England during the reign of William the Conqueror (1066-1087); their most important center was London. An early period of prosperity was ended by a series of massacres following the Third Crusade. Blood accusations became common. In 1190 the entire Jewish populace of York committed suicide rather than surrender to the anti-Semitic mob that was besieging them. Finally the Jews were expelled in 1290 by Edward I. Although Marranos had lived secretly in England since the 16th century, it was not until the Restoration period that Jews could throw off the mask of secrecy and live openly as Jews. There was no ghetto system, nor were there important restrictions on their activity; in 1858 the Jews received the right to vote, and Lionel de Rothschild was admitted to Parliament. English Zionists played an important role in obtaining the Balfour Declaration in 1917. Many Jewish refugees from Central Europe fled to England in the 1930s. There are now some 410,000 Jews in Great Britain.
See also London.

An engraving of Clifford's Tower in York, England. Here, in 1190, the entire Jewish population of York committed suicide rather than fall into the hands of the mob.

EPHOD

Sacred garment, a short coat made of gold, blue, purple and scarlet linen worn by the high priests over their blue robes. The Ephod had two shoulder-pieces, each adorned by an onyx stone on which were engraved the names of six of Israel's twelve tribes. It was held together by an embroidered sash. The breastplate worn by the high priest was attached to the Ephod.

EPHRAIM

The sons of Joseph, Manasseh and Ephraim were adopted by Jacob, their grandfather and became fathers of two of the "twelve tribes." The tribe of Ephraim occupied the mountainous center of the land. Gradually it gained in power and developed the largest army among the twelve tribes. Joshua, who succeeded

Moses as leader of the Jews, was a member of the tribe of Ephraim. It is possible that the great woman judge, Deborah, was an Ephraimite. The Book of Judges tells of a war between Ephraim and the Gileadites under Jephthah. The Gileadites, knowing that the Ephraimites pronounced *shin* (sh) as *s*, trapped and killed many of their enemy by asking the fleeing Ephraimites to pronounce the word *shibboleth*. But after the time of Samuel, Ephraim became the most important of the northern tribes. When Solomon died and his son Rehoboam refused to ease the heavy tax burden on the northern tribes, they broke with the south and formed a separate kingdom. In this Ephraim was the prime mover and rebel. Eventually the whole northern realm was called by that name and is so referred to in the Prophets ("Is Ephraim a darling son unto me?"—Jeremiah 31:20).

EPHRAIM, TRIBE OF

One of the tribes of Israel. It occupied the mountains of the central region of Canaan, and became the heart of the northern Kingdom of Israel, which sometimes is called "Ephraim." Always close to its brother tribe, Manasseh, their emblems were often presented together. Ephraim's emblem was a bullock; its banner, shared with Manasseh, was jet-black. The stone representing (Manasseh and) Ephraim in the High Priest's breastplate was probably an onyx.

EPHRON

The Hittite from whom Abraham bought the cave and field of Machpelah.

EPSTEIN, JACOB

(1880-1959)—Sculptor. Epstein was born in New York, but settled in England in the early part of the century. He was influenced by ancient Egyptian art, and quickly became a significant figure in English, and indeed world, sculpture. His best-known works include Oscar Wilde's tomb in Paris, W. H. Hudson's memorial, London, and the figures decorating the British Medical Association building in London. He executed busts of famous personalities, among them Einstein, Weizmann, and Churchill. Epstein's autobiography is called *Let There Be Sculpture.*

ERUV

In cases where the Sabbath laws might prove burdensome and incline persons to violate them, methods of modifying the religious observances by using legal devices have been created. These accommodations of the Sabbath and festival laws to the daily needs of the people were called *Eruvin* ("combinations"). Since certain provisions of Sabbath laws do not apply to private, enclosed property, a cord or temporary fencing about a street opening or an entire section would render it not public in the accepted sense, but an enclosure. Thus articles could be carried within the enclosed space without breaking the law prohibiting the Sabbath carrying of burdens. When a group of houses faces upon a courtyard, if all the tenants join in purchasing a loaf to place within it, it also attains the status of privacy. Also, since one may not cook for the Sabbath on a festival just preceding it, some food is put aside for the Sabbath on a festival so that the cooking may be considered continuous. These *Eruvin* are not to be misrepresented as evasions of law but as established means of easing legal stringencies whenever this proves necessary.

ESDRAS, TWO BOOKS OF

Books of the Apocrypha, contain many excerpts from the Books of Ezra and Nehemiah. The most famous part of Esdras is the story of Darius' three young pages who, in a contest for a prize, tried to answer the question: what is the strongest thing on earth? The winning answer was: truth.

ESHKOL, LEVI

(1895-1969)—Israeli Prime Minister. Born in the Ukraine, Eshkol settled in Palestine in 1914. One of the founders of the Histadrut, he held various administrative posts in the Mapai party, serving as its secretary general from 1942 to 1945. He also was chief of the financial administration and arms-procurement branch of Haganah and headed the country's water company. After the State of Israel was founded, Eshkol became director general of the Defense Ministry; he also served as head of the Jewish Agency's Land Settlement Department, and later became its treasurer. From 1951 to 1952 he was minister of agriculture; he was minister of finance from 1952 until 1963, when he succeeded David Ben-Gurion as Prime Minister, retaining this office until his death. Particularly noted as a conciliator, Eshkol engineered the series of alignments that resulted in the formation of the Israel Labor Party in 1968, and organized a national-unity coalition to govern Israel during the crisis preceding the Six-Day War.

ESSENES

A sect of isolated Jews who lived near the Dead Sea during the beginning of the Common Era. They believed in escaping from the world and its pleasures, in avoiding marriage and in waiting for the coming of the Messiah. This mysterious group, about four thousand strong, all men of advanced years, lived a simple life, working with their hands for a livelihood. No one is sure what the word signified, though Josephus thought it meant "pious ones." Many Pharisees, the dominant Jewish group of that time, practiced austerity too, but they were far apart from the Essenes, who were a closed brotherhood, with special oaths for all who joined them. It has been difficult to unearth authentic facts about Essene communities, though the recent discoveries of the Dead Sea Scrolls will perhaps provide new insight into this group.

ESTHER

(*Hadassah*) cousin and ward of Mordecai, lived in Shushan, as wife and queen of King Ahasuerus. Encouraged by Mordecai, she approached the mighty Ahasuerus and turned his mind against Haman's plans to kill all the Jews of Persia. These events are described in the Book of Esther and commemorated by the festival of Purim.

See also Purim.

ESTHER, ADDITIONS TO

Book of the Apocrypha, contains additions to the Megillat Esther.

ESTHER, BOOK OF

(*Megillat Esther*) last of the Five Megillot of the Bible, often simply called "The Megillah." It describes how Esther saved the Jews of Persia. It is read on Purim. Many beautiful medieval Megillot, with illustrations and ornaments, mounted on hand-tooled or carved rollers, have been preserved.

ETHICS

In Judaism, ethics and religion have been connected since the earliest times. The ethical principles of the Bible have never been surpassed nor perfectly practised; they include the highest forms of love, peace, truth, righteousness and justice; they demand equality for native and stranger alike; they teach charity and kindness for the poor, the weak, the widow, the orphan and the slave. Jewish ethics were developed further by the Talmud, which held that "the essential is not learning but doing," and *Ethics of the Fathers*, a collection of Mishnaic ethical maxims is one of the most popular pieces of Jewish literature. In the 19th century the *Musar* movement, led by Rabbi Israel Salanter, brought back ethical notions into the intellectualized atmosphere of many yeshivot.

ETHIOPIA

See Abyssinia.

ETROG

A citron or fruit resembling a lemon, one of the four plants used in the celebration of Sukkot, considered one of the most beautiful fruits of ancient Israel.

See also Sukkot, Four Plants of

EVEN-SHOSHAN, AVRAHAM

(1906-)—Israeli lexicographer. Polish-born Even-Shoshan (originally Rosenstein) settled in Palestine in 1925. His chief work, a standard dictionary of modern Hebrew, appeared in 5 volumes in 1941-52. This illustrated dictionary has also been published in an abridged edition.

EXILARCH

(Hebrew, *Rosh Golah*, "Leader of the Exile"; Aramaic, *Resh Galuta*)—Head of the Babylonian Jewish community. Tradition traces the institution back to the exiled King of Judah, Jehoiachin (2 Kings 25:27-30), therefore assigning direct descent from the Davidic line to the Exilarchs. Historically the institution is traceable to the 2nd century. The exilarch was responsible for the internal government of the Jewish community, collecting the taxes and appointing the judges; he was recognized as such by the Babylonian authorities. The Gaon too, was selected by the Exilarch, though, in later periods, the Gaonim made inroads on the power of the Exilarchs and assumed some of their functions. Though the office continued at least until the 13th century, the last Exilarch who is more than a name was Hezekiah (d. 1040).

EXILE, BABYLONIAN

The forced stay of the Jews in Babylonia (about 586-538 B.C.E.) away from their homeland. It occurred after Nebuchadnezzar's victory over Judah and the destruction of the First Temple. Captives from Judah were deported to cultivate agricultural regions of the Babylonian provinces and some were sent to the city of Babylon itself.

See also Babylonia.

EXODUS

The second book of the Bible (Heb., *Shemot*). It tells the story of how Moses brought the Children of Israel out of Egyptian bondage. As near as can be ascertained, the departure took place before the end of the fifteenth century B.C.E. Many Jewish rites and prayers have been termed "a memorial of the departure from Egypt." The book Exodus begins with the death of Joseph and ends at the time of the building of the Tabernacle. It tells of the descendants of Jacob who came to Egypt, the enslavement, and the incidents that raised Moses to leadership. It continues with the story of how Aaron and Moses went to Pharaoh and asked for the release of their brethren and were successful only after the Ten Plagues. The fugitives were saved from an Egyptian attack when the Red Sea miraculously divided. When the Israelites reached Mount Sinai, the Commandments were given by God to Moses to teach his people a code of laws for everyday and for religious use.

EXPULSIONS

Jews were expelled from England (1290), France (1306), Spain (1492), Portugal (1497), and South Italy (1541). Expulsion was often the only alternative to forced conversion, although sometimes even this choice was not offered. In the 19th century the Russian attempt to confine the Jews to the "Pale of Settlement"

Grant of property, confiscated by the Inquisition, to a Cordovan monastery, by Ferdinand and Isabella (autographed).

led to periodical expulsions from Russia proper, coming to a head in the last decade of the century and being responsible for a good deal of the emigration to England and America.

EZEKIEL

Among those Israelites carried into exile by Nebuchadnezzar in 597 B.C.E. was Ezekiel ben Buzi, the third of the major prophets. Ezekiel, who was twenty-five years old at the time, had served in the Temple and therefore was honored by the Jews among whom he came to live. He declared that the Jews in exile were superior to those left behind and his hopes for a revival of their nation rested in the exiled men. He was the first of the great prophets to be close to the people. He blamed the Jews for having brought calamity upon themselves but added that no later generation would be punished for the sins of its predecessors and that the Jews in Babylonia, therefore, could always live in hope. Ezekiel committed his work and prophecies to writing, which we can read in the book of Ezekiel.

EZEKIEL, BOOK OF

Third of the Books of the three Major Prophets of the Bible. It contains the words of the prophet Ezekiel.

EZRA

A priest and scribe whose life and deeds are related in the book of Ezra and the book of Nehemiah, his associate. About 458 B.C.E. King Artaxerxes I of Persia gave Ezra permission to visit Jerusalem to inquire into the religious conditions there and to bring gifts to the Temple. He took with him 18,000 Jewish families. He found the Jews still in Jerusalem had taken non-Jewish wives and he persuaded most of these men to give them up. In 444 B.C.E., after Nehemiah had erected new walls about Jerusalem and brought in many other Jewish families, Ezra again appeared in

Jerusalem. He read to the people the almost forgotten laws of Israel. The rabbis honor Ezra as the man who restored the Torah to Israel; founded the Great Synagogue, the highest religious authority in the land; arranged Torah reading on Mondays and Thursdays, for the benefit of visiting merchants; and established the synagogue as we know it today to replace the village shrines at which Jews were then inclined to worship.

EZRA, BOOK OF

With the Book of Nehemiah, the second book of historical writings of the 3rd division (Ketubim) of the Bible. The book records the major events in the life of Ezra and his teachings.

FACKENHEIM, EMIL

(1916-   )—Theologian. Born in Germany, where he was ordained a rabbi, Fackenheim escaped to Canada in 1940. Since 1948 he has been a member of the philosophy faculty at the University of Toronto. A religious existentialist who is particularly concerned with the theological meaning of the Nazi Holocaust, Fackenheim has written God's Presence in History, Quest for Past and Future, Paths to Jewish Belief, and other books.

FALASHAS

A large tribe of dark-skinned Jews living in Ethiopia. They consider themselves descendants of Menelik, the son of Solomon and the Queen of Sheba. However, it is generally assumed that they were Jewish immigrants who settled and intermarried in central Abyssinia. Their features are not negroid. Until recent times, they believed they were the only Jews left in the world. They always lived apart from non-Jewish neighbors in Ethiopia, allowing none but themselves to enter their homes and enclosures. Though they knew no Hebrew they remembered the laws of Moses, to the extent that they settled near running streams to carry out the laws of personal purity. They had sacrifices similar to those the Bible describes. They knew nothing of the Talmudic ban on mixtures of milk and meat or of the marriage contract (Ketubah) required by Jewish law. But they are essentially observant Jews. They suffered cruel persecutions during the past decades. Professor Jacques Faitlovitch, who studied and wrote about the Falashas, organized a committee to help them in the early part of this century. Many have gone to live in Israel, where they carry on their old trades of weaving, pottery making and other skilled arts.

See also Abyssinia.

FAMILY AND FAMILY LIFE

Jewish family life is notable for its solidarity. The responsibility of children to their parents is defined in the Commandment, "Honor thy father and thy mother," which made an indelible impression on the life of the Jew. The parents were required to educate their children, and in the case of a son, to train him in some useful trade; naturally, the son's education was primarily in the father's hands, while the mother was responsible for the daughter's training. In many areas of the world the family pattern has come to resemble that of the environment, due to assimilation, though Jewish family life, on the whole, still remains stronger than that of the surrounding world. While the Biblical family was polygamous, the Jewish family since the Talmud has been monogamous, which was formally established by R. Gershom's Takkanah (about 1000 C.E.).

FAST DAYS

Jews fast to express repentance or as a sign of mourning. But the main purpose of fasting is to enable man to commune better with God. In addition to the fast day of Yom Kippur, there are also commemorative fast days, of which the four best known are: Tisha B'Av, Taanit Esther, Tzom Gedaliah and Asarah Betevet.

FEDERATIONS OF JEWISH PHILANTHROPIES

The various Jewish Welfare Funds in the cities of the United States and Canada united in 1932 as the Council of Jewish Federations and Welfare Funds. This body conducts unified fund-raising activities, from which some 800 communities benefit. This practice prevents the chaos of each and every organization organizing its own fund-raising campaign. Federation funds ($25 million in 1956) are largely distributed to hospitals and social service agencies.

FEINSTEIN, MOSES

(1895-   )—American Orthodox rabbi. Born in Belorussia, Feinstein came to the United States in 1937 and became the head of the Metivta Tiferet Jerusalem, a major yeshivah in New York City. One of the most important present-day halachic authorities and talmudists, he has written many responsa on questions pertaining to modern science and technology. As president of the Union of Orthodox Rabbis, he is generally regarded as one of the chief leaders of American Orthodoxy.

FEISAL IBN HUSSEIN

(1885-1933)—King of Iraq from 1921. At one time Feisal was ready to come to terms with Zionism, and in fact concluded a mutual aid agreement with Dr. Chaim Weizmann in 1919. However, his moderate attitude later became a hostile one through the influence of the Palestinian Arab faction.

FERTILE CRESCENT

Modern term for the crescent formed by the fertile

lands along the fringe of the Arabian desert, starting in the northeast at the Persian Gulf and including the lands watered by the great rivers: the Tigris and Euphrates (Babylonia, Assyria, Persia), the Jordan (Syria, Phoenicia, Israel), and the Nile (Egypt). Through the Fertile Crescent, Abraham, the Patriarch, and all the great peoples of antiquity have traveled.

FETTMILCH, VINCENT

(d. 1616)—German agitator and anti-Semite, who expelled the Jews from Frankfort in 1614. Ultimately he was deposed and executed, which was ·celebrated by the Jews on Adar 20 as "Purim Winz."

FINLAND

Jews first settled in Finland in the 18th century, when it was under Swedish rule. During the 19th century, when Finland was under Russian domination, Jews were restricted to three towns, and only ex-soldiers and their families were permitted to settle freely in the country. All restrictions were removed in 1917, when Finland became an independent state. Most Finnish Jews are merchants and tradesmen, living in Helsinki, Viborg, and Abo. The Jewish population numbered 1,450 in 1971.

FIRST BORN

The Bible (Exodus 13:2) states: "Sanctify unto Me all the first-born . . . both of man and beast." This was based on God's sparing the Jews when the firstlings of Egypt's children and cattle were struck down with the tenth plague. In ancient times, therefore, first-born sons were consecrated to Temple service. When the Levites were assigned to work in the Temple with the priests, this practice no longer became necessary. Instead, each first son was redeemed on payment of five shekels to a priest or Levite. This ceremony, called *Pidyon Haben*, ransom or redemption of the first-born, is still observed by many Jews.

See also Pidyon Haben.

FIRST FRUITS

Since everything that grows is a gift of God, ancient religions always dedicated the first of any produce to the Lord. The Torah set down a similar principle. A portion of first fruits was burnt on the altar and the rest was given to the priests, Levites, the poor, widows and orphans, all of whom are the people under the special protection of God. On the day after Passover a sheaf ("omer") of barley was offered upon the altar. Thus the first crop, barley, was redeemed, and the people were permitted to eat it. At the close of the harvest season, exactly seven weeks after the cutting of the "omer," there was another offering, of all grains. This was Shavuot time, known as the Harvest Festival, the Feast of Weeks, and the Day of First Fruits, all of which refer to the series of grain

offerings. It was later ruled that these were to be brought not to local shrines but to the Temple in Jerusalem, and that the normal gift was to be a tenth or tithe. In present day Israel, the *Bikkurim* celebration reproduces the joys of the ancient harvest in song and dance.

See also Shavuot.

FLAG

Each of Israel's tribes had its own flag (Num. 2). The Maccabees, in their wars, were said to have carried a banner which bore the first letters of the words, "Who is like unto Thee among the mighty, O Lord!" The flag of the Zionist movement, a central Star of David upon a white field set off by two horizontal blue bands, which was inspired by the *Tallit*, was later adopted by the State of Israel.

FLEISHIG

Food derived from the meat of mammals and poultry. The Jewish dietary laws prohibit the eating of meat and milk products together and require separate cooking and table utensils for the preparation and eating of each.

See also Dietary laws; Kosher.

FLEXNER, ABRAHAM

(1866-1960)—One of America's most distinguished educators. He was born in Louisville and attended Johns Hopkins University in Baltimore. He returned to Louisville to teach high school but in 1891 established a private school for difficult students. The president of Harvard University influenced Flexner to close his school and resume his studies at Harvard. His major interest was methods of teaching, and although his books on college and medical education were written forty years ago, they are still consulted today. As assistant secretary of the Rockefeller General Education Board (1913), he prevailed upon John D. Rockefeller to provide fifty million dollars for improvement of medical education throughout the United States. He induced men to advance great sums to institutions of higher learning. In 1930 Flexner obtained from Louis Bamberger eight million dollars to help establish the Institute for Advanced Studies at Princeton. He became the Institute's first director; Albert Einstein was the first faculty member. Abraham Flexner's brothers, Simon and Jacob, were among the great medical researchers in America.

FOUR MOTHERS

Also called Matriarchs, the wives of Israel's Patriarchs: Sarah, Rebekah, Rachel and Leah.

FRANCE

Jews lived in France even before the destruction of the Second Temple. With the Church's triumph in

France, the position of the Jews worsened, and in 629 they were exiled from part of the country, though they prospered in southern France. In Charlemagne's day numerous Jews were again found in every part of France, active as merchants and physicians. The development of the feudal system deprived the Jews of their lands, and the growth of a Christian merchant class drove them into money-lending. The Crusades took their toll—the entire community of Rouen was exterminated. Meanwhile, Jewish literature and learning had risen; Rashi and the Tosafists lived and taught in France. The French Revolution brought full emancipation to the Jews (1791), though Napoleon did issue some discriminatory decrees. The Dreyfus Case stirred some anti-Semitic sentiment (1894-1906). The fall of France in 1940 to the Nazis meant the deportation of 90,000 Jews to the death chambers; the present population is 350,000, Paris being the center of Jewish life. Jews such as Leon Blum, Rene Mayer and Pierre Mendes-France have been prominent in French public life.

FRANK, JACOB

(1726-1791)—False Messiah and founder of the sect which bore his name. He brought about the burning of the Talmud by Bishop Dembovsky in 1757 and engaged in many public disputes with the rabbis, who had excommunicated him. Ultimately, he was baptized and accepted Catholicism, as did the members of his sect. His daughter Eva succeeded him as the leader of the sect after his death.

Jacob Frank, a false Messiah.

FRANKEL, ZACHARIAS

(1801-1875)—Rabbi and scholar. In 1836 he became the Chief Rabbi of Dresden, and was later appointed president of the Breslau rabbinical seminary, which tried to combine religious and secular education. Frankel took a middle position between the Reform and extreme Orthodox positions; he strongly opposed the Reform attempt to introduce prayer in the vernacular.

FRANKFORT

The Jews of Frankfort were long considered merely as objects to be taxed, and as early as 1462 they were forced into a ghetto. It was not until the start of the 18th century that Frankfort's Jews received any measure of freedom. Frankfort was a leading city of the Reform movement, though Orthodoxy, under Samson Raphael Hirsch, also maintained a strong community. The Jews of Frankfort, especially the Rothschild family, played a leading part in the economic development of the city. There are now only 1,000 Jews in the city.

FRANKFURTER, FELIX

(1882-   )—Associate Justice of the United States Supreme Court since 1939, wherein he has taken a liberal position. He was a professor at Harvard (1914-39), and prior to 1921 was associated with Brandeis in the Zionist movement.

FRANKS, ISAAC

(1759-1822)—A distinguished member of the Franks family which settled in America in pre-Revolutionary days. The Franks family, as well as hundreds of other Jewish families, were active in their support of the newly established United States. Isaac Franks, who

Isaac Franks.

was aide-de-camp to General George Washington, rose to the rank of lieutenant-colonel. In May, 1776, when he was seventeen, he enlisted in a New York regiment. He fought in the near-decisive Battle of Long Island, where he was captured by the British. After three months in the guardhouse, he escaped. From 1777 to 1781 Franks served in the quartermaster's corps. Then he became an ensign (flag-carrier) in a Massachusetts regiment, during which time he saw considerable action and suffered several wounds. After the war

Colonel Franks settled near Philadelphia, then the center of the American government. He was the recipient of many civic honors and positions. When yellow fever struck the city, President Washington moved to the Franks home in Germantown. Despite all his achievements and honors, Isaac Franks died a poor man. He lived on a military pension during the last years of his life. His name has not died out, as many of his descendants, to this day, have found distinction in the law and other professional and business occupations.

FRATERNAL SOCIETIES

Many fraternal societies in America were founded by immigrants from the same areas during the period of large-scale immigration from Eastern Europe. They offered insurance and burial benefits and many took part in important social and cultural activities. The oldest and largest society is B'nai B'rith, which was founded in 1843. Other important orders are Free Sons of Israel, B'rith Abraham, the Workman's Circle, and Farband, the Labor Zionist Order.

FREEHOF, SOLOMON

(1892-   )—American scholar. Specializing in the study of Jewish liturgy and law, Freehof is honorary life president of the World Union for Progressive Judaism and head of the Responsa Committee of the Central Confrence of American Rabbis. He has written extensively in the field of responsa literature, and has also produced commentaries on Psalms and Job as well as books on Jewish preaching and ritual practice.

FREEMASONRY

A world-wide, secret society which calls itself a system of morality veiled in allegory and illustrated by symbols. It is now mainly devoted to purposes of brotherhood and good fellowship. Though it probably developed from the building guilds of the Middle Ages, its tradition claims that Freemasonry was in existence when the Temple was erected by Solomon with the assistance of Hiram, king of Tyre. Its ceremonies therefore contain many allusions to this period, and it uses as passwords Hebrew names and expressions.

FREUD, SIGMUND

(1856-1939)—One of the greatest psychologists and thinkers of our time. He was the founder of modern psychoanalysis, which is a technique for diagnosing and curing mental ills. His theory that mental disturbances can be traced back to subconscious mental processes has influenced the thinking and work of scientists and scholars of many fields. He was born in Moravia and studied medicine at the University of Vienna. Though he settled in Vienna as a general medical practitioner, he devoted an increasing amount of time to the healing possibilities of hypnotism and

Sigmund Freud.

psychoanalysis. His book, "The Interpretation of Dreams," published in 1900, which contended that dreams furnished a key to explain man's behavior, caused great controversies which have persisted to this day. As Freud's work grew and his fame increased, he became the object of controversy and hostility. Freud generally held aloof from Jewish affiliations, though he was active in B'nai B'rith and was on the board of trustees of the Hebrew University. He died in England, where he fled after the Nazis had confiscated all his possessions.

FRISCHMANN, DAVID

(1861-1922)—Hebrew and Yiddish writer. Frischmann was an important critic, author and translator. He was largely responsible for the admission of West European literary criteria into the somewhat provincial Haskalah literature. A prolific writer, his collected works appeared in 23 volumes.

GABIROL, SOLOMON IBN

See Ibn Gabirol, Solomon.

GAD, TRIBE OF

One of the tribes of Israel. Its territory was the mountainous terrain east of the Jordan. The emblem of Gad was an encampment of tents; its banner was grey. The stone representing Gad in the High Priest's breastplate was probably an agate.

GALICIA

An area of Central Europe north of the Carpathian Mountains, with Cracow and Lemberg (Lvov) as its principal cities. Galician Jewry reached its peak during the period of Austrian control over the region (1772-1918). Though the government attempted forced assimilation, the Jewish population, which numbered 225,000 in 1772, remained loyal to its traditions. Galicia was a fruitful field first for Hasidism, then for the Haskalah movement and finally for Reform, which was halted in the 1850's by Moses Shreiber. Galicia was also the birthplace of "Hibbat Zion."

GALILEE

The northern part of the State of Israel is called Galilee (Heb., *Galil*), even as it was in the days of Joshua. Its three subdivisions were mentioned in the Talmud—the valley, Upper Galilee and Lower Galilee. In olden days the trees and streams and fertile soil of this section brought much wealth to the inhabitants. The fisheries of the Sea of Galilee were famous. Wheat, olive oil, barley, wine, honey, flax and fruit were abundant. The Galilean farmers were not learned in Jewish law; hence rose the use of the expression *am ha-aretz*, "people of the soil," to mean the ignorant. It is also recorded that they pronounced Hebrew like the Ashkenazim of today. They were deeply patriotic and proved the fiercest fighters against the tyranny of Rome. As Jews settled in larger numbers in the northern province, academies arose and Tiberias and Safed became two of the four holy Palestinian cities. It was in Tiberias, seat of the Sanhedrin, that Judah the Prince compiled the Mishnah in the year 210. In modern Israel, Galilee has become a region of flourishing agricultural settlements of which wheat and other grain, sheep and poultry are the chief products.

GALUT

("Exile") refers to the compulsory exile of Jews from the land of Israel after the destruction of the Second Temple.

See also Diaspora.

GAMALIEL

This name was borne by several scholars in one line of descent. The first one, who lived during the last decades before the destruction of the Temple, was a grandson of the great Hillel, president of the Sanhedrin and leader of the Pharisees, the party of piety and tolerance. The title "Rabban," meaning "our teacher," was first bestowed upon him. His name is mentioned in the Christian Bible and he was claimed as a teacher, defender, and even supporter of Christians and Christian doctrine. They made him a saint, whose day is August 3. Gamaliel, however, was always a completely devoted Jew, who was tolerant of differences among people. His grandson, Gamaliel II, is remembered for having established the prayer called the Eighteen Blessings, for having ordered simple burials for all Jews and for presiding when the Bible canon was completed. There were four more Gamaliels; the sixth was the last patriarch of the Talmudic period, who was deposed for violating the Roman regulations against building new synagogues and judging between Jews and Christians.

Rabbi Gamaliel surrounded by his disciples. A painting from the Sarajevo Haggadah.

GANZFRIED, SOLOMON

(1804-1886)—Rabbinic scholar. His best known work is the abridgment of the *Shulchan Aruch* called *Kitzur* ("Abbreviated") *Shulchan Aruch*, which is still used widely. An English translation of this work appeared in 1915, and it has been translated into other languages as well.

GAON

The title held by the heads of the academies of Sura and Pumbeditha in Persia, from the 6th to 11th centuries and possibly later. The duties of the Gaon were to direct the study and interpretation of the Talmud, to share with the Exilarch jurisdiction in lawsuits among Jews and to answer those questions which were addressed to him by world Jewry as the highest authority on Jewish law. The Gaonate became the central religious institution of the time, and was largely responsible for the popularization of the Talmud and its study. Famous Geonim were Saadia (928), Sherira (968), and Hai (998).

GARDEN OF EDEN

(*Gan Eden*) the Biblical name for the peaceful, idyllic, original home of Adam and Eve. The Garden of Eden is also called Paradise.

GAZA STRIP

Tongue of land named after Gaza, its chief city, which extends 22 miles along the eastern border of

Egypt with Israel. The Gaza Strip was a base for Egyptian commando (*fedayeen*) raids into Israel, which provoked the Sinai Campaign in 1956.

GEDALIAH

Son of Ahikam; friend and protector of Jeremiah, installed by Nebuchadnezzar as governor of Judea after the destruction of the First Temple. Gedaliah tried to reunite the scattered people of Judah. He was assassinated by Ishmael, prince of the House of David. His death is commemorated by the Fast of Gedaliah (*Tzom Gedaliah*), on the 3rd of Tishri.

GEIGER, ABRAHAM

(1810-1874)—Founder of Reform Judaism. In his "Magazine for Jewish Theology" he demanded a radical reform of Judaism, and convened the first conference of Reform rabbis in 1837. He claimed that Orthodoxy was overlegalistic, and also tried to eliminate the national element in the Jewish religion by praying in the vernacular and by emphasizing the mission of Judaism to the whole world.

GELILAH

The "rolling up" of the Torah scroll after it has been read. The person who receives the honor to perform the *Gelilah* is called the *Golel* ("he who rolls up").

GEMARA

("Study, learning") second part of the Talmud, consists of discussions and commentaries on its first and basic part, the Mishnah. The Gemara, compiled (third to sixth centuries, C.E.), after the completion of the Mishnah, consists of the teachings of the Amoraim. Two distinct versions are in existence, the Palestinian and the Babylonian Gemara.

See also Talmud.

GEMATRIA

This refers to the method developed by Jewish scholars of Talmudic times of adding up the numerical values of all the Hebrew letters in a word and using the sum as a means of interpreting the text. They would see a relationship between words that added up alike. Each letter had its number: for example, *aleph*, one; *bet*, two; *yod*, ten; *kaf*, twenty; *pay*, ninety; *kof*, a hundred; *tav*, four hundred. The word *gematria* is from either the Greek word meaning geometry or the Greek *grammateia*, "letter play." There are many unusual examples in the Talmud and Midrash. Since the value of *sulam*, a ladder, which led from earth to heaven in Jacob's dream, is the same as that for *Sinai*, the rabbis declare that the Torah given on Mount Sinai is the ladder between this and the heavenly realm. When it is said that Abraham came to Lot's assistance with 318 servants, the rabbis say that these were only one man, the steward Eliezer, whose name is computed as 318. In modern times, *gematria* is often employed in a witty manner.

See also Abulafia, Abraham ben Samuel.

GENESIS

(*Bereshit*) first of the Biblical Five Books of Moses (the Torah). Genesis relates the origins of Israel, from the Creation to the death of Joseph. Its 50 chapters are divided into 12 portions for weekly Sabbath readings. The Hebrew name for Genesis (*Bereshit*) is the first word in the book and means "in the beginning." It gives an account of the origins of the world, of man and of the Jewish people. It tells of God's relation to all of mankind; His relation to Israel; His selection of Abraham and his descendants for His service; and God's promise to give to Israel the land of Canaan.

GENEVA

Capital of the Swiss canton of the same name. Jews lived there, as well as in other towns along Lake Geneva as early as the 14th century. The Jewish population in 1962 was approximately 3,000.

GENIZAH

When sacred scrolls, books, parchment, and papers containing the name of God—and most of them did—became soiled, torn, or otherwise unusable, they were not destroyed but put away in a special storage place called *genizah* ("hiding"). These would generally be in the basements or attics of a synagogue. The term *genizah* is particularly applied to the one in the old Ezra Synagogue in Cairo where discarded documents had accumulated over a period of twelve centuries. In 1896 Dr. Solomon Schechter, then teaching at Cambridge, England, and later the head of America's Jewish Theological Seminary, was shown some Hebrew leaves brought from this *genizah* by two women scholars. He recognized one as a fragment of "The Wisdom of Ben Sirah," important non-Biblical book of which no one had ever seen the original Hebrew. Dr. Schechter traveled to Cairo and brought back thousands upon thousands of leaves which have shed light upon every branch of Jewish literature.

GENTILES

Persons who are not Jewish by birth and religion. The word does not refer to a person's race or nationality but to his religious belief. It derives from Latin *Gens*, nation.

GEOGRAPHY AND GEOGRAPHERS

Many Jews provided maps and nautical instruments for the great voyages of discovery at the end of the Middle Ages. Abraham Cresques of Majorca (died 1387) was "Master of Maps and Compasses" to the Infant Juan of Aragon; one of the great productions of the Majorca cartographers was the famous Catalan Atlas.

GERIZIM, MOUNT

The mountain, designated by Moses as a place of assembly and blessing, where Joshua and other leaders of Israel blessed the people. At its foot was the ancient city of Shechem (now Nablus). On Mount Gerizim stood the Temple of the Samaritans, built in the 4th century B.C.E., and destroyed by John Hyrcanus (about 128 B.C.E.). Today the Samaritans still celebrate Passover on Mount Gerizim.

GERMANY

It is probable that Jews were settled in the region now called Germany as early as the 3rd century C.E. During the 9th century Jews were encouraged to settle in the area, and by the 11th century a vital cultural life had developed, particularly in the Rhineland and in such towns as Metz, Worms, Mainz, and Magdeburg. In 1096, however, the Crusaders massacred Jews throughout the region. Jews lived in Germany all through the Middle Ages, and despite persecution and anti-Semitism, developed a healthy Jewish life, since many states employed Jews in various technical capacities and gave them their protection as "Court Jews." In the 18th century Moses Mendelssohn founded the Haskalah movement and Jews began to enter the cultural life of the country. Reform Judaism emerged, and Jewry gave to Germany some of her greatest names in literature, philosophy, public service and scholarship. World War I saw Jews fighting for Germany, and the decade following the Armistice was, in some respects, the happiest for German Jewry. In 1933 Adolf Hitler, maniacal anti-Semite, came to power and put into force a system for the annihilation of world Jewry, succeeding in killing some 6,000,000. Of Germany's prewar Jewish population, some 300,000 managed to emigrate by 1939; the remaining 200,000 all were killed. In 1952 West Germany agreed to pay $822 million in reparations for the property damage done by the Nazis. There are now 30,000 Jews in Germany.

Prayer service in the Old Synagogue in Berlin.

GERSHOM

Oldest son of Moses and Zipporah.

GERSHOM BEN JUDAH

(Rabbenu Gershom, "M'or Hagolah," the Light of the Exile; 965-1028). Greatest rabbinic authority of his period. Gershom was rabbi of Mayence, and there convened a council of rabbis which prohibited polygamy in European lands and forbade a husband to divorce his wife without her consent. He also advocated sympathetic treatment to those who returned to Judaism after compulsory baptism.

GERSHWIN, GEORGE

(1898-1937)—American composer. Gershwin wrote many types of music, ranging from the Piano Concerto in F to scores for motion pictures. His "Rhapsody in Blue" (1922) elevated jazz to the status of "serious" music, while losing none of its popularity. "Porgy and Bess" (1935) is a folk opera based on Negro life, and contains the well-known "Summertime." Other familiar Gershwin songs are "Embraceable You" and "The Man I Love." Ira, his brother, was the author of many of the lyrics George set to music.

GET

("Bill of divorce") a religious divorce. In traditional Jewish life a civil divorce must be followed by the granting of a religious document.

GEZER

Town in Palestine which was a Canaanite center in the 3rd and 2nd millennia B.C.E. At one time conquered by Joshua, the town of Gezer passed from Israel's rule but was later given to Solomon by the Egyptian Pharaoh as dowry for his daughter. Pharaoh Shishak later recaptured the town. During the Middle Ages, Gezer was the site of Mont Gisart, a Crusader castle. In 1945, Youth Aliyah graduates from Central Europe founded a settlement there. Excavation of the ancient town by R. Macalister in 1902-1909 revealed evidence of occupation from the Chalcolithic to the Arab period.

GHETTO

In the Middle Ages, Jews were compelled to live in ghettos—special sections within a city. This compulsory separation of the Jews from the rest of the city existed in Italy and Central Europe during the 14th to the 18th century. Today the term "ghetto" refers to any section of a city that is chiefly occupied by one group of people in a low economic class. The largest Jewish ghettos during the Middle Ages were in Frankfort, Prague, Rome, Venice and Dublin. Christian leaders justified the segregation of Jews on the religious basis that the church forbade intimate relations between Christians and Jews. The effect of compulsory ghettos was, however, the elimination of competition from Jewish artisans and traders. The Jewish quarters generally were crowded and unsanitary and the Jews living in them were easy victims of epidemics and fires.

A street in the Frankfurt ghetto.

Nevertheless, a rich religious, social and cultural life developed in many of the ghettos. The infamous ghetto system was resurrected by the Nazis. The heroism of the Jews forced into the Warsaw ghetto by the Nazis, and who fought valiantly against great odds before they were destroyed, is one of the great stories of courage in modern times.

GIBEAH

Home and capital of King Saul, in the territory of Benjamin, near Jerusalem. Parts of Gibeah, including Saul's dwelling, have been excavated by modern archeologists.

GIDEON

Also called Jerubbaal, of the tribe of Manasseh, one of the most important Judges who ruled in Israel (12th century B.C.E.). He zealously fought idol worship in Israel and battled the hostile neighboring tribes. With 300 men he defeated the marauding Midianites in a surprise attack. He helped unite the tribes of Israel and strengthened them in their belief in One God.

GILBOA, MOUNT

Mountain in Galilee, southeast of the Emek Jezreel, where Saul and Jonathan died in the great battle they lost to the Philistines.

GILEAD

The beautiful and fertile land of the Jabbok River, east of the Jordan and south of the Yarmuk, where the tribes of Reuben, Gad and part of Manasseh settled; home of Jephthah and Elijah. From the time of the Patriarchs, many Biblical events have taken place in Gilead.

GILGAL

A town near Jericho. The Israelites, under Joshua, set up their first camp site in Gilgal after they had crossed the Jordan.

GIMEL

The third letter of the Hebrew alphabet, has the numerical value of 3.

See also Aleph Bet.

GINZBERG, LOUIS

(1873-1953)—Rabbinic scholar. Born in Lithuania, he received a thorough Talmudic education before settling in New York in 1899. In 1908 Ginzberg became professor of Talmud at the Jewish Theological Seminary. He published works on the Aggadah, the Gaonic period, and the Jerusalem Talmud.

GINZBURG, ASHER

(1856-1927)—Critic, philosopher and essayist, better known by his pen name of Ahad Ha-Am. Born in the Ukraine, reared in the Jewish tradition, he was largely self-educated, though he attended several European universities. He settled at Odessa in 1886, where he joined *Hovevei Zion*. His critical essays on the policy of this organization were signed in Hebrew, Ahad Ha-Am ("one of the people"). Founder of the Bene Mosheh league, he was its first president, from 1889 to 1891, and in 1892 he helped establish the *Ahiasaf* publishing society. His *Al Parashat Derakhim* ("At the Crossroads") a collection of his articles, included criticism of the colonization of Palestine based on visits he made there. He founded the periodical *Ha-Shiloah* in 1896 and was its editor until 1903. In this publication, Ginzburg voiced his opposition to what he called "Herzl's political Zionism." Later he lived in London, where he wrote other essays and participated in the negotiations which resulted in the Balfour Declaration. He settled in Tel Aviv in 1922, where he published his memoirs.

Asher Ginsberg.

GLUECK, NELSON

(1900-1971)—American archaeologist. As director of the American School of Oriental Research in Jerusalem in the 1930s and 1940s, Glueck carried out extensive archaeological work in Jordan and Palestine. Concentrating on the Negev from 1952, he discovered and excavated many ancient sites, including King Solomon's copper mines at Wadi Arabah and King Solomon's port city of Ezion-geber near present-day Elath. From 1947 to his death he also served as president of Hebrew Union College.

GOLAN HEIGHTS

Strategic rocky plateau region, bordering on Israel, Jordan, and Syria. During the 1950s and 1960s Syria used the heights as a base for artillery attacks on the vulnerable Israel farms of Upper Galilee. During the Six-Day War Israeli troops stormed and captured the heavily fortified Syrian positions, and Israel retained the area after the war. It was the scene of massive tank battles and very bloody fighting during the Yom Kippur War but remained under Israeli control.

GOLDBERG, ARTHUR J.

(1908-   )—American statesman. The son of poor immigrant parents, Goldberg was appointed Secretary of Labor in President Kennedy's Cabinet in 1961. Prior to this, he had become an expert on labor law, was special counsel to the AFL-CIO, and had taught law at John Marshall Law School and at the University of Chicago. From 1962 to 1965 Goldberg was a justice of the U.S. Supreme Court. He served as U.S. ambassador to the United Nations from 1965 to 1968, and subsequently ran unsuccessfully for the governorship of New York State.

GOLDBERGER, JOSEPH

One of the most noted researchers in the causes of and cures for disease. Born in Hungary, in 1874, Goldberger came to New York City at the age of six. He attended the College of the City of New York and studied medicine at Bellevue Hospital. In 1899 he entered the United States Public Health Service. His first success was the identification of the straw mite that gave United States sailors a troublesome rash. Because he investigated directly instead of at the laboratory, he almost died of typhus fever. His most noted achievement was the discovery of the cause of pellagra, an illness common in the South and certain foreign lands. This disease brought on early weakness, insanity and a lingering death. It was believed at that time that pellagra was a contagious or infectious disease. Goldberger discovered that it was caused by the inadequate diet of the poor—the lack of milk, meat, green vegetables and other vital foods. He determined later that yeast was a cure, but the important preventive factor was proper diet. By going directly to the sick and studying their curcumstances, Goldberger removed a scourge and gained the eternal esteem and gratitude of his fellow citizens. Joseph Goldberger died in 1929.

GOLDMANN, NAHUM

(1895-   )—Zionist leader and public figure. The Russian-born, German-educated, Goldmann served as Jewish Agency representative to the League of Nations in 1935-39. In 1940 he settled in the United States. Goldmann has since served as chairman of the Jewish Agency (1949), chairman of the executive committee of the World Jewish Congress, and president of the World Zionist Organization (1955-68). The German Reparations Agreement of 1952 was due, in large part, to Goldmann's skill as a negotiator. His debate with David Ben-Gurion, Israeli Prime Minister, over the meaning of Zionism aroused much discussion.

GOLDWYN, SAMUEL

(1882-1974)—American film producer; an original founder of Metro-Goldwyn-Mayer (MGM). Goldwyn introduced many stars to the films.

GOLEM

(Heb., lit. "shapeless mass") An automaton created by magical, Kabbalistic means. The Talmud tells of the creation of a golem (Sanhedrin 65b), but the best known by far was that created by R. Judah Low (Maharal) of Prague at the end of the 16th century. The golem legend is the theme of Leivik's play; Capek's "R.U.R." is also thought by some to have been influenced by the legend.

GOLUS

Ashkenazic pronunciation of *Galut*.

GOMORRAH

One of the five Cities of the Plain. It was destroyed because of the wickedness of its people.

See also Sodom.

GOMPERS, SAMUEL

(1850-1924)—One of the founders of the American Federation of Labor. Gompers was bor of Dutch Jewish parents in London and came to New York City when he was thirteen years old. At that time the number of factory workers was rapidly rising and their lack of organization made it difficult for them to achieve higher wages and better conditions. Gompers' activities in unionizing underpaid workers and fighting their battles led to his election in 1886 as president of the newly formed American Federation of Labor. He held this position for thirty-eight years. He considered it the better part of wisdom to form no alliance with either political party. In World War I, he was appointed by President Wilson to the Advisory Committee for the Council of National Defense. Much of the present advance in the status of the American worker can be ascribed to him. His biographers believe that the Judaism he learned in his London childhood gave him his humanity and practical common sense.

GORDIS, ROBERT

(1908-   )—American scholar and theologian. As a professor at the Jewish Theological Seminary for many years and as editor of the periodical *Judaism*, Gordis has made important contributions in biblical research and many other fields of scholarship, and has also written significant works on the problems and meaning of contemporary Judaism. Among his many books are *A Faith for Moderns, Koheleth: The Man and His World, The Book of God and Man: A Study of Job*, and *Conservative Judaism: A Modern Approach to Jewish Tradition*.

GORDON, AARON DAVID

(1856-1922)—Zionist thinker. Gordon created the ideology of the Halutz movement when he demanded that man return to nature and engage in physical labor. This "Religion of Labor" was followed by Gordon himself, who settled in Palestine in 1904, and worked as an agricultural laborer until his death in Daganiah.

GORDON, LORD GEORGE

(1751-1793)—Convert to Judaism. Gordon was born Protestant and elected to Parliament, where he was a staunch opponent of Catholicism. He was converted to Judaism in 1787 and lived an observant Jewish life until his death in Newgate Prison, to which he was sentenced for libeling the Queen of France.

GOREN, SHLOMO

(1917-   )—Israeli Chief Rabbi. As the Israeli army's chief rabbi from 1949 to 1968, Goren introduced a uniform ritual and liturgy for use by soldiers from Israel's many different ethnic communities, and he also solved many halachic problems pertaining to military service and national defense. During the Six-Day War (1967), he was the first rabbi to enter the newly liberated Old City of Jerusalem, and Jews throughout the world were thrilled by news photos showing him praying and dancing before the Western Wall of the Temple, Judaism's most sacred place. Goren became chief rabbi of Tel Aviv-Jaffa in 1968, and in 1972 he was elected Israel's Ashkenazic Chief Rabbi.

GOSHEN

Grazing ground in the land of Egypt, near the Sinai Peninsula, that Pharaoh gave to Jacob and his family. At that time, Jacob's son, Joseph, was second in command to Pharaoh in Egypt. The Exodus of the Israelites from Egypt started from Goshen.

GOTTSCHALK, ALFRED

(1930-   )—American educator. Born in Germany, Gottschalk came to the United States in 1939. Ordained a rabbi in 1957, he joined the faculty of the California School of the Hebrew Union College in 1959 as dean and professor of Bible and Jewish thought. In 1971 he became the president of Hebrew Union College-Jewish Institute of Religion.

GRACE AFTER MEALS

(*Birkat Hamazon*) a traditional Jewish prayer recited after meals.

GRADE, CHAIM

(1910-   )—Yiddish writer. Born in Vilna, Grade came to the United States in 1948, and for many years was a staff writer for the *Morning Journal*, a Yiddish newspaper. In addition to his many poems about the Holocaust, Grade wrote novels depicting the traditional Jewish life of prewar Lithuania, his homeland. Best known are *The Well* and *The Agunah*.

GRAETZ, HEINRICH

The great Jewish historian of modern times lived in Germany, 1817-1891. As a young man he was for a time under the influence of Samson Raphael Hirsch, the leading theologian of his time. He held two professorships: one at the Jewish Theological Seminary in Breslau; the other at the University of Breslau. His most important achievement was the writing of the massive *History of the Jews from Ancient Times to the Present*, which was published in German in eleven volumes, during a period of twenty-two years (1853-1875). Though later historians have found errors in his facts and methods, Graetz is still read and honored for his style, his great knowledge, his vast research, and above all, his ability to see all Jewish history as a unit and not as a disjointed series of episodes. Modern Jewish historians have profited greatly from his monumental work. Graetz also wrote on the Bible, on Zionism, and on general Jewish problems, but his fame rests on the History, now translated into numerous languages including English. On his seventieth birthday the world of scholarship, Jewish and non-Jewish, honored him for his scholarly achievements.

GRATZ, REBECCA

(1781-1869)—Daughter of a distinguished Philadelphia family, Rebecca Gratz is best remembered as the model for the Rebecca of Sir Walter Scott's *Ivanhoe*. Her appearance, her excellent character, and her loyalty to Judaism were related to Scott by Washington Irving when the American writer visited Sir Walter in 1817. At the age of 20 Rebecca was already an official of social welfare societies. For forty years she served as secretary of the Philadelphia Orphan Asylum. She founded the Female Hebrew Benevolent Society, was founder and president of the first Jewish Sunday School in America and in her later years acted as president of the Jewish Foster Home and Orphan Asylum. It is known that Rebecca never married because of her refusal to wed a non-Jew to whom she had been deeply attracted. Her name is associated with educational and charitable institutions in Philadelphia to this day. Her personality remains the most romantic among the noted Jewesses in American history.

GREGGER

A noisemaker used in the celebration of Purim.

An 18th-century silver gregger, made in Poland, complete with bells to add to the confusion when Haman's name is read.

GUATEMALA

Jews first settled in this Central American republic in the 1850's, coming mainly from Germany. Jewish immigration is now limited severely. A thousand Jews live in the country, and they maintain a single synagogue.

GUGGENHEIM, DANIEL

The Guggenheim family was famed in Europe for its industrial and humanitarian achievements. The American branch began with Meyer Guggenheim, who came to America in 1845, at the age of seventeen and who started the enterprises which were to bring the family riches and fame. His son Daniel (1856-1930) is perhaps the best known of the next generation; he was chiefly responsible for the development of the family's mining and engineering projects. As early as 1919 he advocated the federal government's interest in labor relations; and before that he had defended the right of labor to organize. During World War I he was active in stimulating the production of copper for war

purposes; he headed Red Cross drives and helped organize the Third Liberty Loan. He supplied the funds for many free concerts, still given in New York City. Art, music and science received his aid. In 1925 he established and paid for the School of Aeronautics at New York University; a year later he gave almost three million dollars to form the Daniel Guggenheim Fund for the promotion of Aeronautics. He was one of the incorporators of the Conservative Jewish Theological Seminary of America, and a trustee of Congregation Emanu-El in New York City.

GUILDS

Associations of skilled workers. Such associations already existed at the time of the building of the Second Temple (Neh. 3: 8, 31-2). Often, as in the case of the Great Synagogue in Alexandria, members of the various guilds sat in special sections. In the Middle Ages, Jewish guilds existed where there were sufficient numbers of Jews in a particular calling; Jews were excluded from the Christian guilds.

GÜNZBURG FAMILY

Russian financiers, philanthropists, and public figures. Baron Joseph Yozel G. (1812-1878) established the family fortune. Though he settled in Paris, his interest in Russia never flagged, and he was a great force in the industrial development of the country. Baron Horace G. (1833-1909), succeeded his father as head of the Jewish community of St. Petersburg, and was consulted by the Russian government as a leader of that country's Jewry. His son, Baron David G. (1857-1910) was an oriental scholar who published many articles in this field and served as an editor of the Russian Jewish Encyclopedia. In addition to these scholarly activities, he continued the family tradition of public work.

GUT SHABBOS

Greeting meaning "a good and happy Sabbath."

GUT YOM TOV

Greeting meaning "a good and happy holiday."

HABAD

(Initials of *Hochmah*—"Wisdom," *Binah*—"Understading," *Da'at* — "Knowledge") Hasidic sect. The movement, founded by Shneor Zalman of Ladi, was an intellectual reaction against unlearned Hasidism, and was opposed by their leaders and by the *Mithnagdim*, led by the Vilna Gaon. While study of the Torah is preferred to emotional ecstasy, saintliness and joy do play an important role in the Habad philosophy. The present center of Habad activity is New York City, where they are led by Rabbi Menahem Mendel Schneersohn. The movement is also known as the "Lubavitcher Hasidim," after the early center of Habad activity in Russia.

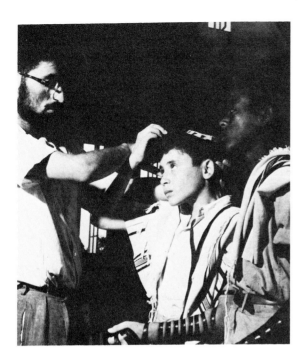

Two boys practicing putting on the Tefillin.

HABAKKUK

Eighth of the Books of the Twelve (Minor) Prophets. The prophet Habakkuk lived in the latter part of the seventh century B.C.E. and foretold the invasion of the Kingdom of Judah by the Babylonians.

HABER, FRITZ

(1868-1934)—German chemist and Nobel Prize winner. His discovery of an efficient means of producing ammonia from nitrogen and hydrogen assured Germany a permanent supply of nitrates for explosives during World War I, besides being valuable as a source of natural fertilizer. In 1933, prodded by the rise of Nazism, he left Germany; his extensive scientific library was left to the Science Institute in Rehovot, Israel.

HABIMAH

(Hebrew for "stage") Israeli Hebrew theatre. The *Habimah* troupe was organized in Moscow in 1917 by Nahum Zemach, and was aided in its early development by the famed Russian director, Constantin Stanislavski. Among its most notable productions was the mystic play, *Ha-Dibbuk*. The theatre moved to Palestine in 1928, and made its home in Tel Aviv. *Habimah* has a repertoire of over one hundred plays, and has made successful tours of Europe and America.

HAD GADYAH

("One Kid") the title of a ballad sung at the conclusion of the Seder celebration.

HADAS

(Myrtle) one of the four plants used in the celebration of Sukkot.

See also Sukkot, Four Plants of

HADASSAH

The largest national Jewish women's organization in America. The small group organized in 1912 by Henrietta Szold now numbers more than 300,000 and

The Hadassah hospital in Jerusalem, Israel.

has a youth auxiliary, the Junior Hadassah. A Zionist group, it was originally called "Daughters of Zion" but changed its designation to Queen Esther's Hebrew name. Its primary purpose is to provide medical services for the State of Israel. Its first modest project was mother and child care for which two nurses were sent from the United States in 1913. Since then Hadassah's medical program has greatly expanded. Now all over Israel it operates hospitals and dispensaries which care for Jew and Arab alike. Its many health stations have helped to drastically reduce the death rate among infants and new mothers and reduce the number of malaria and trachoma cases. Hadassah has also built playgrounds and provided food and health care for thousands of children. In 1939 the Rothschild-Hadassah-University Hospital and Medical School were erected on Mount Scopus (now in Arab hands). It maintains a tuberculosis hospital, the Straus Health Center. Hadassah has extended its program to aid in the education of young immigrants. In the United States it has carried out an educational program for Jewish women, organizing classes in Hebrew, Jewish history and Zionism.

HAFTARAH

After the reading of the assigned portion of the Torah on each Sabbath or other holy day, there is the *Haftarah* reading, meaning concluding reading from the Prophets. Originally only special Sabbaths or holidays were so favored; later all holidays, including fast days, were assigned their prophetic readings. These portions always have some relationship with the Torah readings. The Ashkenazim (German and Eastern Jews) often differ from the Sephardim (Spanish and Orientals) in the selection of the Haftaroth, or one group will read fewer verses than the other. For many centuries the Haftarah was read from a small scroll but it is now recited from a book. The Torah itself is always read aloud from the Sefer, or Scroll. He who is honored with the Haftarah is called "Maftir," or the concluder. It has become the custom to assign the honor to bar mitzvah boys, who spend months learning the chant and the benedictions. Frequently, when there is more than one bar mitzvah on one day in a synagogue, all will have the same reading. Many rabbis deliver a short explanation before the Haftarah, showing its connection in history or sentiment with the portion of the Law read that day.

HAG SAMEAH

Greeting used on holidays, meaning "a happy holiday."

Haganah soldier.

HAGANAH

(Hebrew for "Defense") Underground Jewish self-defense group organized in Palestine in 1920, and ending its existence in 1948, with the establishment of the State of Israel, when it was incorporated into the Israeli Army. *Haganah* members, realizing that the Jewish population was ill-protected by the British forces against Arab attacks, determined to defend their brethren. The Arab riots of 1929 confirmed these pioneers in their determination to strengthen their position. In World War II, 30,000 *Haganah* members enlisted in the British army in the struggle against Nazi Germany. After the War, the *Haganah* aided in the illegal immigration of thousands of Jewish refugees, and the *Palmach (P'lugot Machatz,* Hebrew for "Striking Units") undertook commando activities against the British.

See also Army of Israel.

HAGAR

Maid of Sarah; mother of Ishmael. She and her son were cast out of Abraham's household and sent into the wilderness of Beersheba.

HAGBAAH

"The Lifting Up" of the Torah to the congregation by a worshipper who is thus honored, at the conclusion of the reading.

HAGGADAH

Haggadah, meaning story or narration, is so often applied to the book read at the Passover Seder that many forget its original meaning—the non-legal, fanciful, legendary and proverbial portions of the Talmud. To distinguish it from the Passover Haggadah it is often referred to by the Aramaic form of the word, Aggadah. Ezra the Scribe was the first leader to attempt popularization of the Bible by interpreting its text in parables and legends. The people understood and loved Haggadah and found solace in it in times of hardship. The Geonim and other sages collected the material which they believed strengthened allegiance to the Halachah, the other part of the Talmud, concerned with Jewish law. One-sixth of the Palestian Talmud and a full third of the Babylonian Talmud consist of Haggadah. A great part of Haggadah consists of ethical teachings, as "The Sayings of the Fathers," the book of the Mishnah called *Avot,* which is read on Sabbath afternoons during the spring and summer months. It also contains sections on theology (the study of God and religion), on speculations on the coming of the Messiah, on popular sciences such as astronomy, mathematics and medicine and even on astrology and magic. Many beautiful anecdotes, folk tales and miracle stories are to be found in the Haggadah.

See also Aggadah.

HAGGADAH OF PASSOVER

The book that tells the story of the Exodus from Egypt, explains the Seder symbols, and contains the prayers, psalms and songs used at the Seder, the home service for Passover. It developed as the result of the tradition that commands that each man must retell the story of the Exodus on Passover, discuss its meaning and answer his children's questions, and explain it vividly to them. The subject matter of the Haggadah was added to and altered as the rabbis found necessary; it probably received its present form at the time the Mishnah was compiled (200). New songs were added throughout the centuries. Many commentaries have been written on the Haggadah. A number of beautiful illuminated Haggadahs have been preserved; handwritten manuscripts, with hand-colored illustrations. Hundreds of printed Haggadah editions are known, some dating to the early sixteenth century. Today many beautiful versions of the Haggadah are printed, varying from copies of ancient manuscripts to modern, brightly colored books, prepared especially for children.

HAGGAI

Tenth of the Books of Twelve (Minor) Prophets. The prophet Haggai, after returning to Jerusalem from Babylonian Exile, inspired Zerubbabel and the high priest Joshua to build the Second Temple.

HAGIOGRAPHA

See Ketubim.

HAHAM

(lit., "wise man, scholar")—Title of Rabbi among Sephardic Jews.

HAIFA

Port in northern Israel. Haifa (pop. 155,000), built on the slopes of Mount Carmel, is one of Israel's most beautiful cities, in addition to being a center of industry. The Technion (Technical College), which trains Israel's engineers, was established in Haifa in 1913 through the joint effort of Palestinian, German and American Jews. The city is the maritime gateway into Israel and is the base for Israel's navy and her merchant fleet.

HAKAFOT

(Rounds)—processions with the Torah around the Bimah and the synagogue on Simhat Torah. All the Torah scrolls are taken from the Ark and the men of the congregation take turns carrying them, singing psalms and prayers. Children, waving flags, join the joyous processions.

Hakofot dancers.

HALACHAH

The code of Jewish law is called *Halachah* because this word means "the proper way." It includes every law concerning the Jew's personal and religious con-duct—ethical rules as well as those of ritual practice. *Halachah* signifies the established legislation, according to traditional teachings and the majority vote of the sages, taken after full discussion. The first code was the Torah itself, accepted by the Jews at Sinai; and it is assumed by the rabbis that every law that can be derived from the original verses of the Torah was equally transmitted to Moses. As new customs and ways of living arose, the rabbis provided for them through interpretation of previous traditions. This was the method of the Pharisees, as opposed to the inflexible Sadducees. The Pharisaic method has been employed through Jewish history. This does not mean that any person is empowered by Jewish tradition to decide these matters for himself. It must be done in full accord with time-honored methods. *Halachah*, the legal part of post-Biblical literature, is in contrast to *Aggadah*, the non-legal portions of that literature.

See also Codes of Jewish Law; Talmud.

HALLAH

Today we call the twisted white loaves used on the Sabbath and festivals by the name *Hallah*, which does not mean bread at all. The original meaning in the Bible is the portion taken from the dough of every baking for the priest. It was a kind of tax, to support the priesthood, but no specific amount was mentioned. Later the rabbis established that one forty-eighth of a baker's dough must be given and twice that amount of dough if prepared at home. If the Hallah was not taken from the dough it could later be separated from the finished bread. Although the Bible prescribes that the law applies only to Palestinian products, it was ordained that similar procedures be instituted in all other lands, so that the custom be not forgotten. As there is no way of using the Hallah for the purpose originally intended, today we merely take off a small piece of dough and throw it into the fire. Calling Sabbath loaves "Hallah" perpetuates the legal sanctity of the process. They are made especially beautiful and tasty, and are ridged, twisted, spiraled and otherwise distinguished from weekday bread.

HALLEL

Psalms of praise and prayer, recited between Shemoneh Esreh and the reading of the Torah on the Three Festivals, Rosh Hodesh and Hanukkah.

HALUKAH

(Heb., lit., "distribution")—The system of supporting needy Jews in Palestine with funds collected abroad. This custom is very ancient but was organized most systematically by Moses Alshech for the Jews of Safed in 1600. In the 17th and 18th centuries emissaries (*meshulachim*) were dispatched to the communities outside Palestine to collect funds; often they were men of great piety and scholarship. The rise of Zionism, which insisted upon Jewish colonization of the land and believed in the dignity of labor, ended the *Halukah* system.

HALUTZ

The word commonly used in modern Hebrew for "pioneer," specifically for the young people who settled the new Israel. In ancient Hebrew it refers to an armed man. The Halutz movement began around 1905 but it developed and led to mass migration only toward the end of World War I. Joseph Trumpeldor, who was also a leader in the Jewish Legion, was the leading spirit of the movement. The Halutzim believe in the renewal of the individual through manual labor, especially on the land, to achieve closeness of all Jews to the land of Israel. They came to Israel full of idealism and determination. Most of them had grown up in European cities and were of artisan and middle-class families. In Israel, they cleared swamps, where many of them died of malaria; they worked on their land by day and often stood guard over it by night. They began the process of reclaiming the old Jewish land. Outside Israel the Halutzim established a system called *Hachsharah* (preparation). During the period of *Hachsharah* the Halutz learns how to do agricultural work or whatever else will be required of him on the land. He also learns Hebrew and to live with his comrades in the simple way that will be required of him. Groups with similar religious or economic ideas tend to work together. The movement includes various Zionist youth groups.

HAMADAN

Town in Iran, identified by an ancient tradition with Shushan, the capital of Ahasuerus; a mausoleum in the city is likewise considered by the same legend to be the tomb of Mordecai and Esther. Hamadan is probably Ecbatana, the city from which Cyrus granted the Jews permission to rebuild the Temple (Ezra 6:2). During the Middle Ages, Hamadan was a cultural center of Persian Jewry; its present Jewish population is 4,000.

HAMAN

Prime minister and favorite of King Ahasuerus, plotted to destroy the Jews of Persia. Queen Esther went to the mighty Ahasuerus and exposed Haman's plans. Haman was hanged and the Jews of Persia were saved. The holiday of Purim celebrates this event.

See also Purim.

HAMANTASHEN

Three-cornered pastries filled with poppy seeds or prunes, traditionally served on Purim. Hamantashen is a Yiddish word meaning "Haman's pockets."

A form for baking hamentashen, Poland, 19th century.

HAMETZ

(Leavened bread) during Passover all leavened food is removed from the home. Traditionally, Jews do not eat leavened food during Passover or use dishes and utensils employed during the rest of the year.

HAMISHAH ASAR BI-SHEVAT

This festival, sometimes called Tu Bi-Shevat, because the Hebrew letters spelling "tu" have the numerical value of fifteen (*hamishah asar*), is known as the Jewish new year for trees. It is tree-planting day in Israel. The festival marks both the beginning of Israel's springtime and the last day on which the ancient Biblical tithes could be paid for the produce of the past year. However, the Bible has no mention of the day and its observance. The Talmud cites the custom of planting a cedar for a boy baby and a cypress for a girl. The trees and the children grew up together; and when young people married, poles from the trees dedicated to them were used to hold up the canopy. In all countries, observant Jews eat special fruits on Tu Bi-Shevat and the children dance and sing and hold joyous parties. The status of the day has been elevated since creation of the State of Israel, where it is now a generally observed national celebration.

HAMMURABI

A Babylonian emperor who conquered and united a vast realm four thousand years ago. His most important achievement was the creation of a famous legal code, found engraved on stone in 1901. It has been compared often with the Jewish law of the Bible. There are similarities in the laws concerning property, marriage, inheritance and punishment, but the Jewish laws were more enlightened and humane than those of the Babylonians. There is the law, an eye for an eye, a tooth for a tooth, known as the *lex talionis*. Jewish law has always interpreted this as meaning money damages equivalent to the physical loss; but the Code of Hammurabi suggests that when a man falls out of a tree and kills another man's daughter, the other man is entitled to fall out of a tree in an effort to kill the daughter of the first man. Judaism teaches humane ideas not found in the Hammurabi Code, such as protection of the weak and the poor, limitations of wealth, love of one's neighbor and the stranger within the gates.

HAMOTZI

The words of the blessing over the bread which mean "Who brings forth." As bread is the most basic food, the Hamotzi blessing is the customary one recited before meals.

HANDLIN, OSCAR

(1915-   )—American historian. Born in New York City, Handlin has been a member of the Harvard faculty since 1939. He has written extensively on both general American and American Jewish history, often concentrating on the immigrant experience, and in 1952 was awarded the Pulitzer Prize for his volume *The Uprooted.*

HANNAH

1. Wife of Elkanah. Her prayers for a son, at the sanctuary of Shiloh, were fulfilled. She became the mother of the great judge and prophet Samuel.

2. Martyr who lived under the reign of Antiochus IV, at the time preceding the Maccabean revolt. It is told that Hannah's seven sons bravely gave their lives rather than forsake their Jewish heritage.

HANUKKAH

During the time of Alexander the Great, the Jews in Palestine were not hindered in observance of their religion. But after his death (323 B.C.E.), many of the rulers of Palestine tried to compel the Jews to give up their own religion in favor of Greek paganism. The king most determined to root out Judaism was Antiochus IV. He set up images of Zeus throughout the country and in the Temple itself and sought to force worship and sacrifice to his idols. He forbade Sabbath, festival and dietary observance. To escape death many Jews fled to the hills. The fighting Jews formed an army under Judah Maccabee, whose aged father had struck down a renegade Jew and issued the call to rebellion. After three years, in 165 B.C.E., Judah and his brothers succeeded in defeating the Syrians, cleansing the defiled Temple and relighting the Eternal Lamp. The small jar of pure oil burned for eight days—hence the eight-day observance of Hanukkah (Feast of Dedication). On the first evening a single candle is lit; the number is increased each evening until the last night when the full eight are kindled. Though Hanukkah, which generally falls late in December (Kislev 25), is beloved by young and old for its joyous celebration, the festival is important to all mankind, for this was the first successful insurrection against limitation of religious freedom in history.

See also Maccabees.

HARAN

1. Brother of Abraham; son of Terah, father of Lot.
2. (Charan)—Ancient city in Paddan-Aram (Mesopotamia) where Abraham left his kin to go to the Promised Land. Haran was the home of Rebekah, Rachel and Leah.

HAROSET

A mixture of apples, nuts, cinnamon and wine. It is eaten at the Passover Seder as a reminder of the mortar with which the Jews were forced to make bricks when they were slaves in Egypt.

HASHOMER

(Heb., lit., "The Watchman")—Organization of Jewish workers, founded in Palestine in 1909 to defend Jewish settlements and to press for the employment of Jewish labor. It was later succeeded by the Haganah.

HASID

Deeply religious and compassionate person.

HASIDEANS

(*Hasidim*) Jewish party (sect) at the time of the Maccabees. The Hasideans upheld the Jewish tradition and way of life against the influence of Hellenism.

HASIDIM

Men known by this name are members of a movement called Hasidism which, originating in Poland in the 18th century, gradually spread through Europe and other parts of the world. Its attraction to great numbers of Jews lay in its insistence that even the unlettered Jew could be pious and perfect before the Lord, and that song and dance and pure self-abandonment were proper expressions of the religious impulse. People could thus follow their faith in pure emotion.

Hasidim dancing in front of the Western Wall.

However, Hasidism never attempted to deviate from traditional Judaism, but tried to give it added warmth and acceptance. The founder of the movement, Israel Baal Shem Tov, was a poor man, a mystic, and a lover of his faith and his people. Many of the principles and beliefs that attached themselves to Hasidism, however, were derived from the Kabbalah and its ideas about the relationship between man and God, heaven and earth. Hasidim highly revered their rabbis (Tzaddikim). Many rabbis, headed by the Gaon of Vilna, opposed the movement—hence their title, *Mithnagdim*, meaning opponents. After two great wars and many modern changes, the movement is still important in Judaism.

See also Baal Shem Tov.

HASKALAH

A term applied to the "Enlightenment" movement, which was an effort that began in the 18th century to modernize the lives and thinking of European Jews. It began in Germany and spread to adjacent countries. Before the development of this movement, European Jews continued to live almost as did their ancestors during the Middle Ages. They were isolated from the cultural and social changes that were occurring in the rest of Europe. The *Maskilim* (intelligentsia or enlightened ones) that formed around Moses Mendelssohn propagandized actively for German Jews to adapt themselves to their environment. Mendelssohn, who translated the Torah into German, with special commentaries, was looked upon as the leader of the movement. He was himself an observant Jew, but some of his followers took advantage of their new "freedom" to break away from Judaism. New schools and periodicals arose to spread the Haskalah faith. The pious folk of Austria and Galicia and Poland fought the movement, lest it lead to assimilation. In Russia the Jews, who had witnessed thousands of forced conversions, looked upon the Jewish government official sent to make them *Maskilim* as an apostle of conversion. Writers, magazines and an academic society gained much success in spreading the idea. After the Russian pogroms late in the 19th century, the movement halted its efforts toward making Jews better Russians and substituted new aims leading to Zionism and a better understanding of Hebrew life and literature.

HASMONEANS

This is a name that applies to the Maccabees, the descendants of Hashmon, great-grandfather of Mattathias, father of Judah and his brothers, and to the Maccabean succession of Judean kings who ruled from 141 to 37 B.C.E. In the Maccabean revolt that defeated Antiochus in 165, celebrated in the Hanukkah festival, the fighters sought freedom of religious worship. Later they fought for political independence. Jonathan, youngest son of Mattathias, became the sovereign of Judea, in fact, by taking the office of high priest. In 141 his eldest son, Simon, was chosen Israel's "leader and high priest forever." The Romans recognized the Hasmonean dynasty in 139. But the effort to create a Jewish empire, with a standing army, diplomatic alliances, and emulation of surrounding warlike nations, wrought havoc in the life of the people, creating strange ideas of God and causing religious and political conflict. The popular and pious party was the Pharisees; the aristocratic and politically-minded party was the Sadducees. There was a long succession of kings, fighting one another and fighting Rome, until Herod, who had married into the family, took over and ended the Hasmonean dynasty.

See also Maccabees.

HATAN BERESHIT

("Bridegroom of *Bereshit*") the person honored by being called to the reading of the first portion (*Bereshit*) of the Torah on Simhat Torah, when the reading of the Torah begins anew.

HATAN TORAH

("Bridegroom of the Torah") the person honored by being called on Simhat Torah to the reading of the concluding portion of the Torah.

HATIKVAH

Anthem of the Zionist movement and the State of Israel, based on a poem by Naphtali Hertz Imber. Hatikvah means "The Hope."

HATUNAH

Ceremony and celebration of a wedding. The groom is called Hatan; the bride is called Kallah.

A wedding scene by Moritz Oppenheim.

HAVDALAH

The end of Sabbath or a festival is marked by a ceremony of separation between the holy and the profane or earthly. The Kiddush begins the holy period; the Havdalah ends it—for the Bible says, "Blessed shalt thou be when thou comest in, and blessed shalt thou be when thou goest out." Since Kiddush requires wine, the concluding blessing is made over a glass of wine and a benediction made over a *Besamim* (spice) box; this is interpreted as the effort of the Jew to obtain a final breath of the Sabbath or festival atmosphere. The third and last benediction is recited over a lit Havdalah candle because light was given the universe on the first day of creation. The blessings over spice and lights are employed only after the Sabbath; at the conclusion of festivals the Havdalah is recited over wine alone. Often songs and hymns are chanted following the ceremony. There are many beautiful silver spice boxes in forms of towers, houses, fruits, eggs, baskets and other objects.

HAY

The fifth letter of the Hebrew alphabet, has the numerical value of 5.

See also Aleph Bet.

HAZAZ, CHAIM

(1898-1973)—Hebrew writer. Born in the Ukraine, Hazaz lived in Paris in the 1920s and settled in Palestine in 1931. An outstanding stylist who combined realism and psychological insight with satire, he won both the Bialik Prize and the Israel Prize. His earliest stories deal with Jewish small-town life in the Ukraine during the Russian Revolution. He also wrote extensively about the Yemenite Jewish community, about Jewish life in Palestine during the British mandate, and on other themes, especially the ingathering of the exiles and the ethnic/cultural diversity of the many Jews who have come together in Israel.

HEBREW

The sacred tongue of the Jews is today the everyday language in the land of Israel. Hebrew is one of the Semitic languages (Arabic, Aramaic and Syriac). The peoples among whom the early Israelites lived spoke Hebrew too, though there were different dialects. Aramaic, a related speech, became the common language of the Jews about 250 B.C.E., but the language of prayer remained Hebrew. Then, when the rabbis began the making of the Talmud, they evolved a new type of Hebrew along with the Talmudic Aramaic. "Masorah" is the word describing the effort, from the second to the fifteenth century, to study and standardize Hebrew spelling and grammar. Modern Zionism has helped revive the ancient tongue but the accent, Sephardic, is different from that used by most other Jews of the world. Hebrew can be spoken in two different "pronunciations"—Sephardic, which is most popular and spoken in Israel, and Ashkenazic, the European pronunciation.

HEBREW SCHOOL

Usually refers to afternoon religious schools which meet after the public school session. These schools are usually conducted under the auspices of the synagogue.

HEBREW UNION COLLEGE-JEWISH INSTITUTE OF RELIGION

Rabbinical seminary of the Reform movement. The original Hebrew Union College was founded in 1875 by Isaac M. Wise in Cincinnati. In 1950 it merged with the Jewish Institute of Religion in New York, founded in 1922 by Stephen S. Wise. The combined institution, which also has schools in Los Angeles (founded 1954) and Jerusalem (1963), is the world's largest and oldest school for training rabbis, cantors, and teachers for the Reform branch of Judaism.

Hebrew Union College campus in Cincinnati.

HEBREW UNIVERSITY

There was jubilation throughout the Jewish world when the Hebrew University was opened on Mount Scopus, Jerusalem, in 1925. But in 1948 the Arabs took the site. For many years thereafter the university was compelled to hold classes in other places and build anew in the city proper, dedicating its modern campus at Givat Ram in 1955. The original Mt. Scopus campus was recovered in 1967 as result of the Six-Day War. The university now operates at both locations. The Hebrew University had been first projected by Professor Hermann Schapira of Heidelberg, and it was mentioned at the First Zionist Congress in 1897. But it was not until 1918 that Chaim Weizmann laid the cornerstone. Lord Balfour formally opened the completed institution on April 1, 1925. The Hebrew University began as a group of graduate schools, and still mainly provides courses for higher degrees. The curricula include Judaic studies, science, mathematics, humanities, education, archaeology, medicine, and agriculture. The first president of the University was Dr. Weizmann, later to become president of the State of Israel. The University Press (officially named the Magnes Press since 1949) has published distinguished books on Hebrew literature, archaeology and natural history, and many other subjects. Among supporting institutions outside Israel, the most important is the American Friends of the Hebrew University. The Hebrew University is an honored institution in Israel, a home for the traditional Jewish pursuit of learning, and a spur to the revival of the Hebrew language. In 1973 its total enrollment was 16,000; its staff numbered nearly 1,700. The Jewish National and University Library, located on campus, and forming the university's main library facility, has a collection of more than 2 million volumes.

HEBREWS

A name occasionally applied to Israelites by people of other nations. Today "Hebrews" is sometimes used as a term to designate the Israelites from the time of Jacob's death to the Exodus from Egypt. The Hebrews were later called Israelites and eventually Jews.

HEBRON

One of the most ancient towns of Palestine, home of the Patriarchs, Abraham, Isaac and Jacob. The town is either identical with or very near ancient Mamre. Near Hebron is the Cave of Machpelah, where the Patriarchs were buried. Hebron, in the territory of Judah, was one of the Cities of Refuge. It was David's capital, until his conquest of Jerusalem. There was a Jewish community in Hebron during most of the Middle Ages and through the Turkish period. The modern Jewish community of Hebron was destroyed by the Arabs in 1929 and again in 1936. Hebron was incorporated into Jordan from 1948-1967. It came under Israeli control during the Six-Day War when the West Bank territories were conquered, and in 1968 a new Jewish settlement was established just outside Hebron.

HEDER

Usually a one-room school, privately conducted, often in the home of a teacher, where children receive an elementary Jewish religious education. This form of religious instruction has declined in the United States.

A typical *heder* of the city of Vilna.

HEIFETZ, JASCHA

(1901-   )—Violinist. Heifetz was a child prodigy, giving his first concert performance before he was 5. He is a brilliant virtuoso, and is considered by many the finest violinist today. Born in Vilna, he settled in the U.S. in 1917, and was quickly acclaimed. In addition to his many recordings, he has written a number of original pieces for the violin.

HEINE, HEINRICH

(1797-1856)—One of Germany's greatest lyric poets. During his early years his father and uncle tried to establish this gifted poet as a businessman but their efforts failed. After he studied law, his family insisted he convert to Christianity, as there were few official positions open to Jewish lawyers. But no position was offered him, even though he was achieving worldwide fame as a poet. Always suspicious of Germany's pretenses in the matter of democracy, he went to Paris, and there he was disappointed also in the liberal causes he adopted. Married to an intellectually inferior woman, sick of many of the political struggles of his time, Heine kept on writing even during the last seven years of his life, during which he lay on his "mattress grave," suffering from a disease of the spine. Toward the end of his life, as was the case with many converted Jews, Heine developed a profound loyalty to and interest in his people. When Hitler came into power, Heine's books were burned. Since his lyric, "Die Lorelei," was too popular to be forbidden, its authorship was changed to read "author unknown." Today Heinrich Heine is honored as one of Germany's outstanding poets.

HELLENISM

The Greek civilization which was spread over the Mediterranean region after the end of the 4th century B.C.E. Hellenism, which brought the Jews into close touch with Greek culture, was an important influence on Jewish thought until 350 C.E. The large Jewish community of Alexandria, for example, had adopted the Greek tongue and was familiar with Greek art and literature. The Bible was translated into Greek (the Septuagint), and was interpreted in the light of Greek ethics and psychology. A vast literature in Greek was composed in the Diaspora, partly for missionary purposes and partly for the expression of a Graeco-Jewish philosophy. It reached its peak in the allegorical interpretations of the Bible by Philo, which had decisive influence on Christian theology. The Hellenistic influence often led to the weakening of the observance of the Torah, because the Commandments were explained away as ethical allegories. In Palestine the attempt of a Hellenizing Jewish faction to set up Greek worship in the Temple led to the Maccabean revolt, in which Judaism vanquished Hellenism. Both the Mishnah and the Talmud contain hundreds of Greek words which entered the Hebrew and Aramaic tongues.

HELLMAN, LILLIAN F.

(1905-   )—American playwright. Among her best-known plays are *The Children's Hour, The Little Foxes,* and *Watch on the Rhine.* Her most recent drama is *Toys in the Attic.*

HEROD

Idumean king of Judea, installed by the Romans. He destroyed and supplanted the Hasmonean dynasty, executing his own wife, the beautiful Hasmonean princess Mariamne. This tyrannical king, despite his cruelty, is said to have been a cultured man. He built many magnificent structures in Jerusalem, and is especially remembered for beautifying and enlarging the Second Temple. Herod ruled from 37 to 4 B.C.E.

HERODIAN DYNASTY

The royal House of Herod (of Idumean origin), last kings of Judea before its destruction by the Romans. The Herodians were: Herod, son of Antipater; Herod's sons, Archelaus and Antipas (also called Herod Antipas); Herod's grandson, Agrippa I and his great-grandson, Agrippa II. The Herodians ruled from about 37 B.C.E.-70 C.E.

HERTZ, HEINRICH

(1857-1894)—German physicist and professor. While doing work on Maxwell's electromagnetic theory, Hertz discovered an unusual type of electromagnetic waves, known as radio waves, and now called "hertzian waves." He also taught at the universities of Kiel and Bonn.

HERTZ, JOSEPH HERMAN

(1872-1946)—Chief Rabbi of the United Hebrew Congregations of the British Empire from 1913 to his death in 1946. He was born in Slovakia but his career took him to three continents. He came to New York City at the age of twelve. Here he studied and was ordained in 1894. He served as rabbi in Syracuse, New York. In 1898 he went to Johannesburg, South Africa, where he was soon expelled for British sympathies during the Boer War; but he returned in 1900. After a notable career there, he was called to a New York congregation in 1912, soon relinquishing that post to accept the chief rabbinate of Britain. Hertz visited all the Jewish communities of the British commonwealth as part of his duty. He was present in 1925 at the opening of the Hebrew University and became a member of its Board of Governors. Among the positions to which he was appointed were: president of Jews' College; president, Jewish Historical Society of England; president, Conference of Anglo-Jewish Preachers; member, board of translators, Jewish Publication Society of America; and many British war posts. He supported Zionism and Jewish rights all over the world. Among his writings are *A Book of Jewish Thoughts, Affirmation of Judaism, Daily Prayer Book with Commentary;* and his unsurpassed *Pentateuch and Haftorahs.*

HERZL, THEODOR

(1860-1904)—In his short life, Theodor Herzl became the great founder and leader of the modern Zionist movement. After being admitted to the bar he

Herzl and the Zionist delagation to Kaiser Wilhelm returning from Palestine.

entered the Austrian government service. His greater interests, however, were in his literary and journalistic work. He wrote articles and poems when still a young student, and contributed to various papers and periodicals. He left his legal work and became a well-known playwright and journalist. In 1892 he was the Paris correspondent of a Viennese paper and witnessed the famous Dreyfus trial. He was deeply affected by this exhibition of injustice and anti-Semitism, and from this time on he devoted his life to the fate of the Jewish people. He wrote several books expressing his ideas on a Jewish national home, the best known of which is *The Jewish State.* Herzl approached many important men in behalf of his Zionist aims; among them were Baron de Hirsch, the philanthropist; the German Kaiser, and the Turkish Sultan whose empire included Palestine. Though opposed by some prominent Jewish figures of his time, Herzl's Zionist ideas found many enthusiastic followers, and he united all the smaller groups that had been interested in similar ideas. Herzl called the First Zionist Congress in Basle, Switzerland, in 1897. He organized the Jewish Colonial Trust and conducted a prominent Zionist weekly. He also traveled a great deal in the service of his ideas. He died in 1904 of a heart ailment. In his will he asked that his body rest next to that of his father in Vienna until "the Jewish people will carry my remains to Palestine." In 1949 the new State of Israel brought the body of the beloved leader of early Zionism to its final resting place on Mount Herzl in Jerusalem.

HERZOG, ISAAC HALEVI

The late Chief Rabbi of Israel (d. 1959), like so many distinguished Jews, lived and labored in several countries. Isaac Halevi Herzog was born in Poland in 1888, studied in yeshivot, then in universities in

Paris and England. He became a rabbi in 1910 and a doctor of literature in 1914. After serving the Jewish communities of Belfast and Dublin, he was elevated to the chief rabbinate of the Irish Free State. His learning and piety brought him offers from other lands but he accepted the call to Jerusalem in 1936, following the death of Chief Rabbi Abraham I. Kook. He was known for his devout interest in the Holy Land and zealous participation in the Religious Zionist movement, Mizrachi. He visited the United States and other countries in behalf of Jewish institutions in Israel and Europe, lecturing in English, Yiddish and Hebrew. He wrote many books and articles and completed two of five projected volumes of his monumental work, *Main Institutions of Jewish Law*.

HESCHEL, ABRAHAM JOSHUA

(1907-1972)—American scholar and theologian. Born in Poland, Heschel taught in Berlin until 1938, when he escaped to the United States. After teaching for a time at the Hebrew Union College, he joined the faculty of the Jewish Theological Seminary in 1945 as professor of Jewish ethics and mysticism. Heschel was a religious thinker of great profundity and impact. His teachings, sometimes termed "Neo-Hasidism," drew upon both modern existentialist philosophy and the pietistic tradition of Hasidism. In his many books, among them *The Prophets, Man's Quest for God, Man Is Not Alone,* and *God in Search of Man,* Heschel emphasized that God and man are partners — God constantly reaches out to man, and man responds through faith and the performance of sacred acts.

HESHVAN

Eighth month in the Jewish calendar, also called Mar-Heshvan.

See also Calendar, Jewish; Months, Jewish.

HET

The eighth letter of the Hebrew alphabet, has the numerical value of 8.

See also Aleph Bet.

HEZEKIAH

Thirteenth king of Judah; son of Ahaz, reigned about 720-692 B.C.E. After Assyria destroyed Israel, he supplied Jerusalem with an adequate water system and strengthened its fortifications just before the long Assyrian siege of the city. Hezekiah prayed for delivery while the prophet Isaiah inspired the besieged people to hold out. The Assyrians, beset by plague and other difficulties, withdrew from Jerusalem.

HIGH PRIEST

The highest office in the priestly class *(Cohanim),* a hereditary office. The High Priest lived by the Priestly Code, performing the most sacred tasks in the Temple.

He alone was allowed to enter the Holy of Holies once a year, on Yom Kippur, to pray for all the people of Israel. Aaron was the first High Priest.

HILKIAH

High Priest in the time of King Josiah. He helped the king restore the religious faith of the people.

HILLEL

One of the greatest of early rabbis, Hillel is said to have lived from 110 B.C.E. to the year 10 of the present era (like Moses, he is reputed to have lived 120 years). Born in Babylon, he came to Jerusalem to study when he was forty years old. It is related that he could not at first obtain entrance to the Academy so he peered through a window, where he was discovered, half frozen. His learning and his fame grew and in the year 30 B.C.E. he was appointed president of the Sanhedrin (supreme religious court). There are many reasons for remembering and honoring Hillel. He was a pious man who believed completely in the authority and authenticity of Biblical law, yet managed to make the law accord with the needs of his day. All his judgments were within the framework of tradtion. It was Hillel who expressed the basic dictum of Judaism as follows—"What is hateful unto thee do not do unto thy fellowman"—adding, "This is the Law; the rest is commentary; study it." He also proclaimed the rule that no Jew should separate himself from his community.

HILLEL II

Nasi, formulated the Jewish calendar which, until his time, the 4th century C.E., had been secretly calculated each year and proclaimed by messengers to the Jews of various lands. The present Jewish calendar is based on the formulation of Hillel II.

HILLMAN, SIDNEY

(1887-1946)—American labor leader; president of the Amalgamated Clothing Workers' Union and a vice-president of the CIO. Hillman was a moderate who advocated cooperation between labor and industry.

HIRAM

Phoenician king of Tyre, friend and ally of King Solomon.

HIRSCH, BARON MAURICE DE

(1831-1896)—The most generous giver to Jewish causes in modern history. His wealth, obtained in part from his own family and his wife's, was increased through his activities as a banker and a contractor for British railroads. When he beheld the misery of most of the Jews in the East he gave the Alliance Israelite Universelle, engaged in educating Jews in eastern and

Baron Maurice de Hirsch.

African lands, a million francs (1873); he made up all its deficits until he died. In 1888 he offered Russia fifty million francs for education if that country would ease the hardships of its Jewish citizens but Russia refused. After this he sought out countries in which Jews might settle and till the soil. To assist this movement to Argentina, he organized the Jewish Colonization Association, providing its first capital of $10,000,000 and bequeathing it most of his estate. He also gave large sums to organizations in the United States, Canada and England. It is estimated that Baron de Hirsch gave upwards of $100,000,000 for philanthropic purposes during his lifetime.

HIRSCH, SAMSON RAPHAEL

The distinguished German rabbi, who lived from 1808 to 1888, set himself the task of proving that orthodox Judaism and the modern world were not antagonistic, and that an observant Jew could take his full place in the surrounding culture. He gave new vitality to his religion and his influence is still strong. His chief work, published in 1836, *The Nineteen*

Samson Raphael Hirsch.

Letters of Ben Uziel, which explained and defended Jewish laws and observances, has been translated into English and other languages. Hirsch also wrote a textbook on Biblical and Talmudic doctrines. Through influence in the Reichstag he helped observant Jews form separate communities. To carry out his ideas Hirsch founded a school and edited a magazine. In addition to publishing books expounding the prayers and opposing changes in Judaism, he defended the Talmud and other Jewish writings against German anti-Semites.

HIRSCHBEIN, PERETZ

(1880-1948)—Born in Poland, Hirschbein lived in many countries of Eastern Europe and also traveled extensively throughout the world. He settled permanently in the United States in 1930. The author of several novels and travel books, he was most noted as a dramatist. His plays, though realistic in style, were suffused by a lyrical, idyllic mood. The most famous of his folk dramas is the pastoral romance *Grine Felder* ("Green Fields").

HISTADRUT HA-OVDIM

(Hebrew for "Federation of Hebrew Workers in Israel.") Federation of trade unions founded in 1920, which, by 1972, had 1,161,000 members, including 73,000 Arab and Druse workers. Manual workers, holders of white-collar positions, intellectuals, and self-employed persons all belong to the Histadrut. The Histradrut's Kupat Cholim (Sick Fund) ministers to a million people. Its cooperative marketing company, T'nuvah, markets most of Israel's agricultural produce. Its public work and building firm, Solel Boneh, carries on most of Israel's construction projects and is also active in other countries. Histadrut operates other economic enterprises as well, and in addition publishes two newspapers (*Davar* and *Omer*), supports the *Ohel* theatre, runs a youth organization, and possesses its own publishing house.

HITTITES

Mentioned many times in the Bible as one of the tribes whose territory was to be taken over by the Israelites in the Promised Land. It is less than a hundred years since scholars began deciphering inscriptions on old monuments in an effort to learn more about the Hittites and their language, which turned out to be akin to Latin and Greek. It was learned that these people conquered Babylon about 1900 B.C.E. and created a huge empire. Seven centuries later the empire was destroyed and only a small group in Syria retained the name. Gradually their language gave way to Aramaic, the tongue closest to Hebrew. Interesting comparisons have been made between the Jewish and Hittite codes of law; they have many points of similarity. Anthropologists have speculated that the Jewish physical type had its origin in the Hittites—but there is no firm evidence to support this theory.

HOL HA-MOED

This term refers to the "ordinary" days of Passover and Sukkot. In Israel the Biblical arrangement still holds—the first and seventh day of Passover are holy, the intervening five days ordinary. Outside Israel there are two holy days, followed by four *Hol ha-moed*, and two more holy days; there are two holy days of Sukkot, five days of *Hol ha-moed*, and then the holy days of Shemini Atzeret and Simhat Torah. On the ordinary days, though the prayers retain a holiday character, Jews may work; on the holy days, no regular labor may be done. No weddings are solemnized on the half-holidays, but marriage engagements may be celebrated. On these half-holidays there are additional prayers of joy. On *Hol ha-moed* Sukkot (except on the Sabbath) the synagogue procession is conducted with Lulav and Etrog; on the fifth day there are seven processions about the synagogue, with the chanting of the prayer *Hoshana* ("Save"). This day is therefore called Hoshana Rabba (Great Hoshana).

HOLY CITIES

Although only Jerusalem is known as the Holy City, there were, in fact, four such places in Palestine. Jerusalem was the first, for there was erected the Temple of Solomon. Tiberias in the north is considered holy because the great supreme court of the Jews, the Sanhedrin, was established there; and in Judaism, law and religion are as one. In the sixteenth century schools of the pious were established in the city of Safed; the presence of so many good and learned Jews there from that time on has given sanctity to this city. In the south there is Hebron, now in possession of the Arabs. In Hebron lies the Cave of Machpelah, in which the Patriarchs and Sarah, Rebekah and Leah are buried, a fact which renders the spot forever sacred. Jews who wished to improve their knowledge of Jewish lore and to live the traditional life of saint and scholar gravitated to these four holy cities.

HOLY OF HOLIES

(*Kodesh Hakodashim*) the most holy place in the Tabernacle, and later in the Temple, where the Ark of the Covenant was kept. The Holy of Holies was entered only by the High Priest, once a year, on the holy day of Yom Kippur.

HOLY LAND

See Canaan; Israel.

HOPHNI

One of the sons of the Judge and High Priest Eli, regarded unworthy to succeed his father. Hophni and his brother Phinehas fell in the battle against the Philistines, when the Ark was captured.

HOR, MOUNT

A mountain near the coast of Edom and Kadesh-barnea where the Israelite camp site stood. Aaron died at Mount Hor.

HOREB, MOUNT

Biblical name of Mount Sinai, in Deuteronomy. *See also* Sinai, Mount

HORITES

Ancient people who invaded Syria and Palestine in the 17th century B.C.E. Eventually, their territory was taken by the Edomites (Gen. 14:6, 36:20-30; Deut. 2:12, 22). Egyptian documents of the period call Palestine "Haru," which some scholars have identified with the Horites.

HOSEA

First of the Books of Twelve (Minor) Prophets of the Bible. The prophet Hosea wrote and preached in the 8th century B.C.E. in Israel, at the time of Jeroboam II and the disorder that followed the king's death. He preached against the immorality of his day, reminding the people that God wants men to be just and compassionate.

HOSHANA RABBA

This is the name of the seventh day of Sukkot and means Great Hoshana; for many prayers recited on that day begin with "Hoshana," which means "Save, O Lord!" It is told that on every day of Sukkot, in the Temple, one procession was made around the altar in which each participant carried the four plants of the festival; the Etrog, the Lulav, myrtle and willow, bound together; but on this day many processions were made. Earlier that day the people cut willow branches, a symbol of the fruitfulness of the rain, and decorated the altar in the Temple with them. After seven processions around the altar, they beat willow branches on the ground. Today, in many synagogues, after the processions, the willow branches are beaten on the floor and benches until the leaves are broken off. This old custom is a symbol of man's hope and his trust in the Divine; though trees and plants lose their leaves, God restores them again and He grants them warmth and moisture. In like manner, He renews man's strength. Through the centuries pious men have spent the whole night of Hoshana Rabba in prayer and in the study of the special selections from the Torah, the Talmud and the Zohar. In the Zohar it is said that this day is a "day of judgment," when the decree of Yom Kippur becomes effective; until that day man has the opportunity for repentance and forgiveness. But other sources reveal an independent importance of Hoshana Rabba, that this is a day of blessing for Israel. Toward the end of the morning services of Hoshana Rabba, the Etrog and Lulav are laid aside. The next day, the eighth day of Sukkot, is the holiday of Shemini Atzeret.

HOSHANOT

1. The Hoshana prayers of Hoshana Rabba.
2. The willow-branches used on Hoshana Rabba during the prayer for rain and salvation. In ancient

Israel, the willow was a symbol for the fruitfulness of rain.

See also Aravah

HOSHEA

Last king of the northern Kingdom of Israel (about 734-722 B.C.E.). He allied Israel with Egypt, ignoring earlier treaties with powerful Assyria. Shalmaneser, the Assyrian king, and Sargon II, his successor, overran Israel. Samaria, the capital, held out against a siege that lasted three years. After its fall, Hoshea was taken prisoner and the ten tribes of the Kingdom of Israel were led into captivity and scattered over the lands of the Assyrian Empire.

HOUDINI, HARRY

Born Erich Weiss, in Wisconsin, 1874, Harry Houdini, the most skillful magician of modern times, was the son of a pious synagogue official in Appleton. Houdini's stage name was adopted from a great past practitioner of magic. At the age of twelve he ran off to become a trapeze performer. While still in his twenties he was already a famous magician. By keeping completely serene and breathing slowly he was able to spend minutes in closed crates under water. He would allow men to tie him up in any manner they wished, encase him in a box and lower it by ropes into a freezing river; within a few minutes he was free and on the surface. No handcuff could restrain him, as Scotland Yard discovered. He escaped from a Siberian prison van he had never before looked upon. In hundreds of theatres and many countries he was seen and applauded by millions. He said all his feats were accomplished by skill and not by magic. He fought spiritualists who declared they could move objects by remote control and bring the dead to life and exposed

Harry Houdini.

and duplicated their tricks. Mediums have offered to bring word from him from the other world but they have never succeeded. Houdini, who had survived many physical injuries, died in 1926 as the result of a chance blow by a student with whom he was sparring.

HUGH OF LINCOLN

(d. 1255)—Alleged ritual murder victim. At the age of 8, he disappeared and his body was later discovered in a Jewish well. Nearly 100 Jews were executed without trial for his death. The story is told in Chaucer's *"Prioress' Tale,"* in the *"Canterbury Tales."*

HULDAH

Prophetess, advisor to King Josiah. She was consulted to interpret the meaning of the lost book of the Torah that was found in the Temple during Josiah's reign. Huldah helped Josiah rekindle the people's religious faith.

HUMASH

Short form of *Hamisha Humshe Torah* (the five-fifths of the Torah). The *Humash* is the book containing the Five Books of Moses (and also the Prophetic passages read each Sabbath in the synagogue). The Five Books of Moses are: Genesis *(Bereshit)*, Exodus *(Shemot)*, Leviticus *(Vayikra)*, Numbers *(Bamidbar)* and Deuteronomy *(Devarim)*.

HUPPAH

Wedding-canopy, consisting of a square top cover, often made of silk or satin, supported by four poles which either stand on the ground or are held during the ceremony by four men. The bride and the bridegroom are wed under the *Huppah*.

See also Hatunah.

HUR

Assistant to Moses, who with Aaron, supported Moses' uplifted hands while he prayed for victory during the battle against the Amalekites. Some say he was the husband of Miriam.

HUSSEIN

(1935-   )—King of Jordan. Hussein became ruler of Jordan in 1953 after his grandfather, King Abdullah, was assassinated. In 1967, despite Israeli urgings, he participated in the Six-Day War and as a result lost all his territories on the West Bank of the Jordan River, including the Old City of Jerusalem. During the Yom Kippur War in 1973, except for token involvement, he kept his country out of the fighting. Regarded as one of the more moderate and Western-oriented of the Arab leaders, Hussein has frequently been in conflict with the various Palestinian terrorist groups, and in 1970 his army used force to drive them out of Jordan.

HUSSEINI, HAJ AMIN AL

(1893-   )—Mufti of Jerusalem; violently anti-Jewish and anti-Israel Arab leader. Husseini was responsible for the Arab riots of 1937, and during World War II collaborated with Hitler and arranged the destruction of the Jews in the Moslem areas of Bosnia.

HYKSOS

Semitic people who conquered Egypt after the destruction of the Middle Kingdom. During their rule (c. 1720-1580 B.C.E.) the Children of Israel entered Egypt; their enslavement commenced upon the expulsion of the Hyksos.

HYRCANUS, JOHN

Son of Simon the Hasmonean. As Simon's successor, he ruled from 135 to 104 B.C.E. After his father and two brothers were murdered by Ptolemy, Hyrcanus, then Governor of Gezer, escaped to Jerusalem. There he seized power before Ptolemy was able to gain control. When Antiochus Sidetes captured Jerusalem in 135-4, Hyrcanus was confirmed as High Priest. After defeat of Syria, he regained territory he had been made to cede. He captured Shechem and Mt. Gerizim, then forced the Idumeans to adopt Judaism after he had overrun their territory. The last years of his reign were peaceful.

HYRCANUS II

(d. 31 B.C.E.)—Eldest son of Alexander Yannai. He succeeded Salome Alexandra (67 B.C.E.) who was his mother, and was then driven from the throne and position of High Priest by his brother Aristobulus. He escaped to Petra, obtained support there and returned, defeating Aristobulus. After the death of the Roman emperor Pompey, Hyrcanus supported Julius Caesar and was restored as ethnarch, also being given expanded territory. Taken prisoner by the Parthians during the invasion of Judea (40), Hyrcanus was maimed so he could not qualify for priesthood. Sent to Parthia, he was afforded much honor there by the Babylonian Jewish communities. He returned to Judea but was later accused of treason by King Herod and executed.

IBN EZRA

1. (Abraham) writer of famous Bible commentaries, grammarian, philosopher, astrologer and poet. He lived in Spain and Italy (about 1092-1167 C.E.).
2. (Moses) relative of Abraham, great poet, lived in Granada, Spain (died about 1139). He wrote in both Hebrew and Arabic.

IBN GABIROL, SOLOMON

A distinguished Hebrew philosopher and poet who lived in Spain, 1021 to 1056. Through an accident, his writings, translated from the Hebrew into the Latin, were accepted and discussed by Christian scholastics as the work of an unknown Christian or Arab. His name had been corrupted to Avicebron and it was only a century ago that the true author, Ibn Gabirol, who had not mentioned the Bible or Talmud or anything specifically Jewish in his book (Fountain of Life), was identified. Students have wondered how a man so pious could have written a book which seems totally to ignore Jewish references, but his piety and genius are unquestioned. At twenty, Ibn Gabirol composed a complete Hebrew grammar in perfect rhyme and meter. Continuing his writings, he traveled and lectured throughout Spain. The poetry of Ibn Gabirol is found in the Jewish prayerbook, taken from his long poem, "The Royal Crown." Impressed by Greek philosophy, he is the first Jewish man of learning to have actively introduced the ideas of the Greeks and the Arabs into the western world.

IBN TIBBON, SAMUEL

(1150-1230)—Member of a famous family of translators, who rendered many philosophic and scientific texts from Arabic into Hebrew. Ibn Tibbon is best known for his translation of the Guide of the Perplexed of Maimonides. His work is accurate and clear, and was praised by Maimonides himself, whom Ibn Tibbon consulted on difficulties. He also translated other Arabic works of Maimonides, and wrote some commentaries on the Bible.

IBZAN

Of Bethlehem, one of the Judges of Israel. He judged for seven years.

IMBER, NAPHTALI HERZ

(1856-1909)—Hebrew poet; author of the Zionist anthem "Hatikvah." At one time a pioneer in Palestine, Imber died in poverty in New York City.

INCUNABULA

Books printed before 1500. Nearly two-hundred such Hebrew books are known, the first of them probably printed in Spain, before 1475. About two-thirds of these books, which dealt with Biblical, liturgical or Rabbinic topics, were printed in Italy; many were produced by the Soncino family. The Spanish Inquisition was responsible for the burning of many of these volumes in 1490.

INDIA

The Jewish community in India consists of Jews who have lived in the land for centuries—the Cochin Jews, and of European and Iraqi Jews, who are more recent settlers. The "Bene Israel" believe themselves descended from the Ten Lost Tribes. The Jews of India are to be found in all occupations, ranging from the millionaire landowner to the poverty-stricken day laborer. Nearly 25,000 Indian Jews settled in Israel in the late 1940s and the 1950s. There are now 14,500 Jews in India, most of them living in Bombay.
See also Bene Israel

INHERITANCE

The Jewish laws of inheritance have always been unique. The oldest son must receive a double portion, even when the father would like to favor another son. There were exceptions, however. Jacob was chosen over the older Esau, and Ephraim over Manasseh; but special reasons are given for the changes. David was the youngest in his family, but he had been divinely chosen to become king. Joseph, who was next to the youngest among twelve sons, rose to become second in power over Egypt, hence ruled over Reuben and the other brothers. Daughters were considered as having left the homes of their fathers, to be provided for in full by their husbands; but Moses issued a special decree that daughters could share the estate when there were no sons. Although Solomon reached the throne despite the existence of an older brother, later kings of Israel and Judah—whenever this was possible —passed the rule to their firstborn sons. Today Jewish laws of inheritance have been modified, or made to accord with the laws of the land; and Jews leave their possessions to charity, education and other causes as well as to their children.

INQUISITION

In 1231 Pope Gregory IX set up a court to inquire into the activities of men and movements breaking away from the Church. Its interest was first limited to known Christians. After a while the court extended its attention to the Jews, especially those who had been converted and then returned to Judaism. When the Spaniards offered the Jews the choice of baptism or death, many only pretended to accept Christianity, forming the class called Marranos. By special dispensation of the Pope, a Spanish Inquisition was organized under Ferdinand and Isabella (the same rulers who sponsored Columbus), and headed by Torquemada, one of the cruelest and most savage persecutors in history. Men were accused and were never told the names of their accusers. They were subjected to tor-

A procession of officials and victims of the Inquisition in Goa, in an auto-da-fe.

ture and permitted no defense. Thousands were "relaxed" (released) to non-religious courts and burnt to death before huge crowds. The Inquisition spread its tortures to many other lands. Not until 1820 was this savagery in the name of religion abolished in Spain.

See also Auto-da-fè; Marranos.

IRAN

See Persia.

IRAQ

Fertile land between the ancient Euphrates and Tigris where the great Babylonian, Assyrian, and Syrian empires flourished. Both the office of the Exilarch and of the Gaon existed in Iraq (formerly Mesopotamia) until the 12th century. In 1917 the British conquered the country and ended Turkish rule, permitting Jews to rise to responsible positions. However, when Iraq gained independence in 1932 the Jews were once again treated badly. Iraq attacked Israel in 1948, and 123,000 Jews subsequently left the country. Iraq also fought against Israel in the 1967 and 1973 wars. There are now 2,500 Jews in Iraq, the majority living in Baghdad.

IRELAND

Handfuls of Jews have lived in Ireland since the 12th century, but the present Dublin community was not founded till 1822. At the end of the 19th century some East European Jews emigrated to Ireland. 5,400 Jews now live in Ireland, mostly in Dublin and Belfast. Robert Briscoe who served as lord mayor of Dublin in 1956-57 and 1960-61, was the first Jew to hold this office and also had been the first Jew to serve in the Irish Dail (parliament).

IRGUN

(Full name: *Irgun Zvai Leumi,* Hebrew for National Military Organization) Palestinian underground movement founded in 1937 by members of the Betar youth organization, and the Zionist-Revisionist movement. Its main activities were retaliation against Arab attacks on Jews, and sabotage against the British Mandatory administration. The Jewish Agency disavowed both the means and goals of the organization, which, from 1943 on, was headed by Menahem Beigin. After World War II the Irgun was especially active in the organization and success of the "illegal" immigration of Jewish D.P.'s ("displaced persons") to Palestine. Despite initial friction, the Irgun merged with the Haganah upon the establishment of the State in 1948. The *Herut* (Hebrew for Freedom) party continues to make the organization's traditional demand for a more aggressive foreign policy in the Knesset, Israel's parliament.

ISAAC

Second son of Abraham and only son of Sarah, he is the second of Israel's Patriarchs and occupies a prominent place in Jewish prayer and tradition. His name means "one laughs," because his aged parents, especially Sarah, laughed unbelievingly at the angel's promise of a son. The story of Isaac is told in less detail than those of the other two patriarchs, Abraham and Jacob. He seems to have been a quiet man who sought peace and trusted in God's will. Isaac is remembered as the child who had such faith in God and in his father Abraham that he was willing to be sacrificed at their behest. The meaning of this incident (the *akedah*, binding of the altar of sacrifice) is treated in great detail in Talmud and Midrash and it is the portion of the Torah read on the second day of Rosh Hashanah. At the age of forty Isaac married Rebekah, who bore him twin sons after twenty years of marriage; Jacob and Esau. Isaac was a farmer and cattle-breeder. He lived in the Negev, until famine drove him to move on. The Philistines made life difficult for him and his herds but finally they realized that Isaac was a blessed man and peace was made at Beersheba. Isaac turned blind in his old age and was deceived into slighting Esau, his older and favorite son, and giving the blessing and the birthright to Jacob, who later became the third patriarch. Isaac lived to see Jacob's return from Haran, where he had fled from his brother's wrath, and the old man saw his sons in peace with each other before he died in Hebron (Mamre) at a very old age. There the brothers buried him in the Cave of Machpelah.

ISAIAH

In the section of the Bible called Prophets the first entire book devoted to one prophet is the book of Isaiah. Some think the latter portion of this Book, which offers comfort to the dispersed and exiled Jewish people, was written by another Isaiah and not "the son of Amoz." Isaiah ben Amoz began his activity about 738 B.C.E., and ended in 701. Probably influenced by the words of Amos and Hosea, he also denounced the unrighteousness of his brethren and promised their punishment at the hands of conquering Assyria. Isaiah constantly counseled Israel to form no alliances with any of the nations but to rely on their faith and trust in God. The Midrash explains the differences in style and attitude in the later chapters by saying that God urged the prophet, after so many years of scolding the Jews, to bring the sinners some hope for the future. Because of his magnificent writing and his great vision, Isaiah is often called the greatest of the prophets. Best known are Isaiah's prophecies of final peace in the world—"they shall beat their swords into plowshares, and their spears into pruning hooks."

ISH-BOSHETH

Also called Ishbaal, fourth son of King Saul. After Saul's death he ruled over part of Israel, while David ruled over the tribe of Judah. Ish-bosheth reigned for about two years.

ISHMAEL

The firstborn son of Abraham, was born to Hagar, his wife Sarah's slave. Fourteen years later Sarah gave birth to Isaac. When Isaac was weaned, Ishmael mocked the child and Ishmael's conduct toward Isaac finally led to the expulsion of the older son and his mother from Abraham's household. Some commentaries assert that Ishmael, though the son of a slave, demanded the double portion of the inheritance granted the firstborn son of the first wife, and that he heaped insults upon his little half-brother. The Bible relates how Hagar and Ishmael wandered in the desert, "the wilderness of Beer-sheba," suffering from thirst, and how Hagar despaired and feared her son would die. Then an angel of God appeared and comforted Hagar and asked her to be of good cheer. The angel promised to make a great nation of Ishmael and bade Hagar open her eyes and hold up her child. Hagar looked up and saw a well and Ishmael was saved. The mother and son settled in the wilderness of Paran, where Ishmael became a great hunter. Hagar selected for him a wife from Egypt. From this marriage four sons and a daughter were born; the daughter later married Esau, son of Isaac. The Arabs look upon Ishmael as their father; they believe him to be a prophet of Mohammed and describe him as a great missionary who converted many pagans to the belief in one God and who, through his son Kedar, was the direct ancestor of Mohammed.

ISLAM

Monotheistic religion proclaimed to the Arabs by Mohammed. Islam borrowed many elements of its belief and law from Judaism, and the Jewish prophets are considered the forerunners of Mohammed by the Koran, the Islamic Bible. Though Islam theoretically recognized that Jews are not to be considered "infidels," and should enjoy religious freedom, many Arab leaders, following the example of Calif Omar (633-644), introduced oppressive legislation against the Jews; at times there were forced conversions on a wholesale scale. There were, however, many periods in which the persecution of Jews by Moslems was rare. Medieval Jewish philosophers were sometimes influenced by contemporary Moslem thought.

ISRAEL

The name given to Jacob after he had "striven with God"—really with God's angel. "Children of Israel" is an old historic name for the Jewish people and has served to unite the ancient tribes, the descendants of the sons of Jacob—Israel. The Land of Israel, (now the portion of it that became the modern state in 1948) was once the name of all Palestine. The whole land was included in the first kingdom of Israel, from the time of King Saul to the death of Solomon, 933 B.C.E. Then the land was divided into two kingdoms, the northern kingdom of Israel and the southern kingdom of Judah. The capital of Judah was Jerusalem. Judah remained loyal to the great religious heritage of Israel and to the dynasty of David and Solomon. The kingdom of Judah consisted only of the tribe of Judah and the small tribe of Benjamin; the northern kingdom of Israel included the ten other tribes. In the kingdom of Israel governmental problems were confused and difficult. Frequent changes of rule took place and many political murders were committed. Four different cities served as capitals and royal residences and the prophets thunderingly denounced the kingdom's frequent return to idol worship. King Jeroboam II, who reigned from 782 B.C.E. to 745 B.C.E., defeated his enemies and brought some external power back to the kingdom; but still it remained internally weak, as is evident from the writings of the prophets Amos and Hosea. In 722 B.C.E. the Assyrians crushed the revolt of Hoshea, the last king of Israel, and put an end to the duration of the kingdom. Some of the people of Israel found refuge in Judah, but the greater part of the Ten Tribes, concerning whose disappearance there have been many fanciful guesses, were permanently scattered.

See also Israel, State of .

ISRAEL BEN ELIEZER

Founder of Hasidism.

See also Baal Shem Tov.

ISRAEL, STATE OF

In the first words spoken by God to Abraham ("Get thee out of thy country, unto the land that I will show the . . ."), the meaningful connection between the Jewish people and the land of Israel was established. Out of this relationship, God promised, would come a "blessing" for all the children of man. Jews who live in America and other lands, whose homes, ties and loyalties are rooted in these lands, are grateful for the restoration of Israel for those Jews, especially the homeless ones, who desire to go there. The modern movement to re-establish Israel as a homeland for Jews began in the nineteenth century with the efforts of Theodor Herzl. After World War I, Great Britain, through Lord Balfour, promised creation of a national homeland for Jews in Palestine. But for political and other reasons, Britain did not keep its promise and actively fought statehood and additional Jewish immigration to Palestine. After World War II the sorely pressed British gave in and turned the problem of Palestine over to the United Nations. In 1947 the United Nations officially divided Palestine into Arab and Jewish states. The Arabs, angered, invaded Israel. The Israelis, less than a million strong, having

Chaim Weizmann, the first President of Israel, addressing the first Knesset of Israel.

no other choice, fought with valor and determination and defeated the armies raised by 40,000,000 Arabs. The United Nations arranged a truce, which the Arabs violated. Another truce was imposed and modern Israel's peculiar boundaries remain in accord with the situation at the time of the cease-fire. Arab hostility against Israel continued in the decades that followed, and Israel was forced to fight three more wars of self-defense: the Sinai Campaign of 1956 against Egypt, the Six-Day War of 1967 against Egypt, Syria, Jordan, and Iraq, and the Yom Kippur War of 1973 against Egypt, Syria, and Iraq, and in addition had to remain constantly on the alert to defend itself against terrorist attacks both within and outside its boundaries. Despite this, however, the State of Israel has grown and prospered. After statehood it experienced a tremendous influx of new immigrants from many countries, especially Europe and the Arab world, and in 1972 its population numbered 3,164,000, of whom 2,636,000 were Jews, 343,900 Moslems, 77,300 Christians, and 37,300 Druze. Israel's total area (not counting the territories occupied after the Six-Day War) is 7,992 square miles, and the main natural resources are copper, phosphate, potash, and asbestos. The capital of Israel is Jerusalem; Tel Aviv-Jaffa is the country's largest city, and Haifa is its main port. In 1972 Israel's gross national product amounted to $3.4 billion. Israel's principal trading partners are the United States, Britain, West Germany, the Netherlands, Japan, and France. Her most important exports are citrus fruits, polished diamonds, textiles, chemicals, mining products, and food products; her main imports are industrial materials and equipment, fuels and lubricants, agricultural and transport equipment, and cereal grains. Israel is a parliamentary democracy. The chief of state is the President, elected by the 120-member Knesset (parliament) for a 5-year term. The head of the government is the Prime Minister. Israel celebrates her Independence on May 14.

See also Israel.

ISRAELI, ISAAC

(c. 855-c. 955)—North African philosopher and physician. One of the pioneers of medieval Jewish philosophy, Israeli wrote several significant philosophical works, including the *Sefer ha-Yesodot* ("Book of Elements"), in Arabic. Primarily a compiler rather than an original thinker, he helped bring the philosophy of Plato and Aristotle to the attention of the Jewish community of his day. He also wrote important treatises on medical subjects.

ISRAELS, JOZEF

(1824-1911)—Dutch painter. Israels is thought by many to be the leading Dutch painter of the last two centuries. Like Rembrandt's work, which he admired, many of his paintings deal with Jewish subjects, such as *A Son of the Ancient People, The Scribe,* and *Jewish Wedding Feast.* Israels was the leader of the Hague School of Painters. While his main artistic field was painting, he turned author in *Spain,* a volume describing a trip to Spain and North Africa.

ISSACHAR

Ninth son of Jacob, fifth son of Leah, ancestor of the tribe of Issachar.

ISSACHAR, TRIBE OF

One of the tribes of Israel. Its territory was the fertile eastern section of the Emek Jezreel and the northern hills, near the tribe of Zebulun. Issachar's emblem was a donkey; its black banner depicted the sun and the moon. The stone representing Issachar in the High Priest's breastplate was probably a sapphire.

ISSERLES, MOSES

(1525-1572)—One of the leading Talmudists of Polish Jewry. Isserles ("Rama") is best known for his notes to the *Shulchan Aruch* which contain the opinions of Ashkenazic scholars, as distinguished from Caro's work, which is based on Sephardic authorities and practices. Isserles was also a student of philosophy and Kabbalah.

ITALY

Jews first settled in Italy in the 2nd century B.C.E., and a Jewish community has existed there until the present day. Earlier prosperity was followed by persecution, and in 1555 the Jews were confined to a ghetto, forced to wear a Jewish "badge," and discriminated against economically. Full equality was restored only in the second half of the 19th century. Jews have held responsible positions in the country, including that of Prime Minister. During World War II, Nazi persecution of Jews was common. There are now 31,000 Jews in Italy.

See also Rome.

IYAR

Second month in the Jewish calendar.

See also Calendar, Jewish; Months, Jewish.

JABBOK

River of ancient Gilead which flows into the eastern bank of the Jordan. Jacob, on his return from Haran, wrestled with the angel on the bank of the Jabbok, where he was named Isael.

JABESH-GILEAD

Town east of the Jordan, in Gilead, saved by King Saul, in his first battle, from its enemies, the Ammonites. At the time of Saul's tragic death in the battle of Gilboa, the brave men of Jabesh-gilead saved the bodies of Saul and his sons from the Philistines and buried them in Jabesh-gilead.

JABIN

Canaanite king whose general, Sisera, was defeated by Deborah and Barak in a battle at Mount Tabor.

JABOTINSKY, VLADIMIR

(1880-1940)—Leader of the Revisionist movement in Zionism and founder of the Jewish Legion, he was born in Odessa, 1880. He gained fame as a journalist when he covered World War I for a Moscow paper. Early in life he devoted himself to spreading the Zionist ideal. In the early years of 1900 he was the foremost Zionist speaker and writer in Russia. In 1915 he prodded the British Government to organize all-Jewish fighting units in Palestine. Jabotinsky remained in Palestine, where he organized a self-defense corps (Haganah) against the Arabs. For this the British sentenced him and his comrades to long prison terms. But he was soon released and his first act was to announce that many of Weizmann's policies needed revising. Thus he became a "revisionist." He traveled and spoke in Europe and America, contending that Zionists should concentrate on rapid mass immigration into Palestine despite British objections and that the immigration effort should be safeguarded by Jewish military and police units. During the Hitler period he

Vladimir Jabotinsky in the uniform of the Jewish Legion.

fought with an angel and maintained himself in the struggle. The angel gave him his new name—Israel ("he who strove with God"). Thus Israel became the name of his descendants, the sons of Israel. Jacob preferred Joseph to all his sons. The sons were jealous of Joseph and sold him to a caravan which took him to Egypt. Later, during a famine, Jacob and his family migrated to Egypt where Joseph had become a great statesman. Pharaoh gave the land of Goshen to Jacob and his sons and Jacob died there a very old man. His sons, according to his wish, buried him in the Cave of Machpelah, near Hebron.

JACOB BEN ASHER

(1269-1343)—Talmudic scholar and codifier. Jacob was the son of Rabbi Asher, a famous Talmudic scholar who was also his teacher. In 1303 he fled with his father from Germany to Barcelona, Spain, where he lived in poverty, refusing to accept the post of rabbi. His great work was a code of Jewish law called the *Arba Turim* (Hebrew for "Four Rows," after Ex. 39:10) because it contained four parts: *Orah Hayim*, on Jewish ceremonial law and prayers; *Yoreh Deah*, on dietary laws and other matters; *Even Ha-Ezer*, on marriage laws; and *Hoshen Mishpat*, on civil law. This work was often based on the *Mishneh Torah* of Maimonides, but was more practical, as it dealt only with actual conditions and omitted all laws concerning sacrifices and Temple service. The legal decisions of the *Tur* were arrived at by an examination of the decisions of Rabbi Alfasi (Rif), and Rabbi Asher (Rosh), who as Rabbi Jacob's father, is always referred to as "my master, my father." Rabbi Joseph Caro based his *Shulchan Aruch* on this earlier work.

inspired a campaign for sending "illegal" immigrants into Palestine. A linguist with unusual literary ability, Jabotinsky produced highly praised novels, histories and language studies. He died in New York in 1940.

JACOB

Son of Isaac and Rebekah, he was the third of the Patriarchs. He received his name because at birth he held onto the heel (*akev*) of his slightly older twin brother, Esau. The story of Jacob is told in dramatic detail in the Bible. For a "mess of pottage" Esau sells him his birthright. On his mother's instigation he deceives his old, blind father to obtain the blessing which was intended for Esau, the firstborn. To escape Esau's vengence, Jacob fled to Haran. On his way he had his famous dream in which God promised to help him and lead him back and make his descendants into a great people. In Haran, Jacob served Laban, a cattle and sheep breeder, for fourteen years in order to marry his daughters and six more years for a herd of his own. Leah bore Jacob many sons, and Rachel, whom he loved above all, bore him two sons, Joseph and Benjamin. After twenty years of service with Laban, Jacob and his family returned to his home. While crossing the Jordan Jacob

Page from Jacob Ben Asher's "Orah Hayyim", printed at Ixar, 1485.

JAEL

Heroic Kenite woman who slew Sisera, general of the Canaanites, on his flight from the victorious Barak.

JAFFA

Just north of this ancient Palestinian seaport lies the modern city of Tel Aviv. After Israel again became a nation, the cities were united; but Tel Aviv, built over the sand dunes, is young and modern, whereas Jaffa shows its ancient Arab origin. Long ago it served as a port for Jerusalem and received wood from Lebanon for building the Temple. It was often the scene of bloody battles and sieges. Though the rocks in the harbor made it dangerous for ships, the city was conquered by sea and destroyed several times. It lay in ruins from about 1350 to 1700. Napoleon captured Jaffa in 1799 and many of its inhabitants were massacred. As time passed the city was transformed into a haven for Jews. Moses Montefiore bought an orchard near the city in 1855 to encourage Jewish agriculture; in 1869 Mikveh Israel, an agricultural school, was established nearby. Because of the Arab attacks on the Jews in 1921 and thereafter, Jaffa Jews began to move northward to Tel Aviv, which, founded in 1909, had outstripped its neighbor. Tel Aviv became the leading freight and passenger port.

JAIR

Of Gilead, Judge of Israel who defeated the Ammonites and judged for twenty-two years.

JAMAICA

Though originally a Spanish colony, this island in the West Indies was never controlled by the Inquisition, and so became a haven of refuge for many Marranos. In 1655 the island was captured by the British, the Jewish Acosta arranging the surrender terms. The colony flourished most in the 18th century, and the Jews there shared in this prosperity. In 1831 all restructions were removed from the Jewish settlers, but the Jewish colony grew smaller in the 19th century. At present, some 600 Jews live on the island, the majority of them in the city of Kingston.

JANOWSKY, OSCAR

(1900-   )—American historian and sociologist. Born in Poland, Janowsky came to the United States in 1910, and has taught at City College since 1948. Among his many works are *The American Jew* and *The American Jew: A Reappraisal.*

JAPHET

One of Noah's three sons. According to Biblical tradition, he is the ancestor of the Indo-European peoples.

JASTROW, MARCUS

(1829-1903)—American rabbi and philologist. As a rabbi in Poland, the country of his birth, he participated in the Revolution (1861) and was expelled by the authorities. He came to America and served as a rabbi in Philadelphia, becoming a leader of Conservative Judaism. His main philological work was the *Dictionary of the Targumim, the Talmud Babli and Yerushalmi, and the Midrashic Literature.*

JAVITS, JACOB K.

(1904-   )—American political figure. A leading liberal Republican, Javits has represented New York State as member of Congress, 1946-54, and as Senator, since 1956. He has been strongly pro-Israel, and has been active in Jewish affairs, serving as a member of the Board of Overseers of the Jewish Theological Seminary.

JAVNEH (YAVNEH)

In ancient writings there is frequent mention of this town, which the Greeks called Jamnia. It had a harbor on the Mediterranean and was the scene of many battles. Judah Maccabee, Pompey, Augustus, Herod, Salome and the Empress Livia were all involved in its history. But it is famous in Judaism for an additional reason. When Jerusalem was destroyed by the Romans in the year 70, Johanan ben Zakkai famous scholar and member of Israel's supreme lawmaking body, the Sanhedrin, fled to Javneh with a group of sages. These men formed the new Jewish high court. Emperor Vespasian readily gave permission to found an academy in the city—a most fortunate event for the Jews, for without its new spiritual center, Israel could not have survived. However, the city was destroyed during the Bar Kochba revolt and those who did not escape were made captive. The sages established another center in Usha about 135. In Judah Hanasi's time it moved again, to Sepphoris, and it also met at Tiberias and Bet-Shearim. The scholars of Javneh made great contributions to the Mishnah.

JEBUSITES

Strong tribe hostile to the Israelites during the time of Saul and David. David and his general, Jaob, captured the fortified city of Jerusalem from the Jebusites.

JEHOAHAZ

1. Also called Shallum, seventeenth king of Judah, son of Josiah. After a reign of three months, he was taken captive by Pharaoh Necho and died in Egypt, in 608 B.C.E.

2. Eleventh king of Israel, son of Jehu (ruled about 815-798 B.C.E.). During his reign the rulers of Damascus threatened Israel, but their defeat by the Assyrians removed this threat.

JEHOASH (JOASH)

1. Eighth king of Judah (about 836-796 B.C.E.), son of Ahaziah, saved by Jehoiada from his scheming grandmother, Queen Athaliah. When Joash was six years old, Jehoiada called the nobles of Jerusalem and presented Joash, their rightful king. The nobles revolted against Queen Athaliah. Joash cleansed the Temple of idols, rid the country of Baal and put an end to the cruelties of Athaliah.

2. Twelfth king of Israel (about 798-782 B.C.E.), son of Jehoahaz, warred successfully against Aram and battled with Judah.

JEHOIACHIN

Also called Jeconiah, nineteenth and next to the last king of Judah (about 597 B.C.E.) before the Babylonian Exile, son of King Jehoiakim. He was imprisoned by Nebuchadnezzar and together with his family and many important citizens, deported to Babylon.

JEHOIADA

Faithful priest who helped save Prince Joash from his scheming grandmother, Athaliah, and later helped put Joash on the throne of Judah.

JEHOIAKIM

Also called Eliakim, eighteenth king of Judah (about 608-597 B.C.E.), second son of King Josiah, succeeded his brother Jehoahaz. Jehoiakim was an irreverent king. He ignored the warnings and prophecies of Jeremiah. In his 11-year rule the yoke of Egypt was replaced by that of Babylon. Jehoiakim led the revolt against Babylonia that resulted in the destruction of Jerusalem and the Temple.

JEHORAM (JORAM)

1. Ninth king of Israel (about 852-842 B.C.E.), son of Ahab and Jezebel, successor to his older brother Ahaziah. Jehoram continued his parents' cruelties and worshipped the idol Baal. Jehu, an officer in his army, revolted and slew him. Jehu succeeded Jehoram.

2. Son of Jehoshaphat; fifth king of Judah (about 851-843 B.C.E.), married Athaliah, daughter of Ahab and Jezebel. He was an unpopular king. Influenced by the House of Ahab, he encouraged worship of Baal. He died of a painful disease, as predicted by the prophet Elijah.

JEHOSHAPHAT

Fourth king of Judah (about 876-851 B.C.E.), ruled at the time of King Ahab of Israel. He fought idolatry, sending priests and Levites to teach the people of Judah their religion. Judah flourished under his reign.

JEHOSHEBA

Daughter of King Jehoram of Judah, aunt of Prince Joash whom she and her husband, the high priest Jehoiada, hid from the scheming Queen Athaliah.

JEHU

Tenth king of Israel (about 842-815 B.C.E.). He slew the idolatrous Queen Jezebel and rid Israel of the House of Ahab and Baal's priests. Anointed by the prophet Elisha, who had a great influence on him, he was the first king of Israel to forbid idol worship.

JEPHTHAH

Judge in early Israel. He drove the invading Ammonites out of Gilead and became the leader of the Gileadites. Later he led the men of Ephraim to victory over the Ammonites. He helped unite and strengthen the tribes of Israel.

JEREMIAH

The second of the so-called major prophets is Jeremiah, born near Jerusalem, 650 B.C.E. The destruction of Jerusalem by the Babylonians took place in 586; Jeremiah died some years later. He was a shy and thoughtful youth, who found his call to prophecy difficult and painful. At the age of twenty-six he began preaching against the evils he witnessed in the cities and in the country; for forty years he never ceased preaching, despite abuse and imprisonment. He attacked idol worship in the very halls of the Temple and he stood up bravely against kings. When Jeremiah's secretary, Baruch ben Neriah, wrote down his prophecies of doom, King Jehoiakim had the scroll destroyed. But Jeremiah had them all rewritten. He protested Judah's plan to ally with Egypt or Assyria. He said these nations could not be trusted and would betray their Judean "allies." When Babylonia besieged Jerusalem he advised surrender, knowing the city could not hold out. But still they would not listen. After the destruction some Jews took Jeremiah to Egypt, where he may have been killed by his own people. Though his book consists mainly of prophecies of ruin for his sinning brethren, there are chapters offering hope and consolation.

A drawing of the prophet Jeremiah by Michelangelo.

81

JEREMIAH, EPISTLE OF

Sixth chapter of the Book of Baruch, part of the Apocrypha. Baruch was the loyal disciple of Jeremiah.

JERICHO

Ancient fortified city in the Jordan valley near Jerusalem. In the Book of Joshua it is told how the walls of Jericho crumbled under the blowing of the Israelites' mighty trumpets. Jericho has been excavated in modern times.

JEROBOAM

First king of the northern Kingdom of Israel (about 937-915 B.C.E.). He had revolted against King Solomon and fled to Egypt. During the reign of arrogant Rehoboam he returned. When the kingdom split into two, he led the rebellious northern tribes in establishing the Kingdom of Israel and became its king.

This seal belongs to the period of Jeroboam and was found at Meggido. The line above the lion reads "Shema." The line underneath reads "Seal of Jeroboam."

JEROBOAM II

Great grandson of Jehu; thirteenth king of Israel (about 782-741 B.C.E.), at the time of the prophet Amos. Amos criticized Jeroboam's prosperous reign because of the great differences between the rich and the poor of the kingdom. Amos also warned Jeroboam against the mighty Assyrians.

JERUSALEM

Jerusalem includes the Old City, inhabited mainly by Arabs, and the New City, built and occupied by Jews in the 19th and 20th centuries. Jerusalem is very old, dating back to the 18th century B.C.E. David, after taking it from the Jebusites, made it the Jewish capital. It has been conquered and retaken, destroyed and rebuilt, more often than any other city in the world. The Romans ploughed it over after the Bar Kochba revolt of 135 and renamed it Aelia Capitolina. All through Persian, Mohammedan, Mamluk, Tartar, and Turkish control, Jews continued to live there despite hardships. The Crusaders burned all Jews they found in the city in 1099. Nevertheless, other Jews

came in to replace them. In 1917 the Turks were driven out of the Holy Land by General Allenby; and the history of Jerusalem since that date is the story of modern Zionism. In 1949 Jerusalem became the capital of the new State of Israel. Jordan, however, had taken over the Old City during the War of Independence (1948). Jerusalem remained divided for the next two decades. It was reunited again after Israel's victory in the Six-Day War (1967). Its present population (1971) is 301,300, including 79,100 non-Jews. Jerusalem is recognized as a holy city by three of the most important religions of the world—Judaism, Christianity and Islam.
See also David, City of

JESHURUN

Poetic name for Israel, meaning "courageous one," or "righteous one."

JESSE

(Hebrew, *Yishai*) of Bethlehem, father of David, descendant of Ruth and Boaz.

JESSEL, GEORGE

(1898-   )—Prominent entertainer and toastmaster. Has been outstandingly active on behalf of the State of Israel Bond campaign, the United Jewish Appeal and various community drives.

JETHRO

The noble Kenite priest of Midian; father-in-law of Moses, who found refuge with Jethro after he fled from Egypt. Jethro accompanied Moses during the wanderings in the wilderness. He helped install the first judges of Israel to assist Moses in his difficult tasks.

JEW

(*Yehudi*) originally the name for a member of the tribe of Judah. After the return from Babylonian Exile, the name for all Israelites became Jews (*Yehudim*).

JEWISH AGENCY

When, in 1922, Great Britain took the Mandate for Palestine from the League of Nations, "an appropriate Jewish Agency" was formed "for the purpose of advising and cooperating with the Administration of Palestine in such economic, social and other matters as may affect the establishment of the Jewish National Home and the interests of the Jewish population . . ." This task was entrusted by the British to the Zionist Organization. Soon thereafter the Agency was enlarged to include non-Zionists, since all world Jewry was interested in helping Jews find a home. A Council was set up, with representatives from twenty-six countries. The rise of the State of Israel has revived the organization which is now part of the world Zionist movement, with offices in Jerusalem.

JEWISH BRIGADE

Infantry brigade formed as part of the British army in September 1944 consisting of Palestinian Jews. The Brigade, commanded by Brigadier A. P. Benjamin, first saw action in February 1945 in north Italy. Later,

Members of the Jewish Brigade during a lull in the fighting on the Italian front.

the Brigade made the first contact with Jewish survivors of the concentration camps and Jewish underground movements, on the Italo-Austrian-Yugoslav border and encouraged them to emigrate to Palestine. It was disbanded in February 1946, having lost 44 men in action.

JEWISH COLONIZATION ASSOCIATION

In 1891, history's most generous donor to Jewish causes, Baron de Hirsch, formed the Jewish Colonization Association, providing an initial fund of two million pounds. Its aim was to bring impoverished European and Asiatic Jews to new, uncultivated lands. The present large Jewish community in Argentina is due to (J)ICA, as the organization came to be called. Moisesville, first Argentinian colony, was bought and built in 1890. Loans and gifts were distributed from a central office in Buenos Aires. In Brazil the Baron de Hirsch colony became a refuge from the Nazis. ICA helped organize the Jewish Agricultural Society in the United States. It aided Jewish farm settlement in Canada. Later it offered aid to agricultural settlements in Palestine, including the colonies first brought into being by Baron Edmund de Rothschild. Assistance was also given Jews seeking to return to the land, in Russia, Romania, Poland, Lithuania, Latvia, Austria and Turkey.

JEWISH LEGION

When the Turks took up arms against the Allies in World War I, Jewish military leaders, notably Vladimir Jabotinsky and Joseph Trumpeldor, suggested all-Jewish units to fight the then rulers of Palestine. In Egypt, over 600 Jews were permitted to organize as the Zion Mule Corps, commanded by Colonel John H. Patterson and later by Trumpeldor. They fought in the disastrous Dardanelles-Gallipoli campaign. The battalion was disbanded. Jabotinsky then visited several countries to request recruitment of a Jewish company to fight in Egypt and Palestine. Permission was finally granted by England in July, 1917. Sixty members of the former Mule Corps were the first to join the new battalion. Thousands of volunteers, recruited in the United States, were trained in Canada. A dozen more countries sent recruits, there being a thousand from Palestine itself. Popularly called the Jewish Legion, this detachment helped bring about collapse of the Turkish armies. The Legion pursued the foe across the Jordan, taking 4,000 prisoners, and then made a triumphal entry into Jerusalem, on September 28, 1918. The Jewish units held the land until 1920. But despite its promises, Great Britain never offered these soldiers land grants, such as were given other British Colonial troops. There were attempts made to reorganize the Legion but they failed.

JEWISH MUSEUMS

See Museums, Jewish.

JEWISH NATIONAL FUND

(Hebrew: *Keren Kayemet Leyisrael*) In 1884 Professor Hermann Schapira of the University of

Forest in Israel planted by the Jewish National Fund.

Heidelberg, at a conference of the *Hovevei Zion*, (Lovers of Zion), proposed a land-purchasing agency for Palestine. He repeated the proposal at the first Zionist Congress in 1897 but it was not adopted until late in 1901. Later the Jewish National Fund was formed in London, to be conducted by representatives of the World Zionist Organization. Its headquarters were in various European cities until it moved to Jerusalem in 1921 where it has remained. The Fund has steadily carried on the aims for which it came into being—acquiring land as national property, drainage, afforestation, installation of water systems and giving long-term leases to settlers willing to cultivate the soil. The land purchased has remained the possession of the entire Jewish people. In Israel today there are hundreds of colonies on Jewish National Fund land. They pay no rental for several years and then a small, graduated annual sum. The Fund has helped immeasurably to solve the difficult problems of rehabilitating Israel.

JEWISH OATH

Special form of oath, often degrading, taken by Jews during the Middle Ages. Jewish witnesses took this oath, usually over the Sefer Torah or Tefillin. The oath was abolished in France in 1846 and in Germany during the 19th century. England never knew the oath, though a special oath was adopted which exempted the Jew from a form to which he conscientiously objected (1677).

JEWISH THEOLOGICAL SEMINARY OF AMERICA

Located in New York City, the JTS is the rabbinical school of the Conservative movement. It was founded in 1887 by Sabato Morais, who served as its first president, and was reorganized in 1902 under the presidency of Solomon Schechter. In the years since it has became a major educational institute. The New York campus, which adjoins Columbia University and Union Theological Seminary, has the rabbinical seminary, a teachers' institute, and one of the world's finest libraries of Judaica. In addition JTS now encompasses schools in Los Angeles (University of Judaism) and Jerusalem (Schocken Institute).

The Jewish Theological Seminary

JEWISH WAR VETERANS

American organization of Jewish men and women who have served in the armed forces. It was established in 1896, and reached its present form in 1929. The Jewish War Veterans were recognized by the U.S. Veterans Administration as the official agency for the care of sick Jewish soldiers. The organization had 105,000 members in 1970.

JEZEBEL

Queen, wife of King Ahab of Israel, Phoenician princess from Tyre. She sought to replace Israel's religion with Baal. She encouraged Ahab in his injustices and cruelty. She persecuted the prophets. Elijah opposed her. His successor, the prophet Elisha, encouraged the revolt of Jehu against Jezebel and her son, Jehoram. Jezebel was slain by Jehu.

JOAB

Capable and devoted general of King David. He was victorious in many battles and helped conquer Jerusalem, then a Jebusite fortress.

JOB

For thousands of years the character of Job has been a symbol of patience and trust in God. The Book of the Bible bearing his name teaches that a good man may lose his family, his wealth and his health and still can turn hopefully to his Father in heaven. The Book opens with a prologue in which Satan tells God that any man with Job's blessings can remain faithful to his Maker, but if he were to encounter difficulties he would lose his faith. God permits Satan to inflict a series of hardships on Job. His children die sudden deaths, his wealth is destroyed and he is afflicted with a dread form of leprosy. But Job's piety never falters. He cries out his despair, curses the day he was born, but never doubts God's rightness. "Though He slay me, yet will I trust Him; but I will argue my ways before Him." His friends taunt him and try to make him say that he has sinned or that God is unjust. But Job insists on his innocence and God's justice. In the end of the Book God Himself appears and declares that suffering is no proof or indication of sin on the part of the sufferer. Job is granted a new family, renewed health and riches. The Book of Job is considered a literary masterpiece.

JOCHEBED

Wife of Amram, of the tribe of Levi, mother of Moses, Aaron and Miriam.

JOEL

Second Book of the Twelve (Minor) Prophets of the Bible. Joel described with scientific accuracy a terrible plague of locusts that had taken place, and drew moral lessons from this experience.

JOHANAN

Son of Mattathias; brother of Judah Maccabee; one of the leaders in the revolt against Antiochus.

JOHANAN BAR NAPPAHA

Scholar and teacher, one of the founders of the Palestinian Talmud. Rabbi Johanan, a student of Judah Hanasi, headed his own school at Sepphoris but, after a scholarly disagreement, left and joined the academy of Tiberias. There he met Simeon ben Lakish. Impressed by the mind and personality of Simeon, he convinced him to join him and become a scholar. The famous discussions between Johanan and Simeon are recorded in the Talmud.

JOHANAN BEN ZAKKAI

Great Tannaitic scholar, helped preserve the traditions of Torah at the time of the destruction of the Temple, founder of the academy of Javneh, died about 80 C.E. It is said that he had his students carry him out of besieged Jerusalem in a coffin, to enable him to seek permission from the Roman general, who later became Emperor Vespasian, to found the school at Javneh.

JOHN OF GISCALA

(Johanan of Gush-Halav; 1st century C.E.) Military leader and patriot. He fought the Romans in Galilee, and after Vespasian's conquest, fled to Jerusalem where he became a leader of the defenders of the city and fought with the greatest bravery. When the Temple fell, John was captured and taken to Rome for the triumphal procession of Vespasian and Titus; he died in a Roman prison.

JOINT DISTRIBUTION COMMITTEE

The American organization that did most to aid needy Jews overseas during war and persecution was the Joint Distribution Committee. It was created in 1914 after the outbreak of World War I, to raise and expend funds as a central agency for three committees which had been working separately. It assisted Jews suffering from the war; provided relief immediately thereafter; helped rebuild Jewish communities and helped revive the people's will to live. The committee did everything possible to rescue the victims of Nazism, before and during World War II. After the war it aided the survivors, saved refugees, established religious schools, provided men and means for healing and hygiene, cared for thousands of orphans and conducted rehabilitation programs. Hundreds of thousands were given support. The work of the "Joint" is one of the noblest humanitarian efforts in history. Its activities, for Israel and for the rest of the Jewish world, are now continuing through the United Jewish Appeal, which annually calls upon the Jews of the world to assist the unfortunate and persecuted of their race.

JONAH

Fifth of the Books of Twelve (Minor) Prophets of the Bible. It is a narrative (the other Later Prophetic writings are mainly orations) relating how Jonah, son of Amittai, of the tribe of Zebulun, avoided God's command to go to the Assyrian capital Nineveh and preach against its wickedness, by taking a sea voyage. During a storm, he was thrown overboard and was swallowed by a great whale who spewed him out near Nineveh, where Jonah fulfilled his mission. The book of Jonah is read on Yom Kippur.

JONATHAN

1. Noble warrior prince, son of King Saul, victor of many battles against the Philistines. Though his father bitterly turned on David, Jonathan remained David's loyal friend. Both Saul and Jonathan fell in the battle of Mount Gilboa. David wrote a beautiful song lamenting the deaths of Saul, his king, and of his friend, Jonathan.

2. Son of Mattathias; brother of Judah Maccabee; military leader and High Priest of Judea.

JORDAN

The best known stream in the world is not the mighty Amazon or Mississippi, but the short river that cuts through Israel. Though the State of Israel has only partial control of the Jordan it is looked upon as forever bound up with the history of the Jews. Beginning at Mount Hermon in Galilee, it flows down through swampland (now being drained in part by Israeli engineers), through the Seas of Merom and Kinnereth, and then flows with innumerable twistings into the Dead Sea. The short stream, less than seventy miles long, drops from above sea level to almost 1300 feet below. Because of this rapid fall the Jordan became the site for the Rutenberg power project, now halted by Arab hostility. During most of its course the Jordan flows between sharply sloping banks and thickets almost impossible to penetrate. The streams to the east and west flow into it and thus give it as great an importance for Israel as the Mississippi and its tributaries for the United States.

JOSEPH

Eleventh son of Jacob; first son of Rachel, father of Ephraim and Manasseh. Joseph was sold by his jealous brothers into Egyptian slavery. In Egypt his ability to interpret dreams led him to become second in command to Pharaoh. Through his wisdom Egypt was saved from famine. He was reunited with his father and brothers when they came to Egypt to escape the famine. Joseph, one of the most beloved Biblical figures, has inspired artists and writers throughout the ages.

JOSEPHUS

Flavius Josephus, who lived from 37 to 102 C.E., was one of the world's greatest historians, remembered

Medieval drawing of Josephus.

with mixed emotions by the Jewish people. His books are the only source of what happened in Jerusalem during the Roman siege. About this episode and others it is suspected that on occasion he invented tales to throw a favorable light on his own doubtful conduct. In any case, he enjoyed the full favor of the Romans until his death in Rome. Josephus was of priestly descent, a Pharisee, who on a mission to Rome in 65 gained the good graces of Empress Poppaea. The next year he was made military governor of Galilee, commanding over 100,000 troops. Suspecting his favoritism toward the Romans, the other Jewish commanders tried to have him removed. During the siege he attempted to bring General Titus and the Jews to terms. After the Roman victories, he followed their armies until he was able to settle in Rome and there write his histories and memoirs. Though the citizens of the city tolerated him, hatred was shown him by the Jews. He then tried to justify his military conduct in his autobiography. Josephus' history of his people proved completely favorable. He also replied vigorously to Apion, first notorious Jew hater of his time. Josephus' reputation as a historian was greatest during the Middle Ages.

JOSHUA

Son of Nun, was the successor to Moses. His story is told in the Biblical Book bearing his name. After guiding his people through the wilderness for forty years, Moses could only see but not enter the Promised Land. The great leader died on Mount Nebo, after instructing his aide and general, Joshua, to lead the people on, and bidding him and the priest Eliezer to portion out the land. Joshua, under Moses' direction, already had defeated the Amalekites. He and Caleb had been the only spies, out of the twelve Moses had sent to Canaan, who brought reports that encouraged the people to hope for victory against Canaan. Of all those who left Egypt, only Moses, Caleb and Joshua remained. Under Josh-

ua's guidance the Israelites leveled the walls of Jericho; they captured many cities, made a pact with the Gibeonites and finally achieved victory and peace. Joshua inspired and admonished the people to remain faithful to God and to His commandments which He had given them through Moses. Joshua died at the age of 110, honored for his courage, faithfulness and zeal for God. He became the subject of many Midrashic tales and has been glorified in paintings, novels, poems and music. Because the Book of Joshua resembles the Book of Moses and continues the story of Moses, some scholars attach it to the Torah to form the Hexateuch (Six Books).

JOSIAH

In the southern kingdom of Judah, formed in 933 B.C.E. when the land of the Israelites was divided in two parts, there was a succession of kings, good and bad, descended from David. The last great king of Judah was Josiah, who reigned from 638 to 608. Josiah was only eight years of age when the murder of his father brought him to the throne. During his day the people had forgotten the Law of the Lord; and it was a most important event when the "Book of the Law" was discovered in the Temple in 621. At once Josiah set about reviving Jewish traditions. He abolished various forms of idolatry, one of which permitted child sacrifice. He abolished many "high places" used for worship by the Israelites, and established the Temple in Jerusalem as the only national shrine. Worship of the golden calf, taken from the religion of Egypt, was forbidden. But this peaceful and prosperous reign came to an end when the Pharaoh treacherously murdered Josiah. The throne was held successively by Josiah's three sons. During the twenty-two years of their reign Judah was lost and the Jews were led into exile. But Josiah's reforms were not in vain; they helped the exiled Jews maintain their religion in foreign countries.

JOSIPPON

A chronicle of Jewish history written in the 8th century in southern Italy. Its presumed author, Joseph ben Gorion, was confused by Christian scholars of the 16th-17th centuries with Josephus Flavius. The work, written in a vivid Hebrew, deals mainly with the period of the Second Temple.

JOTHAM

Eleventh king of Judah (about 737-735 B.C.E.), son of Uzziah, became ruler when aging Uzziah was stricken with leprosy. He continued to fortify Judah as his father had done. He lived at the time of the prophets Micah, Hosea and Isaiah.

JUBILEE

The word jubilee refers to a Biblical law in Leviticus and is not related to the Latin word meaning "shout for joy." The Hebrew origin of "jubilee" is *yovel*, meaning a ram, a ram's horn or the blast of a trumpet. According to the Biblical law of that name, on every fiftieth year after the Jewish occupation of Canaan, all slaves were to be freed and all lands returned to their original owners or heirs and land was to lie fallow. Another law required that the land lie fallow every seventh year—a matter that caused difficulties for Israel in 1955, seven years after the new State had come into being. According to the Bible, ancestral lands should remain inalienable (never to be transferred from the families owning them), and that vast estates were not in keeping with the idea that God alone owned the world and all within it. The law of jubilee was cited by Henry George, the American economist, to justify his "single tax" program. He argued, as had many other reformers before him, that every increase in value of the land should be taken over for the use of the entire community.

See also Sabbatical Year.

JUDAH

The name Judah is often used to refer to all descendants of the people of Israel, for the ten tribes of the North disappeared and the Jews (from the word Judah) of today are descended from the southern kingdom, which consisted almost entirely of the one tribe, Judah. The territory of the tribe in southern Israel was at first very small but it grew as Judah took over other tribes and land. When the northern kingdom separated from Judah, no break occurred in the dynasty of kings established by David. Hence Judah remained more secure and enduring than the North. From 933 B.C.E. to 586 B.C.E. nineteen kings and one queen (Athaliah) ruled over Judah. Unfortunately, the kings formed alliances with untrustworthy neighboring rulers. Although the prophets protested, in 705 Hezekiah joined with Egypt and Babylonia and was promptly attacked by their enemies, the Assyrians. Later, when Assyria grew weak, it was conquered by Pharaoh Necho of Egypt, who killed King Josiah and conquered Judah. In 586 B.C.E., the Babylonians came and destroyed the first Temple and the capital of Judah and sent the Jews into their first exile —an exile that was to last seventy years. The kingdom of Judah, which had lasted 350 years, had ended. Judah the man, was the fourth son of Jacob, who suggested that the brothers sell rather than kill Joseph.

JUDAH HALEVI

The greatest Jewish poet since Biblical times, Judah Halevi was born in Spain in 1075 and is said to have died under the horse of an Arab rider at the walls of Jerusalem, 1141. His poems, devoted to God, to faith, to land and to people are unsurpassed in literature. Though he is best known for his lyrics on human love, love of God and love of the Holy Land, he was also a notable Talmudic scholar, philosopher and practicing physician. Three hundred of his poems are preserved. As theologian and philosopher, Judah Halevi

A page from the first edition of the Kuzari. The dialogue form of the writing can be seen. On the side of the page stand the words: "Said the Kuzari," and "Said the Haver" (meaning rabbi), introducing their statements.

is famous for his *Sefer Hakuzari*. This book, published in 1140, is in the form of a dialogue with the King of the Khazars, living in what is today called Crimea. The king examines all the religious faiths and then accepts Judaism as his own religion. The book is based on the reported conversion of the Khazars to Judaism.

See also Khazars.

JUDAH HANASI

The great rabbi who compiled the Mishnah in the beginning of the third century C.E. He is known as "Judah the Prince," "Rabbi," or as "Rabbenu Hakadosh" (our holy rabbi). Before he succeeded his father Simeon ben Gamaliel II as Patriarch (Nasi), head of Israel's scholars, he had studied with the great rabbis of his time and had also acquired an excellent general education and a knowledge of languages. He served his high office humbly and unselfishly. He showed clemency and understanding to those who appeared before him and his own interpretations of the law were lenient. He reinforced the respect for the office of Nasi, and the people saw embodied in him the great power of the Sanhedrin. His life's work was the compiling and writing of the Mishnah. He collected and arranged, reduced and brought up to date the vast number of post-Biblical laws and interpretations derived from the Bible—the "oral" Torah, based on the "written" Torah. He organized all these within the six major divisions of the Mishnah, the great basis of the Talmud. It is said that Judah Hanasi was a friend of a Roman emperor, probably Antonius, and that he was highly respected by the Roman officials. Among his own people he was beloved and honored for his purity and brilliance, his compassion and humility. When Judah died, no one was willing to announce the news to the people. Finally it had to be told and a rabbi said: "Angels and men contended for possession of the Tables of the Covenant; the Angels won and took the Tables."

JUDAH MACCABEE

The Jewish revolt against the Syrians eighteen centuries ago was led by Judah Maccabee. After Alexander the Great had conquered the known world, many Jews "hellenized"—that is, they tried to live like the Greeks, or like the Syrians who imitated the Greeks. King Antiochus Epiphanes ("Madman"), seeking to hasten the assimilation of the Jews, set up an altar to Zeus in the Temple and threatened death to all who refused to perform his pagan rites. A rebellion against this cruelty was started by Mattathias, a priest in the small town of Modin. Mattathias died soon after, leaving the command to Judah, his third son. Judah was called Maccabee (Hebrew for "the Hammer"). The loyal Jews formed a small army which, though unequipped and untrained, fought brilliantly against the well-trained and well-equipped armies of Antiochus. After the Syrian garrison in Jerusalem was defeated and the Temple was cleansed, there occurred the miracle wherein a one day's supply of holy oil lasted for eight days. Judah kept on fighting, but finally the exhaustion of his troops and the overpowering number of his enemy brought about his defeat and death in 160. To this day Maccabee remains a word signifying the highest degree of patriotism and courage. Hanukkah celebrates the successful revolt against the Syrians by Judah Maccabee and his followers.

See also Maccabees; Hanukkah.

JUDAISM

The name of the religion of the Jewish people, apparently first used in the 1st century C.E. by Greek-speaking Jews to describe their religion as distinct from the religion of their neighbors, Hellenism. As the centuries passed, the term Judaism was used by Jews and non-Jews alike to distinguish it from other religions. Orthodox Judaism, Conservative Judaism, Reform Judaism and Reconstructionism are comparatively new terms used to describe the various branches of American Judaism. In general, these groups all accept the basic ethical, moral and social principles of Judaism and draw their inspiration from the same Biblical and Rabbinical writings. They differ on the place of the law in Judaism, particularly the laws dealing with rites and ceremonies.

1. Orthodox Judaism maintains strictly the traditional laws of the Bible as they were interpreted and developed by the early rabbis in the Talmud and other works of Jewish law (the Rabbinic tradition).

2. Conservative Judaism accepts the authority of Jewish ceremonial and ritual laws and believes that these laws strengthen the Jewish community socially and spiritually. But it has adopted a number of important modifications meet the conditions of modern life.

3. Reform Judaism maintains that the laws of the Bible and the Talmudic tradition may be changed (reformed) or developed to meet the needs of new situa-

tions, and that this process of development must continue. Reform Judaism has modified many rituals and observances.

4. Reconstructionism accepts from Orthodox Judaism the stress on a maximum of Jewish life and from Reform Judaism the concept of need for development. It maintains that it is important for the Jew to gain knowledge of Judaism and to participate meaningfully in Jewish life.

JUDEA

Name of the Second Commonwealth after the Babylonian Exile. Judea was bounded by Samaria on the north, Edom (Idumea) on the south, the Mediterranean on the west, and the Jordan and Dead Sea on the east. Judea was governed by priests and in its latter days ruled by kings of the Hasmonean and Herodian dynasties. Judea was independent only a short time, under the Hasmoneans (Maccabees). It became a vassal of Persia, Syria and later of Rome. It existed from approximately 539 B.C.E.-70 C.E.

See also Hasmoneans; Herodian Dynasty.

JUDEO LANGUAGES

As Jews migrated to many parts of the world they adopted and developed many languages and dialects, a number of which are still used today. The most familiar and widely used is Yiddish, also called Judeo-German. During the Middle Ages, Judeo-Greek, which was written in Hebrew characters as is Yiddish, was heard in the Greek world along the Mediterranean. Parts of the Bible were translated into this dialect. Various Jewish dialects also developed in Italy, similar to the oldest forms of the Italian language, just as Yiddish resembles the Middle High German of long ago. These dialects are called Judeo-Italian. In Persia and Central Asia Jews spoke a Judeo-Persian tongue, which preserved many words no longer used in ordinary Persian. The Judeo language most common among Jews (next to Yiddish) is Judeo-Spanish, or Ladino. Spoken in the Balkan states and North Africa, Ladino is today the second language of thousands of Jews. Spanish Jews carried their version of Spanish with them when they were exiled in 1492 and spread its use in the lands to which they traveled. Ladino has adopted Turkish, Italian, Greek, Slavic and other foreign words.

JUDGES

Various kinds of judges have played a great role in Jewish history; but the term first brings to mind the Biblical Book of Judges. Here the term refers to tribal leaders in spiritual and military matters who also served as judges in the contemporary sense. This system was first suggested to Moses by his father-in-law, Jethro, and judges took the responsibility for countless minor cases off Moses' shoulders. Among the great judges, leaders of early Israel, described in the Book of Judges, were priests like Eli, prophets like Samuel and Deborah, and soldiers like Gideon and Jephthah. Later, in the Kingdom of Judah, judges were appointed in the great cities and the High Priest in Jerusalem was the judge in all religious matters; he also held an exalted position in the king's government. The Talmud describes the later court system in which members of the various courts were appointed by the highest religious authority on the basis of knowledge, wisdom and righteousness. The election of judges was never held for political reasons only. The Talmud says that judges must be "wise, humble, fearful about sinning, of good reputation, and popularly accepted." Their way of life, their conduct and appearance had to command respect. No man who had seen a crime or knew any of the parties involved could serve as a judge in a particular case. The standards of these courts were very high and the position of a judge was lofty and carried grave responsibility.

JUDGES, BOOK OF

(Shofetim) second book of the Early Prophets (Nevi'im Rishonim) of the Bible. It records the period of the twelve Judges, Israel's history from the death of Joshua to the birth of Samuel.

JUDITH

The title of one of fourteen books that constitute the Apocrypha, the works similar to Biblical writing that were not, however, included in the Bible. It tells of a beautiful Jewish woman, Judith, who saved her people from the Assyrian general, Holofernes. His army had beseiged the city of Bethulia, where Judith, a highborn, pious widow lived. When the siege was at its worst and the defenders were at the point of surrendering, Judith bravely went to meet Holofernes. She induced him to feast and drink with her. When he was helplessly drunk she put him to death with his own sword. The panicky soldiers fled and Bethulia was saved. The spoils were divided among the citizens but Judith donated her share to the Temple. Judith never married again but spent her days doing good deeds until her death in 105. Some of the great paintings in European museums show the brave Judith killing Holofernes. Dramas and operas have been inspired by this story. Although there are other Judiths in Jewish lore, it is the heroic Judith after whom girls are named.

JUSTINIAN

(483-565)—Byzantine emperor whose intolerance to religious minorities included much anti-Jewish legislation. The Jew became a "second class" citizen, and many religious practices were outlawed. Synagogues were closed in Africa (535) and some Jews were forcibly converted. His policies led the Jews and Samaritans of Caesarea to revolt in 556, but the uprising was put down.

JUSTUS OF TIBERIAS

(1st century C.E.)—Leader in the war against the Romans in 66. He was a moderate, however, and opposed Josephus' policies. Later, Justus became a literary rival of Josephus and wrote an account of the war which did not portray his opponent in a complimentary light; Josephus attempts to answer some of these charges in his *Autobiography*.

KABBALAH

(Hebrew for "Tradition")—Jewish mystical philosophy. There are many examples of deeply mystical speculation in the Talmud and the Midrash, many of them centering around Rabbi Simeon bar Yohai, whom tradition considers the author of the *Zohar*. This book was presented to the public in the 13th century and became the classic work of Kabbalists. *Pardes Rimonim* was written by Moses Cordovero in the 16th century as an explanation of the doctrines of the Zohar; another prominent Kabbalist was Rabbi Isaac Luria ("Ari") who, however, left no printed works. There are two types of Kabbalah: "speculative," which is theoretical and philosophic, attracting the thinker, and "practical," which taught its students to change the course of nature by use of the Divine Name of God. The Kabbalah had a vital influence on Hasidic

An amulet supposed to give good luck, with formulas derived from the Zohar and other mystical teachings.

thought, and is being studied today as a valuable source of Jewish thinking about God, man, and the world.

See also Sefer Yetzirah; Zohar

KADDISH

At first the Kaddish (from the Hebrew root meaning "holy") was recited at the end of a study session. Later, it became part of synagogue worship, the final words of a prayer service. It was not until much later that it was made the mourners' prayer. The original intent of the prayer was to plead for the speedy coming of the Messiah and of God's rulership over all men. Most of it is in Aramaic, the spoken language of ancient Jewry. For parents who have died it is recited at every service of every day for eleven months; and though it contains no mention of the dead or of death, it expresses faith in final comfort and healing for all men. When the original Kaddish was taken from the house of study to the house of prayer, it was what we today call the half-Kaddish. Petitions that were added to the prayer are for God's acceptance of the prayers and for peace on earth. There is a special form called the burial Kaddish, and another, recited after study, known as the Rabbinical Kaddish *(Kaddish Derabbanan)*. About the year 1400 it became the custom to recite the Kaddish on every anniversary of a death. It is said for father, mother, husband, wife, sister, brother or child.

KADESH-BARNEA

Oasis in the Sinai desert, south of ancient Canaan, where Miriam was buried and from where Moses sent the first scouts to Canaan. Kadesh-barnea was a central camp site of the Israelites during their forty years of wanderings. It was the starting point for their final march to Canaan.

KAF

The eleventh letter of the Hebrew alphabet, has the numerical value of 20.

See also Aleph Bet.

KAFKA, FRANZ

(1883-1924)—Czech author; a major figure in world literature. Kafka's writing is largely symbolic and portrays the plight of modern man in the face of anonymous, superior and cruel powers. His major works, all written in German, are *The Castle, The Trial* and *The Metamorphosis.* Kafka's diaries have shown his Jewish awareness.

KAHAL

The administrative body of the Jewish community of fourteenth-century Germany and that of sixteenth-century Poland. In the Kahal the rabbi was the highest and most respected paid official. He presided over educational matters, courts and elections. But he was responsible to the Kahal officials, and in many communities statutes were drawn to limit the rabbi's power. Other paid officials were the head of the yeshivah, sexton, judges, scribe and physicians and nurses. The Kahal collected taxes, conducted the law courts, was in charge of educational and ritual affairs and, of course, organized the government of the Jewish community it constituted. It represented it and mediated between it and the outside government. The dignitaries of the Kahal, in its early stages, were elected. Later, in its state of decay, elections became less democratic. But in the time of its flowering, methods of election and government adhered to the highest democratic, moral and technical standards. During the eighteenth century the Kahals slowly decayed and in 1812 they were dissolved and replaced by "overseers of the synagogue."

KAHANE, MEIR

(1932-   )—American rabbi and political leader. Born in Brooklyn, Kahane became an Orthodox rabbi in 1957. In 1968, concerned about the plight of both Soviet Jewry and the impoverished Jews of America's inner cities, he founded the Jewish Defense League. He soon became a highly controversial figure because of his right-wing ideology, his criticism of the Jewish establishment, and his advocacy of the mass emigration of American Jews to Israel. Kahane's views are elaborated in his book *Never Again* and in his many journalistic writings.

KALISCHER, ZVI HIRSCH

(1795-1874)—Rabbi and early Zionist thinker. As early as 1832 this pupil of Rabbi Akiba Eger declared that the Jews must return to Palestine and bring about their own redemption. His *D'rishat Zion* ("Searching After Zion") appeared in 1862 and called for the formation of agricultural and colonizing societies to settle the barren lands of Palestine. He was the driving force behind the establishment of the Mikveh Israel agricultural school, the first in the land, in 1870.

KAMMERKNECHTSCHAFT

(German for "Servitude to the Royal Chamber Term indicating the status of the Jews in the Holy Roman Empire during the Middle Ages. It meant that the Jews were under the direct control of the Emperor and that their taxes belonged to his private treasury. The term is first found in 1157, and fell into disuse after 1400.

Mordecai M. Kaplan.

KAPLAN, MORDECAI M.

(1881-   )—American rabbi, philosopher and educator. Kaplan founded the Reconstructionist Movement, which emphasizes that Judaism is not only a religion, but a civilization. He has taught at the Jewish Theological Seminary of America since 1909, and was dean of its Teachers' Institute.

KAPPAROT

(Hebrew plural for Kapparah, meaning "atonement")—A custom which originated in Gaonic times, and became widespread in eastern Europe. It consisted of swinging a chicken around the head, and praying that the slaughter of the chicken substitute for the punishment due the individual. Later, money which was donated to charity took the place of the chicken. The ritual is performed on the morning of the day before Yom Kippur.

Kapparot ceremony before the Day of Atonement, Germany, 1520.

KARAITES

(From the same root as *Mikra*, meaning Holy Writ) —A Jewish sect who based their Judaism solely on the Bible and not on Rabbinic law as taught in the Talmud. Anan ben David founded the small sect in Babylonia about 767. He abolished the prayers used by the Rabbanites (the majority who opposed him), and forbade any connection with them whatsoever. The Karaites, always trying to convert the traditional Jews to their belief, were without restraint in their attacks on the Rabbanites. (Among those who replied in like manner was the famous Saadia Gaon). Whereas most Jews managed to have a Sabbath of light and joy, the Karaites, who refused to have any lights in their homes, spent the day in darkness and gloom. The movement spread into many countries, developing new forms of self-denial. In Russia they proclaimed themselves completely distinct from the Jews and thus were granted all rights held by Christians. The Russians believed them to be descendants of the ten lost tribes. Today there are few remaining Karaites.

Abraham Firkovich (1728-1812), famous Karaite scholar. He held various posts in the Crimea and owned a collection of ancient Biblical manuscripts. These are now in the Leningrad Library.

KARLITZ, AVRAHAM YESHAYAHU

(1878-1953)—Rabbi and Talmudist, known by his pen-name, "Hazon Ish." Born in Grodno, Poland, he emigrated to Palestine in 1935 from Vilna, and settled in Bene Berak, north of Tel Aviv. There he founded a yeshiva which attracted students from all the land. A modest man, he held no official position, but was consulted on all problems—religious and political—which perplexed the religious segment of the *Yishuv*.

KASHRUT

("Fitness, worthiness") refers generally to any object or person which meets all traditional Jewish requirements. Specifically it refers to foods which are considered kosher.

See also Dietary laws; Kosher.

KATZ, MANÉ

(1894-   )—Artist. The Russian-born Katz settled in France in the 1920's where he has lived since, except for a stay in the United States during World War II. Originally a painter of melancholy scenes, he has lately turned to a happier art. Many of his paintings have been exhibited in Europe and America.

KATZIR, EPHRAIM

(1916-   )—Fourth President of Israel. Born in Russia, Katzir came to Palestine in 1925. He received his Ph.D. from the Hebrew University in 1941, was a research fellow at the Brooklyn Polytechnic Institute and Columbia University, and in 1948 became head of the biophysics department at the Weizmann Institute of Science. In 1966 he also became the chief scientist of the Defense Ministry. A renowned researcher whose main work has been in the field of proteins, Katzir was elected the fourth President of the State of Israel in 1973.

KAUFMANN, YEHEZKEL

(1889-1963)—Israeli scholar. Born in the Ukraine, Kaufmann settled in Palestine in 1928 and for many years was a professor at the Hebrew University. Kaufmann made many important contributions in the field of biblical studies. Most importantly, he put forward the view, elaborated in his *The Religion of Israel*, that Jewish monotheism was not the product of a slow evolution from paganism but appeared suddenly and decisively as the beginning of a new phase in the world's religious development.

KAYE, DANNY

(1913-   )—American comedian. Kaye, born Kaminski, has achieved world-wide fame mainly through the medium of motion pictures, which have made him a beloved figure to children and adults alike. In addition to being a talented singer and dancer, he is a brilliant mimic.

KEDESH

City of Refuge in the territory of Naphtali.

See also Cities of Refuge.

KEDUSHAH

("Sanctification") a dramatic daily prayer that acknowledges the majesty and holiness of God. It is recited in the form of alternate chanting by the cantor or reader and the congregation. The Kedushah is based on the visions of Isaiah and Ezekiel.

KEHILLAH

The Hebrew word *Kehillah* means community. It was used to describe closely knit Jewish groups in European cities and countries. Efforts have been made to create *kehilloth* in American cities. The most ambitious of these took place in New York, from 1908 to 1919, following the false accusation by a police commissioner that half the city's criminals were Jews. The city's Jews, mainly immigrants and their children, had previously organized a great number of social, religious, charitable, educational and labor institutions. Representatives of these met on February 27, 1909, with Rabbi Judah L. Magnes, later to become chancellor of the Hebrew University, presiding. Under his leadership the *Kehillah* assisted religion and religious education, arbitrated Jewish quarrels, helped Jews find employment, gathered statistics and improved the common welfare. Despite some opposition it might have continued to this day had not World War I diverted the people's interests to other pressing matters in Jewish life. The nearest thing to *kehilloth* today is the federation of Jewish charities and community councils in the larger American cities.

KEREN HAYESOD

(Hebrew for "Foundation Fund")—The Keren Hayesod was founded in 1920 by the Zionist Organization as a fund for the development of a Jewish national home in Palestine. In practice, it provides for all the expenditures of the Jewish Agency, except the purchase and development of land and the expenses of the headquarters organization. It is active in over seventy countries, and its headquarters are in Jerusalem.

KEREN KAYEMET LEYISRAEL

See Jewish National Fund.

KETIVAH TOVAH

A greeting used on Rosh Hashanah, meaning "may you be written down well." It refers to the belief that on the New Year each man's fate for the coming year is written down by God in the Book of Life.

KETUBAH

The Hebrew word meaning "something written," refers to a contract, specifically to the Jewish marriage contract which obligates the husband to pay or to have paid a certain sum to his wife in the event of divorce or his death. The sum became a first lien upon all the husband's property, "even to the cloak upon his shoulders." The minimum payment was two hundred *zuzim*, a considerable amount in former days, but it could be made as high as the groom wished. The *Ketubah* obligated the husband to provide ransom if his wife were taken captive and to support the children of a divorced wife. Although a marriage without the *Ketubah* was not considered complete, all its provisions were enforced nevertheless. The wife had to hold the document in her possession or obtain another if the first were lost, on pain of not being permitted to live with her husband. When the famous Rabbenu Gershom (960-1040) forbade divorce without consent of the wife, much of the need for the original *Ketubah* disappeared. The trend to decorative colored *Ketubot* persisted throughout the Middle Ages. Today they are usually printed forms, with blanks for names and other information. The language used is still the original Aramaic, the spoken language of ancient Jewry.

KETUBIM

("Writings") the third and last division of the Bible. Kebutim contains eleven Books, arranged in three parts. The first part, the three poetical Books, contains: Psalms, Proverbs and Job. The second part, the Five *Megillot* (Scrolls) contains: Song of Songs, Ruth, Lamentations, Ecclesiastes and Esther. The third part, the historical writings, contains: Daniel, Ezra-Nehemiah, and Chronicles I and II. The Greek name for Ketubim is Hagiographa ("sacred writings").

KHAZARS

A Turkish or Finnish people who settled in the lower Volga region and at one time extended their empire to the borders of Persia, the Byzantine Empire, the Dnieper and the Don. In the period 786-809 their king, Bulan, and many nobles were converted to Judaism; the masses of the nation never accepted Judaism, how-

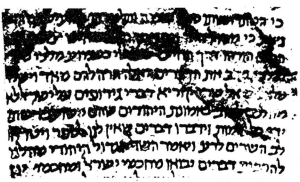

A letter in Hebrew from a Khazar Jew, dated 950 C.E. In this letter are recounted the incidents that led to the conversion of the Khazars to Judaism and events that took place in Khazaria during the tenth century.

ever. This conversion provides the background for Judah Halevi's famous *Sefer Hakuzari* which preaches the superiority of the Jewish religion. Hasdai ibn Shaprut claimed that he had received a letter from the last of the Khazar kings but most scholars doubt its authenticity.

KIBBUTZ

(Hebrew for "collective settlement")—Collective settlements, almost entirely agricultural in character, which are found in Israel. Land, buildings, machinery, etc., are held in common and the collective is responsible for the health, education, and social welfare of its members. The first *Kevutzah* (a *Kibbutz* is unlimited as to the number of members it may accept, while a *Kevutzah* does limit itself) was Daganiah, founded near the Lake of Galilee in 1910. As of 1962, over 25,000 Israeli men and women lived on 73 *Kibbutzim* and *Kevutzot*.

KIDDUSH

At the beginning of each Sabbath and every festival day when the evening service is concluded, the cantor, and later the householder at home, sanctify the day over a cup of wine. The exception is the first two days of Passover, when no *Kiddush* is recited at the synagogue, since the *Seder* is peculiarly a home observance. The *Kiddush* was transferred to the synagogue in Babylonia, where there often was not sufficient wine for the use of all Jewish families. However, in those days and thereafter, the synagogue was itself considered a second home, since travelers and homeless folk slept and ate there. Beautiful *Kiddush* cups were designed for the ceremony, in keeping with the Jewish effort to beautify all religious customs and objects. Every *Kiddush* contains the blessing over the wine, as well as a special recitation for the Sabbath, the festival, or both if they coincide. The melodies are more or less standard throughout the world as with all Jewish religious chants, variations have been created by cantors and composers.

KIDDUSH CUP

The special cup for the wine to be blessed at the *Kiddush* ceremony either in the synagogue or at home.

Kiddush cups are usually made of silver and often beautifully decorated.

KIMCHI, DAVID

(1160-1235)—Hebrew grammarian and Bible commentator. Radak (*Rabbi David Kimchi*) lived in Narbonne, in the south of France, all his life. There he wrote the *Mikhlol*, a Hebrew grammar which went beyond all previous books on the subject, and long remained the standard work. His Biblical commentaries have preserved his fame through the centuries. They are written in a clear Hebrew, and join the grammatical and philosophic studies of Spanish Jewry with the Midrashim and traditions of the earlier rabbis and Rashi. These commentaries were often translated into Latin, and were widely consulted when the Bible was translated into the modern languages. Kimchi took the side of Maimonides in the controversy concerning the study of philosophy.

KINGS

(*Melachim*)—The name of the two Biblical Books that follow the two Books of Samuel. In Samuel, the story of Saul and David, the first anointed kings of Israel, is told. The Books of the Kings begin with David's last days, his difficulties with his rebellious sons and the crowning of his favorite son, Solomon. After the story of Solomon and his death the division of the kingdom is described. Then follow the detailed parallel accounts of the northern kingdom of Israel and the southern kingdom of Judah, covering 400 years and ending with the destruction of the first Temple and the Babylonian empire. Since Samuel and Kings tell a continuous story, some translations have treated them as a single work. In the Bible, Joshua, Judges, Samuel and Kings belong to the larger division of Prophets. Kings provides much information about four centuries of Jewish history and, in addition, a large store of prophetic writings. The chroniclers, throughout Kings, refer to other sources, now lost; such as the "Book of the Chronicles of the Kings of Israel," and the "Book of Chronicles of the Kings of Judah," the "Book of Jashar," and the "Books of the Acts of Solomon." It seems that the kings had their separate recorders apart from the records of the Temple. Though folklore is interwoven into the history of Kings, the ancient historians were careful and methodical. They were not slaves of despots but possessed of a free, religious spirit that allowed them to condemn even the deeds of the great kings. Modern archaeological findings have confirmed the reliability of these ancient historians.

KINNOT

(Lamantations) a special service observed in the synagogue on Tishah B'Av, in commemoration of the destruction of the Temples, during which the Book of Lamentations is read.
See also Lamentations

KIRIATH-JEARIM

("Town of forests") a town on the border of Judah and Benjamin. After the Philistines had captured the Ark, they abandoned it at Kiriath-jearim. There priests watched over it until David took it to Jerusalem.

KISHINEV

City in Russia, site of an infamous pogrom in April 1903, which inspired Bialik's "City of Slaughter" and which brought about the establishment of Jewish self-defense. During World War II the Jewish population was annihilated.

KISHON, EPHRAIM

(1924-   )—Israeli satirist. Born in Budapest, Kishon settled in Israel in 1949. His popular column of political and social satire appears regularly in the newspaper *Maariv*. In addition he has written plays and films. Several collections of his writings have been published, including *Look Back, Mrs. Lot; Noah's Ark, Tourist Class;* and *Unfair to Goliath*.

KISHON, RIVER

Small river north of Mount Carmel and near Mount Tabor. During the rainy season it sometimes swells to a torrential stream. A sudden storm that increased the Kishon's power was an important factor in the defeat of Sisera, as described in Deborah's Song. The prophet Elijah slew Baal's priests near this river.

KISLEV

Ninth month in the Jewish calendar.

See also Calendar, Jewish; Months, Jewish.

KISSINGER, HENRY

(1923-   )—American statesman. Born in Germany, where he experienced Nazi persecution as a youth, Kissinger came to the United States in 1938. After receiving his Ph.D. from Harvard in 1954, he worked for the Council on Foreign Relations, soon becoming known as a leading expert on defense policy and international affairs. He joined the Harvard faculty in 1957, and at various times also served in an advisory capacity to the Eisenhower, Kennedy, and Johnson administrations, and to Gov. Nelson Rockefeller. Kissinger became President Nixon's principal advisor on foreign policy in 1969, and in 1973 was appointed Secretary of State. He was retained in this office by President Ford. During Kissinger's tenure in the State Department, American foreign policy underwent a dramatic turnabout. Kissinger worked to secure peaceful relations with both Russia and China. He played a key role in negotiating a settlement of the Vietnam War, for which he received the Nobel Peace Prize in 1973, and also served as a trusted intermediary through whom Israel and Egypt were able to negotiate interim disengagement agreements in the Sinai following the Yom Kippur War. Kissinger's Middle East policies have sometimes been criticized because they seem intended to enhance America's relations with Egypt and the other Arab countries at Israel's expense.

KITZUR SHULCHAN ARUCH

Shortened popular edition of the *Shulchan Aruch*, widely used as a handbook on Jewish law by Orthodox Jews.

See also Shulchan Aruch.

KLAUSNER, JOSEPH

(1874-1959)—Scholar and historian. Klausner was an early Zionist, and edited *Hashiloach*. In 1925 he was appointed professor of Modern Hebrew Literature at the Hebrew University of Jerusalem and in 1945 became professor of Second Temple History. His published works deal mainly with Modern Hebrew Literature and the Second Temple period and have become standard works in these fields. Klausner was Editor-in-Chief of the *Encyclopedia Hebraica* and exercised a great influence in Jewish scholarship.

KLUTZNICK, PHILIP M.

(1907-   )—American realtor and public figure. Klutznick has served as the international president of B'nai B'rith (1953-59), president of the American Friends of the Hebrew University, and general chairman of the United Jewish Appeal. In 1961 President Kennedy appointed him United States representative to the Economic and Social Council of the United Nations, with the rank of minister. He remained in this post until 1963.

KNESSET

(lit., "assembly")—Parliament of the State of Israel.

KOF

The nineteenth letter of the Hebrew alphabet, has the numerical value of 100.

See also Aleph Bet.

KOHUT, REBEKAH

A grand lady of American Jewry, she devoted more than fifty years of her life to social and educational work. Born in Hungary in 1864, Rebekah was brought to the United States at the age of three. Her father was a rabbi and led congregations in several American cities. Returning east in 1886 from California, Rebekah met in New York the well-known Talmudic scholar, Alexander Kohut. The father of eight children, Dr. Kohut had recently been made a widower by the death of his wife. Rebekah fell in love with him and they were married the next year. She reared her stepchildren with devotion and assisted her husband in

Rebecca Kohut.

composing his sermons and completing his Talmudic lexicon. When Dr. Kohut died, seven years after their marriage, Mrs. Kohut lectured on Jewish subjects, taught immigrants, and then opened schools for boys and girls. These schools brought her both wealth and fame. Among the offices she held were: president, World Council of Jewish Women; president, National Council of Jewish Women; executive director, Columbia Grammar School; vice-president, Jewish Conciliation Court of America; and organizer for the war-time Federal Employment Clearing House. Mrs. Kohut wrote the story of her life in four volumes.

KOL NIDRE

When one thinks of Yom Kippur, the first remembrance is of the extraordinary prayer that is thrice recited at the beginning of the Yom Kippur evening service. *Kol Nidre* and its music existed in Gaonic days, long before the Inquisition in Spain which many think brought it into being. The prayer declares null and void any vows an individual takes in regard to his own person, but not those he takes in regard to other persons. Enemies of the Jews have falsely described the prayer as an invitation to annul honest obligations. Some people have believed that *Kol Nidre* was devised so that the Marranos might disavow the faith forced upon them by the Spaniards; this is untrue. However, it did serve sometimes as a disavowal of forced conversion. The music of *Kol Nidre* is among the most celebrated in all Jewish liturgy. It reflects the solemn mood of the chanter and of the sacred eve on which it is recited.

KOLLEK, THEODORE

(1911-   )—Israeli political leader. Teddy Kollek was born in Vienna. He emigrated to Palestine in 1934, occasionally returning to Europe thereafter on educational missions to youth groups. From 1940 to 1947 Kollek served in the Political Department of the Jewish Agency. During the War of Independence he was sent to America to buy weapons. From 1952 to 1964 he was director general of the Office of the Prime Minister of Israel. He also headed the Government Tourist Corporation and was one of the founders of the Israel Museum. Kollek was elected mayor of Jerusalem in 1965. After the Six-Day War, he superintended the reunification of the city, displaying much tact and goodwill in his effort to normalize relations with the Arab populace. During his administration Jerusalem has undergone considerable growth and modernization.

KOOK, ABRAHAM ISAAC

First Chief Rabbi of the Holy Land after the British Mandate, Abraham Kook was born in Latvia in 1865 and died in Jerusalem, 1935. After a career as a brilliant rabbinical student and leader of Russian Jewish communities, Kook became rabbi of Jaffa in Palestine in 1903. He established a yeshiva there in which the Talmud and all related branches of Jewish lore were studied. In legal matters he showed an ability to relate the traditional law to the conditions of the time, without violating

Rabbi Abraham Isaac Kook.

tradition. In 1919 Rabbi Kook was appointed head of the Ashkenazic congregations of Jerusalem and became Chief Rabbi two years later. During World War I he was stranded in London, where he occupied an important pulpit. He helped form British opinion for the issuance of the Balfour Declaration. Rabbi Kook wrote extensively on a variety of subjects—Jewish law, legendry, philosophy, Kabbalah and many others. The religious Zionist Party, Mizrachi, established a foundation, Mosad Harav Kook in his memory. The function of this foundation was to publish the Chief Rabbi's manuscripts. It has since published a great amount of additional scholarly material. Rabbi Kook is buried on the Mount of Olives, now in Arab hands.

KORAH

A demogogic Levite who, with Dathan and Abiram, led an unsuccessful revolt against Moses and Aaron. The three and all who were associated with the rebellion were engulfed by the earth.

KORCZAK, JANUSZ

(1878-1942)—Polish author and educator. Trained as a physician, Korczak devoted himself to working with the poor. In 1911 he became the head of the Jewish orphanage in Warsaw. Through his compassionate concern, his respect for children as individuals, and his innovative pedagogical techniques, he quickly won the love and admiration of the youngsters who were placed in his care. His ideas on child psychology, elaborated in such books as *How to Love a Child* and *The Child's Right to Respect*, have been very influential, especially in Israel. He was also the author of numerous extremely popular stories for children. During the Nazi occupation of Poland, Korczak, together with 200 Jewish children whom he refused to leave, though he could have saved himself by doing so, were exterminated in the gas chambers at Treblinka.

KOSHER

("Proper" or "prepared") refers to food prepared in accordance with Jewish law and practice, also used to designate the animals (and their flesh) which are cloven-footed and chew the cud, and fish that have both fins and scales.

See also Dietary laws; Kashrut.

KROCHMAL, NACHMAN

(1785-1840)—Polish historian and philosopher. One of the most important figures in 19th cent. Jewish thought, Krochmal was a leader of the Jewish Enlightenment (Haskalah) in Eastern Europe and a founder of the "Science of Judaism." He pioneered in the application of modern scientific and critical methodology to the study of Hebrew literature. His philosophical views are outlined in his *Moreh Nevukhei ha-Zeman* ("Guide for the Perplexed of the Time"). He saw Jewish history as a reflection of the soul and spirit of the Jewish people, and laid out a concept of the Jewish mission that had great influence on many later Jewish thinkers, especially in the Reform movement His systematic defense and elaboration of the fundamentals of Judaism in accordance with western philosophical systems was also of great influence.

KURDISTAN

Region in Central Asia. Tradition has it that Jews settled in the area as early as the time of Ezra. They were always treated poorly, and with the establishment of Israel the majority of Kurdistan's Jews emigrated there.

LABAN

Brother of Rebekah, wealthy sheep and cattle breeder of Haran, who gave work and refuge to his nephew Jacob. He was the father of Jacob's two wives, Leah and Rachel.

LACHISH

Ancient fortress between Jerusalem and Gaza overlooking the main road connecting Egypt and the land of Israel. It was conquered by Joshua. Later Lachish was taken by Nebuchadnezzar. It became the strong southern frontier fortress of the Persians during their rule of Judea. It has been excavated in modern times.

LADINO

Spanish-Jewish language. Ladino was for Sephardic Jewry what Yiddish (a German-Jewish language) was

Spanish in Hebrew characters (Ladino). Title page of Bahya ibn Pakudah's *Duties of the Heart*.

for East European Jewry: a tongue for daily intercourse and folk-literature. Ladino is written with Hebrew letters, and the first printed book in the language appeared in Constantinople, in 1510. It is still spoken in centers of Sephardic Jewry such as Turkey, North Africa, and Israel.

See also Judeo Languages.

LAG BEOMER

(l-g in Hebrew has the numerical value of thirty-three)—The thirty-third of the forty-nine days between Passover and Shavuot, known as the period of the "counting of Omer" (*Sefirah*). These were the days of the barley harvest in Israel, and the *Omer* is an ancient measure of barley. The counting of Omer (*Sefirah*) is part of the prayer service during this period. It is a time of mourning and sad memories, so signified by ancient tradition that hair could not be cut and weddings could not take place. But on Lag Beomer this period is interrupted by gayety, and weddings could take place and hair was cut. It is said that in the period of Omer during the Bar Kochba revolt, the students of Rabbi Akiba were stricken with plague and that on this day the plague ceased. In Israel on this day pilgrims go to Meron, the Galilean village, to visit Simeon bar Yohai's grave. At midnight bonfires are kindled and the pilgrims dance and sing until dawn. This custom of dancing around bonfires on this day has also spread to other parts of Israel. Lag Boemer is not mentioned by scholars or Geonim. It is celebrated as a sort of half-holiday and its character has been developed by traditions and observances.

LAMED

The twelfth letter of the Hebrew alphabet, has the numerical value of 30.

See also Aleph Bet.

LAMENTATIONS

Generally ascribed to the prophet Jeremiah, the Book of Lamentations (*Echah*) is the third of the Five Scrolls in the Bible. A mournful poetic lament on the destruction of the Temple in 586 B.C.E., it contains moving descriptions of the desolation of Jerusalem. The book is read aloud, with a special grieving chant, at the evening and morning services on Tisha B'Av.

LAMM, NORMAN

(1927-)—President of Yeshiva University. Born in Brooklyn, Lamm became an Orthodox rabbi in 1951. In addition to serving in the congregational rabbinate and in national Jewish organizations, he taught philosophy at Yeshiva, founded the journal *Tradition,* he is the editor of Ktav's "Library of Jewish Law and Ethics." In 1976 he became the fourth president of Yeshiva University, his alma mater. Among Lamm's best-known books are *Faith and Doubt, The Royal Reach,* and *A Hedge of Roses.*

LANDSMANSHAFTEN

Societies set up, mainly in the United States, by emigrants from the same town or district. These societies extended social, cultural, and economic aid to their members. Landsmanshaften were founded in the United States primarily in the later years of the 19th century, when this country saw a great emigration from Europe, and their language was almost always Yiddish. Similar organizations have recently been set up in Israel.

LAW, CODIFICATION OF

The Talmud, the primary source of Jewish law, is not arranged as a code. The demands of practical life made the drawing-up of codes based on Talmudic law necessary, and so, some time after the final revision of the Talmud, the *Halachot Pesukot* and the *Halachot Gedolot* were issued. The most comprehensive code is Maimonides' *Mishneh Torah,* which classified all Jewish law, and which served as a model for later codifiers. The most authoritative code is Joseph Caro's *Shulchan Aruch,* to which were added the comments of Moses Isserles containing the practice of Ashkenazic Jewry. Caro's code was based upon the works of Isaac Alfasi, Maimonides, and Jacob ben Asher *(Arba Turim)*, and was accepted by world Jewry.

See also Codes of Jewish Law,

LAWS OF NOAH

See Noahide Laws.

LAZARUS, EMMA

(1849-1887)—American poetess. Her Jewish consciousness flowered during the great emigration from Russia in the 1880's, and she turned to Jewish themes for her poetry, writing *Songs of a Semite* and *By the Waters of Babylon.* The poetess learned Hebrew and translated the work of Judah Halevi into English. Perhaps her most famous poem is the familiar *The New Colossus,* which is engraved on the base of the Statue of Liberty in New York, and which contains the lines,

"Give me your tired, your poor,
Your huddled masses yearning to be free . . ."

LEAH

Wife of Jacob, older sister of Rachel, daughter of Laban. Laban tricked Jacob into marrying her instead of Rachel. Leah was the mother of Reuben, Simeon, Levi, Judah, Zebulun, Issachar and Dinah. She was buried in the Cave of Machpelah. Leah is one of the Four Mothers of Israel.

LEBANON

1. Two beautiful mountain ranges, called the Lebanon and Anti-Lebanon, named for their snow-capped peaks. The Lebanon's highest peak is 10,200 feet high. The cedars and cypresses of Lebanon were famous for their beauty. King Solomon built the Temple with wood from the cedars of Lebanon.

2. The new republic at the northern border of the State of Israel (between Syria and the Mediterranean). Lebanon was established in 1942.

LECHAH DODI

Beautiful song welcoming the Sabbath. The author, Solomon Halevi Alkabetz (1540), calls Sabbath the beautiful bride.

LE-CHAYIM

A toast, wishing life and health.

LEESER, ISAAC

(1806-1868)—A rabbi, translator and editor who was born in Germany. He came to America when he was seventeen years of age. In 1829 Leeser became cantor of the Sephardic Congregation Mikveh Israel of Philadelphia. Because he introduced prayers in English and the English sermon, some Orthodox Jews thought him a "Reformer," though some Reformers considered him an opponent. In 1843 Leeser established the *Occident and Jewish Advocate*, first Jewish informational periodical in America. He founded Maimonides College in Philadelphia, which opened in 1867. He translated the Bible into English and for more than half a century it was a standard in America until appearance of the Jewish Publication Society version. With Rebecca Gratz he founded the first Jewish congregational Sunday School that has remained in existence continuously—now the Hebrew Sunday School Society of Philadelphia. For his Sephardic congregation he provided a set of Hebrew-English prayerbooks; and he prepared a daily prayerbook for the Ashkenazim. No communal enterprise failed to receive his encouragement and assistance. His life was devoted to the education of Jews in Judaism and the interpretation of Judaism to the non-Jew.

LEHMAN, HERBERT H.

(1878-1963)—American statesman, banker, and philanthropist. He was Lieutenant Governor of New York State for two terms (1928-32) and Governor of the State (1932-42). Lehman was a vigorous proponent of the New Deal philosophy and fought for civil rights in his career as United States Senator (1949-57). He was also the Chairman of the Board of Overseers of the Jewish Theological Seminary of America.

Herbert H. Lehman.

LE-SHANAH TOVAH

Greeting used during Rosh Hashanah and the Ten Days of Penitence. It means "a happy New Year."

LEVI

Third son of Jacob and Leah, ancestor of the tribe of Levi, the Levites and the *Cohanim*.

LEVI, TRIBE OF

One of the tribes of Israel. The tribe of Levi, dedicated to Temple service and the education of the peo-ple, received no portion of land in Israel—its portion was the Torah. Levi's banner was white, black and red; its emblem was the Urim and Tummim (priestly equipment). The stone representing Levi in the High Priest's breastplate was probably a garnet.

LEVI BEN GERSHON

(also known as Gersonides and Ralbag; 1288-1344)—Philosopher, Bible commentator and mathematician. He practiced medicine in Avignon and was even more rationalistic than Maimonides. Gersonides' main work is *Milchamot Adonai* which is an Aristotelian interpretation of Judaism. He also wrote commentaries on Aristotle and a work on astronomy. The *Camera Obscura* was developed by Gersonides, as was "Jacob's Staff," a valuable nautical instrument.

LEVIATHAN

A legendary sea-monster referred to in the Bible. In Rabbinic literature it is used symbolically for power in general. At the Resurrection it will be killed by God and the righteous will feast on its flesh.

LEVIN, MEYER

(1905-   )—American author who has frequently written on Jewish and Zionist themes. Among his many books are *Yehudah*, one of the first novels to be written about kibbutz life; *The Old Bunch*, describing Jewish life in Chicago; and *The Settlers*, a panoramic fictionalized account of the resettlement of Palestine in modern times. Levin is also the author of *Compulsion*, based on the Leopold-Loeb murder case, and many other novels, as well as a dramatization of the diary of Anne Frank and translations of famous Hasidic tales. Since 1958 he has lived in Israel.

LEVIN, SHMARYAHU

(1867-1935)—Zionist leader and orator. Levin was ordained a rabbi and received a university education as well. He worked for the reform of Hebrew education in Russia and was a member of the first Russian Duma. Levin was a member of the Zionist Executive (1911-18) and was a leader of the movement in America during World War I. Together with Bialik he founded the Dvir Publishing Company in Berlin (later, of Tel Aviv).

LEVITES

The members of the lower priestly caste of Temple servants. They were the descendants of Levi, third son of Jacob, and had received no portion of land in Canaan. In the latter days of the Temple, Levites served under the *Cohanim* and were subject to their orders. They had many duties; they cared for the holy scrolls; they educated the young; they also prepared animals for the sacrifices. They provided the music for the ceremonies and they performed many additional menial tasks. It is said that at times, when the

Cohanim, the priests, turned away from their religion and its duties, the Levites zealously guarded the faith and the ritual and preserved the great belief in one God. Josephus, Philo and the Apocrypha tell in detail the duties performed by the Levites. The Talmud describes the long period of preparation before a Levite could carry out his sacred duties in the Temple. Their livelihood was paid from the people's tithes, the tax of one-tenth that was brought to the Temple. The same priestly laws imposed upon the *Cohanim,* the redemption of the first born and family purity, also apply to the Levites. Today when the Torah is read in the Synagogue, according to tradition the first worshiper called up for the reading is a "Kohen" (priest), the second a Levite, and only then is this honor accorded to the "ordinary" Israelite.

LEVITICUS

The third book of the Torah, it is primarily concerned with the laws of the priesthood; the Hebrew name of the book is *Vayikra.* It is the shortest of the Five Books of Moses, but it contains the greatest number of laws. Leviticus is divided into chapters stating regulations on the offering of sacrifices, on consecrating priests, on conducting the yearly Day of Atonement (Yom Kippur), on vows, on taxes, on personal purity, and on holiness. Among the laws of purity are those concerned with cleanliness and Kashruth. The "laws of holiness" are not only concerned with religious ritual. In them, for example, is repeated the command: "Ye shall be holy, for I the Lord your God am holy." In the nineteenth chapter, among the laws of love of all fellowmen, are the famous sayings: "Thou shalt love thy neighbor as thyself," and "Thou shalt love him (the stranger) as thyself; for ye were strangers in the land of Egypt." Many ceremonial laws, such as the dietary laws and those on ritual bathing, are still observed today. The great ethical laws of Leviticus have had a great impact on Western civilization: the laws stressing the holiness of the home, duties to all mankind, justice and charity, and the sanctification of God's name.

LEVY, ASSER

(d. 1681)—When twenty-three Jews arrived from Brazil at New Amsterdam in 1654, this young man was about twenty years old. He resented Governor Stuyvesant's declaration that the colony desired no Jews, for all the newcomers were full-fledged Dutch burghers and should have been accorded every right. Levy was particularly irked when the Governor imposed a special tax upon the Jews in place of the customary military service. When he and a friend were refused the right to stand guard, they performed this duty nevertheless and then demanded and obtained full rights of citizenship for all. Levy became a fur trader with the Indians, opened taverns, acquired real estate and was granted a license to serve as a butcher—with the provision that he be excused from slaughtering hogs.

Not only did he achieve the respect of his Christian neighbors but he was honored for advancing funds for building a Lutheran church. When the English captured the city and renamed it New York, Asser Levy took the oath of allegiance to the British king, continuing to hold his high place in the community. He died in 1681.

LEVY, URIAH PHILLIPS

Born in Philadelphia in 1792, Levy was a United States naval officer. He was the son of a patriot soldier of the Revolution. He became a cabin-boy when he was only ten years old and later served an apprenticeship at sea and studied navigation. At the age of twenty he was already the captain of a schooner. Shortly before the War of 1812 his sailors mutinied and stranded him on an island. He was captured by the British and compelled to serve on a British sloop. He refused an offer to enlist in the British navy and returned to the United States. Levy volunteered his services in the War of 1812 and received an appointment as assistant sailing master. He helped break through the British blockade and bring an American envoy safely to France. He also sank twenty-one enemy ships. But he was taken captive once more by a British vessel and made a prisoner until the end of the war. Levy had many adventures on distant shores. Among his achievements was the suppression of piracy in the Gulf of Mexico and the slave trade along Honduras Bay. He refused a flattering offer by the Emperor of Brazil to command the Brazilian navy. Levy saw bitter times also in the service. He seems to have been

A portrait of Uriah Phillips Levy.

retired from active service for over ten years at the rank of captain. At a special court trial he was reinstated, when evidence was brought that he had been demoted for anti-Semitic reasons. After his reinstatement he rose to the highest honors attainable in the navy at that time. Long an admirer of Jefferson, he purchased his home, Monticello, and left it to the government after his death in 1862. He is said to have abolished flogging in the navy. In 1961, a chapel named after Levy was opened at the Norfolk, Virginia, Naval Base.

LEWISOHN, LUDWIG

(1883-1955)—American novelist, critic, and professor. Lewisohn wrote novels dealing with Jewish problems (*The Island Within, The Last Days of Shylock*), books of criticism, and several volumes concerning Zionist ideology and biography. From 1948 he taught comparative literature at Brandeis University; in Waltham, Mass.

LILIEN, EPHRAIM MOSES

(1874-1925)—Austrian artist. Lilien was the first Jewish artist to become active in the Zionist movement. His portraits of Theodor Herzl and his illustrations for the Golden Book of the Jewish National Fund helped to arouse Zionist sentiments among Jews throughout the world. He was also noted for his sensitive etchings of Jewish life in Palestine during the early part of the twentieth century.

LIPPMAN, WALTER

(1889-1975)—American author and journalist. He founded the *New Republic* in 1914, and was its editor until 1919, and was editor of the *New York World* until 1931. For many years he wrote a political column for the *New York Herald Tribune* that was syndicated in over 250 newspapers in 25 countries. Lippman was considered one of the most prominent political and economic writers in the United States; his works included *The Good Society, The Public Philosophy,* and *A Preface to Morals.*

LIPSKY, LOUIS

(1876-1963)—American Zionist leader and writer. In 1899 he founded the *Maccabean*, the first official paper of this country's Zionist Organization. Lipsky held high office in all the major American Zionist agencies, and was considered the dean of American Zionist. His last book (1956) was *A Gallery of Zionist Profiles*, a collection of essays and biographies.

LITHUANIA

Until the 16th century the Jews of Lithuania were protected by royal charters and propered, but the "Jewish Badge" was introduced in 1566 and many economic activities were restricted. Lithuania was a center of Jewish scholarship, producing the Gaon of Vilna and other great Talmudists; it was also a center of the Haskalah movement. At the outbreak of World War II there were 175,000 Jews in the country, most of whom were killed by the Nazis; 25,000 Jews now live in Lithuania, which is a member state of the U.S.S.R.

LONDON

Jews first settled in London at the end of the 11th century. In 1290 London Jewry shared in the general expulsion of England's Jews, though a secret community of Marranos existed through the 16th century. By the middle of the 17th century Jews were readmitted to the country. In 1835 Sir David Salomons became Sheriff, and in 1855, Lord Mayor; Lionel de Rothschild was elected Member of Parliament for the city in 1847. The mass immigration from Russia in the 1880's greatly increased the London Jewish community. The newcomers settled in large numbers in the East End, where they engaged mainly in the tailoring and cabinet-making industries; a trade union movement and Yiddish press and theater soon came into being. 280,000 Jews now live in London.

See also England

LOPEZ, RODERIGO

(1525-1594)—Marrano physician to Queen Elizabeth. He was accused of plotting to poison the queen and his execution aroused anti-Jewish feeling; it was once thought that the character of Shylock in *The Merchant of Venice* reflected the anti-Semitism stirred up at the time.

A drawing showing Roderigo Lopez supposedly planning to poison Queen Elizabeth I.

LOT

Nephew of Abraham, son of Haran, from Ur. He accompanied Abraham to Canaan. He and his family lived in Sodom and were the only ones saved when the city was destroyed. His wife, however, who looked back at Sodom despite the angel's command, was turned into a pillar of salt.

LUBIN, DAVID

He made significant contributions to the solution of economic problems of American agriculture. Born in Poland in 1849, he came to America at an early age and began his remarkable career. His store in Sacramento was the first "one-price" establishment west of the Mississippi. The farmers who were his customers confided their financial difficulties to him and he became active in their behalf. Through his efforts the California Fruit Growers Exchange was founded, which bought and sold the produce of many farmers; he also arranged for farmers to be financed by rural credit banks. He offered many other suggestions for easing the lot of the shipper, including extension of the parcel post service. His crowning triumph was the International Institute of Agriculture in Rome, which aimed at raising world prices of farm goods. At first the United States, England and France refused their cooperation. But King Victor Emanuel of Italy helped to further the project and in 1905 forty nations met in Rome to discuss general agricultural problems. Today the number of member nations has doubled. The Institute is the clearing house for international farm statistics. Lubin, who died in Rome in 1919, was a devout Jew and believed that his economic idealism was learned from his Judaism.

LULAV

A palm branch, one of the four plants used in the celebration of Sukkot. During the synagogue service, the branch is waved in all directions to show that God is to be found everywhere.

See also Sukkot, Four Plants of

As in ancient days, Jews all over the world celebrate the holiday of Sukkot by blessing the *lulav* and etrog.

LURIA, ISAAC

(1534-1572)—Kabbalist; also known as "Ari." Luria lived in Safed, where he gathered round himself a band of followers who adopted his ascetic life and who spread the teachings of their master. These teachings had a great influence on subsequent mystical thought;

Luria himself was regarded as a saint and miracle worker. He wrote nothing save three Aramaic Sabbath songs and a few poems in Hebrew; our whole knowledge of his teaching is derived from the works of his disciple, Chaim Vital.

LUZZATTI, LUIGI

(1841-1927)—The first Jew to become prime minister of Italy. He taught political economy at the Milan Technical High School and in 1866 became professor of constitutional law at the University of Padua. At twenty-eight he was appointed secretary to one of the most important ministries in the Italian government. For many years he made brilliant contributions to Italy's economic and financial policies. He helped establish basic laws on commerce, customs and tariffs. He furthered Italian cooperation with neighboring lands. In Parliament he was acclaimed as an outstanding administrator and noble orator. Luzzatti defended the civil rights of Jews in many countries, particularly those of the Roumanian Jews. He helped in his official capacity and also personally. In 1921 he sent an encouraging message to the agricultural settlements of Palestine and in 1925 he felicitated Lord Balfour when the Hebrew University was dedicated. Luzzatti wrote many books and essays, his best known work being *God In Freedom*, a book on religious liberty.

LUZZATTO, MOSES CHAIM

(1707-1747)—Kabbalist and poet. He imagined that heavenly visions came to him, and that he was the Messiah, or the forerunner of the Messiah. The Italian rabbinate, fearing the damage which could be done by a false Messiah, forced him to desist in his claims. His poetical and dramatic works had a great influence on modern Hebrew poetry, and his *Messilat Yesharim*, a work on ethics, is considered a classic.

LYDDA

City southeast of Jaffa; important center of Jewish revolt in Roman times. After the destruction of the Temple, Lydda was a refuge for scholars and became a seat of Jewish learning. An academy of Tannaim was established there. Today, the modern city is an important railroad junction and boasts one of the largest and most modern airfields in the Middle East.

MAARIV

The Evening Service, first of the three daily services (in the Jewish calendar, the day begins after sunset). The prayers of Maariv are recited after sunset.

MACCABEES

The name applied to members of the Hasmonean dynasty. The word is derived from *Maccabee* ("the Hammer"), the name given to the brave Judah, son of the Hasmonean priest Mattathias. Judah and his brothers fought the war which began with the famous revolt against the Syrians' religious oppression and later developed into struggle for independence. After the rededication of the Temple, in 164 B.C.E., the nation was divided between the supporters of the Hasmonean policy of aggression and the minority that wanted peace. Among these latter were the Hellenists. When Judah Maccabee died, 161 B.C.E., he had temporarily secured his people's liberty. But his brother Jonathan, who took over the high priesthood and rule, had to continue the fight against the Syrians. After Jonathan's murder in 142, his brother Simon rid Israel completely of the Syrian influence. During the following period of peace, the high priesthood became hereditary in the Maccabean family. During the reign of John Hyrcanus, Simon's son, dissension arose and the people formed three parties, the Pharisees, the Sadducees and the Essenes. A series of plots and murders and civil conflicts under Hasmonean reign in the years that followed well nigh wrecked the Jewish state. The Roman general Pompey, on his conquering expedition, made Judea a tributary to Rome and took the then Maccabean ruler, Aristobulus II, captive to Rome. Confusion followed and the cruel Herod, who had married the Hasmonean princess Mariamne, put all her relatives to death, thus ending the dynasty. Today we remember largely the early days of the Maccabees, the brave sons of Mattathias, and we call Hanukkah the "Feast of the Maccabees."

See also Judah Maccabee.

MACCABEES I AND II

Books of the Apocrypha, a record of the religious thought, historical events and legends of the time of the Maccabees.

MACHPELAH

The cave and field near Hebron which Abraham bought from the Hittite, Ephron, for the burial of Sarah. The cave became the burial place for all the

Interior view of the cave of Machpelah.

Patriarchs and for Rebekah and Leah. It is now in Arab territory, a sacred sanctuary of the Moslems who also consider Abraham their ancestor.

MACHZOR

("Repetition" or "cycle of the year") prayer book for the High Holy Days and the Three Festivals, containing the prayers, poetry and passages from the Scriptures to be recited on those days.

MAFTIR

("the concluder") originally the term referred to the person who concludes the portion of the Torah read in the synagogue on the Sabbath and holidays and who recites the reading from the Prophets (the *Haftarah*). It has now been extended to refer to the concluding Torah portion itself.

See also Haftarah.

MAGGID

The word *maggid* means a teller or narrator. Very early in the history of Judaism the text of the Bible used to be expounded at some length in sermons in which stories, parables and moral teachings were related. After a while this interest in *derush,* or preaching (the Midrash developed from that custom) was limited to two sermons by the rabbi, one before Passover and one before Yom Kippur. Then arose the popular traveling preacher, Maggid, who provided the Jews with the inspirational stories they desired. These men would scold and comfort the people in the same discourse and often the audience alternated between laughter and tears. They would invent parables of such interest that many, such as those of Jacob Kranz, the Dubno Maggid, are preserved to this day. Each Maggid had a considerable knowledge of Jewish lore and could quote from it as adequately as could a rabbi. Some congregations hired Maggidim on a permanent basis. They would deliver lectures after the evening prayer and usually on Sabbath afternoons. For the traveling Maggid the returns were very meager; he delivered his talk without previous invitation and then hoped for donations. To many Jews of Europe, who had few forms of recreation, and for a long while to immigrant Jews in America, the Maggid proved a most valuable institution.

MAGNES, JUDAH LEON

(1877-1948)—First president of the Hebrew University in Jerusalem. Magnes served as a Reform rabbi in New York's Temple Emanuel and was active in communal affairs. During World War I he was an uncompromising pacifist, which weakened his influence in Zionist and communal matters. He settled in Palestine in 1921 and helped establish the Hebrew University. Magnes advocated Arab-Jewish understanding.

MAH NISHTANAH

The opening words of the "Four Questions" asked by the youngest member of the family at the Passover Seder service. The "Four Questions" query the differences between the Passover night and other nights. "Why do we eat matzah? Why do we eat herbs? Why do we dip in salt water? Why do we recline instead of sitting erect?"

MAIMON, SOLOMON

(1754-1800)—Philosopher. Maimon was a boy genius who, having received a thorough Jewish education, emigrated to Germany, where after undergoing many hardships he entered philosophic-scientific circles. His critique of Kant established him as the most penetrating of that philosopher's critics. Maimon's autobiography gives an interesting picture of Jewish life at the time and is a vivid personal document.

MAIMONIDES

Also known as Rambam and Moses ben Maimon, Maimonides was the great philosopher, codifier and leader of the Jews of the Middle Ages. He was born in Cordova, Spain, 1135. His family had to flee Moslem persecution when he was only thirteen. As a youth he amassed a vast store of knowledge taught him by his mother and father, a distinguished scholar. Later, eminent Arabic teachers taught him philosophy and the natural sciences and trained him to become a physician. The family travelled to many places until they found refuge in Egypt, near Cairo. By that time Maimonides was an established scholar and a rabbinical authority. He had written many treatises, including his brilliant Commentary on the Mishnah, which contains his famous Thirteen Articles of Faith. He was devoted to the Jews who suffered persecution under the Islamic tyrants who tried to convert them. Though active as a Jewish scholar he had a great medical practice and wrote many medical works. Many of the new Sultan's potentates were his patients and he exerted his influence on behalf of the persecuted Oriental Jews. Among his great later works were the *Mishneh Torah (Yad Hachazakah)*, a fourteen-volume code of Jewish law which summarized the spiritual and intellectual content of the Talmud and the *Moreh*

Autograph signature of Moses Maimonides on an appeal for the redemption of captives, Cairo, 1172.

Nevuchim (Guide to the Perplexed), his great philosophic work which attempts to establish harmony between ritual and ethical teachings on the basis of reason. When he died in 1204 it was said: "From Moses to Moses, there has risen none like unto Moses."

MALACHI

Last of the Books of Twelve (Minor) Prophets of the Bible. Malachi (his real name is uncertain), a prophet of the fourth century B.C.E., spoke out against the evils of his time and proclaimed that all men are brothers, children of the One God, and that men should deal justly with one another.

MALAMUD, BERNARD

(1914-   )—American writer. Malamud's novel *The Fixer*, based on the case of Mendel Beilis, a Russian Jew who was charged with the ritual murder of a Christian child, was awarded the Pulitzer Prize. Among his other best-selling books are *The Natural, The Assistant,* and *The Tenants.*

MALTA

Catacombs with Jewish symbols prove that Jews lived on this Mediterranean island during Roman times. After 1530, when the island was handed over to the Knights of St. John, Jewish slaves captured in the raids on Turkish and Moorish shipping were brought there, and during the 17th and 18th centuries a community of slaves existed on the island. The present Jewish community numbers around forty, all of them Sephardim.

MAMRE

1. Dwelling place of the Patriarchs, Abraham, Isaac and Jacob, either identical with Hebron or very near it. Abraham built an altar there.
2. Abraham's ally who helped him rescue Lot after the Canaanite kings had taken him prisoner.

MANASSEH

1. Older son of Joseph; grandson of Jacob, ancestor of the tribe of Manasseh.
2. Fourteenth king of Judah, son of Hezekiah, ruled about 692-641 B.C.E. Under his early rule idol worship flourished in Judah. Though he freely submitted Judah to Assyrian rule, he was temporarily taken captive to Assyria.

MANASSEH, PRAYER OF

Book of the Apocrypha, a poem of penitence written in captivity, ascribed to King Manasseh of Judah.

MANASSEH, TRIBE OF

One of the tribes of Israel. It first settled in the north of Canaan, east of the Jordan. Later it joined its brother tribe, Ephraim, in the central region of Canaan. They shared the jet-black banner. Manasseh's emblem was a unicorn. The stone representing (Ephraim and) Manasseh in the High Priest's breastplate was probably an onyx.

MANASSEH BEN ISRAEL

(1604-1657)—Instrumental in gaining readmittance to England for Jews. He became a rabbi at sixteen and while serving in Amsterdam wrote a book reconciling passages in Bible and Talmud. He was also author of *Hope for Israel*, a book dealing with his people's martyrdom and their hope for betterment. When Oliver Cromwell ruled England (1649-1660), his

Drawing of Manasseh Ben Israel.

Puritan supporters showed marked favor toward the people of Israel, some saying Britain's troubles were due to mistreatment of the Jews. Manasseh's book was sent to Parliament with a request that Jews be allowed to live and worship in England. Invited to visit the country, the rabbi was held up by a war between the countries. Later, some Puritans, who had advocated the laws of Moses as the basis for their constitution, obtained another invitation for Manasseh. Although Parliament then decided the original expulsion in 1290 had been illegal, new difficulties arose. Holland authorities feared to lose their Jews. Manasseh then wrote his widely influential *Vindication of the Jews*. Marranos began to filter into England, gradually forming a tolerated community, and Manasseh's efforts yielded their fruit.

MANDATE

The Balfour Declaration of 1917 committed the British government to help establish in Palestine "a national home for the Jewish people." In July, 1922 the Council of the League of Nations, meeting in London, declared that England should govern Palestine under a Mandate, and strive to accomplish the aims of the Balfour Declaration. Growing opposition to the Mandate reached its peak after World War II, and the British ended their rule of Palestine on May 15, 1948, a day after the independence of the State of Israel had been declared.

MANE-KATZ (EMANUEL KATZ)

(1894-1962)—Artist. The Russian-born Katz settled in France in the 1920s where he lived thereafter, except for a stay in the United States during World War II, until shortly before his death. He died in Israel. Originally 'a painter of melancholy scenes, he later turned to a happier art. Many of his paintings have been exhibited in Europe and America, and on his death he left many of them to the city of Haifa.

MANGER, ITZIK

(1901-1969)—Yiddish poet and dramatist. Born in Poland, Manger escaped to England in 1939, then lived in New York, and settled in Israel in 1967. In addition to his many poems on various themes, Manger, in his *Megile Lider,* attempted to create a traditional Purim spiel in modern form.

MANNA

Food from heaven that miraculously fell with the dew of the night near the camps of the Israelites during their wanderings in the barren wilderness. Manna is described as similar to the manna of the tamarisk tree, still found in the Sinai Desert.

MAOZ TZUR

("Rock of Ages") a song sung at Hanukkah; the melody dates back to a German song of the 16th century.

MAPAI

(Formed by the initials of *Mifleget Poale Eretz Yisrael,* Hebrew for "Party of the Workers of Israel") Israeli socialist-labor party. It was founded in 1930 to foster "the rebirth of the Jewish people in Palestine as a free laboring people . . . and to build a society based on labor, equality, and liberty." In 1935 Mapai became the strongest party in the Zionist Organization, and has remained so till the present, just as it has always been the strongest party in the State of Israel. In 1949, Mapai received 35.8% of the votes for the first *Knesset;* in 1951, 37%; and in 1955, 30%. By forming coalitions with other parties, Mapai has been the dominant force on the Israeli political scene. Much of its strength has also been due to its dynamic leader, David Ben-Gurion, Israel's first Prime Minister.

MAPPAH

1. Decorative cover or mantle for the Torah, consisting of a headpiece, with two openings for the rollers of the Torah, and the covering piece itself.
2. Name of a code of law arranged by Moses Isserles, Ashkenazic scholar, published in Krakau, 1578. *Map-*

pah ("Tablecloth") is a supplement to the *Shulchan Aruch* ("The Prepared Table"), the code of law arranged by Joseph Caro, in Safed.

MAR

Hebrew word meaning "mister" or "sir."

MAR SAMUEL

Samuel bar Abba, also called Yarhinaah ("The astronomer"), one of the most important Babylonian scholars (about 180-257 C.E.); head of the academy of Nehardea. He and his colleague and friend, the great Rav, initiated work on the Babylonian Talmud (Gemara) which established Babylonia as the important center of Jewish life. Mar Samuel was also a physician and an astronomer. He drew up the first calendar for Babylonian Jewry. A humble man, he regarded Rav (Abba Arekha) as superior to himself.

See also Abba Arekha.

MARCUS, DAVID

A United States Army colonel who died in defense of Jerusalem during the Israel War of Independence in 1948. Born in 1903, he was the youngest of eight children, who were orphaned in their early years. At the West Point Military Academy, Marcus was a champion welterweight boxer. For several years he was stationed at Governor's Island in New York. While there he studied law. He left the Army to become an assistant United States district attorney. He was Commissioner of Correction for New York City when he returned to the service at the beginning of World War II. Promoted to colonel, he served as judge advocate general (chief legal officer) of the southeastern armies, with headquarters in Australia. He saw considerable combat duty. In Germany and elsewhere Colonel Marcus had witnessed the fearful sufferings of his people. After World War II, at the request of the Jewish Agency he went to the Holy Land to train recruits. He returned home but returned to Israel when the Arabs attacked. Just outside Jerusalem he was shot and killed, probably by a hasty sentry. When his body was returned to America, a large public funeral was conducted for David Marcus and he was buried at his beloved West Point.

MARIAMNE

The beautiful, gentle Hasmonean princess who was executed by her husband, Herod, the Idumean king of Judea, in 29 B.C.E.

MAROR

Bitter herbs which are eaten at the Passover Seder meal as a reminder of the bitterness of slavery in Egypt.

MARRANOS

Spanish word meaning "swine" applied to those Jews who were compelled to adopt Christianity but remained secretly faithful to Judaism. The Spanish Inquisition was established in 1480 to deal with them and the forced conversion of Portuguese Jewry in 1540 extended the Inquisition to that country. Many Marranos migrated, first to Turkey and Italy and later to the South of France, Amsterdam, Hamburg and London. These Marrano communities played an important role in international commerce and included men of distinction in every field.

Yom Kippur Machzor in use during the period of the Spanish Inquisition. It was elongated so that the Spanish Jews (who pretended to be Christians) could hide it in their wide sleeves and escape detection.

MARRIAGE CEREMONIES AND CUSTOMS

It is a very ancient custom for the bride and bridegroom to fast on the wedding day until the ceremony. The wedding usually takes place in a synagogue; since the 14th century the ceremony has been performed under a "Huppah," or canopy. The groom places a gold ring without a stone on his bride's finger and says, "You are hereby bethrothed to me in accordance with the laws of Moses and Israel." At the conclusion of the ceremony the bridegroom breaks a glass, in memory of the destruction of Jerusalem. Orthodox Jews prepare a marriage feast for each day of the following week, at which the "seven blessings" are recited.

MARSHALL, LOUIS

One of America's most distinguished constitutional lawyers, Louis Marshall was born in Syracuse, New York, in 1856. He studied at the Law School of Columbia University. At the time of his examination for the bar, one of the men on the Board of Examiners invited Marshall to become a partner in his law firm. Later he joined this firm, which then became Guggenheimer, Untermyer and Marshall. Louis Marshall argued some of the country's most memorable constitutional cases before the courts. He was an unrelenting battler for human rights. He helped investigate slum conditions and immigration problems and served as mediator and arbitrator in the clothing industry. He did much for relief of World War I victims, helped build Palestine and fought anti-immigration and anti-alien measures. Marshall led the struggle for minority rights at the Versailles Peace Conference in 1919. These rights would never have been attained by the Jewish delegations had not Marshall first brought about some unity among the various Jewish representatives. He was at the forefront of those who combatted publishers of anti-Semitic literature. He was active in or president of many American Jewish institutions of all religious divisions. The State College of Forestry at Syracuse bears his name. He died in Switzerland in 1929.

MARX, KARL

(1818-1883) — German philosopher and creator of modern Socialism. He was baptized as a child by his parents and brought up as a Christian. The Marx home was a center of culture where English and French were spoken and Voltaire was read. The young Marx's radical activities forced him to flee to Paris in 1843, and, in 1849, to London, where he lived till his death. His two outstanding literary achievements were the *Communist Manifesto* (1848) and *Das Kapital* (1867), which are among the most influential

Karl Marx.

books of the last century. Marx saw history as the continual struggle between oppressors and oppressed, and considered economic factors all-important in this struggle. His references to the Jews are usually derogatory and anti-Semitic.

MASORAH

The word *Masorah* stems from a root meaning "to hand down." From Ezra's time to the year 1425, the scholars who preserved and corrected the traditional Bible text are known as Masoretes. The Talmud relates that a copy of the Bible as we know it today was placed in the Temple for the use of copyists. Through carelessness, however, many scrolls were copied with errors. As errors could not be permitted, the Masoretes combed through the scrolls, discovering every altera-

tion, misspelling and obscurity. One may see their corrections in the margins of the Hebrew Bible today. They counted the letters, spaced the words (which had been written solidly), and spaced sentences and paragraphs. Above all, it was necessary to have all letters accounted for, as the Mishnah sometimes derived laws from certain letters that copyists frequently omitted. Since the same consonants might be read in various ways, the Masoretes invented the vowel points. The complete system of vowels and accents came into being in the eighth century. When the notes of Masoretes were too numerous to set in the margins they were gathered into books. It is because of the Masoretes that we have today a standard Hebrew Bible, known as the Masoretic text.

MASSAH

A place near Mount Sinai, in the Sinai Desert, where Moses brought forth water from a rock for the thirsting, troubled Israelites.

MATTATHIAS

Hasmonean priest of Modin, father of the five Maccabees. He inspired the victorious revolt against Antiochus Epiphanes of Syria (165 B.C.E.), and is one of the heroes of Hanukkah.

MATZOT

The eating of unleavened bread (*matzot*) during the week of Passover is commanded in the Bible. No details are given about their baking beyond the statement that the Israelites left Egypt so hurriedly that they did not have time to leaven their bread and so baked unleavened cakes. The Talmud, however, supplies full directions for baking matzot. The dough of flour and water is to be spread very thin, and perforations are to be made to prevent rising. A special wheel was devised to make the holes. There were community matzah bakers even in the Middle Ages but today it is

A drawing showing the baking of matzah.

rarely prepared except in large bakeries. Most matzot of past centuries were round; though some were triangular and in other shapes. The square form is best for machine baking. In 1942 a United States baker sold V-shaped matzot, for Victory! A special type of matzah is *matzah shemurah* which is carefully watched through all its operations, even in the growing of the wheat.

See also Passover.

MEDICINE

Jews have excelled in medicine throughout the ages. Biblical and Talmudic regulations concerning the proper killing of animals and their fitness as food resulted in the accumulation of a practical knowledge of animal anatomy by the Rabbis. The Talmud reveals that clinical observation had attained a high standard, treatment with drugs was quite elaborate, and that surgery was used when necessary. In the 10th-12th centuries Jews contributed to the development of Arab culture by translating Greek medical works. Some Jews, such as Hasdai Ibn Shaprut, Shabbetai ben Abraham Donolo in Sicily, and Maimonides, were noted physicians. During the later Middle Ages Jews were forbidden to practice medicine, but many disregarded the ban. Modern medicine owes a great deal to the discoveries made by Jews such as Paul Ehrlich, who discovered Salvarsan, Jonas Salk, the originator of an anti-polio vaccine, and Sigmund Freud, the father of psychoanalysis.

MEGGED, AHARON

(1926-)—Israeli writer. Born in Poland, Megged came to Palestine in 1926. He attended high school in Tel Aviv and was a member of Kibbutz Sedot Yam from 1937 to 1950. From 1969 to 1971 he served as cultural attache at the Israeli Embassy in London. Megged is the author of plays, short stories, children's books, and novels, including *Fortune of a Fool* and *The Living on the Dead,* and has received many distinguished awards and prizes.

MEGIDDO

Ancient fortified town in the Plain of Jezreel where Barak defeated the Canaanites and where Josiah was killed by Pharaoh Necho. King Solomon's stables were excavated at this site.

MEGILLAH (SCROLL)

Today this refers usually to the Book of Esther. Megillah was the name for any book handwritten on parchment or animal skin. Later a large book was called "Sefer" as (Sefer Torah), and a small one "Megillah." The Sefer scroll was held on two rolls, while the Megillah was held on just one roll and could be spread out like a letter. Though five Books of the Bible are

each called *Megillah*: the Song of Songs, Ruth, Lamentation (*Echah*), Ecclesiastes (*Kohelet*), and Esther, it is Esther that is generally known as *the Megillah.* The Megillah, the story of Queen Esther, is read in the synagogue on the joyous festival of Purim. Whenever the name of the wicked Haman (from whose vicious plot Queen Esther saved her people, the Jews of Persia) is read, the children boo. The Megillah used in the synagogue is as plain as the Torah scroll; but for home use there are also illustrated editions. Some medieval Megillot have beautiful illuminations; others have engravings and woodcuts. Some are kept in beautiful cases of carved wood, tooled silver or fine filigree work. Purim is a joyful festival and Jews have derived joy from the Megillah for many centuries.

MEGILLOT, THE FIVE

(The Scrolls) five of the Books of the last division (*Ketubim*) of the Bible. The Five *Megillot* are Song of Songs, Ruth, Lamentations, Ecclesiastes and Esther.

MEIR

Rabbi, great Tannaitic scholar and teacher of the 2nd century C.E., brilliant contributor to the Mishnah, disciple of Rabbi Akiba. Meir developed a distinctive manner of logical argument and a beautiful and concise style. Some popular sayings of Rabbi Meir are included in Ethics of the Fathers (*Pirke Avot*). Meir's wife was Beruriah, the scholarly daughter of Rabbi Haninah ben Tradyon.

MEIR, GOLDA

(1898-)—Prime Minister of Israel. Born in Kiev, Golda Meir emigrated to the United States in 1906 and settled in Palestine in 1921. Active in the labor

Golda Meir, fourth Premier of Israel.

movement and in politics almost from the moment of her arrival, she became executive secretary of the Working Women's Council in 1928 and in 1934 joined the executive committee of the Histadrut, eventually becoming the head of its Political Department. In 1946 she also served as acting head of the Jewish Agency's Political Department when Moshe Sharrett was arrested by the British. Following the establishment of the State of Israel, Meir became the new nation's ambassador to Russia. On her return to Israel in 1949 she was elected to the Knesset, retaining her seat until her retirement in 1974. She served as labor minister from 1949 to 1956, was Israel's foreign minister from 1956 to 1965, and then became secretary general of Mapai and later of the Israel Labor Party. In 1969 Golda Meir succeeded Levi Eshkol as Israel's Prime Minister. A very popular figure both in Israel and among world Jewry, Meir worked hard to strengthen Israel's friendly relations with the United States, and displayed great courage and energy in leading her country during the extremely difficult period of the Yom Kippur War. Since her retirement she has devoted herself to writing her memoirs.

MELAVEH MALKAH

Means "escort of the queen" (on her departure) and is the name for the fourth meal and festive gayety at the end of Sabbath. Just as the Sabbath begins with "receiving the queen," so it has become the custom to bid farewell to the holy day with a special ceremony. The Talmud refers to a fourth ceremonial meal in addition to the three eaten on the Sabbath day. Though the laws of the Sabbath were not observed after nightfall and the Havdalah prayer, many rabbis considered the day not really ended until after the fourth meal was taken. This custom was to symbolize how the Jew wished to hold on beyond the allotted time to his beloved Queen, the Sabbath. This after-dark meal is also called King David's feast, because it is told that David had been warned he would die at the conclusion of a Sabbath, and that he celebrated and rejoiced at the end of each Sabbath he survived. In Eastern Europe, particularly among the Hasidim, it was the custom to feast and sing at the Melaveh Malkah. The custom is still observed in many places today.

MEM

The thirteenth letter of the Hebrew alphabet, has the numerical value of 40.

See also Aleph Bet

MENAHEM

One of the last kings of the Kingdom of Israel (about 741-737 B.C.E.). He assassinated and succeeded Shallum. Menahem cruelly taxed the people to collect a large tribute for Assyria and contributed to Israel's eventual annexation by Assyria. The prophet Hosea depicted the times of Menahem.

MENDELE MOCHER SEFORIM

("Mendele the Book-Seller".) The pseudonym of Shalom Jacob Abramowitz (1836-1917), the "grandfather" of modern Hebrew and Yiddish literature. He was born and educated in Lithuania. His extensive travels through Russian Poland and nearby parts gave him an excellent knowledge of the life and literature of his people. For some time he earned his livelihood by teaching in a Hebrew School, always gathering more knowledge of men and books. He learned German, and from reading natural science in that language was able to describe the latest discoveries in classical Hebrew.

Sholem Yaakov Abramovich.

Fame came to him with publication of his first novel, and its translation into Russian. After this he ceased using Hebrew and devoted himself to Yiddish, even though many considered it a non-literary language. His Yiddish books give a realistic and sympathetic picture of the humor and tragedy of Jewish life in Eastern Europe. As a result of his writings, Yiddish was enriched and became a respected member in the family of languages. In his very late years he reverted to Hebrew.

MENDELSSOHN, MOSES

(1729-1786)—Perhaps the first Jew of modern times whose interests embraced both Judaism and modern culture and whose achievements in both fields were recognized by the non-Jewish world. He was born in Dessau, Germany, where he received a traditional Jewish education. When he went to Berlin he studied literature and philosophy. His books on philosophy and art, written during the early part of his life, brought him international renown. He became the most important literary figure in Germany, as he advocated the ideas of enlightenment. In 1763 the government granted him the privileged status of a "protected" Jew and the Jewish Berlin community honored him by exempting him from all Jewish taxes. After Mendelssohn felt compelled to explain publicly that his philosophic beliefs were not in contradiction to his religious faith, he became more active in behalf of Jews. He translated the Bible into German. He opened one of the first Jewish day schools. He encouraged Jews to study Hebrew. He used his reputation to fight for Jewish rights wherever they were threatened. Felix Mendelssohn, the composer, was his grandson.

MENDOZA, DANIEL

(1764-1836)—Born in London, Mendoza was a faithful Jew and one of the great champions of the ring. He was known as the "Star of Israel," and is considered by many as the father of modern boxing, for it was he who taught English fighters to substitute precise sparring, quick footwork, quick thinking and other defensive tactics for the heavy slugging then the vogue. His style of fighting and the victories he won aroused a new interest in pugilism throughout the British Isles. Mendoza was only five-foot-seven, but had powerful muscles and a huge chest expansion. He won all his battles until he tangled with one John Jackson in 1795. Jackson was too big for him. In addition to this, he resorted to such tactics as grabbing Mendoza's long hair and pummeling him at will. Mendoza's last fight took place when he was fifty-seven; he was beaten by a fighter who was fifty-one. After this he engaged in tours and exhibits, designed to demonstrate that men could defend themselves with their fists instead of relying on murderous weapons.

MENE TEKEL

(*Mene, Mene, Tekel Upharsin*) handwriting that appeared on the wall at King Belshazzar's feast. Daniel interpreted these words to mean that God had judged the king and found him wanting, and that the overthrow of the Babylonian Kingdom by the Medes and Persians was approaching. Belshazzar was slain that night, and soon the Persians took Babylonia.

See also Daniel.

MENORAH

The seven-branched golden candelabrum of the Tabernacle was called *Menorah*. In the Temple of Solomon there were ten golden and some silver menorahs. Each of these had a central shaft and bowl, with three more at each side; olive oil and wicks provided the illumination. A representation of the original Temple menorah is to be seen on the Arch of Titus in Rome. To celebrate Hanukkah, an eight-branched menorah was devised. This generally consisted of four lamps on each side of the upright shaft, from which projected another lamp for the *Shamash*. There are many kinds of Hanukkah Menorahs, many of which are highly decorative. Today a great variety are manu-

The giant Menorah which stands in front of the Knesset in Jerusalem. It was a gift from the people of England to the State of Israel.

factured, ranging from the simple tin containers to silver and chromium candelabra for home use, which are almost as large as the synagogue Menorahs.

MENUHIN, YEHUDI

(1916-   )—American violin virtuoso. Menuhin was a brilliant child prodigy, making his concert debut at the age of 8. After these early successes, he studied under Adolph Busch and Georges Enesco. Despite the lure of public acclaim, he devoted the years 1936-7 solely to study. This period added mature artistry to the brilliance of Menuhin, and he has been considered one of the world's leading violinists since then.

MESHA INSCRIPTION

Stone on which King Mesha of Moab (2 Kings 3:4f.) recorded his victory against Israel. It was discovered in 1868 at Diban, the capital of the Moabite kingdom, and is now in the Louvre Museum, Paris.

MESOPOTAMIA

See Iraq.

MESSIAH

The word Messiah comes from the Hebrew *mashiach* ("anointed") and was applied in the Bible to persons who reached high office and were anointed with oil. Today the word refers to a kingly personage who will arise to lead the world to eternal peace and establish the kingdom of God on earth. The coming of a redeeming king is not mentioned in the Bible. Yet leaders appearing to possess the qualities of the idealized King David were always greeted as such. Some years before the present era, Jews began to believe that a personal Messiah would come to rescue them from the many hardships they were suffering. The idea developed that he would be a military as well as spiritual leader. In Talmudic times many miraculous abilities were ascribed to the Messiah. Maimonides, however, asserted that he would be an ordinary human being, but so much wiser than the rest that he would be able to impress upon them the word of God. Many false Messiahs were accepted by suffering Jews during the Middle Ages. Subsequently, this mistaken acceptance caused so much misfortune and disappointment that rabbinical leaders have discouraged speculation about the exact time of the Messiah's appearance.

MESSIAHS, FALSE

Pseudo-Messiahs and false prophets were numerous from the period of the Crusades, among them David Reubeni and Solomon Molcho, who appeared in 1524.

Shabbetai Zevi.

The most famous of these pretenders was Shabbetai Zevi, who announced himself as Messiah in 1648. Since the 18th century only occasional false Messiahs have arisen, the last famous one being Jacob Frank.

MEXICO

Marranos arrived in Mexico at the beginning of the 16th century; the Inquisition followed them, and in 1528 two Jews were burned publicly. The Marranos were absorbed into the native population, and the present Jewish community consists of Mexican Indian Jews and of European immigrants. The majority of Mexico's Jews are engaged in trade and industry. There are many cultural institutions and a large percentage of the children receive a Jewish education.

MEZUZAH

Part of the *Shema* consists of these words from Deuteronomy: "And thou shalt write them upon the doorposts of thy house and upon thy gates." What then should be written upon every doorpost (*mezuzah*)? Declarations of God's love and man's devotion to Him; and man's responsibility for observance of the divine commandments, with resulting reward or punishment. Therefore a parchment with the Biblical verses expressing these thoughts is placed in a small elongated box of metal, wood or plastic and the box is attached to the right (entering) doorpost. It, too, is called

An artistic mezzuzah holder.

Mezuzah, after its location. Except for storerooms, schools and places of worship, it has been the custom to set *Mezuzot* on the doorposts of every inhabited room. Many pious Jews touch the *Mezuzah* on entering or leaving the house and then kiss their fingers. Not only can the *Mezuzah* on the door help strengthen Jewish faith and loyalty, but it can inform the wayfarer that a Jewish family lives within.

MICAH

Sixth of the Books of Twelve (Minor) Prophets of the Bible. Micah, a humble peasant from Gath, prophesied in Judah at the time of Isaiah. He cried out against injustice and dishonesty. "What doth the Lord require of thee," said Micah, "save to do justice, and to love mercy, and to walk humbly with thy God?" Micah, like Isaiah, envisioned a future time when war would cease and all men would be at peace.

MICHAEL

Angel and messenger of God, patron angel of Israel.

MICHAL

Daughter of King Saul, one of the wives of David. Michal helped David escape when Saul pursued him.

MICHELANGELO (BUONARROTTI)

(1475-1564)—The most famous of the great Florentine artists of the Renaissance. Many of his works, such as the marble statues of David and of Moses deal with Biblical subjects. His grandest pictorial work, the frescoes on the ceiling of the Sistine Chapel in Rome, deals with Biblical topics as well.

MICHELSON, ALBERT ABRAHAM

One of history's most distinguished scientists, Michelson was born in Germany in 1852. When he was three years old his parents moved to California and later to Nevada. When he was not yet sixteen he applied for admission to the Naval Academy at Annapolis. Another boy was given the appointment; but President Ulysses S. Grant, despite the fact that he had already named his permitted ten midshipmen-at-large, gave Michelson an eleventh appointment. He was a brilliant student and for several years after he was commissioned he taught physics and chemistry at the Academy. He went abroad to continue his studies and when he returned he became professor at Case School of Applied Science and at Clark University, later becoming head of the department of physics at the University of Chicago. In 1918, when World War I broke out, Michelson returned to the Navy, with the rank of lieutenant commander. The first important paper by the young scientist appeared in 1878, entitled "On a Method of Measuring the Velocity of Light." He calculated the speed of light with greater accuracy than had ever been attained before. Scores of papers followed, adding immensely to the world's scientific knowledge. Michelson invented the interferometer, which measures the wave length of light, a navy rangefinder and a method for computing the diameter of a star. His experiments helped provide a basis for Albert Einstein's theories. In 1907, he was awarded the Nobel Prize. He died in 1931, renowned as one of America's greatest physicists.

MIDIAN

1. Land of the Midianites (and Kenites) in the Sinai Desert. Moses, after slaying the Egyptian taskmaster, fled to Midian where he found refuge with Jethro.

2. Son of Abraham and Keturah, ancestor of the Midianites.

MIDRASH

(From the Hebrew root *darash*, "to seek out.") A way of analyzing the text of the Bible that developed early in Jewish history. Its purpose is to search for the deep, inner truth of the Bible. When it is employed to clarify a law, it is called Midrash Halachah. When it interprets the ethical and spiritual significance of the text, with illustrative anecdotes, it is called Midrash Aggadah. Since the Bible was the only guide in Jewish life, new meanings and teachings had to be derived from it when necessary. In the Midrash, Jewish preachers have for many centuries found support for their religious messages. There are several collections of *Midrashim* to the Books of the Bible. The most important is the *Midrash Rabbah* (Great Midrash), which covers the Torah and the Five Scrolls (Song of Songs, Ruth, Lamentations, Ecclesiastes, Esther). Together with other compilations these writings have instructed and comforted generations of listeners and readers. There are also some minor collections. *Midrash Galut* depicts the ten exiles suffered by the Jews. Hundreds of small books of *Midrashim* exist, and these have been assembled by modern scholars. Almost every important incident in the Bible has this kind of commentary.

MIDRASH AGGADAH

This type of Midrash has for its aim the preaching of religion and morals, and uses the Biblical text very freely. Important events in sacred history, such as the birth of Moses, the departure from Egypt and the giving of the Torah, become the center of detailed explanations in the Midrash. Many of these Midrashim were public sermons, which were later collected and edited. The Midrash not only taught and admonished, it also comforted the people and promised the nation a glorious future. The Midrashim were produced in Palestine and Babylonia at the time when the two Talmuds also were created there, though some were written at a later date.

MIDRASH HALACHAH

A technique of reading the Bible which aimed at deducing *halachot* (laws) from the words of the Scripture. The principles of this technique were enunciated by Hillel and R. Ishmael, to which was opposed the school of R. Akiba, who favored a more liberal interpretation of the text.

MIDRASH RABBAH

A collection of Midrashim on the five Books of the Pentateuch and the five *Megillot*. The most popular and oldest of these Midrashim is *Bereshit Rabbah*, which deals with the book of Genesis.

MIDRASH TANHUMA

This Midrash, which deals with the Pentateuch, derives its name from R. Tanhuma (4th century). Each section often commences with the words "Yelamdenu Rabbenu"—"May our Rabbi teach us," and the Midrash is sometimes referred to as "Midrash Yelamdenu." The work has always been very popular and seems to have been revised many times. In its entirety it does not seem to be older than the time of the Geonim (9th century).

MIGRATIONS

Beginning with Abraham, who commanded by God to leave the land of his birth and journey to the land the

Lord would show him, the Jewish people has been involved in an unbroken series of migrations. These unending migrations have created the legend of the Wandering Jew. Jews have migrated from the lands where they were born for a variety of reasons. In many cases they were driven into exile (for example, from Palestine to Babylonia, Rome, etc.); in other cases, they were expelled (from England, France, Germany). Jews have also migrated to improve their economic and social status (the Jews from Eastern Europe who came to the United States during the period of 1830 to 1933). The Jews themselves are commanded to treat aliens as their own, and to remember that they themselves were once strangers in Egypt. Wherever Jews have lived in peace, they have maintained institutions to care for their brethren in search of a home.

MILCHIG

Milk and foods such as cheese and butter derived from milk, which, traditionally, cannot be eaten together with *fleishig* (meat).

See also Dietary Laws; Kosher

MILSTEIN, NATHAN

(1904-   )—American violinist. Milstein was born in Russia, and received his musical training there. By the year of his arrival in the United States, 1928, he was already a concert violinist. Since then, his reputation has grown steadily.

MINHAG

(Heb., "custom") — Local customs often acquire, through long usage, a binding character. The Talmud itself recognized some such customs, and a large number of such customs were collected by Moses Isserles and inserted by him in the *Shulchan Aruch*. Many new *Minhagim* were adopted by Isaac Luria and later by the Hasidim.

MINHAH

The Afternoon Service, the third (in the Jewish calendar, the day begins after sunset) of the three daily services. The Minhah prayers are recited in the afternoon up to sunset.

MINYAN

In the Bible it is understood that where the word *edah*, a congregation, is mentioned, it means not fewer than ten men. Hence Jews cannot conduct a public service and recite special benedictions such as the Kaddish unless ten Jews over bar mitzvah age take part. Where there are but nine persons of that age, a minor may be employed as the tenth. The Talmud declares that any locality which has ten men always available for required religious services, is to be considered truly a great city. These men were particularly needed on weekdays when so many persons were working; on the Sabbath there was rarely any difficulty in obtaining them.

MIRIAM

Sister of Moses and Aaron, prophetess. She watched over the baby Moses in the bulrushes of the Nile and arranged for Pharaoh's daughter, who found the baby, to employ Jochebed, Moses' mother, as his nurse. Miriam led the Hebrew women in grateful singing and dancing after the crossing of the Red Sea.

MISHNAH

About the year 200 C.E., Judah Hanasi, also known simply as "Rabbi," and his colleagues collected and organized the vast material of oral traditions and laws that had been passed on and developed throughout many generations of rabbis and scholars. This was the "oral" Torah, an elaboration and addition to the major laws of the "written" Torah, the Bible. As new situations arose in different periods of Jewish history, it became necessary to clarify the Torah. The laws and discussions which resulted from these clarifications became known as Mishnah, which means "second reading," or "to study by means of repetition." Before Judah Hanasi's work, many separate Mishnot existed, one of the most famous being Rabbi Akiba's Mishnah. Judah Hanasi's brilliant arrangement became the final collection of the oral laws and traditions and provided the accepted standard. Some changes were made in the Mishnah by later generations but it is essentially the same now as it was at the time of the great Rabbi. Its language is somewhat different from the earlier Biblical Hebrew and it contains many Greek, Latin and Aramaic words. The Mishnah is divided into six divisions, termed "orders" *(sedarim)*. Many commentaries have been written on the Mishnah, the most famous of which is that by the great scholar and philosopher Maimonides.

See also Sedarim; Talmud.

MISHNEH TORAH

1. ("Repetition of the Law") early Hebrew name for Deuteronomy.
2. Name of Maimonides' great code of Talmudic laws, systematically arranged and codified, also known as *Yad Hachazakah.*

See also Maimonides.

MITZRAIM

1. Hebrew name for Egypt.
2. Noah's grandson, ancestor of the Hamitic peoples.

See also Egypt.

MITZVAH

The word used for a meritorious deed, whether in connection with ritual or moral conduct. It is derived from a Hebrew word meaning, among other things, "command." Hence it is often defined as a "divine commandment" or "divine precept." Since the word also signifies "join together," a mitzvah is a bond between God and Man. When the sages counted up all the mitzvot in the Torah, they amounted to 365 negative commands ("Thou shalt *not*") corresponding to the number of days in a year, and 248 positive precepts ("Thou shalt") corresponding to the number of parts in the body. Later a division was made between mitzvot laid down in the Torah and those enacted later by the rabbis. No one was to gain profit of any kind through observance of a mitzvah, which was designed only to improve man's moral character and nothing else. As stated in Proverbs: "In all thy ways acknowledge Him, and He will direct thy paths."

MIZRACH

1. (East) the east wall of the synagogue. The congregation usually faces east, as a symbol of its hopes for the restoration of the Temple on Mount Zion in Jerusalem.

2. A drawing on parchment or paper, or a tapestry, hung on the east wall of a room.

A mizrach.

MIZRACHI

A Zionist organization of religious Jews dedicated to the building of Israel as a state in harmony with the Torah and to the strengthening of traditional Judaism throughout the world. It was founded in Vilna in 1902. Among the well-known rabbinical founders were Reines, Mohilever and Berlin (Bar-Ilan). The organization spread throughout Europe but was particularly strong in Poland. The American branch was established in 1911. Both in Israel and the world at large Mizrachi endeavors to strengthen traditional Judaism, both in education and observance. Though it has its own publications, schools and institutions, it has always cooperated with other Zionist groups. The world office of the movement is in Jerusalem. Mizrachi merged recently with its labor affiliate, *Hapoel Hamizrachi*. The American organization is known as the Religious Zionists of America.

MOAB

Ancient kingdom of the Moabites, east of the Jordan and the Dead Sea, opposite Jericho. There were alternate periods of peace and warfare between Israel and Moab. Ruth, David's ancestor, was a Moabite. Moab was destroyed by Assyria.

MODIN

Village in the Judean hills, home of the Hasmonean priest Mattathias and his sons, the Maccabees. The Maccabean revolt started in Modin.

MOHEL

One who performs the ceremony of circumcision. The person performing this function must be qualified both by piety and training.

See also B'rit Milah; Covenant.

MONASH, JOHN

(1865-1931)—Australia's most honored soldier, Monash was a nephew of the famed historian, Heinrich

Sir John Monash.

Graetz. The first Jew to attain rank of general in the British imperial armies, he commanded Australian forces in World War I and had the war continued would have been put in command of all British forces.

Sir John (he was knighted) was born in Melbourne, where he received college, law and civil engineering degrees. In 1912, when the Australian army was re-organized, he was made a colonel. He served with distinction at Gallipoli as a brigadier. Then he proceeded to France as a major general, commanding a division. Soon he was heading all his country's expeditionary troops as a lieutenant general. It was told of Monash that as a commander he never committed a tactical error. On "Anzac Day" in 1919 he was wildly cheered by the London crowds before returning to his home and his engineering projects. In 1928 he accepted the office of president of the Australian Zionist Federation. And in 1929 a grateful government elevated him to the rank of full general.

MOND FAMILY

(1839-1909)—Ludwig Mond, a chemist, came to England in 1862 from Germany. By 1873 he had established (together with J. T. Brunner) what was to become the largest alkali factory in the world. Mond made many discoveries of great scientific and commercial value, and founded the Davy-Faraday Research Laboratory of the Royal Institution. In addition to these scientific activities, he was a noted art collector. His son, Alfred Mond (1868-1930), made Lord Melchett in 1928, was a noted industrialist, scientist, and Zionist leader. Entering his father's chemical firm, he rose to be its head. In his industrial undertakings he put into practice his ideas of employer-laborer cooperation, ultimately founding the Empire Economic Union. After the First World War Mond became active in Zionist affairs, donating large sums of money and personally serving the cause as joint chairman of the Jewish Agency.

MONTAGU FAMILY

Samuel Montagu (1832-1911), the first Lord Swaythling, was a British banker, economist, and politician, and a Jewish communal leader. He was often consulted by the British government on matters of finance, and was a Liberal member of Parliament for many years. Montagu was a warm supporter of Orthodox Judaism. His son, Edwin Samuel Montagu (1879-1924), entered the British cabinet in 1914 and was appointed, a few years later, Minister of Munitions. As Secretary of State for India from 1917 to 1922 he laid the foundations of Indian self-government and gained for himself a reputation for great statesmanship. His sister, Lilian Helen Montagu (1873-1963), was a founder of Liberal Judaism in England and of the World Union for Progressive Judaism. Ewen Edward Montagu (1901-   ) served in British naval intelligence during World War II and wrote a best-selling book about his espionage activities, *The Man Who Never Was*.

MONTEFIORE, CLAUDE

(1858-1938)—English scholar and theologian. The great-nephew of Sir Moses Montefiore, Claude Montefiore wrote extensively on rabbinical Judaism and early Christianity. He founded an important scholarly journal, the *Jewish Quarterly Review*, and was also one of the founders of Liberal (Reform) Judaism in England. Montefiore was especially noted for his favorable view of Jesus as a teacher whose views and aspirations were within the mainstream of the Judaism of his time.

MONTEFIORE, MOSES

(1784-1885)—A remarkably generous Jewish philanthropist. Sir Moses was born in Italy but came early to London. One of twelve Jewish brokers on the London Exchange, he retired in 1821 to carry on his charitable activities. In 1837 he was elected sheriff of London and knighted by Queen Victoria. Then in 1846 he was made a baronet. He held other high offices, long serving his people as president of the Board of Deputies of British Jews. Always a completely loyal and observant Jew, Montefiore made seven trips to Palestine. He advocated return of the Jews to farming there and established institutions of charity. When in 1840 Jews were imprisoned in Damascus on the common false charge that they had used human blood for religious purposes, he obtained a retraction from the Mohammedan ruler and then a statement from the Pope denying the accusation against the Jews. Montefiore interceded in many other cases where Jews or Judaism were falsely assailed. An impressive royal celebration marked his hundredth birthday.

Sir Moses Montefiore.

MONTH

(*Hodesh*) in the Jewish calendar a month consists of 29 or 30 days, the period of time between one new moon and the next.

See also Rosh Hodesh.

MONTHS, JEWISH

The Jewish year begins with Rosh Hashanah on the first of Tishri, which is the seventh month. There are 12 months in the Jewish calendar: Nisan, Iyar, Sivan, Tammuz, Av, Elul, Tishri, Heshvan, Kislev, Tevet, Shevat, Adar. In leap years a 13th month is added: Adar Sheni or Veadar.

See also Calendar, Jewish.

MORAIS, SABATO

(1823-1897)—American rabbi. Born and educated in Italy, Morais came to the United States in 1851. He succeeded Isaac Leeser as spiritual leader of Congregation Mikveh Israel in Philadelphia. A staunch exponent of traditionalism, Morais was disturbed by the widespread religious indifference of most American Jews and by the rapid growth of the Reform movement. Eager to counteract both these trends, he played a major role in founding the Jewish Theological Seminary (1886), serving as its first president until his death. He is thus regarded as one of the key figures in the early history of Conservative Judaism.

MORDECAI

Guardian and cousin of Queen Esther. He once saved King Ahasuerus from assassination. He influenced Esther to save the Jews of Persia from Haman's plot against the Jews. After Haman was hanged, Mordecai became second in command to the king.

MORGENTHAU FAMILY

Henry Morgenthau (1856-1946) was born in Germany, and came to America as a child. In this country he studied law, ultimately becoming a diplomat in the service of the United States. Morgenthau was ambassador to Turkey (1913-16), commissioner to Poland to investigate the persecution of Jews there (1919), and chairman of the Greek Refugee Settlement Commission of the League of Nations (1923), as well as one of the organizers of the International Red Cross. His son, Henry Morgenthau, Jr. (1891-1967), served as Secretary of the Treasury under President Franklin D. Roosevelt from 1934 to 1945. In this post he was an important shaper of New Deal policies and later kept the country financially healthy during World War II. Morgenthau always energetically promoted Jewish causes also, and was a leading figure in both the United Jewish Appeal and the Israel Bond Drive. His son, Robert Morris Morgenthau (1919-   ), served as U.S. attorney in New York and ran as Democratic candidate for the governorship of New York State in 1962.

MORIAH, MOUNT

The mountain where God tested Abraham by commanding him to sacrifice his son Isaac. In David's time, Mount Moriah was called Mount Zion. Later Mount Zion was also called Temple Mount *(Har Habayit)*, because the Temple of Jerusalem stood there.

MOSES

The great leader and lawgiver of Israel, the man of God who freed the people from Egyptian bondage and led them through the wilderness to Mount Sinai, where he was given the Ten Commandments. His life

Moses bringing down the Decalogue. From the Sarajevo Haggadah.

story is one of the most dramatic in the Bible. When he was a baby he was set adrift on the Nile by his mother to escape Pharaoh's edict that all Hebrew male children were to be slain. The daughter of Pharaoh found him and raised him at the royal court. Nonetheless he identified himself with his ill-treated brethren and on one occasion slew an Egyptian overseer who had brutally attacked an Israelite. Moses was forced to flee Egypt and he found refuge with Jethro, a priest in Midian. Eventually he returned to Egypt with his brother Aaron and, acting as the instrument of God, called down the ten plagues which finally forced Pharaoh to release the Hebrews from bondage. He led his people through the desert to Mount Sinai, then on to the Promised Land, which Moses saw from Mount Nebo before his death. Under Moses the religion of Israel differed from all other faiths of the time; it was a covenant between the people and God. The tribes of the Israelites could not have grown into one nation without the influence of the great laws brought down from Mount Sinai and the power of a God-inspired leader such as Moses.

MULLER, DAVID HEINRICH VON

(1846-1912)—Orientalist. Muller was professor of oriental languages at Vienna University, and also taught at the Vienna Rabbinical Seminary. He visited South Arabia on an archaeological expedition and wrote much on archaeology and Semitic languages, especially those of South Arabia.

MUNI, PAUL

(1895-1967)—American actor. Born Muni Wiesen-freund, he first appeared on the Yiddish stage. After his success there, Muni became a noted Broadway and motion picture star. Though often a portrayer of criminal characters, as in *Scarface*, he also appeared in the title roles in *The Story of Louis Pasteur* and *Emile Zola*. Other extremely popular Muni films are *I Am a Fugitive from a Chain Gang, Juarez,* and *The Last Angry Man*. His last Broadway appearance was in *Inherit the Wind*.

MUNK, SALOMON

(1803-1867)—Orientalist. After studying in Berlin, he settled in Paris in 1828, and after ten years was appointed to the oriental department of the *Bibliotheque Royale* (Royal Library). From then on, he devoted himself to Judaeo-Arabic literature of the Middle Ages, writing much on Biblical and general Semitic studies as well. Munk's greatest achievement was his identification of Solomon Ibn Gabirol as author of the *Fons Vitae* (Fountain of Life). In his later years he was appointed professor of Hebrew at the College de France.

MUSAF

(Additional Service) a collection of prayers recited after the Morning Prayer *(Shaharit)* and the reading of the Torah. Musaf is said on Rosh Hodesh, Sabbaths and on holidays.

MUSAR MOVEMENT

See Ethics.

MUSEUMS, JEWISH

The first collection devoted specifically to Judaica was that of M. Strauss, who exhibited it in 1878 in Paris. The pioneer Jewish museum was established in 1897 in Vienna. The Jewish Museum in New York was organized in 1947 on the basis of the collection of the Jewish Theological Seminary; it is housed in the former Warburg family mansion on Fifth Avenue. Other important museums include the Bezalel National Museum in Jerusalem, the Tel Aviv Museum (housed in the home of Meir Dizengoff), and the Mocatta Museum and Library in London.

MUSICAL INSTRUMENTS OF BIBLE

Musical instruments are mentioned in the Bible in more than a hundred passages, but it is often difficult to identify them accurately because of the lack of contemporary Jewish paintings or drawings. Probably the most familiar instrument is the *Shofar*, which is made from a ram's horn and is still sounded at the New Year and at the close of the Day of Atonement.

See also Shofar.

NABATEANS

Arab tribe which settled in the region of Edom (Southeast Israel) in the 6th century B.C.E. As they controlled the road from Elath to Gaza they grew quite powerful, and once stretched their rule as far north as Damascus. Though living in a desert, they were able to develop methods of water conservation and agriculture which are being studied in Israel today. The Israelis hope to learn from the experience of the Nabateans in farming the desert.

NABLUS

The modern successor of the Canaanite Shechem. It is situated between Mount Gerizim and Mount Ebal and is the Holy City of the Samaritans. The present town is in Jordanian territory and has always been strongly anti-Jewish. According to Jewish tradition, Shechem contains the tomb of Joseph and a well dug by Jacob. The present population of Nablus is about 30,000.

NABOTH

The owner of a vineyard which King Ahab desired. Queen Jezebel enabled Ahab to secure the vineyard by falsely accusing Naboth of blasphemy and having him stoned to death. The prophet Elijah rebuked Ahab for this cruel injustice.

NACHMANIDES

(1194-1270)—Nachmanides is Rabbi Moses ben Nachman of Gerundi, who was born in Spain but settled and died in Palestine. Like many other Jews of his time he was both Judaic scholar and physician. He wrote on rabbinical law and literature but his commentary on the Books of Moses is his outstanding work. Nachmanides was skilled in refuting the arguments of renegade Jews who attempted to force the conversion of other Jews to Christianity. In 1263 King James of Aragon commanded him to argue in public against a convert from Judaism who called himself Pablo Christiani. This was a difficult situation, for the Jewish disputant had to hold his own without saying

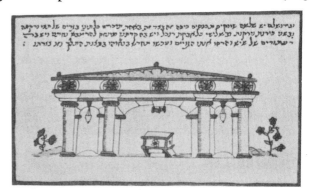

Nahmanides' synagogue in Jerusalem. From the *Casale Pilgrim,* a sixteenth century guide to the holy places of Palestine.

anything that could be considered an insult to Christians and their beliefs. But Nachmanides spoke so calmly and capably that he overcame his opponent. However, the monks involved were not satisfied; despite the king's refusal to accept their findings, the rabbi was found guilty of blasphemy and sentenced to banishment. After wandering through Europe he made his home in Palestine in 1267 whither many disciples flocked to him. He continued his prose and poetic writings and labored mightily in behalf of the Jewish community.

NADAB

1. Oldest son of Aaron; one of Israel's first priests.
2. Second king of the northern Kingdom of Israel (about 915-914 B.C.E.), son of Jeroboam. He warred against the Philistines. Nadab was assassinated by Baasha, who succeeded him.

NAHUM

Seventh of the Books of the Twelve (Minor) Prophets of the Bible. Nahum prophesied the fall of the mighty Assyrians and the destruction of Nineveh, the great Assyrian capital.

NAOMI

Israelite mother-in-law of Ruth the Moabite; ancestor of King David. The Book of Ruth tells how Naomi, after the death of her husband and sons, returned to Bethlehem, followed by the faithful Ruth.

See also Ruth.

NAPHTALI

Sixth son of Jacob, second son of Bilhah, ancestor of the tribe of Naphtali.

NAPOLEON

Napoleon Bonaparte had many contacts with Jews. In 1798, when embarking on his expedition to Egypt against the Turks, he proclaimed his intent to restore the Jewish kingdom. He also encouraged the enlistment of Jews in the French army of Egypt. He acknowledged that Jews in France were living in humiliating circumstances and sought to help them. In 1806, Napoleon called together the Assembly of Notables in Paris for those who "professed the Jewish faith and dwelt upon French territory." Napoleon aimed to revive the supreme Jewish court, the Sanhedrin. He also attempted to analyze the Jewish faith but without much success. His letters contained some odd proposals. Jews were to stop being polygamous (they had ceased taking more than one wife centuries before); they were to undertake useful occupations and own their own homes (which they had always done whenever governments permitted); and they must abstain from usury (a practice of very few Jews and indulged in to a far greater extent by

Medal struck in commemoration of the Sanhedrin convened by Napoleon, 1807.

non-Jews). Furthermore, every third Jew was to marry a Christian, to insure assimilation. Despite decrees of this strange character, Napoleon was hailed as a liberator by the Jews, for other emancipating decrees and for improving the status of other European Jews.

NASI

("Prince, eminence"—referred to by the Romans as "patriarch") originally the head of the Great Sanhedrin. From the time of the destruction of the Temple until the 5th century, the Nasi, who was always a great Palestinian scholar, was the recognized spiritual leader of all Jews, the spokesman of the Jewish community of the land of Israel and head of its highest court. This system of leadership is often referred to as the Patriarchate. The title Nasi was inherited by the scholarly descendants of Hillel.

See also Zugot.

NASSER, GAMAL ABDEL

(1918-   )—President of the United Arab Republic. Nasser was an Egyptian officer in the Israel War of Independence of 1948. In 1954 he became Premier of Egypt, and a leader in the movement to unify the Arab world, culminating in the merger of Egypt and Syria into the United Arab Republic. In 1961 Syria seceded from the U.A.R. and declared its independence. Nasser, who rules his land as a virtual dictator, is an outspoken opponent of the State of Israel.

NATHAN

Prophet, advisor to King David and King Solomon. Nathan helped plan the building of the Temple. He anointed King Solomon.

NAZIRITE

Related to the Hebrew root (*nadar*) meaning "to vow." "Nazirite" refers to a Jew who vowed never to drink anything alcoholic, cut his hair, touch or lay his hand on a corpse. The Talmud decrees that the vow of a Nazirite must be limited in time; no one was to be allowed to restrict himself for too long a period. If anyone accidentally violated this vow, he would have to shave his head, offer a sacrifice and begin his Nazirite period again. Ancient peoples used to think a man's strength was in his hair (as in the story of Samson). Sometimes an entire group of people would become Nazirites, and upon occasion a man would undertake only one part of the vow. For example, Absalom, whose refusal to cut his hair brought about his death. The institution of the Nazirite continued throughout the Talmudic period but finally died out. Many rabbis disapproved of this form of self-discipline.

NEBO, MOUNT

A mountain in Moab. From its heights, the aging leader and prophet of Israel, Moses, saw the Promised Land of Israel before he died.

NEBUCHADNEZZAR (II)

Also spelled Nebuchadrezzar, King of Babylonia (about 604-561 B.C.E.), destroyed the First Temple and Jerusalem. He conquered Judah and led its people into captivity to Babylonia.

A tablet from the period of Nebuchadnezzar which dates and mentions the fall and sack of Jerusalem.

NEGEV

Southern part of Israel, stretching from Beersheba in the north to Elath at the country's southern tip. The Negev was settled in the earliest times; by the time of Abraham, Isaac, and Jacob, a caravan route linked the Negev and Egypt. Solomon mined the Negev's copper, just as modern Israel does today. Around the beginning of the Common Era the area was settled by the Nabateans, who discovered how to farm the Negev successfully by conserving the available water and using it for irrigation. Jews began resettling the Negev in modern times, and after the Egyptian army was driven out of the area in the War of Independence, it experienced considerable development. Many kibbutzim have been established, and the mining industry is active. The population of the Negev, which covers nearly 5,000 square miles, or 60% of the total area of the State of Israel, is 62,000. The region produces cotton, peanuts, almonds, citrus fruits, and sisal, as well as copper from the mines at Timna, natural gas from the fields at Zohar, and phosphates,

as well as some other minerals. The most important towns of the Negev are Dimona (the site of Israel's main atomic reactor), Arad, Mitzpe Ramon, the port city and tourism center of Elath, and Beersheba, known as the "capital" of the Negev, which has grown phenomenally since the birth of the State.

NEHARDEA

Oldest of the three most famous Babylonian academies, founded in the 2nd century C.E. It contributed greatly to the Babylonian Talmud.

NEHEMIAH

The leader who joined Ezra in governing Judea and in saving the Jewish community there about 445 B.C.E. He tells his story in the Biblical book named after him. Nehemiah, cupbearer to Artaxerxes I of Persia, received permission to go to Jerusalem to repair its walls, damaged by surrounding enemies. He completed that task in the face of great hardships and personal attacks in only fifty-two days. Then Nehemiah drove the foreigners out of Jerusalem and brought in Jews. He was first to sign a new covenant to observe the laws of the Torah, which he and Ezra offered the Jews. He fought Sabbath violation and intermarriage. He refused pay for his work and sought no permanent office; all he desired was to elevate the spirit of his people. When he died, about 412, he was mourned as one of the most selfless benefactors in the history of Jewry. His book (originally united with the Book of Ezra) contains many striking passages. It tells the entire story of his appointment by the king and the incidents that conclude with the full repair of the city walls. There is the inspiring account of the re-acceptance of the Torah by the people. His other reforms are also recounted and there is an honor roll of the aristocrats who worked with Nehemiah to rebuild and reconsecrate the Holy City.

NETHERLANDS

At the end of the 16th century Marranos settled in Amsterdam, the capital of the Netherlands. The Jews of Holland were economically successful and maintained a vigorous cultural life. They were rarely, if ever, discriminated against, and formal equality came in 1796; rabbis were paid by the state and Jews were elected to Parliament. Despite the opposition of the Dutch, the Nazis annihilated practically the entire Jewish community of Holland, and there are but 30,000 Jews left in the Netherlands today.
See also Amsterdam.

NEW YORK CITY

Jews first settled in New York City in 1654, when 23 settlers arrived from Brazil. Until the 1880s immigration was steady, but the great Russian immigration brought the Jewish population to 1,500,000 by 1914;

the present Jewish population is 1,836,000 (1971). The Greater New York area, including several nearby suburban counties, encompasses a total Jewish population of 2,381,000 (1971). New York City is by far the largest Jewish community in the world, and it is also the largest urban Jewish community in history. Jews are active in many professions, and trades. Most American Jewish institutions maintain their headquarters in New York, among them the Jewish Agency, the American Jewish Committee, the World Jewish Congress, the Union of American Hebrew Congregations, the United Synagogue, the Union of Orthodox Jewish Congregations, and many others. Many Jewish books are published in New York, as are most Jewish periodicals. In addition, such major Jewish educational institutions as the Jewish Theological Seminary, Yeshiva University, and the New York School of Hebrew Union College - Jewish Institute of Religion, are located in the city, as well as the Jewish Museum, the Yivo Institute, and one of the world's major Judaica collections, maintained by the New York Public Library. Approximately one-half of school-age children receive some Jewish education, either in day schools, Talmud Torahs, or synagogue schools.

NEW ZEALAND

Jews first settled in New Zealand in 1829. Despite the small size of the Jewish community (5,000 in 1971), it has produced many men eminent in public life. Among these are a prime minister, another cabinet minister, and a chief justice, in addition to members of Parliament and many mayors.

NIETO, DAVID

(1654-1728)—English rabbi. Nieto was distinguished as a poet, philosopher and physician, in addition to being one of the most capable men ever to hold the office of "Haham" of London. He wrote in many languages and on many topics, including an attack on the Inquisition and a philosophic defense of Judaism (*Matteh Dan*).

NIGGUN

(Melody, music) refers to the musical form for the chanting of prayers and the wordless songs sung by the Hasidim and others.

NINEVEH

Ancient capital of the Assyrian empire. Both Israel and Judah paid tribute to Nineveh. The prophet Jonah was commanded to travel to this city to preach. Nineveh was destroyed by the Babylonians and was never rebuilt.

NISAN

First month in the Jewish calendar.

See also Calendar, Jewish; Months, Jewish.

NISSIM, YITZCHAK RACHAMIN

(1895-   )—Israeli Chief Rabbi. Born in Baghdad, Nissim was one of the leaders of Iraqi Jewry until 1926, when he settled in Jerusalem. For many years he was an adviser to the Sephardic communities and rabbis of Palestine, and from 1955 to 1972 he was Sephardi Chief Rabbi of Israel, bearing the official title *Rishon le-Tziyon*. Rabbi Nissim is the author of many important responsa.

NOAH

The story of Noah and the Flood is told in Genesis and is one of the best remembered of Biblical episodes. Noah, being the only righteous man in a sinning generation, was instructed by God to build an ark for the rescue of his family and himself and several of every animal species from the impending flood. When the waters receded, the Ark landed on Mount Ararat, all disembarked, and the world began to resume its customary appearance. Then God, with the rainbow as a sign, promised that never again would a flood cover the earth. The rabbis related hundreds of legends about Noah. In order to explain his unusual goodness in a corrupt world, one said that Noah was able to talk the moment he was born. They tried to guess how long it took him to build the Ark—from five to 120 years. All during this period he warned the people of his generation about the impending destruction if they did not mend they way. It was said that when angry mobs tried to board the vessel, the wild animals Noah had brought together fought them off. One story relates that a lion attacked Noah, who always limped thereafter. But most commentators like to remember the ending of the flood, when the dove brought back the olive twig to prove that the flood had subsided and the world and the elements were finally at peace again. The dove and the olive branch are to this day the symbols of peace.

NOAH, MORDECAI MANUEL

(1785-1851)—An extraordinary and colorful character on the American Jewish scene. He was born in Philadelphia in 1785. It was he who petitioned New York State to sell an island in the Niagara River for settlement by immigrant European Jews. He wished to call the settlement Ararat, after the mountain in the story of the Biblical Noah. Though his appeal to world Jewry to join in his efforts proved a failure, the nature of his project to solve the Jewish problem makes Noah a forerunner of Herzl and others who sought a state for Jews. He was an outstanding diplomat. In 1813, appointed consul to Tunis in North Africa, he devoted himself to raising the standing of his young country in Mediterranean lands and to gain freedom for American sailors captured by African pirates. In New York he served as sheriff, judge, and surveyor of the port. Noah was a writer and journalist. He also wrote dramas. Some historians praise him for his good

Mordecai Manuel Noah.

at work—Jews being blamed for difficulties in French life and diplomacy. In the early Zionist Congresses, Nordau labored closely with Herzl. He presented the Basle Program at the First Congress, which first proclaimed the need for a Jewish state. He declared, in speeches and articles, that it was impossible for the

Max Nordau.

intentions and good sense; others consider his actions an effort to combine showmanship with statesmanship.

NOAHIDE LAWS

The laws God commands all people, including non-Jews, to obey; they must avoid idol worship, gross immorality, bloodshed, blasphemy, robbery, injustice to other men and eating flesh cut from a living animal. These rules were laid down by God to Adam and Noah and their descendants—hence the name Noahide. In Palestine there was a regulation that no non-Jew be permitted to dwell there unless he observed these laws. The rabbis demanded that this minimum be accepted by all men. Many later centuries used the Noahide laws as the basis for their theories of "natural law." The Declaration of Independence statement about the "laws of nature and of nature's God," is based on the Noahide concept. Various sects have tried to prove that if all mankind observed only these seven rules of conduct, most of the problems of modern times could be solved, or might never have arisen.

See also Codes of Jewish Law; Halachah

NOD

The land east of Eden where Cain fled after he murdered his brother Abel. Cain lived in Nod as a wanderer.

NORDAU, MAX

One of the great early leaders of the Zionist movement. He was born in Hungary in 1849 and died in Paris in 1923. He received a Jewish education and in 1875 became a physician. But all through his teens he displayed skill in prose and poetic composition and as a newspaper correspondent. His many books on history, social problems and art sold widely. Nordau met Herzl in Paris in 1892. There they saw anti-Semitism

Jews to be merged with the European nations. But because he, as a person, reminded the suffering East European Jews of the "assimilators" in Central Europe, they refused to accept his preachments. His efforts to help Zion, and the quarrels that followed, sapped his health and he died in hardship and poverty.

NORWAY

The Jewish community in Norway dates from the 1850s, when regulations prohibiting the settlement of Jews in the country were relaxed. The Jewish population of the country numbered some 1,500 individuals at the beginning of World War II. About half were killed by the Nazis during their rule of Norway (1940-45). At present, approximately 750 Jews live in the country.

NUMBERS, BOOK OF

(*Bamidbar*) fourth of the Biblical Five Books of Moses (the Torah). Numbers records the 40 years of Israel's wanderings in the wilderness. Its 36 chapters are divided into 10 portions for weekly Sabbath readings, Its name is derived from an event it describes in the opening chapters, the "numbering," or counting of the Israelites.

NUMISMATICS

In Biblical times money was silver, which had to be weighed in every case. The standard unit of weight was the "shekel" (14.5-16.5 grams). Gold was used in exceptional cases only. Coined money first appeared in Palestine in the time of Darius (522-486 B.C.E.), who issued coins bearing his own image. A national Jewish coinage is first found during the Hasmonean period under Simon Maccabee (142-135 B.C.E.). The second period of Jewish coinage set in during the revolt of 66-70 against the Romans; coins struck bear the motto *"Lecherut Yisrael"* (For the Freedom of

Israel). The last Jewish coins struck before modern times were by Bar Kochba and bear palm branches, an *etrog*, a *lulav*, grapes and Hebrew inscriptions.

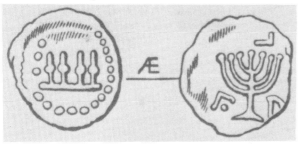

Bronze coin from the reign of Antigonus Mattathias (40-37 B.C.E.). This is the first known appearance of the candle-stick as a Jewish symbol.

NUN

The fourteenth letter of the Hebrew alphabet, has the numerical value of 50.
See also Aleph Bet.

OBADIAH

1. Fourth Book of the Twelve (Minor) Prophets of the Bible. Obadiah prophesied the destruction of Edom and the restoration of Israel.

2. Ahab's steward who courageously risked his life hiding many prophets in caves to save them from Queen Jezebel's persecutions.

OCHS, ADOLPH SIMON

The man who raised the *New York Times* to its high place in world journalism was Adolph Ochs, who was born in Cincinnati in 1858. After working at various occupations Ochs obtained control of a paper in Chattanooga, Tennessee, at the age of twenty. This venture proved so successful that he journeyed to New York in 1896 to advance his fortunes there. The *Times* was then in financial difficulty and Ochs was asked to reorganize the company. Three years later he paid off all its debts and became the controlling stockholder of the newspaper. He bought and sold other journals but his major interest was always the New York paper which published "all the news that's fit to print." Ochs gave millions of dollars to publish important learned volumes, to educational institutions and to synagogues and churches. He received many honorary degrees and other awards. After his death in 1935 his son-in-law, Arthur Hays Sulzberger, became the president and publisher of *The New York Times*. Sulzberger is now chairman of the board, and his son-in-law Orvil E. Dryfoos is president and publisher.

OHEL MOED

Hebrew name for the Tabernacle that housed the Ark during Israel's wanderings in the desert.
See also Tabernacle.

OHOLIAB

Assistant to Bezalel in the building of the Ark and the Tabernacle.
See also Bezalel.

OLAM HAZEH, OLAM HABA

Olam Hazeh means "this world." *Olam Haba* means "the world to come." The latter may refer either to some heavenly realm or to the expected age of righteousness on earth following the final divine judgment. The prophets of Israel always expressed their hopes for the time when the glory of David's reign would return. Later writers thought the change would be a supernatural one and that then a world altered for the better would bring them solace and happiness. The Talmud asserts that the righteous among all nations will inherit *Olam Haba*. The names of the two worlds respectively sometimes appear as *Olam Hasheker* ("world of falsehood") and *Olam Haemeth* ("world of truth").

OMER

Measure of grain in ancient Israel. An Omer of grain from the first harvest was taken to the Temple as a thanksgiving offering. The first harvest of the year took place during the 49 days between Passover and Shavuot, and was called the period of Omer or *Sefirah* (counting). No one ate of the new grain until the giving of Omer.

OMRI

Sixth king of the northern Kingdom of Israel (about 889-875 B.C.E.), father of Ahab. Israel flourished under Omri's reign. He established trade with the Phoenicians and reconquered Moab. Omri left the old capital Tirzah and built Samaria, the new capital city.

The Moabite Stone.

ONEG SHABBAT

("Joy of the Sabbath; rejoicing of the Sabbath") an hour of social gatherings and cultural activities on Friday evenings or Sabbath afternoons. The modern form of Oneg Shabbat was initiated in Israel (then Palestine) by the poet C. N. Bialik. Refreshments are often served for Oneg Shabbat, probably deriving from the ancient custom of the *Se'udah Shelishit*, the third and last prescribed Sabbath meal, which was often accompanied by festivities and singing.

OPATOSHU, JOSEPH

(1886-1954)—Yiddish writer, Born in Poland, Opatoshu came to the United States in 1907. For many years he was on the staff of *Der Tog*, a Yiddish newspaper. He was the author of many stories on Jewish life in America and Poland and on Jewish history. His son, David Opatoshu (1914-   ), is also an author and in addition has led a distinguished career as a film and stage actor.

OPHRAH

Ancient town near Shechem where Gideon the Judge lived and was buried.

OPPENHEIM, MORITZ

(1799-1882)—German artist. One of the most prosperous portraitists of his time, Oppenheim, because of his financial success, was known as "the Rothschild of the painters." In addition to his paintings on biblical themes and his many portraits of famous personalities, both Jewish and gentile, Oppenheim is famous for his series of genre paintings on Jewish motifs, depicting traditional Jewish family life and customs.

ORLINSKY, HARRY MAYER

(1908-   )—American biblical scholar. Born in Canada, Orlinsky has been professor of Bible at Hebrew Union College—Jewish Institute of Religion in New York since 1943. Renowned as a historian and a biblical philologist, he is the editor of Ktav's "Library of Biblical Studies," was the only Jewish consultant for the revised Protestant Bible translation in 1952, and was editor-in-chief of the new Jewish Publication Society translation of the Torah (1962). His numerous scholarly articles and books include a major study of the Book of Isaiah as well as *Ancient Israel, Understanding the Bible Through History and Archaeology,* and *Notes on the New Translation of the Torah.*

ORAL LAW (TORAH)

Post-Biblical laws founded on the laws of the (written) Torah. The laws of the Oral Torah were passed on by word of mouth, from generation to generation, until they were collected and edited in the Mishnah. The Oral Torah—the Mishnah—is the basis of the Talmud.

See also Mishnah; Talmud

ORDINATION

(Semichah) the authority given to rabbis to decide on questions of Jewish law. In modern times, rabbis receive ordination after completing an intensive course of study at a seminary or a Yeshiva.

See also Semichah.

tional restrictions against Jews were being reduced and the founders of ORT (Organization for Rehabilitation and Training) desired to prepare Jews for the new opportunities. ORT established trade schools for Jews; it sought to help those forced out of their jobs by government or social changes. After World War I there were 100 ORT schools in Poland, Lithuania and Russia, attended by 10,000 students. In addition to teaching trades, ORT set up agricultural cooperatives to help bring the Jews back to the land. The work continued in Germany and France and soon there were branches throughout the world. With the rise of Naziism the work became twofold—training Jews untroubled in their lands of residence, and providing for those who had become refugees and might prove too great a burden for mere charity. It tried to meet each emergency as it arose. During World War II, ORT conducted training schools in Europe and in North and South America. Its work continues and assures a more balanced community wherever Jews reside.

OTHNIEL

Son of Kenaz; Caleb's younger brother, of the tribe of Judah, first Judge of Israel. He delivered Israel from King Cushan-rishathaim of Aram.

OZ, AMOS

(1939-   )—Israeli writer. Born in Jerusalem, Oz is a member of Kibbutz Hulda, where as a young man he worked as a laborer in the cotton fields and now teaches literature in the kibbutz secondary school. A combat veteran of the Israeli army and a visiting fellow at Oxford from 1969 to 1970, Oz is the author of three novels, *My Michael; Elsewhere, Perhaps;* and *Touch the Water, Touch the Wind;* the novellas *Crusade* and *Late Love;* and numerous short stories and political, social, and literary essays.

PADDAN-ARAM

Region along the upper Euphrates where the city of Haran was situated. Haran was the home of Rebekah and Laban and his daughters, Leah and Rachel.

PALESTINE

Name for the land of Israel, the territory west of the Jordan from Dan to Beersheba. The name is a derivation from the word Philistine and was first used by the Greeks, and later by the Romans (Palestina). The name is not mentioned in the Bible.

PALMACH

(Hebrew abbreviation for *P'lugot Machatz*—commandos.) The offensive branch of the Haganah. These troops were underground fighters from 1941 to 1948, when they were integrated into the Israeli Defense Army. The corps was originally organized in 1941 to aid the British fight off the German threat to the Middle East; it did not disband after the crisis had passed, however, and with the conclusion of World War II began underground activities against the British. During the Israel War of Independence "Palmachniks" won distinction in the battles for the Negev and for Jerusalem.

PAPYRUS

Documents written on this paper made from reeds have been discovered which cast much light on Jewish history. The Elephantini papyri record the life of the Jewish community in this Egyptian border garrison-town of the 5th century B.C.E. Many other papyri, written from the 3rd century B.C.E. to the 7th C.E., have been discovered. Most of them are written in Greek; there are bills of divorce, contracts, and petitions to the government among them. From these papyri we learn how the Jewish community of the time was organized, what its rights were, and how it lived.

PARAN

Wilderness in the Sinai Peninsula near the Gulf of Aqaba where Hagar and Ishmael lived after they were cast out of the household of Abraham.

PARASHAHS, FOUR

The word *Parashah* refers both to a section or paragraph of the Bible and to the portion of the Torah read during services. Ashkenazic and Sephardic Jews both use the word to mean the written paragraphs in the Torah, but when referring to the section read at the services, the Ashkenazic Jews usually use the word *Sidra*. The Four Parashahs, a term used by all Jews, are those sections of the Torah read from a special Torah scroll on four special Sabbaths preceding Passover. The first is *Shekalim*, recalling the half-shekel offering in the wilderness, on the Sabbath before, or on the first day of, Adar. The next is *Zachor* (Remember) read before Purim. The prophetic reading is about the Amalakites because Haman is presumed to be a descendant of that wicked tribe. The third is *Parah*, the Sabbath next to the last Sabbath of Adar, or the last Sabbath if the next month, Nisan, begins on a Sabbath. It commemorates the custom of mixing the ashes of a red heifer with water, to be used to purify one who has touched a corpse. The last is *Parashat Ha-Hodesh*, which comes before Passover. It contains the laws of the Passover festival. These parts of the Torah are recited after those ordinarily read, and always from a second scroll. They remind the Jew of four significant teachings of the past: freewill offering, by means of the shekel; remembrance of evil men, whom Israel must avoid; the necessity of maintaining personal purity; and the Passover holiday of freedom, and the month Nisan in which it falls.

PAROCHET

The curtain which hangs before the Ark in the synagogue. It is usually made of beautiful cloth and is artistically decorated. It often bears the letters *Kaf* and *Tav*, the initials of *Keter Torah* (Crown of the Torah). Its color is usually red or blue. On the High Holy Days a white Parochet is used.

PARVE

Also called *minnig;* foods such as eggs, fish, fruit and vegetables which, according to Jewish dietary laws, can be eaten with either milk or meat dishes. These foods are considered neutral *(parve)*.
See also Dietary Laws.

PASSOVER (PESACH)

Passover celebrates Israel's deliverance from Egyptian bondage; it begins on the fifteenth of Nisan. It is one of the three pilgrimage festivals when, in ancient times, every Israelite family sent a representative to Jerusalem to sacrifice at the Temple. The Hebrews were freed not merely to gain personal and political independence but to go forth "to serve the Lord" and to receive the Torah, which liberated their souls. The

Present-day Samaritans in Israel, who claim descent from the tribes of Ephraim and Manasseh, have their own customs. Here they bake matzot for Passover.

most important Passover observance is the eating of *Matzot*, unleavened bread. The Jews were so eager to be free when they went out of Egypt that they left in a great hurry. They had no time to mix yeast with their dough and wait for it to rise; instead, they just mixed flour and water together and baked it in flat, thin loaves. The Bible has commanded the Jews to eat no other bread but *Matzot* all the eight days of the holiday to remind them of the going out of Egypt. The Seder dinner is marked by the reading of the Passover story, legends, hymns and blessings, all of which are in the *Haggadah*. Most Jews consider Passover the happiest occasion of the Jewish year.

PATRIARCHATE

Refers to the leadership of the *Nesiim* (sing. *Nasi*; the scholarly heads of the great Palestinian academies) who led the Jewish community of the land of Israel after the destruction of the Second Temple and until about 425 C.E. Their spiritual and legal authority was generally accepted and supported by voluntary taxation by Jews throughout the ancient world.

See also Nasi.

PATRIARCHS, THE THREE

The fathers of the Jewish people, Abraham, Isaac and Jacob.

PAY

The seventeenth letter of the Hebrew alphabet, has the numerical value of 80.

See also Aleph Bet.

PEACE

When Jews meet or part, the word they frequently utter is *Shalom*, peace. Every prayer service contains a plea for peace. Though the Israelites often had to fight for their land and their lives, priests and prophets always exhorted them to seek peace and pursue it. A favorite Bible quotation is from Isaiah: "They shall beat their swords into plowshares and their spears into pruninghooks; nation shall not lift up sword against nation, neither shall they learn war any more." Often the prophets preached non-resistance, in preference to a war which would reward neither the victor nor the loser. Israel's leaders opposed many useless wars, though not such as was waged for Jewish existence by the Maccabees. When the Temple was built, no metal tools were used on it, lest iron, a symbol of arms, touch the altar. When the Talmud mentions ancient Jewish military heroes, it likes to picture them as students and scholars and performers of good deeds. And when the Egyptians were drowning in the Red Sea, God forbade the Israelites to sing, for "the works of My hands are drowning." In America rabbinical groups have frequently issued peace pronouncements and have joined non-Jewish groups to form peace committees.

PEKAH

One of the last kings of the northern Kingdom of Israel (about 736-734 B.C.E.), overthrew Pekahiah. He organized an alliance against the Assyrians; he also warred against Judah. Pekah was overthrown by Hoshea.

PEKAHIAH

One of the last kings of Israel (about 737-736 B.C.E.), son of Menahem. He was assassinated and succeeded by Pekah.

PENTATEUCH

Greek name for *Humash*; the Five Books of Moses; the Torah.

See Humash.

PERES, SHIMON

(1923-   )—Israeli political leader and defense expert. Born in Poland, Peres came to Palestine in 1934. During the War of Independence he headed the naval branch of the Defense Ministry. He became the ministry's director general in 1953, and from 1959 to 1965 was deputy minister of defense. From 1970 to 1974 he served as minister of communications, and in 1974 he became defense minister in Yitzhak Rabin's cabinet. Peres is regarded as one of the prime architects of Israel's growing defense industry and nuclear capability, and he supervised the reorganization and reequipping of Israel's armed forces after the Yom Kippur War.

PERETZ, ISAAC LEIB

The most widely read and praised Yiddish and Hebrew author of his time was Isaac Leib Peretz, a Polish Jew who lived from 1851 to 1915. After writing successful prose and verse in Hebrew, he gave up literature for the law for ten years. Then he returned to writing, using Yiddish as his means of expression. He left his village for Warsaw, where he became secretary of the Jewish community, editing manuals and monthlies when not engaged in communal labors. For these and other periodicals he wrote a vast number of stories and sketches. He portrayed the hardship and bitterness of Jewish life in Eastern Europe, but never failed to contrast the sufferings of the Jews with the kindliness and decency of their inner lives. One of his stories concerns a town where no one ever died, since no one truly lived while in it. Another tale is that of "Bontche Shveig", the tormented, long-suffering Jew who, when asked in heaven to request anything he desired as a reward for his refusal to complain on earth, begged the angel only for a roll with butter. When Peretz died his funeral was attended by more than 100,000 people.

PERSIA

Great empire of antiquity that overthrew Babylonia, ruled over Media, Lydia, Persia and Babylonia and their possessions. The Persian kings, Cyrus the Great and Darius I, helped the Jews return to Judea and rebuild the Temple. Persia's King Xerxes was probably King Ahasuerus, husband of Esther. Persia was overthrown by Alexander the Great of Macedonia. Today the original territory of Persia is modern Iran. The Babylonian Talmud was edited in Persian territory. Benjamin of Tudela reports that there were large communities in the 12th century, though the position of the Jews worsened afterwards. The social and economic status of the Jew in modern Iran is very low,

A page from a Judeo-Persian manuscript.

people, and Pharisaism became equivalent to Judaism. Loyal as the Pharisees were to tradition, they were the most flexible of Jews and interpreted the law with recognition of the needs of the times. They were more lenient and liberal than their chief opposing party, the Sadducees, who were inclined to interpret Biblical injunctions literally. The Sadducees rejected the idea of a human soul, life after death, and the coming of the Messiah. Though the general beliefs of the Pharisees are still held today, the name Pharisee dropped out of usage during the 2nd century C.E.

PHILISTINES

A people who settled in the southwest portion of Canaan. From their name comes the word *Palestine*, which for so many centuries meant the territory known as Israel. The Israel of today is a part of this same ancient territory. The Philistines were sea people, whose many ships sailed from Crete and who embarked on many naval and military ventures. From the monuments discovered in modern times, it is evident

A stone relief from Thebes shows a group of Philistine prisoners of Rameses III. In hieroglyphics the Philistines were called "peles et." The name Palestine was derived from this word.

that they were a tall, handsome people who resembled the Greeks and that they were excellent traders and devotees of art. (Oddly enough, today the term Philistine is used to describe a person who has little appreciation of art.) Late in the period of the Judges these people began threatening the Israelites. Possessing iron spears and chariots, they were superior in warfare to the Israelites, who were more lightly armed. The Philistines seem to have joined the ancient Canaanites among whom they lived and to have adopted their religion. The Philistines invaded Israel, enslaved many of the people and were on the way to subjugating the entire land when Saul, having been anointed king, gathered an army which helped rout them. David defeated them completely. Under Egyptian, Babylonian, Persian and Alexandrian domination the Philistines gradually disappeared as a separate national group.

causing a large immigration to Israel. 80,000 Jews now live in Iran.

PERSKY, DANIEL

(1887-1962)—Hebrew author and journalist. Persky, who came to New York from Russia in 1906, devoted his entire life to the furtherance of Hebrew education and literature in America. He was known best for his delightful weekly column in *Hadoar*, a Hebrew periodical.

PESUKE DEZIMRA

("Passages of Song") passages from the Psalms and Book of Chronicles recited before the morning service *(Shaharit)*.

PHARAOH

("The Great House" in Egyptian) originally name and title of honor of the rulers of Egypt. Pharaoh later came to mean simply "King." The Pharaoh at the time of the Exodus was Ramses II.

PHARISEES

One of the three parties in Israel during the time of the Second Temple was the Pharisees, which means the separatists, and probably refers to those who by their loyalty to Jewish law and observance distinguished themselves from the less observant Jews. The Pharisees comprised the overwhelming majority of the

PHILO JUDAEUS

(20 B.C.E.-40 C.E.)—An Alexandrian philosopher and interpreter of the Bible, descended from an aristocratic and priestly family. He was acquainted with such subjects as mathematics, music, poetry, language

Traditional tomb of Hiram, King of Tyre.

study and philosophy. As a devoted Jew, he once traveled to Jerusalem to pray and bring offerings to the Temple. In 40 C.E. he led a delegation to the Roman emperor to plead against the anti-Semite Apion (against whom the historian Josephus was to write a book). Philo's books, written in Greek, attempted to uphold the dignity and worth of the Jewish law. In commenting on the Torah, Philo employed a vast number of odd symbols and dug unusual meanings from the plain words of Moses. His influence on Judaism, Christianity and Mohammedanism was tremendous. Many later philosophers were guided by his modes of thinking and interpretation.

PHINEHAS

1. Third High Priest of Israel, son of Eleazar, grandson of Aaron, zealous opponent of idol worship. After the Israelites conquered Canaan, Phinehas lived in Ephraim.

2. One of the sons of the Judge and High Priest Eli, regarded unworthy to succeed his father. Phinehas and his brother Hophni fell in the battle against the Philistines when the Ark was captured.

PHOENICIA

The Phoenicians are important in Jewish history because of their close personal and linguistic relationship to the Israelites. From Hiram, King of Tyre, came the splendid metal work in Solomon's temple. His country was mainly the shore territory north of Palestine, which today is called Syria. Inscriptions found at Carthage indicate that the people of Tyre, or the Sidonians, as the Bible knows them, were of a Semitic language group. The tablets found at Amarna, in Egypt, in the last century speak glowingly of the city of Tyre; and the prophet Ezekiel knew it as a great and prosperous city. It was well fortified and offered strong resistance to the successful Assyrian invaders of Israel and its neighbors. Since the Phoenicians lived near the sea, they traded extensively. It is believed they invented the science of navigation. The Phoenicians are said to have colonized many cities and islands of the Mediterranean. They may even have carried on their activities in ancient Britain. They are famous for their alphabet, which may have been the earliest known; it had twenty-two characters, like the Hebrew, and forms the basis for the Greek and Western scripts. Though our information about these people is fragmentary, we know that they added much to the world's knowledge of trade, government, language and diplomacy.

PIDYON HABEN

(The redemption of the first-born son) a ceremony that takes place 30 days after the birth of the first son. As a first son belongs traditionally to the service of God, he is symbolically redeemed by his father by an offering of money (5 shekels) to a *Cohen*, a descendant of the Biblical *Cohanim*, who were dedicated (instead of the first-born) to the service of God.

See also First Born.

PINSKER, LEON

(1821-1891)—Zionist thinker. Pinsker, a physician by profession, originally believed that the Jews should

Leon Pinsker.

strive to assimilate into the populations surrounding them. By 1881 he had changed his mind, however, as he saw the strength of anti-Semitism, and in 1882 he published *Auto-Emancipation*. This book argued that anti-Semitism will be a permanent feature of any society that contains Jews. Pinsker urged the return of a segment of the Jewish people to Palestine, to bring about the rebirth of the Jewish nation in their traditional homeland.

PINSKI, DAVID

(1872-1959)—Yiddish writer. Born in Russia, Pinski emigrated to the United States in 1899, and settled in Israel in 1949. He wrote extensively on themes from the whole far-ranging panorama of Jewish history. Among his best-known works are the plays *The Eternal Jew* and *King David and His Wives* and the novels *The Family Zvi, Arnold Levenburg,* and *The House of Noah Eden.*

PIRKE AVOT

(*Ethics of the Fathers*) one of the best known parts of the Mishnah, wise sayings of the great rabbis and teachers; often read or studied on Sabbath afternoons, starting with the Sabbath after Passover until the Sabbath before Rosh Hashanah. *Pirke Avot* is included in many *Siddurim.*

PISGAH

Mountain in ancient Moab, northwest of Mount Nebo, often referred to as part of Mount Nebo and as the place where Moses died and was buried.

PITHOM AND RAAMSES

The two Egyptian cities built by the enslaved Israelites, probably for the Pharaoh Ramses II. Pithom and Raamses were "store-cities," where great storehouses were built and filled with food and Pharaoh's treasures. At Pithom, modern archaeologists have uncovered massive walls built of "bricks without straw," as described in the Biblical Book of Exodus.

PIYUT

Piyut refers to poetry used in the synagogue. Though the prayerbook had been more or less stabilized in the sixth century, every change in Jewish life led to the writing of new prayers and songs. The first *Piyutim* were probably written during a time of persecution and they were intended to give inspiration and hope for the future. Poetic hymns were added to every regular prayer and service. Worship was thus made more attractive. In composing the *Piyutim,* new words and new grammatical structures were devised. So difficult did the altered language become that commentaries had to be written to explain them. The early poems used alphabetical acrostics, that is, lines began with the successive letters of the Hebrew alphabet; often the writers performed the same feat backwards.

Then, under Arab influence, the Jewish poets used rhyme, and later meter as we know it today. As a result of many years of such rhymed writing, nonreligious Hebrew poetry got its start. Modern Hebrew poets have adopted some of the medieval techniques. In the high holiday prayerbooks (*Machzorim*) are many of the *Piyutim;* some of them have excellent English translations.

PLAGUES, THE TEN

The ten successive plagues visited upon Egypt to compel Pharaoh to set the Israelites free. A recital of these plagues is a traditional part of the Passover Seder.

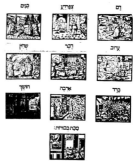

An artist's rendition of the Ten Plagues.

POALE ZION

(Hebrew for "Workers of Zion") A Socialist Zionist labor party formed in 1903, in Austria. Similar groups were formed in the United States, Russia, Palestine, and England. They tried to unite Zionist and social-democratic ideas, forming a world association in 1907. Three of Israel's political parties were born of the *Poale Zion:* Mapai, Mapam, and Achdut Ha'avodah. The Histadrut, too, was created by members of *Poale Zion.*

POGROM

The word pogrom is Russian for "riot" or "disturbance." Because of the violent attacks on the Jews in Russia during the nineteenth century it has come to

Jewish victims of the Russian pogroms.

127

mean attacks on Jews. In 1881 murderous assaults on Jews went on throughout Russia, with soldiers and policemen looking on indifferently. Reactionaries in that country were trying to allay discontent by blaming the Jews for all the difficulties they were having. Jews were accused of hating Christianity and plotting enslavement of all mankind. Though the czar denounced the pogroms as the work of anarchists, his officials established commissions to investigate Jews. The Jews were accused of having no fatherland, of forming a state within a state. Eventually, a government commission placed the blame on the government itself and pogroms ceased for twenty years. But in 1903 an organized massacre took place in Kishinev, with fearful destruction. After that, pogroms were regularly used as a means to fight revolutionary movements. The Soviet regime abolished pogroms, but Jews still remain scapegoats in Russia, as has been revealed in many reports published since the end of World War II.

POLAND

Jews first settled in Poland in the 9th century. There was a great influx of Jews from Germany during the 12th and 13th centuries, when Poland, like many other countries developing in Eastern Europe, was eager to make use of the Jews for economic purposes. Coins bearing Hebrew words were issued in that period, and many Jews were prosperous landowners. The church, however, advocated discrimination against Jews, and those demands were often met; in 1496 a ghetto was established in Cracow. Ritual murder accusations and riots became frequent in the 16th century, and the ten years between 1648 and 1658 saw hundreds of communities destroyed. By this time Polish Jewry had developed the Yiddish language, and the Talmud was studied intensively in the Yeshivot which sprung up. Later, Hasidism found a fertile field in Poland. In the early 19th century it appeared that the condition of the Jews would be bettered, but anti-Semitic trends prevailed, and there was a pogrom in Warsaw in 1881. Zionism attracted many, as did immigration to the United States. In 1939 Poland had 3 million Jews, but the entire community was destroyed by the Nazi regime. The postwar Polish community numbered about 30,000. In the outbreak of anti-Semitism that followed the Six-Day War (1967), most of these were forced to leave the country. There are now barely 8,000 Jews in Poland, the great majority elderly.

POOL, DAVID DE SOLA

A prominent rabbi of the oldest congregation in the United States, was among the notable Jews honored during the tercentenary (300 year) celebration of American Jewry in 1954. Descendant of the Sephardic rabbinical family Meldola, he was born in London, England, in 1885, and educated in England and Germany. He has been serving as the Rabbi of the Spanish and Portuguese Synagogue, Shearith Israel of New

York, since 1907. Famed for his brilliance and devotion, he has aided many Jewish organizations. From 1919 to 1922 he was in Palestine as the regional director of the Joint Distribution Committee. He has been the chairman of the committee on religious activities for the National Jewish Welfare Board, director of the Jewish Education Association, president of the Union of Sephardic Congregations, president of the Synagogue Council of America and president of the New York Board of Rabbis. He also served on the advisory committee of the National Youth Administration. Dr. Pool has written two books on the history of American Judaism. One is *Portraits Etched In Stone*, which reconstructs, through the history of their tombstones, the lives of early American Jews buried in the old Chatham Square cemetery of his congregation. The other, written in collaboration with his wife, Tamar de Sola Pool, is the story of his synagogue, called *An Old Faith In the New World*, and is virtually a history of American Jewry and a description of the three-century old customs and observances still followed in his synagogue.

POPES

Historically, the Catholic popes have demanded both toleration for the Jews and a weakening of Jewish influence. The first pope to lay down this balanced policy towards the Jews was Gregory I (590-604). Many popes, however, have departed from this policy; among the most noted was Innocent III (1198-1216), who guided the 4th Lateran Council to extreme anti-Jewish measures. Other popes, such as Clement VII (1523-33), called "Saviour of the Jews" and friend of David Reubeni and Solomon Molcho, protected and defended the Jews. Pope John XXIII (1958-1963) modified a number of unfavorable references to Jews in the Catholic liturgy.

Procession of Jews meeting Pope Martin V. at the Council of Constance, 1417.

PORTUGAL

Jews settled in Portugal as early as 300 B.C.E. The Jews of Portugal lived peacefully for many centuries and produced distinguished officials and doctors, until 1497, when almost the entire community was forced to convert to Christianity by Manoel II. Many were persecuted and killed by the Inquisition. Jewish freedom of worship was reestablished only in 1910. Aside from Marranos, the Jewish population of Portugal is 600, mainly in Lisbon.

See also Marranos.

POTIPHAR

Official at Pharaoh's court who bought the young Joseph from the Midianites. He made Joseph overseer of his household. His wife falsely accused Joseph and caused him to be thrown into prison.

POTI-PHERA

Egyptian dignitary and priest of On; father of Asenath, Joseph's wife.

PRAYER

In Judaism prayer is regarded as a means to a direct approach to God, to recognize His power and submit to His will, and as a way to turn one's thoughts to a better tomorrow. That is why *kavanah* (extreme attention and devotion) is required of him who prays. Though it is preferred that a Jew join a *Minyan* of ten men to pray, he may say his prayers alone, even in the open fields. Hebrew is the tongue prescribed, but a Jew may pray in any language. There are three services each weekday, four on Sabbaths and festivals, five on Yom Kippur. The prayer for the dead, *Kaddish*, may be recited at every *Minyan*. In many lands there is a prayer for the government. The *Kedusha* (Sanctification) is part of every *Shemoneh Esreh* (Eighteen Blessings—standing prayer) repeated by the cantor. Many prayers derive from ancient Palestinian life. Thus rain is prayed for at the fall Sukkot festivals, and there is a prayer for dew on Passover. One prays at the beginning of a journey and at its happy conclusion. The Priestly Blessing is also part of the service. Though once publication of prayers was forbidden, there are now many different kinds of *Siddurim* ("orders" of service) for ordinary days and Sabbaths, and *Machzorim* ("repetitions" of service) for the holidays.

PRIESTS

("*Kohanim*"—also translated sometimes as princes or ministers.) Those who were consecrated to serve in Temple-worship and to mediate between God and Israel. They presumably are descendants of Aaron, the first High Priest of Israel. They were sometimes simple Levites, the tribe assigned to the service of the sanctuary. Moses, Aaron and Miriam were of the tribe of Levi. It is said that the Levites were faithful·to God in the wilderness when other Israelites rebelled. In the

A reconstruction of the regalia of the Cohanim.

period of the Kings the legitimacy of a priest *(Kohen)* was proven by descent from Zadok, David's High Priest, and the ordinary Levites served under his guidance. Only the High Priest (the *Kohen Gadol*) could enter the "Holy of Holies" in the sanctuary. He had to be a man of high moral character and dignified bearing. He wore special linen robes befitting his high office. In the later period the High Priest became politically one of the most powerful men in the kingdom. The status of the *Kohanim* was above the Levites and high above the common people who were simply called *Israel*. Though some scholars have cast doubt on the purity of descent of today's *Kohanim*, they still are accorded the honors due to the priests. They are still the first to be called to the reading of the Torah and they bestow the ancient Priestly Blessing. In traditional Judaism they still redeem the firstborn and they obey the old special Biblical laws of the priesthood concerning marriage and physical purity.

See also Cohen.

PRINTING

Davin de Caderousse, a Jew of Avignon, France, was studying printing in 1444, about twelve years before Gutenberg's Bible was printed. Much early printing by Jews was done in Italy, Portugal, and Spain. The Soncino family was the most noted family of printers (they did books of both Jewish and non-Jewish content); Daniel Bomberg was à famous Venetian printer of the 16th century. The Romm family of Vilna won distinction in the 19th century, producing superior editions of the Talmud. Today, Israel is the center of Jewish printing, and many new type faces are being designed.

PROPHETS

The second Biblical division *(Nevi'im)* contains all the Books of the Prophets. It consists of two parts: I, the "early" prophets, Joshua, Judges, Samuel and Kings; and II, the "latter" prophets, Isaiah, Jeremiah, Ezekiel, and the twelve "minor" prophets; ("minor" refers to the smaller size of these books). The "early" books relate Israel's history, from the death of Moses to the Babylonian exile in 586 B.C.E., and are considered written by the prophets themselves—the divinely inspired men. The "latter" books contain the words of the fifteen prophets whose names they bear and relate stories from their individual lives. The Israelites believed that God spoke through their prophets. They respected them, though they did not always listen to their words or obey them. These men were not fortune tellers, or foretellers of the future. They were inspired and wise and knew the results of the nation's wrong doings, of unwise alliances, and, above all, of religious and moral wrongs. The prophets considered themselves and were considered by the people the guardians of Israel's spiritual purity and piety and its national well-being. They did not only upbraid and warn the people, they also foretold God's majestic and loving plan of the Messianic era. The late chapters of Isaiah and many other passages of Prophets show that these men also knew how to uplift Israel and how to provide the people with comfort and hope.

PROPHETS, TWELVE

Whereas the latter "major" prophets are but three, Isaiah, Jeremiah and Ezekiel, there are twelve "minor" prophets. All their recorded sayings are considered as one Book of the Bible. They include Hosea, Joel, Amos, Obadiah, Jonah, Micah, Nahum, Habakkuk, Zephaniah, Haggai, Zechariah and Malachi. The only Book related as a story is, Jonah. But incidents in the lives of other prophets are told, notably of Hosea, whose entire thinking was governed by his family problem. These prophets beheld visions; they warned of punishment for iniquity and for detailed, specific crimes against God and man. They depicted and criticized the sorry and often sinful state of Israel and the nations that oppressed them. They also prophesied the golden, peaceful Messianic age. Micah repeats the words of Isaiah on peace: "And they shall beat their swords into plowshares . . ." The last words in Malachi sum up much of the teaching of all these twelve prophets: "Remember ye the law of Moses My servant, which I commanded him in Horeb for all Israel . . . Behold, I will send you Elijah the prophet before the coming of the great and terrible day of the Lord. And he shall turn the heart of the fathers to the children, and the heart of the children to their fathers."

PROSELYTES

The fact that, on one hand, Jewish law requires great caution in admitting non-Jews as proselytes, and on the other, the tolerant attitude of Judaism towards other monotheistic religions, results in a tendency against missionary activity. There have been periods of mass proselytization, however; such were

the Second Temple period, during the reign of the Hasmonean kings, and the period of the Roman Empire, particularly during the 1st century, C.E.

PROSKAUER, JOSEPH M.

(1877-1971)—American judge. Proskauer served on the New York State Supreme Court (1923), and in the State Appellate Division (1927-30). During his presidency of the American Jewish Committee (1943-49) it became a supporter of the establishment of a Jewish state in Israel.

PROVERBS

That a Book called "Proverbs" is in the Bible indicates Israel's love of pithy words of wisdom (meshalim). Mishle, as the Biblical book is called, comes from mashal, which also means a comparison. The Talmud, and indeed all Jewish literature, is filled with proverbs. The Book of Proverbs is part of the so-called Wisdom Literature of the Hebrews, which also includes Job, Ecclesiastes and part of the Apocrypha. One of the latter is called "The Wisdom of Solomon"—since that ancient king is reputed to be the author not only of Ecclesiastes, Song of Songs and Proverbs, but of many collections gathered centuries after his death. Proverbs contains verses on how man should conduct his life, on fear of the Lord, on the glories of virtue and pitfalls of vice, and on the varieties of human character. The last chapter, on the "woman of valor," paints so pleasant a picture of the housewife that it is included in the Friday night prayers. Meshalim (comparisons, anecdotes, wise sayings) have always been used by Jewish lecturers and preachers—from Rabbi Meir to Jacob Kranz, the "Dubno Maggid."

PSALMS

The first Book of the Sacred Writings, the third and last division of the Bible, is the 150-chapter Book of Psalms. Although they are often called the Psalms of David, many of them bear the names of other authors. The Book is admired by many religious groups for its great range of religious thought and emotion. It contains a collection of blessings and prayers, poetic statements in praise of God and confession of sin. The Hebrew name Tehillim means "songs of praise." There are five Books of Psalms which correspond to the number of Books in the Pentateuch, according to the Midrash on Psalms. Most of the individual psalms begin with captions describing their contents—a song, meditation, prayer, or hymn of praise. Their forms and wording are among the most impressive in all literature. Many of the psalms have been included in the prayerbook. In the morning service a succession of psalms are read; one begins the afternoon (Minhah) service; and a special group called Hallel (Praise) is recited on the festivals and the New Moon. There are many other psalms in the prayerbook. The twenty-third psalm ("The Lord is my shepherd") is considered by many to be the most beautiful.

PSEUDOPIGRAPHA

Books similar to Biblical writings, but excluded from the Bible. Many of these books were written under the names of famous Biblical figures, to make them more acceptable.

See also Apocrypha.

PTOLEMY

Name borne by the first Greek king of Egypt, and by all subsequent rulers of the Ptolemaic dynasty. Ptolemy I (ruled 305-285 B.C.E.) conquered Palestine in 319-8. The Greek translation of the Bible called the Septuagint was promoted by the second of the Ptolemies (285-246 B.C.E.), called Philadelphus. The administration of the territory of Judea was much improved by the Ptolemies, and their system, unchanged by Seleucids or Hasmoneans, remained in effect until the Roman occupation of the land.

PUMPADITA

(Also Pumbeditha) one of the three most famous Babylonian Talmudic academies, founded in the 3rd century C.E. and for eight centuries a foremost seat of Jewish learning.

PURIM

("Feast of Lots") a holiday that celebrates the rescue of the Jews of Persia from Haman's evil plot to destroy them. Haman, a favorite of King Ahasuerus, was angered by Mordecai, a cousin of Queen Esther, who refused to bow down before him. Haman cast lots to choose the day of destruction of Mordecai and all the Jews of Persia, and succeeded in getting Ahasuerus to give his approval. The Book of Esther, which is read

A display of Purim items.

on Purim, recounts the courage of Queen Esther, who risked her life to expose Haman to the King. Purim is a joyous holiday and is celebrated with parties, costume plays and *Shalach Manot* (exchange of gifts).

See also Adloyada.

RABBAN

Honorary title of the presidents of the Sanhedrin in their capacity as teachers of law.

RABBANA

Honorary title bestowed upon Exilarchs and outstanding Talmudic scholars in Babylonia.

RABBI

Rabbi means "my master" or "my teacher." The word was not used as a title until the first century of this era. At that time it applied only to men ordained in Palestine; those ordained outside the land were known simply as "Rav," a master or teacher. The title of highest honor was that of Rabbenu, "our master and teacher," granted first to Judah Hanasi, who compiled the Mishnah, and to the most celebrated scholars of each generation since his time. Rabbis of Talmudic time did not receive salaries but worked in trades and professions and as laborers, except for those who worked in the various courts. The rabbi was highly respected for his knowledge of Torah. He spent no time in idle talk. But never was the rabbi "divine," an intermediary between God and man; he was in the best sense a teacher guiding his people to the divine way. Only in the fifteenth century did it become customary to pay him a salary. After this, the duty of the rabbi became clearly defined. He headed and supervised the communal court, all ritual functions of everyday life, the schools, the institutions of learning and the synagogue. He guided the charitable and religious organizations of the community and he gave counsel and comfort readily to all. Besides all these activities, the rabbi engaged in the study of the Torah.

RABBINICAL SEMINARIES

Institutions established in the 19th century to train rabbis versed in the secular culture and scientific method of the day. The traditional European yeshiva was unwilling to change its system of education to meet the demands of the Enlightenment and modern life, and so new institutions were considered necessary. Rabbinical seminaries were founded as early as 1829 (Italy) and 1830 (France); the renowned seminary of Breslau was established in 1854, and that of Berlin in 1873. In addition to producing a new type of rabbi, these schools gave many scholars the opportunity to teach and publicize their new doctrines and methods.

RABBINISM

The tradition of safekeeping, study and interpretation of the Torah, founded by Ezra and the Soferim and carried on to the present day by rabbis, scholars and teachers. The greatest work embodying this tradition is the Talmud.

RABIN, YITZHAK

(1922-   )—Prime Minister of Israel. Born in Tel Aviv, Rabin graduated from the Kadourie Agricultural College and in 1940 joined the Palmach. He commanded a brigade during Israel's War of Independence (1948) and afterwards studied at a military college in England. From 1956 to 1959 Rabin headed Israel's Northern Command. He was head of the army's Manpower Branch from 1959 to 1960, became deputy chief of staff in 1960, and in 1964 became chief of staff, the highest rank in the Israel Defense Forces. During the Six-Day War (1967), the Israeli army, under Rabin's command, won one of the most brilliant victories in military history. Rabin became ambassador to the United States in 1968. Returning to Israel in 1973, he was elected to the Knesset, and in 1974, he was chosen to succeed Golda Meir as Israel's Prime Minister. He resigned in 1977.

RABINA BAR HUNA

Great seholar (Amora) who, with Rav Ashi, collected and edited the Babylonian Talmud. Rabina was Ashi's assistant and, after Ashi's death, his successor. Rabina died in 499 C.E.

See also Ashi.

RACHEL

Younger daughter of Laban, favorite wife of Jacob, sister of Leah. She was the mother of Joseph and Benjamin. Her tomb is near Ramah and Bethlehem. She was one of the Four Mothers of Israel.

Rachel's grave.

RAMAH

1. City in the territory of Ephraim, home of Samuel.
2. A fortress between Judah and Israel, near Jerusalem. Rachel's grave is near Ramah.

RAMOTH-GILEAD

City of Refuge, in the territory of Gad, in Gilead, east of the Jordan; scene of many battles between Israel and Aram.

See also Cities of Refuge.

RAMSES (II)

Pharaoh at the time of the Exodus of the Jews from Egypt.

RAPHAEL

Angel and messenger of God, healer and performer of miracles.

RAPOPORT, SOLOMON JUDAH

(Known from his Hebrew initials as *Shir*; 1790-1867) —Rabbi and thinker. He is one of the founders of "Jewish Science," which introduced scientific, critical methods into Jewish studies. Rapoport upheld the orthodox position, vigorously opposing the reforms of Geiger.

RASHI

The greatest commentator on the Bible and Talmud; born in Troyes, France, in 1040, and died there in 1105. By combining the Hebrew initials of his full name, Rabbi Solomon son of Isaac becomes "Rashi," (the name affectionately and respectfully bestowed upon the great commentator). As a very young boy he gave evidence of his fine and retentive mind and everyone marveled at the extent of his learning. He left

The Rashi chapel in the city of Worms, the synagogue where the great commentator worshipped.

Troyes at an early age to study in Worms. (There he married, though he was poor and still a very young student.) Later, Rashi was elected Rabbi of Troyes and he worked without pay. He founded a yeshiva which became famous and had many students. Rashi was the author of treatises on many subjects; but his fame is based on his brilliant commentaries on much of the Bible and the Talmud, which scholars consider an indispensable guide to the understanding of the great books. Rashi's commentary combines both Halachic (legal) and Aggadic (in the style of tales and fancy) elements. It has been translated into Latin, and English and is used by scholars throughout the world and also by those who seek a first introduction to Talmudic learning. Many legends are woven around the great Rashi—but he was hardly the miracle-man of legend. The true miracle of his life was the devotion, the brilliance and long labor he exhibited in expounding the meaning, language and religious values of the Bible and Talmud.

RAV

("Master, teacher") title of Babylonian scholars and rabbis who were not ordained in the land of Israel. The Orthodox rabbi of today is sometimes referred to as Rav.

See also Abba Arekha; Rabbi.

RAVA

(280-352)—Babylonian Amora, dean of the Mahoza Academy. The Talmud is replete with the discussions between him and his contemporary, Abbaye.

See also Amora.

READING, MARQUESS OF

(Rufus Daniel Isaacs; 1860-1935)—English statesman, diplomat and lawyer. He was the first Jew to be Viceroy of India, Lord Chief Justice, Foreign Minister or Attorney General. The Marquess possessed a strong Jewish consciousness and was chairman of the Palestine Electric Corporation.

REBEKAH

Daughter of Bethuel; wife of Isaac, mother of Jacob and Esau, one of the Four Mothers of Israel. Believing Jacob more deserving than Esau, she helped him to deceive the aging, blind Isaac and to receive the firstborn's blessing instead of Esau. Rebekah was buried in the Cave of Machpelah.

RECONSTRUCTIONISM

Philosophy originated by Mordecai M. Kaplan in the 1930's, which proclaims Judaism a civilization, and not merely a religion. Judaism, as a religion, is declared one of the manifestations of Jewish civilization, as are its folk-ways, language, literature. God, in reconstructionist thought, is no longer a personal deity, but is identified with "that aspect of reality which elicits the most serviceable traits." The movement supports the rebuilding of the land of Israel, the fountain-head of Jewish civilization, and, at the same time, stresses the importance of strengthening Jewish community life all over the world. It has issued various prayerbooks, and publishes the *Reconstructionist* magazine in New York City.

RED SEA

The oceanic gulf which extends from the Indian Ocean to the Gulf of Suez, the scene of the miraculous crossing by the Israelites, under Moses' guidance, in their escape from Egypt and Pharaoh's army. In Hebrew the Red Sea is called *Yam Suf* (Sea of Reeds).

REFORM JUDAISM

Movement within Judaism which declares that the Jewish religion has constantly changed and developed, and that this development must continue in our age. The Reform movement originated in Germany following the Napoleonic granting of rights to Jews. The early Reform congregations shortened the synagogue service, prayed and preached in German, and used the organ. Among their most noted leaders was Abraham Geiger, who demanded a thoroughgoing rejection of Talmudic ritual and practice. In 1873, Isaac Mayer Wise founded the Union of American Hebrew Congregations and brought Reform Judaism to the fore in the United States. In recent years, American Reform Judaism has gradually reintroduced ceremonies and traditions which earlier Reform had declared primitive. Zionism, too, once rejected by Reform, has now won the approval of many Reform Jews.

REHOBOAM

Son of Solomon, became king at the age of 16 (about 937-920 B.C.E.). He arrogantly ignored the people's plea for easing their taxes and burdens. The northern tribes revolted and, under Jeroboam, founded the northern Kingdom of Israel. The southern tribes, consisting of the tribes of Judah and Benjamin, remained loyal to Rehoboam and formed the Kingdom of Judah.

REINHARDT, MAX

(1873-1943)—German theatrical producer. Originally an actor in Berlin, Reinhardt (whose real name was Goldmann) developed into an outstanding producer. His ideas have deeply influenced the modern theater, particularly in staging and decor. After World War I, he created in the Salzburg Festivals a world theatrical center. Fleeing Germany in 1933, Reinhardt became a United States citizen in 1940.

REMBRANDT VAN RIJN

(1607-1669)—This famous Dutch painter, who lived in the Jewish quarter of Amsterdam for 17 years, was attracted by Biblical subjects and Jewish types; 37 of his 200 male portraits are of Jews. Rembrandt illustrated a book of Manasseh ben Israel in addition to painting his portrait. Never did a non-Jewish artist penetrate so deeply and with so much sympathy into the Jewish world as did Rembrandt.

RENAISSANCE

The cultural reawakening of Europe which occurred in the 15th century was aided by the activity of Jewish translators of a century or two earlier; Anatoli, Faraj, and Kalonymos ben Kalonymos. They translated Arab philosophy and science into Latin. Later, Pico della Mirandola was influential in the revival of the study of Hebrew in the 15th century, while Judah Abravanel wrote a widely-read philosophical work,

Dialoghi di Amore. Jews were not important in Renaissance art, though they were active in the musical world of the period. The influence of the Renaissance was especially strong among Italian Jews, who supported with their great wealth many scholars, artists, and musicians.

RESH

The twentieth letter of the Hebrew alphabet, has the numerical value of 200.

See also Aleph Bet.

RESPONSA

This means simply responses to questions, and corresponds to the Hebrew word *teshuvah*, a reply. Responsa refers to the answers given by individual rabbis to questions concerning special cases and points of Jewish law arising in any given condition and time. Since Jewish law covers virtually every activity of man, the collections of Responsa offer more than a knowledge of legal matters; they are a record of economic, political and social conditions of the Jews of many countries and in various periods. Thousands of collections of Responsa have been published and more are coming to light. Responsa were first collected and recorded in post-Talmudic times when the Geonim took over the spiritual and scholarly rule of the Jewish people (early eleventh century C.E.). The legal codes of the Middle Ages and later periods took into consideration the decisions by the great rabbis of the past and present. Solomon ben Abraham Ibu Adret, for instance, who died in 1310, left over 3,000 notable Responsa and his collection is often consulted by those interested in the history of the Jews in Spain. Though the *Shulchan Aruch* of Joseph Caro, completed in the sixteenth century, became the code of record for all Jews, it was impossible to cover every possible occurrence in Jewish life. Hence, among Talmudic scholars the tradition of the Responsa continues to this day.

RESTORATION

The name used to refer to the period after the return of the Jews from Babylonian Exile to Judea (about 538-432 B.C.E.). During the time of the Restoration, Jerusalem was rebuilt and the foundation was laid for the Second Temple and for the Second Commonwealth. At this time Ezra and the *Soferim* founded the Rabbinic tradition.

REUBEN

Oldest son of Jacob and Leah. He saved his brother Joseph from death at the hands of his jealous brothers. He is the ancestor of the tribe of Reuben.

REUBEN, TRIBE OF

One of the tribes of Israel. Its territory was east of the Jordan, today the Kingdom of Jordan. The tribe's emblem was a mandrake; its banner was red. The stone representing Reuben in the High Priest's breastplate was probably a sardius (ruby).

REUVENI, DAVID

(about 1400-1535) Traveller; presumed emissary from the Ten Lost Tribes and forerunner of the Messiah. He appeared in Palestine, Egypt and Italy in 1524 and declared that he had been sent by his brother, king of the tribe of Reuben, to obtain assistance in a war

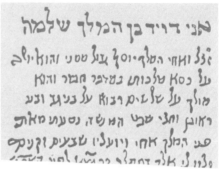

A letter of David Reubini, claiming that he represented a Jewish kingdom in the desert.

against the Turks. At first received cordially by Jew and Christian alike, he finally died a prisoner of the Inquisition in Spain. His most famous disciple was Solomon Molcho, who was hailed by some as a prophet, by others as the Messiah, and was finally burned by the Inquisition in Mantua, Italy.

REVEL, BERNARD

The man who planned the growth of Yeshiva University, including the medical college which was opened in 1955, was Dr. Bernard Revel. A brilliant student of rabbinics and secular lore in his native Russia, Revel came to the United States in 1906 and soon gained

Bernard Revel.

134

higher degrees at American schools of learning. At first engaged in the oil industry, he was induced to return to New York in 1915 to take the leadership of the Rabbi Isaac Elchanan Theological Seminary. Though dividing his time between the institution and his business, he was able to reorganize the Yeshiva, as the Seminary was called, completely, and in 1921 he began devoting all his time to it. In 1915 he established a high school, at which younger boys might combine their Jewish and general studies. In 1920 he took over its Teachers Institute from the Mizrachi Organization. In 1928, despite tremendous opposition, he reached his aim of a college of liberal arts and sciences, first of its kind under Jewish auspices. His great contribution to Jewish thinking was the proof that Orthodoxy could be practiced by Jews in any environment. Bernard Revel died in 1940 at the age of 55.

RIBICOFF, ABRAHAM

(1910-   )—American politician. A member of the Democratic party, Ribicoff served as a representative from Connecticut from 1948 to 1952, as governor of the state from 1954 to 1960, as Secretary of Health, Education, and Welfare from 1961 to 1962 in President Kennedy's cabinet, and has been a senator from Connecticut since 1962. He is particularly known for his interest in social reform and his defense of the rights of minorities.

RICKOVER, HYMAN G.

(1900-   )—A director of American naval scientific research, Rickover was responsible for helping to develop the world's first nuclear-powered submarine. Though his direct methods and harsh criticism have sometimes made him unpopular in the Navy, his views have wide influence.

RIMMONIM

The silver ornaments, with bells, which adorn the top of the Torah scrolls. The Hebrew word *rimmonim* means "pomegranates." In many synagogues the *Keter Torah* (crown) replaces the *Rimmonim* on special holidays.

ROMANS

Great conquerors of the ancient world, first allies and later enemies of the Hasmonean kings, protectors of the Herodians under whom Judea became a complete vassal of Rome. The Jews repeatedly revolted against Rome. In the Jewish War, Vespasian conquered them in Galilee (66 C.E.). Titus destroyed Jerusalem and the Temple, in 70 C.E. Hadrian's general, Severus, cruelly stamped out Bar Kochba's revolt (132-135) and many Jewish martyrs were put to death. Later Roman rulers were more friendly towards the Jews. Jews migrated to Rome where they became Roman citizens. Under Roman auspices, the first Jews settled as pioneers of trade in parts of Western Europe.

ROME

Capital of Italy, and home of the oldest Jewish community in Europe. Jews had settled in Rome as early as the 2nd century B.C.E.; the defeat of the Jews in Palestine by the Roman armies in 68-70 and 132-35 C.E. led to the presence of many more Jews in the city as prisoners of war, who, after their release, stayed in Rome. The Jewish community was permitted to maintain its synagogues, support its rabbis and schools, and entertain visiting scholars from Palestine. The anti-Jewish legislation which was introduced with the rise of Christianity did not greatly affect the Jews of Rome, as they were under the special protection of the Pope. Great scholars, such as Rabbi Nathan (author of the *Aruch*, a Talmudic dictionary) lived in the city. The community reached its peak in the early 16th century, when the popes had Jewish physicians attending them. In 1555, however, the ghetto was introduced to Rome, as were compulsory wearing of the Jewish badge, and economic restrictions. Jews received full emancipation only in 1870. The present Jewish population is 12,000.

See also Italy

ROSENWALD, JULIUS

(1862-1932)—One of the great American philanthropists. He was born in Illinois in 1862. His early business years were spent in New York. Later he returned to Chicago, where he manufactured men's clothing. He became interested in the young Sears-Roebuck mail order business when it ordered 10,000 suits from his company. He and his family invested in the firm and later purchased a controlling interest. In 1910 Sears retired and Rosenwald became president. Rosenwald was particularly concerned with the welfare of the American Negro. He established in 1917 the Julius Rosenwald Fund, the capital and interest of which were to be expended in twenty-five years on educational and welfare work among Negroes. He also gave to many Jewish causes, extending from his home city of Chicago to the Ukraine in Russia. War relief and institutions in Palestine were included among the causes aided by his generosity. He gave five million dollars to the University of Chicago, helped labor unions, national defense and every worthy cause that came to his attention. In 1929 he loaned $50,000 to the International Ladies Garment Workers' Union to help them combat sweat shops. In his participation in civic life he regularly allied himself with liberal and progressive forces.

ROSENZWEIG, FRANZ

(1886-1929)—German theologian. Raised in an assimilated family Rosenzweig, as a young man, contemplated converting to Christianity, but committed himself to Judaism after undergoing a spiritual experience while attending a Yom Kippur service. His theological writings, the most important of which is *The Star of Redemption*, have had great influence on both Jews and Christians.

ROSH HASHANAH

("Head of the year") The Jewish New Year. It is celebrated by Orthodox and Conservative Jews on the first and second days of Tishri and by Reform Jews only on the first day of Tishri. In the Bible, Rosh Hashanah is described as the day of the sounding of the Shofar (the ram's horn), and also as the Day of Memorial (the birthday of the world and of God's creation), or the Day of Judgment. It begins the Ten Days of Penitence which end on Yom Kippur, the Day of Atonement. The High Holidays, Rosh Hashanah and Yom Kippur, are also called the "Days of Awe," the days when the sound of the Shofar calls man to self-judgment and summons him to prayer, repentance and good deeds. The synagogue service of Rosh Hashanah dramatizes man's frailty and his need to take stock of his deeds and duties. Among the traditional customs of Rosh Hashanah are the dipping of bread in honey to symbolize hope for a good and sweet new year to come. Hymns and poems in the days' liturgy express movingly "the mighty holiness of the day." Many of them were written in medieval times, such as the *Unetaneh Tokef* prayer, which says: "On Rosh Hashanah it is written and on Yom Kippur it is sealed, how many are to pass away and how many are to be born; who shall be tranquil and who disturbed; who shall be abased and who uplifted . . ." But Rosh Hashanah is not only a Day of Awe; it is also one of festive joy. It is not a sad holiday. Jews believe that prayer, repentance and good deeds will please God and lead to a fruitful and happy New Year.

ROSH HODESH

(Beginning of the month) also called New Moon (the new moon determines the beginning of the Jewish month). Rosh Hodesh, in ancient Israel, was a sacred rest day, like the Sabbath; now it is a half-holiday. The Torah is read and special prayers are recited in the synagogue.

ROTH, CECIL

(1899-1970)—Born in England and a member of the Oxford University faculty for many years, Roth settled in Israel in 1964. He wrote important scholarly works on Jewish art, the Marranos, the Italian and British Jewish communities, and many other subjects. Among his most outstanding books are *The Jews in the Renaissance* and *A History of the Marranos*. He was also the editor-in-chief of the *Enyclopaedia Judaica*.

ROTH, HENRY

(1906-   )—American novelist. Roth's *Call It Sleep* is perhaps the most outstanding account of Jewish immigrant life on New York's Lower East Side and is also renowned for its innovative literary technique. First published in 1934, it was little known until the 1960s, when it was rediscovered by critics and the reading public.

ROTH, PHILIP

(1933-   )—American writer. Roth's many works include *Goodbye Columbus*, a collection of short stories about middle-class Jewish life, and the best-selling novel *Portnoy's Complaint*.

ROTHSCHILD, MAYER AMSCHEL

(1743-1812)—Founder of one of the world's richest banking houses. The name means Red Shield, for the family lived for centuries in the House of the Red Shield, on Jews' Street of Frankfort, Germany. Mayer Amschel learned about finance in another bank and in 1760 opened his own in Frankfort. At that time the landgrave, or ruler, of the province of Hesse-Cassel was William IV—the very man who earned a fortune by hiring out his mercenary Hessian troops to the British during the American Revolution. As agent and banker for the landgrave, Rothschild made many profitable investments which gave his own fortune a favorable start. So trustworthy was he considered that

The Rothschild family's original house in the ghetto of Frankfurt-am-Main.

when William was compelled to flee invading French troops, he left $3,000,000 in money and jewels with Rothschild; this was all returned with profit. Mayer Amschel had nineteen children. He was wise enough to settle his sons in five European capitals so that the business became widespread and interlocking. It is said that his third son, Nathan Mayer (1777-1836), who lived in England, learned of Waterloo through carrier pigeon before any other Englishman knew of it. There are many other stories related of this family; but their truest distinction is their honesty and charity and their devotion to Judaism.

RUBINSTEIN, ARTHUR

(1886-   )—Pianist. The Polish-born Rubinstein was a child prodigy, going on a concert tour at the age of 12. Though he first appeared in the U.S. in 1907, this great virtuoso was widely acclaimed here only after his concert tour of 1937. In 1940, he settled in America. In addition to his many recordings, Rubinstein has also composed pieces for the piano and chamber music.

RUMANIA

Jews first settled in the region now known as Rumania in the 2nd century C.E. There were additional waves of immigration to Rumania in the 14th century (from Hungary), the 16th century (from Spain), and the 17th century (from Poland). During the 19th century Jews played an important role in the establishing of a modern economy in Rumania; however, they remained subject to severe discrimination and many left the country. During World War II nearly half of Rumania's 800,000 Jews were killed. Over 200,000 Rumanian Jews have gone to Israel since 1948. The country's present Jewish population is 100,000. The Communist government of Rumania, though it restricts and controls Jewish communal and organizational activity, has followed a policy of increasing, though cautious, tolerance vis-a-vis both Rumanian Jewry and the State of Israel.

RUSSIA

Jews have lived in the southern parts of Russia since classical times. In the 8th century the Khazars converted to Judaism. The Jewish population of Russia increased considerably in the 18th century when Russia absorbed many territories that had formerly been part of Poland. Russian Jewish history, from the earliest times to the present, is marked by extreme anti-Semitism, forced conversions, and severe economic restrictions. The Pale of Settlement, which limited the area in which Jews might settle, was established in 1835; it remained in force until 1915. However, Jewish life within the Pale was vigorous and productive. The Talmud was studied intensely, and both Hasidism and Zionism attracted many. Large numbers of Russian Jews emigrated to the United States, starting in the 1880s. Others participated in the movement to resettle Palestine, and many of the leaders of modern Israel are of Russian birth or ancestry. Jews were active in the revolutions of 1917, but though the Soviet constitution guarantees religious freedom, Jews are allowed almost no cultural expression. In addition, the Soviet government follows an anti-Israel policy and is the main backer of the Arab states. There are now about 3,000,000 Jews in Russia, many of whom have strong Jewish sentiments. In the 1960s and 1970s there was a great awakening of Jewish consciousness and assertiveness among Soviet Jews, especially the young generation. Many have been imprisoned by the Soviet government, and others were persecuted because of their desire to emigrate to Israel. They are encouraged by widespread support in the United States and other Western countries. Since 1966 more than 100,000 Russian Jews have managed to settle in Israel.

RUTENBERG, PINHAS

(1879-1942)—Zionist and electrical engineer. Rutenberg was an active revolutionary in Czarist Russia, participating in the Russian Revolution of 1917 as a Menshevik. After imprisonment by the Bolsheviks he emigrated to Palestine, where he was granted a concession for the generation of electric power for almost all of Palestine by the British Mandatory government. This necessitated the building of a hydro-electric power project at the joining of the Yarmuk and Jordan rivers, which was accomplished by his Palestine Electric Company.

RUTH

The young Moabite widow who faithfully followed Naomi, her Israelite mother-in-law, home to Bethlehem. She married Boaz who saw her glean in his field. She was an ancestor of David. Her story is told in the Book of Ruth.

RYBACK, ISSACHAR

(1897-1935)—Russian artist. Born in the Ukraine, where his father was killed in a pogrom, Ryback studied art in Kiev, St. Petersburg, and Berlin, then settled in Paris in 1920s. Influenced by the French Cubists and the German Expressionists, he worked in several different genres, including illustrations for children's books. His paintings on the Jewish shtetl life of his youth are particularly noteworthy.

SAAD AL-DAULA

(d. 1291)—Physician and statesman at the court of the Mongol ruler in Baghdad and Tabriz. In 1289 he became Vizier of the entire Mongol Empire, and remained in this position until his murder in 1291 by Moslems and Mongols who were jealous of the success of a Jew. His death set off a series of anti-Jewish riots.

SAADIA GAON

The title Gaon, always added to Saadia's name, was given to the intellectual leaders of the Jews in Babylonia. Saadia was born in an Egyptian village in 882. He received a Jewish and Arabic education and he started his literary and scholarly work when he was a very young man. Because of threats by the powerful Karaite sect, which he attacked in his writings, he fled to Palestine in 915. There he resided in Tiberias until 928. So great was his fame as a scholar that the authorities in the city of Sura, Babylonia, seat of one of the outstanding Jewish academies, offered him the position of Gaon. Saadia had a strong sense of righteousness. When he found himself in conflict over an injustice perpetrated by a lay official, he went to Baghdad where he stayed seven years, until he felt the time suitable to return. Saadia revived the study of the Talmud and rabbinics in Babylonia. He was distinguished in a remarkable number of fields: as a dictionary maker, a student of word origins, a commentator, translator and philosopher. His translation of the Bible into Arabic, with commentary, had a powerful influence on Arab-speaking Jews and their Mohammedan neighbors. His greatest work, written in Arabic, is the *Beliefs and Opinions*—a complete recounting of the faith and morals of his people. He wrote the book in Arabic to make it possible for those Jews of his time who could not read Hebrew, and possibly for his educated Moslem neighbors, to become acquainted with the ideas of Judaism. Saadia Gaon died in Surah in 942.

SABBATH (SHABBAT)

The day of rest, the only day of observance mentioned in the Ten Commandments. Sabbath, even though it comes every week, is the most important holiday in the Jewish calendar. When the command to keep the Sabbath was given, it was the first time in history that every seventh day was set aside for rest and holiness. Later, other religions emulated that law. When the leaders of the French Revolution tried to make each tenth day the time for rest it was argued that one in seven was the minimum requisite to health and good work. The Jewish Sabbath, however, is not devoted to mere repose of the body. It is also a time for knowing God, the Creator; a time for thoughtful man to try to understand the process of Creation and to learn that all men have the same father. Thus man attains a feeling of brotherhood, a sense of justice, a love of peace. In a traditional Jewish household everyone, even the animals, is given this day of rest. The Sabbath observances, the special meals, the prayers, prescribed by law and custom, all increase the holiness of the day. Blessings, song and study add sanctity and glory to the day. In the new State of Israel, Shabbat (Saturday) is the official day of rest, and the whole country joins in its observance.

SABBATH LIGHTS

Candles kindled by the woman of the household as she recites a blessing on Friday evening in honor of the coming of the Sabbath. If there is no woman in the home, the lights may be kindled by a man.

SABBATICAL YEAR

The seventh year during which no agriculture was allowed and all outstanding debts were cancelled. It was observed in this manner in Israel during the time of the Second Temple.

See also Jubilee.

SABBETIANS

Followers of Shabbetai Zevi, a false Messiah who died in 1676. Many of his adherents maintained their allegiance to him, though he had adopted Mohammedanism before his death. The Donmeh sect was led by Jacob Querido, who also converted to Islam while preaching that Shabbetai Zevi would reappear to save Israel. Other leaders of the Sabbetians were Abraham Cardozo in North Africa and Mordecai Mochiah of Germany. Some 1,500 attempted a pilgrimage to Palestine, which was unsuccessful. Finally, the rise of Hasidism captured the attention of the popular mind.

SABORAIM

Scholars and teachers who lived in Babylonia about the beginning of the 6th century C.E. They supplemented and finished the editing of the Babylonian Talmud, most of which had been collected and written down by Rav Ashi and Rabina.

See also Talmud, Babylonian

SACHAR, ABRAM

1899-   )—American historian and educator. Born in New York City, Sachar was an organizer of the B'nai B'rith Hillel Foundation and served as its national director from 1933 to 1948. He was the founding president of Brandeis University and became its chancellor in 1968. He has written several historical works, including the 1-volume *History of the Jews*.

SACHS, NELLY

(1891-1970)—German poetess. Born in Germany, Nelly Sachs fled to Sweden in 1940 and lived there for the remainder of her life. Her poems, mostly written after World War II, express an undying faith in the vitality and indestructibility of the Jewish people. In 1966 she was co-recipient of the Nobel Prize for literature with S. Agnon. Many of her best poems are collected in the volume *O the Chimneys*.

SADDUCEES

(*Tzeddukim*) Jewish party (sect) during the reign of the Hasmoneans and at the time of the Roman rule of Judea (about the end of the 2nd century B.C.E.

through the 1st century C.E.). The Sadducees were the party of the priests and kings. They believed in the strict word of the Torah and rejected Oral Torah, the teachings of Ezra and the Soferim. The party opposing the Sadducees was the Pharisees.

SAFED

Town in Upper Galilee. In the 15th century Safed became a center of Kabbalism as it housed Isaac Luria and Chaim Vital. Joseph Caro wrote the *Shulchan Aruch* in Safed and the city was one of the "Four Holy Cities" of Palestine. Its present population is 9,000 and it has become an art center in modern Israel.

SALK, JONAS E.

(1914-)—American scientist. Salk, working at the University of Pittsburgh, led to the development of the polio vaccine named after him, which gives immunity against paralytic poliomyelitis. In 1957 he was awarded the Nobel Prize in Medicine.

SALOME ALEXANDRA

Wise and able queen of Judea (76-67 B.C.E.), wife and successor of the Hasmonean King Alexander Jannaeus.

SALOMON, HAYM

(1740-1785)—A Polish Jew who came to America and provided the money which brought success to the American Revolution. He arrived in New York about

Statue of Robert Morris, George Washington, and Haym Salomon.

1772, soon becoming a successful merchant. In 1778 he was arrested as a spy by Sir Henry Clinton, the British commander, and charged with accepting orders from General Washington to destroy the fleet and stores of the enemy. He was turned over to the Hessians to serve as interpreter. In this capacity he was able to liberate French and American prisoners and to escape to Philadelphia when discovered. There, as a broker in bills of exchange, he helped the French finance their expeditions against the British. Later he aided Robert Morris, superintendent of finance, in raising money for the patriots' cause. He loaned his private fortune to the new government, but Congress has never acknowledged the debt and his descendants have not established their claim. A biographer, Charles E. Russell, declared: "All Americans of all races may acclaim Haym Salomon as a patriot, a benefactor to his country, an inciter of patriotism to members of his race, to his countrymen of all races and to their later generations."

SALONIKA

Greek port city. A Jewish community was found in the city as early as 50 C.E. by the Christian Apostle Paul. After 1492 exiled Spanish and Portuguese Jews flocked to the city, then under Turkish rule, and made it a center of culture. Such men as Ephraim Caro and his son, Joseph (compiler of the *Shulchan Aruch*), Judah Beneviste, and Joseph Taytasak, a noted Kabbalist, set in motion an active religious and intellectual life. A schism due to Jacob Frank's stay in the city in the 17th century was healed, and the community began to flourish once again in the 18th century. Until 1912, in fact, the predominantly Jewish population of Salonika (about 80,000) prevented ships from docking and unloading in the harbor on Saturday. After World War I, however, there was a large Greek immigration into the city, while World War II saw the extermination of almost the entire community. At present, there are some 2,000 Jews in Salonika.

SALVADOR, FRANCIS

A prominent American patriot, who was born in England in 1747 of a distinguished Portuguese Jewish family. He came to America in 1773, where he purchased a large farm in South Carolina. He made many friends among the patriotic rebels whom he joined. He was elected a member of the Provincial Congress, which later became the General Assembly of the new state of South Carolina in 1775, and he served on many important committees. Salvador was the first Jew to become a representative in a popular assembly in America. He bitterly opposed the British refusal to accept petitions of the Congress for redress of wrongs inflicted on colonists. When South Carolina formed its own army, Salvador served on the committee to provide the soldiers' pay. When the American Revolution started in 1776, it was British policy to incite the

Indians against the white settlers. In July of that year, while their fleet was stationed off Charleston, they aroused the Cherokees to massacre. Salvador rode to the military commander to sound the alarm. He was already hated by the (pro-British) Tories, who fought the rebels with the Indians' help. Salvador became a commander of the revolutionary forces. On August 1st the combined Tory and Indian troops fell upon the patriots. Salvador was shot from his horse and scalped. His name is mentioned in every history of South Carolina.

SALVADOR, JOSEPH

(1796-1873)—French scholar. Trained as a physician, Salvador committed himself to Judaism even though only one of his parents was Jewish. He wrote many books on Judaism and Christianity, interpreting Judaism along historical and rational lines as adaptable to the needs and standards of modern times, and attempting to outline a universal creed for all mankind. Salvador's biography of Jesus, which was profoundly influential throughout the 19th cent., was one of the first books to emphasize the Jewish background of Jesus' life and thought.

SAMARIA

(Shomron) capital of the northern Kingdom of Israel built by King Omri (9th century B.C.E.). Elijah, Amos, Elisha, Hosea and Micah preached in Samaria. The city was destroyed by the Assyrians, after a three year siege; with it fell the Kingdom of Israel, 722 B.C.E.

SAMARITANS

The Samaritans were a group who developed in Central Palestine out of Babylonians, Cuthites and Assyrians who were brought there to replace the Jews who were exiled in 722 B.C.E. by the Assyrians. The Samaritans were semi-pagans, who adopted some Jewish customs and later proclaimed themselves the only true Jews. When the first Jews returned from exile in Babylonia in 537, the Samaritans hindered the rebuilding of the land and the Temple. They knew only the Books of Moses and Joshua of the Bible. To them God was merely the ruler of Canaan. Instead of Mount Zion, they proclaimed the holiness of Mount Gerizim. Their efforts to hurt the returning Jews proved futile; but in the natural course of events Jews intermarried with them and the families were as much Samaritans as Hebrews. Slowly the numbers of Samaritans dwindled, until today there are not more than two hundred and fifty of them. They live in Nablus and carry on their rituals on the mountain top they have made into a shrine.

SAMBATYON

A mythical river which rested on the Sabbath. The river is mentioned by Josephus, Pliny and Rabbi Akiba, and allegedly circled the land of either the Ten Lost Tribes or the Sons of Moses.

SAMECH

The fifteenth letter of the Hebrew alphabet, has the value of 60.

See also Aleph Bet.

SAMSON

Judge and hero of the tribe of Dan, from Zorah, famous for his great strength whose secret source was said to be in his long hair. He was betrayed by Delilah and was taken captive to the land of the Philistines. He was blinded and his hair was cut. In a final display of his great strength, he destroyed the Philistines' temple, killing thousands of his tormentors and himself.

SAMUEL

(11th century B.C.E.) A great priest, seer and leader. The story of his life is recorded in the first book of Samuel. His mother, Hannah, in gratitude for this only son, dedicated him to the service of God and brought him to the High Priest Eli in Shiloh as soon as he was weaned. It was the young Samuel who received the divine message that the Ark of the Covenant would be taken in battle by the Philistines because of the sinfulness of Eli's house. When the prophecy came true, Eli died, shocked, on hearing of the Philistines' victory. Samuel took his place. He went to Ramah where he lived for twenty years, esteemed as a great seer. Samuel and his disciples worked to free the people from the Philistine tyranny, and they spread the spirit of revolt throughout the country. Samuel anointed Saul, the first king in Israel, and Saul led the people in the great battle against the Philistines and threw out the invaders. Later, Samuel recognized Saul's willfull temperament and under the guidance of God he chose David to be the next king. The struggle between Saul and David is related in great detail and the story of Samuel's later life is told only in relationship to that conflict. It is clear that Samuel was the leader who kept his people alive and free in a time of great crisis. He gave them encouragement in adversity and quieted them and looked wisely into the future. The prophet Jeremiah compared him to Moses, as one who interceded for his people; and it is generally accepted he is next to Moses among great Biblical figures.

SAMUEL, MAURICE

(1895-1972)—American writer. Born in Rumania, Samuel spent his early years in England and came to the United States in 1914. A forceful and effective exponent of the Zionist point of view, Samuel did many translations from Yiddish and Hebrew and was a talented, extremely literate writer. His works include *The World of Sholom Aleichem*, *The Prince of the Ghetto*, *Blood Accusation*, *The Gentleman and the Jew*, and *Light on Israel*.

SANDMEL, SAMUEL

(1911-   )—American scholar. A member of the Hebrew Union College faculty since 1952, and its provost from 1957 to 1966, Sandmel began his career as a specialist in Philo and Hellenistic literature and is today one of the foremost Jewish students of early Christianity. Among his many outstanding books are *We Jews and Jesus, A Jewish Understanding of the New Testament,* and *The First Christian Century in Judaism and Christianity.*

SANHEDRIN

From the Greek word meaning "assembly" *(synedrion),* the Talmudic term for a court is derived. The tractate of the Talmud entitled *Sanhedrin* describes a lesser court of twenty-three members and a Great Sanhedrin of seventy-one. The Sanhedrin interpreted the law and judged civil and criminal cases. It is reported that when the members of the court took their places in the semi-circle, every scholar took his proper seat without conflict of precedence. The Great Sanhedrin originated most likely in the Hasmonean era, about 141 B.C.E., and endured until the time of the destruction of the Temple. It was replaced by the limited rule of the patriarchs, who tried cases and made religious and legal decisions. To guarantee that all religious and social views were represented in this ancient democratic assembly, the court had both Pharisees and Sadducees in its membership. It met in a chamber of the Temple readily available to all interested parties. Attempts to re-establish the Sanhedrin failed. Napoleon planned the formation of a new Sanhedrin to speak for all Jews but the effort was not successful.

See also Zugot.

SAPIR, PINHAS

(1907-1975)—Israeli political leader and financial expert. Born in Poland, Sapir became a Zionist as a youngster and emigrated to Palestine in 1929. For many years, during the British mandate period, he headed the country's water-supply company, and was also active in the labor movement. During the War of Independence he headed the quartermaster branch of Haganah. After statehood he served as director general of the Defense Ministry and of the Finance Ministry. In 1955 he became minister of commerce and industry. He became minister of finance in 1963. He resigned in 1968 to become secretary general of the Israel Labor Party, serving concurrently in the cabinet as minister without portfolio. He became minister of finance again in 1969, holding this post until his death.

SARAH

From Ur in the Chaldees, wife of Abraham. She was a beautiful woman of great courage and piety. Late in life she bore Abraham a son, Isaac. She was buried in the Cave of Machpelah. Sarah is the first of the Four Mothers of Israel.

SARAI

Name of Sarah before God's covenant with Abraham.

SARGON (II)

Assyrian king, son of Shalmaneser. The city of Samaria fell to him after a three-year siege. He completed the destruction of the Kingdom of Israel and forced its people into captivity.

SARNOFF, DAVID

(1897-1971)—American broadcasting executive. Born in Russia, Sarnoff came to America in 1900. Orphaned at an early age, he learned how to use the telegraph key and worked as an operator for the Marconi Company. In 1912, Sarnoff picked up the radio report of the sinking of the *Titanic.* For three days he stayed at his post, receiving national acclaim for his achievement. Thereafter, he rose high in the Marconi Company, and in quick stages became president of the Radio Corporation of America, which had absorbed Marconi. He built RCA into America's largest electronics manufacturer, and in 1926 founded the National Broadcasting Co. as an RCA subsidiary. In both World Wars, Sarnoff helped supply the armed forces with electrical and electronic equipment. After serving on General Eisenhower's staff as a brigadier general, he was awarded the Order of Merit.

David Sarnoff.

SASSOON FAMILY

Anglo-Indian family, eminent in commerce, society and philanthropy. The family's fortunes were founded by David (1792-1864), who settled in Bombay and acquired a virtual monopoly of the opium trade. The family later moved to England, where many were admitted to the nobility.

SAUL

First king of Israel (about 1040 B.C.E.), anointed by Samuel. He united the tribes in the fight against hostile neighbors, especially the strong Philistines. At first he favored young David who cheered him with his harp and songs. Later he turned against David. To avoid being taken alive by the Philistines, Saul killed himself by falling on his sword in the battle of Mount Gilboa.

SCHARFSTEIN, ASHER

(1890-   )—American publisher. Born in Russia, Scharfstein came to the United States in 1921. In 1924 he founded the Ktav Publishing House, Inc. in New York City. Under his aegis as president, the firm soon became the leading North American publisher of scholarly studies, textbooks, and educational aids in the field of Judaica. Scharfstein was also the editor-compiler of two books, *Tikun LaKorim* and *Encyclopedia for Readers of the Torah*.

Asher Scharfstein.

SCHATZ, BORIS

(1866-1932)—Sculptor. In 1906 Schatz, an artist of considerable repute and professor at the Academy of Visual Art at Sofia, Bulgaria, founded the Bezalel School of Arts and Crafts in Jerusalem. As director of the school until his death, he had a great influence on Israeli art. One of his best-known works is a statue called "Mattathias the Hasmonean."

SCHECHTER, SOLOMON

One of the world's greatest modern Jewish scholars, he was born in Roumania in 1850 and died in New York in 1915. Son of a pious scholar, he received a good rabbinical education. As a young man he continued his theological and secular studies in Vienna and later in Berlin. His brilliance came to the attention of Claude G. Montefiore, who invited him to London in 1882 to become his rabbinic tutor and continue his scholarly work there. Later, appointed reader in rabbinics at Cambridge University, he wrote and lectured widely, visiting the United States as lecturer in 1895. His world fame was based on his discovery of the lost Hebrew original of the book of *Ecclesiasticus* (The Wisdom of Ben Sirah) and of other originals of important Judaic documents in the Genizah of the Cairo synagogue. (A *genizah* is a storeroom for worn or unused books and leaves in the holy tongue, Hebrew.) This brought Schechter an honorary degree from Cambridge, a professorship in Hebrew at the University College, London, and in 1901 an invitation to become president of the Jewish Theological Seminary of America, which was being reorganized. Dr. Schechter became a leader of what is now called Conservative Judaism, which takes a middle position between Orthodoxy and Reform. He organized the United Synagogue of America, today comprising hundreds of Conservative congregations. His works, *Some Aspects of Rabbinic Theology*, *Studies in Judaism* and other books and essays brought him equal fame with his Genizah discoveries. Few men have written so clearly and brilliantly on the history, teachings and literature of the Jewish people.

SCHIFF, JACOB H.

Renowned as financier and philanthropist, born in Frankfort, Germany, in 1847, the son of a distinguished old family. He came to New York at the age of eighteen in 1865. Like his father, he went into the banking business, rising quickly. He married the daughter of the president of Kuhn, Loeb and Company and in 1885 became head of that company when Loeb retired. Schiff helped reorganize and develop railroads and other corporations and he arranged large loans to foreign governments—except to Russia, which was maltreating its Jews. His contributions to hundreds of Jewish and non-Jewish causes brought him the respect and honor of all America. He helped Herzl and others rebuild the Holy Land; the Haifa Technion could not have been built without his generous aid. He aided educational institutions such as the Jewish Theological Seminary, the Hebrew Union College, the New York Public Library, and Harvard and Columbia Universities. He subsidized the publication of the English translation of the Bible and the Classics Series by the Jewish Publication Society of America. Without his support there might have been no *Jewish Encyclopedia* and other works whose authors he supported. When he died in 1920, his passing was mourned by millions throughout the world.

SCHNEERSOHN FAMILY

Family of Hasidic rabbis and scholars. Shneor Zalman of Ladi (1747-1813) was a pupil of Dov Ber of Meseritz and founded the *Habad* movement within Hasidism. This movement, in contrast to other wings of Hasidism, emphasized the importance of study and learning. Shneor Zalman was the first of the Schneersohn dynasty, which has led *Habad* since his day. Dov Ber of Lubavitch (d. 1828) succeeded him, and he himself was succeeded by his son-in-law, Menahem Mendel Schneersohn (d. 1866), a great Talmudist and the author of the volumes of responsa called *Tzemah*

Tzedek ("The Plant of Righteousness"). The *Habad* movement was transplanted to America after World War II, with the arrival here of Rabbi Joseph Isaac Schneersohn (1880-1950), who established *yeshivot* and other institutions after the *Habad* tradition. The present leader of *Habad*, or "Lubavitcher, Hasidim," is Rabbi Menahem Mendel Schneersohn (b. 1902). Under his direction the movement, based in the Crown Heights section of Brooklyn, has experienced great growth in the United States and abroad, and has initiated a program of reaching out to non-Hasidic, and even non-observant, elements of the Jewish community, especially among the younger generation. *See also* Habad.

SCRIBES

(Hebrew, *sofer*)—From the time of the Talmud the scribe has been a professional writer of the Torah and other documents. At an earlier period the scribe was a learned man (Ezra the Scribe, for example) and was an authority both on the text and on the interpretation of Scripture. The *Soferim* of this period played a decisive role in the development of Jewish law.

See also Soferim.

SEALS

During the Biblical period, both documents and jars were often closed by a man's personal seal. These seals, of which over one hundred have been discovered, bore their owner's name; in later periods, such decorations as the *Menorah* were added. Often, the seal was copied onto a signet ring. The custom of using personal seals lasted well into the Middle Ages, when animals, such as the lion, became a family's sign. The State of Israel has adopted a seal which pictures a *Menorah* bordered by olive branches.

SEDARIM (OF THE MISHNAH)

("Divisions, orders") the six divisions of the Mishnah, each of which is subdivided into tractates (*massechtot*), chapters (*perakim*) and paragraphs. The six Sedarim are:

1. *Zeraim* (Seeds): laws concerning agriculture.
2. *Moed* (Festival): laws regulating the Sabbath, festivals and fast days.
3. *Nashim* (Women): laws concerning marriage and divorce.
4. *Nezikim* (Damages): civil and criminal laws.
5. *Kodashim* (Holy Matters): laws concerning Temple services, sacrifices and *Shehitah*.
6. *Toharot* (Purities): laws of ritual purity and cleanliness.

SEDER

The Passover service at home which celebrates the liberation of the Jewish people from Egyptian bondage. In recent times community Seders are held as well as the home Seders. Seder means "order."

A Persian Passover Seder.

SEDER DISH

The platter, often beautifully tooled and designed, which holds the foods eaten during the Seder ceremony. The foods are: (1) a lamb's shank bone, symbolizing the paschal sacrifice; (2) a roasted egg, symbolizing the sacrifice brought to the Temple on festivals; (3) green herbs, usually parsley, symbolizing spring; (4) *Haroset;* (5) *Maror.* A separate dish often holds the *Three Matzot,* said to stand for the three branches of Israel: *Cohen* (the priest), *Levi* (the Levite) and *Israel* (the people).

See also Haroset; Maror; Matzot.

SEFER YETZIRAH

(Heb., lit., The Book of Creation)—Modern scholarship ascribes this mystical work to the 3rd-6th centuries, though there is a tradition that it was written by Abraham or by Rabbi Akiba. The book contains a system of cosmology which emphasizes the mystical powers of numbers and of the letters of the Hebrew alphabet; it became a basic book of Kabbalah and was the subject of many commentaries.

See also Kabbalah.

SEFIRAH

Period of Omer, also a time of remembrance of the sufferings of Rabbi Akiba and his students and other scholars under the Roman Emperor Hadrian. According to tradition no weddings or parties are held during the Sefirah period, except on Lag Beomer.

See also Lag Beomer; Omer.

SEIR

Mountainous territory south of the Dead Sea stretching to the Gulf of Aqaba. Esau (Edom) settled there after he lost his birthright. Seir was renamed the Land of Edom. Mount Hor, where Aaron died, is in the region of Seir.

SEIXES FAMILY

Gershom Mendez Seixes (1745-1816) served as rabbi of the Sephardic Congregation Shearith Israel, of New York, for fifty years, and was rabbi of Mikveh Israel Congregation in Philadelphia (1780-4), as well. A prominent clergyman, he took part in George Washington's inauguration as first president of the United States. One of his sons, David G. Seixes (1788-1880) was a well-known educator, while another, Benjamin Mendez Seixes was among the founders of the New York Stock Exchange.

Gershom Mendes Seixas.

SELEUCIDS

A dynasty of Syrian kings founded by Seleucus Nicator, one of Alexander the Great's generals. Antiochus III conquered Palestine about 200 B.C.E. and pursued a lenient policy towards the Jews. The policies of Antiochus IV were more repressive; he tried to destroy Judaism completely. His efforts caused the Hasmonean revolt, in which the Jews freed themselves from Seleucid domination by 128 B.C.E.

SELIGMAN FAMILY

Family of American bankers. Members of the family have served on national and state commissions. Edwin R. A. Seligman (1861-1939) was professor of economics at Columbia University and edited the *Encyclopedia of the Social Sciences*.

SELIHOT

Prayers of penitence asking for forgiveness of sins. A special group of *Selihot* prayers are recited in the synagogue during the Ten Days of Penitence (from Rosh Hashanah to Yom Kippur). *Selihot* are also recited in advance of Rosh Hashanah.

Selihot—prayers of repentance—as found in a 19th-century European prayer book.

SEMICHAH

The Hebrew word *semichah* means the laying on of hands, usually upon the head, and is a symbolic act of blessing and consecration. Religious leaders and the priests in Israel were thus ordained in ancient times. In the Bible Moses ordained Joshua in that manner and their successors continued this custom until 135, when the Roman Emperor Hadrian made ordaining or being ordained punishable by death. The masters then began the custom of ordaining merely by bestowing the title Rabbi. Later, when the original ceremony was revived, it could be carried out only in Palestine; but with the development of large communities in Babylonia and elsewhere it became customary to ordain scholars outside the Holy Land. Yet Jews continued to go to Palestine in the hope that the Patriarch would bestow upon them the title Rabbi as opposed to the lesser title *Rav*, or *Hakim*. Palestinian ordination ended in the eleventh century, the time of the Crusades. In 1538, Jacob Berab passed judgment that if all the wise men of Palestine agreed to ordain a scholar that would start the chain of ordination again. He gathered together twenty-five sages of Safed to ordain him; then he passed his ordination on to others. But the Jerusalem rabbis resented his slighting them and a controversy followed which destroyed Berab's movement. Today the candidates for the rabbinate still receive *semichah*, following a thorough examination in Jewish law and literature. Though the laying on of hands is no longer part of the ceremony, the ancient term still is used. The custom of laying on of hands (upon the head) is still preserved in the blessing of children.

SEMITES

A term applied to the people who speak the related groups of tongues known as the Semitic languages. The term is derived from the name Shem, the son of Noah who is the reputed ancestor of the Jews, Arabs and Aramaeans. The Nazis and others have used the term Semitic race in unfavorable contrast to the Aryan race. Modern anthropologists and biologists have made clear that there are no racial Semitic or Aryan types; that these terms have meaning only as language classifications. Jews are not members of a Semitic race; the Jews of today are a mixed race. Hebrew, Arabic, Aramaic, Ethiopic and others constitute the Semitic languages.

SEPHARDIM

One of the great divisions of Jewry is the Jews of Spanish or Portuguese descent (also called Spagnoli). In 1492 and 1497, great persecutions and the final expulsion of Jews from Spain and Portugal led to mass migration. Spanish and Portuguese Jews fled to Italy, Southern France and to many parts of the Ottoman Empire, North Africa, the Balkans and the Middle East, where some of them settled in Palestine. The refugees were joined later by Marranos, the term used for their brethren who converted to escape the tortures of the Inquisition but held to their Jewish customs in secret until they were able to flee to friendly countries. Further migrations occurred, until Sephardic communities were established in many European countries and in the Americas. They created great cultural centers in Cairo, Salonika, Jerusalem and Safed. They held on to their specific customs and pronunciation of Hebrew, differing from that of the Ashkenazim, the other major division of Jewry. Today the modern Hebrew spoken in Israel is Sephardic. Many Sephardim have preserved their old language, Ladino, which is close to Castilian Spanish. It is used for everyday speech and as a literary medium, much as Yiddish is used by many Ashkenazim. Everywhere the Sephardim went they founded their own synagogues and communal institutions and maintained their distinct traditions, apart from the Ashkenazic Jews. Many prominent Sephardim were early settlers in this country. Some of them were shareholders in the Dutch West Indies Company and they protected the rights of all the Jews in New Amsterdam. Great old Sephardic congregations still exist today, such as Shearith Israel in New York (founded 1654 in New Amsterdam) and Mikveh Israel in Philadelphia (founded in 1740 and built by Jewish patriots of the American Revolution).

SEPPHORIS

(*Tzippori*) one of the largest and best fortified cities of Galilee; its capital in Roman times. After the destruction of the Temple, prominent citizens, priests and scholars found refuge there. In the 2nd and 3rd centuries, Sepphoris was a seat of Jewish learning.

See also Javneh.

SEPTUAGINT

("Seventy" in Latin)—The name of the oldest Greek translation of the Bible. A legend tells that seventy Jewish scholars were placed in separate rooms to render the Torah into Greek. When they compared their finished manuscripts, all the versions were identical—a proof of the correctness of the version. The entire Bible was not translated at one time. The Torah was translated about 300 B.C.E. Some portions of the Septuagint are freely translated; others contain additional material in the nature of commentary. But the results of this translation were of tremendous importance. The Bible could now be read by Jews who did not know Hebrew and by the educated people of all the nations, because Greek was the general language of that period. The later revisions of the Septuagint text by the Church fathers brought about a certain amount of confusion in religious camps; so many variations existed. Today the Septuagint is still a great aid to Biblical scholars. It is a guide to the way Hebrew was pronounced in ancient times, and despite confusing additions to the original text, much has been learned about difficult words and phrases in the original Hebrew. At the time the translation of the Septuagint was completed, the Jewish community of Alexandria instituted an annual holiday in its honor.

SERMON

The sermon during services is a unique custom of Judaism which has been adopted by other religious groups. The sermon is usually based on a verse from the Bible which is applied to present times. The popularity and the function of sermons have varied over the centuries.

SETH

Third son of Adam and Eve, born after Abel's murder and Cain's exile to Nod; father of Enosh.

SE'UDAH SHELISHIT

Last of the three prescribed meals of Sabbath, held at the end of the day. *Se'udah Shelishit* is often accompanied by special festivities and singing.

SHAATNEZ

By this word of obscure origin, the Bible (Lev. 19:19, Deut. 22:11) describes the mixing of wool and flax in the making of clothes, and bans the wearing of such garments. Some medieval commentators said this law symbolizes the sinfulness of man's presumptuous mixing of substances which have been created separate.

SHABBAT BERESHIT

The Sabbath immediately following Simhat Torah on which the yearly cycle of the Torah reading is begun. It is named for the first portion of the Torah, which begins with the word *Bereshit* (In the beginning), and which is read on this Sabbath.

SHABBAT HAGADOL

The Sabbath which immediately precedes the holiday of Passover. It is generally accepted that it is called *Shabbat Hagadol* ("the Great Sabbath") because the portion from the prophet Malachi read on that day includes the verse: "Behold I will send you Elijah the prophet before the coming of the *great* and terrible day of the Lord" (3:23). On this Sabbath it is customary for the rabbi to deliver a special discourse on the laws and observance of the holiday of Passover.

SHABBAT SHALOM

Greeting on Sabbath, meaning "may you have the Peace of Sabbath."

SHABBAT SHUVAH

The Sabbath that falls between Rosh Hashanah and Yom Kippur. It is called *Shabbat Shuvah* (the Sabbath of Return) because the portion read from the Prophets on that day begins with the words, "Return, O Israel, unto the Lord thy God." On this Sabbath it is customary for the rabbi to deliver a sermon on the laws and principles of *teshuvah* (repentance).

SHABBETAI ZEVI

See Messiahs, False; Sabbetians.

SHADCHAN

A marriage broker; his fee was a percentage of the dowry. The profession, though still surviving, hardly flourishes as it did in the Middle Ages or in Eastern Europe in more modern times.

SHADRACH, MESHACH, ABED-NEGO

Daniel's three friends who miraculously survived the fiery furnace into which they were cast by King Nebuchadnezzar of Babylon.

SHAHARIT

Morning Service, the second of the three daily services (in the Jewish calendar, the day begins at sunset). The prayers of *Shaharit* are recited early in the morning.

SHALACH MANOT

Exchange of gifts on the day of Purim. Children receive *Shalach Manot*, usually sweets, on Purim.

See also Purim.

SHALLUM

1. King of Israel (about 741 B.C.E.). He assassinated Zechariah, the son of Jeroboam II. Shallum ruled for only one month. He was assassinated and succeeded by Menahem.

2. King of Judah, also called Jehoahaz.

See also Jehoahaz.

SHALMANESER (V)

Assyrian king who led the three-year siege of Samaria, capital of the northern Kingdom of Israel, and took captive its last king, Hoshea. His campaign led to the destruction of the Kingdom of Israel (about 722 B.C.E.).

The black obelisk was set up by Shalmanesser III in his palace at Nimrud. It is inscribed with the story of his battles.

SHALOM

(Peace) the traditional Jewish salutation used in greetings and farewells.

SHALOM ALECHEM

1. Traditional greeting which means "peace be unto you."

2. Beautiful Sabbath song, sung on the eve of Sabbath (Friday evening).

SHALOSH REGALIM

(The Three Festivals of Pilgrimage) Passover, Shavuot and Sukkot. In ancient times these festivals were observed by making pilgrimages to the Temple in Jerusalem.

SHAMGAR

Hero and third Judge of Israel, son of Anath. He defeated the Philistines.

SHAMIR

According to Jewish legend, the miraculous little worm which could split the greatest stones, used by King Solomon in building the Temple. Iron tools could not be used in building this sacred house because they were symbols of war. The legends of the Shamir are many and very colorful.

SHAMMAI

Brilliant scholar and teacher of the 1st century B.C.E., Av Bet Din, colleague and opponent of the great Hillel. Hillel and Shammai were the last of the five Zugot (pairs) of the Great Sanhedrin. Shammai kept to the letter of the law and was strict, while Hillel was more lenient and gentle. Some of their brilliant discussions and those of their schools were recorded in the Mishnah.

See also Zugot.

SHAMOS

1. (Sexton) also called *Shamash*, the man in charge of the synagogue building, and aid at services.

2. The "helper" candle used to light the other eight candles of the Hanukkah Menorah.

SHARETT (born Shertok), MOSHE

(1894-1965)—Israeli political figure and diplomat. Sharett came to Palestine with his family in 1906, and in 1913, upon graduation from high school, went to Turkey to study law. Upon his return to Palestine, he became active in economic and political affairs. From 1933 to 1948 he was head of the Political Department of the Jewish Agency. In 1948, when the provisional government of Israel was established, he was appointed foreign minister, and represented the young state in the United Nations sessions of 1949-50. A political moderate. Sharett was Prime Minister of Israel from January 1954 to November 1955, and then served as foreign minister again until 1956. In 1960 he was elected chairman of the Jewish Agency Executive, serving until shortly before his death.

Moshe Sharett.

SHAVUOT

This is the Feast of Weeks and takes place seven weeks after Passover and after the beginning of the counting of Omer. These seven weeks were the time of the gathering of the grain harvest in ancient Israel. So Shavuot is the Feast of First Fruits (brought to the Temple) and of this early grain harvest. It falls in Sivan, late May or early June. But its major significance is *Zeman Mattan Toratenu*, the "Time of the Giving of Our Torah," for on Shavuot Moses ascended Mount Sinai and received the Ten Commandments. As Passover is the birthday of the Jewish nation, so Shavuot is the birthday of the Jewish religion. We eat honey and milk foods on Shavuot because of the phrase in the Song of Songs, "Honey and milk shall be under your tongue." The sages interpret this as a hope that the words of the Torah will be as pleasant and acceptable to ears and hearts as are milk and honey to the tongue. The special reading for Shavuot is the Book of Ruth; Ruth was the ancestor of King David. In the story of Ruth, relating her acceptance of the Jewish faith, there is an account of the early grain harvest in ancient Israel and of how poor people were helped during the reaping. One tradition has it that David was born and died on this festival. Every Jew who observes Shavuot can imagine that he too stood at the foot of Mount Sinai and received the Ten Commandments.

See also First Fruits.

SHAZAR, ZALMAN

(1889-1973)—Third President of Israel. Born in Belorussia, Shazar came to Palestine in 1924. On his arrival he joined the staff of the newspaper *Davar*, becoming its editor-in-chief in 1944. Shazar was Israel's minister of education and culture from 1949 to 1951, and was a member of the Jewish Agency Executive from 1952 to 1963. In 1954 he also became head of the education and culture department of the World Zionist Organization. In 1963 Shazar was elected Israel's third President, serving until his death. Shazar was a writer and scholar of distinction, and a recipient of the Ussishkin Prize. His works include

Zalman Shazar.

a major study of the Frankist movement, two volumes of biographical profiles of outstanding personalities, and his beautifully sketched autobiographical reminiscences, *Morning Stars.*

SHEBA, QUEEN OF

The wise and wealthy queen who came to visit King Solomon because the fame of his wisdom and splendor had reached her in her faraway Arabian kingdom. She declared that what she had seen for herself far exceeded the reports she had heard.

SHECHEM

Ancient city northeast of Samaria, seat of Jeroboam, first king of the northern Kingdom of Israel. Many Biblical events took place in Shechem. Joseph is said to be buried there. Joshua assembled the tribes at Shechem to speak to them before his death. It was one of the Cities of Refuge.

See also Cities of Refuge.

SHEHITAH

Shehitah ("the slaughtering ritual") has compelled Jews from their earliest days to put their animals to be used for food to death in a quick and humane manner. By the method of Shehitah an animal dies almost immediately and with a minimum of pain. The rules are many and only a learned man can become a *shohet,* a ritual slaughterer. After he has proved his piety and learning to a rabbi, he is granted a certificate. The *shohet's* knife must be smooth and sharp and without a fault in the cutting edge. The *shohet* must make the cut in a prescribed area of the animal's neck and there must be no pausing, no downward pressure, no burrowing and no tearing of the flesh. A close examination of the animal's vital organs is made to see if there is evidence of disease or injury which would make the animal not kosher. In the past the need for Shehitah was one of the factors that made Jews draw together and organize their communities.

See also Shohet.

The "kosher" stamp shown here were used in a European Jewish community in the 19th century.

SHEITEL

Wig worn by some Orthodox married women. Jewish law states that married women should not display their hair in public, and the *sheitel* was devised to satisfy both aesthetic and halachic demands.

SHEKEL

Weight in very ancient times with which metal was weighed, in later Biblical times the coin and money-value of Israel and Judah. The yearly tax to help maintain the Temple was half a shekel.

SHEM

Oldest of the three sons of Noah. According to Biblical tradition, he is the ancestor of the Semitic peoples.

SHEMA

("Hear") the first word of the prayer which forms the central concept of the Jewish religion: "Hear, O Israel: the Lord our God, the Lord is One."

SHEMINI ATZERET

This is the name for the eighth day of the Sukkot festival and is generally translated as "Eighth Day of Solemn Assembly." Though the Sukkah is still used on this day, the sages considered the festival unrelated to the preceding days. Shemini Atzeret was marked by special sacrifices in the Temple, by special benedictions and readings from the Psalms. Though Sukkot itself, and indeed all the festivals, are known as "seasons of rejoicing," on Shemini Atzeret the joy is redoubled. It does not, however, take on the character of Simhat Torah, the ninth day of the Sukkot season, when the jubilation reaches its peak. The major feature of the morning service is the beautiful hymn or prayer for rain; it is chanted by the cantor, dressed in the same kind of white garment he wears on Yom Kippur. Without rain the Holy Land could not exist, and when it came it was greeted with rapture. On Shemini Atzeret, Jews in Israel and throughout the world insert in the Eighteen Blessings the phrase: "Thou causest the wind to blow and the rain to fall." This phrase is repeated in every Amidah until Passover.

See also Simhat Torah; Sukkot.

SHEMONEH ESREH

(Heb., lit., "Eighteen Benedictions")—Prayer drawn up by the Great Assembly which is the central feature of the three daily prayers. A 19th benediction, dealing with heretics, was inserted by Gamaliel (100 C.E.). The contents of the prayer divide into three sections: (1) Praise of God; (2) Petitions for individual and national needs; (3) Thanksgiving. The *Shemoneh Esreh* is recited standing and in a whisper; the reader repeats the prayer, at which time the *Kedushah* and Priestly Blessing are inserted.

See also Amidah; Eighteen Blessings.

SHESHBAZZAR

Prince of the House of David, sometimes identified as Zerubbabel. He led the first Jews back to Judea at the time of King Cyrus.

SHEVAT

Eleventh month in the Jewish calendar.

See also Calendar, Jewish; Months, Jewish.

SHIELD OF DAVID

(Hebrew, *Magen David*)—This is made of two triangles interlaced to form a hexagram and is accepted today as a Jewish symbol. But it was used earlier by Chinese, Hindus, Egyptians and many other ancient peoples. It was first found on a Hebrew seal of the seventh century, B.C.E., and thereafter on synagogues, tombstones, Jewish catacombs in Rome and in many other places. By the sixteenth century it seems to have been used widely. The shield gradually displaced the *Menorah* as the prime emblem of Judaism. In the Middle Ages the Kabbalists looked upon it as a mystical representation of the upper and lower worlds, the visible and the invisible, the rise of man and the coming of the Messiah. Other interpretations assert that the *Magen David* refers to the days of the week, the planets and the four directions. Today the Shield of David is seen in synagogues, on objects for ritual use and on Jewish seals. The Nazis compelled Jews to wear it as a badge of identification. In Israel the Red Magen David represents the counterpart of the Red Cross.

SHILOH

Town in Ephraim where Joshua established the first sanctuary of the Ark. After the death of Eli, Shiloh was destroyed by the Philistines.

SHIN

The twenty-first letter of the Hebrew alphabet, has the numerical value of 300.

See also Aleph Bet.

SHIR HAMAALOT

1. (Song of Ascents, Song of Steps)—The title of 15 Psalms from the Biblical Book of Psalms (120-134). These Psalms were probably sung on the Three Pilgrimage Festivals and by the Judeans returning from Babylonian Exile. At the time of the Second Temple, the Levites sang these Psalms on fifteen designated steps of the Temple.
2. Refers specifically to Psalm 126 sung at Grace after Meals on the Sabbath and festivals.

SHIVAH

(Seven) Traditional seven-day mourning period. Mourners refrain from work and sit *Shivah* at home during this period.

SHIVAH ASAR BETAMMUZ

(Fast Day of the Seventeenth of Tammuz) Fast day observed in commemoration of the first break in the wall of Jerusalem by the Babylonians in the year 586 B.C.E.

SHOFAR

A ram's horn, used in ancient times to signal an alarm or to assemble the people. The Shofar is sounded on Rosh Hashanah and Yom Kippur. Its stirring notes are understood as an announcement of the New Year and as a divine summons to repentance and improvement. The three notes sounded on the Shofar are called *Tekiah* (blowing), *Teruah* (alarm) and *Shevarim* (tremolo).

See also Musical Instruments of Bible.

SHOHET

Slaughterer of animals and fowls in accordance with Jewish ritual. The *Shohet* must be an observant Jew who has thoroughly studied the laws of *Shehitah* and who has received a written license from a rabbi, certifying that he has been examined and approved.

See also Shehitah.

SHOLOM ALEICHEM

This great Yiddish writer was born in a Russian village in 1859, the son of a poor, scholarly innkeeper. When he died in New York in 1916, thousands came to mourn and honor him. Using the pen name Sholom Aleichem, which is the usual Hebrew greeting and means "peace be with you," he achieved fame as one of the most distinguished and beloved writers in the Yiddish language. His admirers included Gorky and Tolstoy and other great literary figures and critics of his time. Though he grew up in poverty and in the care of a scolding stepmother, he was a gay youngster, known for his humor and warmth and for his story telling and imitations. He received both a Jewish and general education and by the time he was seventeen he earned his keep as a teacher. He served as a government rabbi and also conducted a business. But in 1900 he began to devote himself fully to his literary work. After the horrors of the 1905 pogroms, he emigrated with his family and settled in Switzerland. He went on extended lecture tours all through Europe and in the United States. His writings depict many unique characters and describe scenes of Russian life that have

Sholom Aleichem.

now vanished. Tevye der milchiger (the milkman), Menachem Mendel, the proverbial optimistic "Shlemiel," and all their fellow-characters have become immortal in world literature. During the past decade a Sholom Aleichem revival has occurred. Books and articles have been written about him and his world and new translations of his work have appeared.

SHULAMIT

("Peaceful one") the shepherdess whose loveliness is extolled in the Song of Songs.

SHULCHAN ARUCH

Famous code of Jewish law, first published about 1565 in Safed, Palestine. It was written by Joseph Caro (born in Toledo, Spain, 1488, died in Safed, 1575). The *Shulchan Aruch* (based on the *Arba Turim* by Jacob ben Asher), which deals with ritual and legal matters, is simply arranged so that it can be used by everyone. *Shulchan Aruch* means "the set table"—the laws are arranged so that everyone can help himself to them, as he would to food at a prepared table.

SHUSHAN

(Or Susa) capital of ancient Persia, scene of the events described in the Book of Esther.

SHUSHAN PURIM

A half-holiday which occurs the day after Purim. It celebrates the festivities which took place in the city of Shushan, the scene of the Purim story, after the Jews were saved.

See also Purim.

SIDDUR

Prayer book, a volume containing the prayers for daily and Sabbath worship, arranged in a given order. The Siddur also contains some prayers for the holidays. Saadia compiled the first Siddur in the 10th century.

SIDRA

See Torah, Reading of

SIFRE EMET

(Books of "Truth") the three poetical Books, the first part of *Ketubim* (the third division of the Bible), containing Psalms, Proverbs and Job. *Emet* ("truth") is formed by the Hebrew initials of the three Books in reverse order.

See also Ketubim.

SIMHAT TORAH

("Rejoicing of the Law") In all lands outside Israel there are two days of Shemini Atzeret, the end of the

celebrating the joy of the Torah in song and dance on Simhat Torah.

Sukkot holidays. The second is called Simhat Torah. In the land of Israel both festivals are observed together. On Simhat Torah the reading of the Torah for the year is completed and then begun anew. Both at evening and morning services the Torah scrolls are taken from the Ark and carried about the synagogue, with song and dance, festivity and joy. Every man in the synagogue is called up to a Torah reading; and even the youngest boys who usually are not called in this ceremony come up together and recite the blessings, often under a large *Tallit*. The reader of the year's last portion of the Law is called the "bridegroom of the Torah," and he who begins the first portion of the new reading is called the "bridegroom of Genesis." In many synagogues there is a special children's procession on the eve of Simhat Torah and the children carry the scrolls of the Torah, large and small ones, wave flags, sing and participate in the services and receive gifts. This is truly a day of joy in the Torah for all Jews—from those who adhere to a gay ceremony in their house of worship to the Hasidim who pray and feast all night and day and whose dancing and joyful worship overflow into the street.

See also Shemini Atzeret.

SIMEON

Second son of Jacob and Leah, ancestor of the tribe of Simeon.

See also Simeon, Tribe of .

SIMEON, TRIBE OF

One of the tribes of Israel. Its territory was south of the tribe of Judah and included Beersheba, the southernmost point in Israel. Its emblem was the city of Shechem; its banner was green. The stone representing Simeon in the High Priest's breastplate was probably a topaz.

SIMEON BAR YOHAI

Tannaitic scholar and teacher of the 2nd century C.E., student of Akiba. Simeon had to flee from the

Romans, and for 13 years hid in a cave. Simeon was a mystic. Legend has it that he was the author of the *Zohar* (great work of Kabbalah which appeared in Spain in the 13th century). On Lag Beomer, the day of Simeon's death, pilgrims visit his grave at Meron, near Safed.

SIMEON BEN LAKISH

Great Amora, scholar and teacher, one of the founders of the Palestinian Talmud, colleague and friend of Johanan bar Nappaha. Many legends exist about Simeon. He is said to have been a circus animal-trainer and perhaps a leader of a band of highwaymen before he became a great rabbi. Simeon's brilliant discussions with Johanan bar Nappaha are recorded in the Talmud.

SIMON

Son of Mattathias, head of Judea and High Priest; brother of Judah Maccabee.

SINAI, MOUNT

The mountain in the Sinai Desert where Moses received the Ten Commandments.

SINAI CAMPAIGN

Throughout 1955 and 1956, Egyptian-backed terrorists known as fedayeen, based in the Gaza Strip, conducted raids against civilian targets in Israel. In addition, Egypt began to build up its forces in the Sinai Peninsula, refused to permit Israeli ships to pass through the Straits of Tiran, and formed a joint military command with other Arab states. In this atmosphere of increasing tension and danger, Israel decided to take military action. Operation Kadesh was initiated on October 29; within less than 100 hours, Israeli forces had defeated the Egyptians at all points, occupying the Gaza Strip and the whole Sinai Peninsula to within 10 miles of the Suez Canal. In the process they captured 6,000 Egyptian soldiers and vast quantities of munitions and military equipment. The Egyptian dead numbered 1,000; the Israeli, 171. A cease-fire was declared on Nov. 5. U.S. and Soviet pressure soon forced Israel to withdraw from the occupied areas, but a UN Emergency Force was organized to patrol the frontier and keep the Straits open for Israeli ships.

SINGER, ISAAC BASHEVIS

(1904-   )—Yiddish novelist, the brother of Israel Joshua Singer. Born in Poland, where he was educated in a yeshivah, I. B. Singer came to the United States in 1935. For many years thereafter he was a staff writer for the *Forward*, a Yiddish newspaper. Singer's enigmatic novels and stories, in English translation, have enjoyed wide popularity. Among his best-known work are the novels *Satan in Goray*, *The Magician of*

Lublin, *The Slave*, and *The Family Moskat*, the short-story collections *The Spinoza of Market Street* and *Short Friday*, the memoir *In My Father's Court*, and children's books like *Zlateh the Goat* and *Mazel and Shlimazel*.

SINGER, ISRAEL JOSHUA

(1893-1944)—Yiddish novelist, the brother of Isaac Bashevis Singer. Born in Poland, where he worked as a journalist, I. J. Singer came to the United States in 1933. A realistic writer in the traditional vein, he specialized in panoramic family novels covering several generations and encompassing an entire era or society within their broad scope. His best-known works are *The Brothers Ashkenazi*, *The Family Carnovsky*, and *Yoshe Kalb*.

SIRAH

Book of the Apocrypha, also called *Ecclesiasticus*, containing wise sayings and rules for conduct.

See also Ben Sirah.

SISERA

General of the Canaanite King Jabin, defeated by Deborah and Barak in a battle at Mount Tabor. He fled and was killed by a Kenite woman, Jael, in whose tent he sought refuge.

SIVAN

Third month in the Jewish calendar.

See also Calendar, Jewish; Months, Jewish.

SIX-DAY WAR

In May 1967 Syria, backed by Russia, accused Israel of planning to attack. Ostensibly to aid Syria, powerful Egyptian forces moved into the Sinai Peninsula. Declaring that Egypt intended to destroy Israel, President Nasser expelled the UN Emergency Force and closed the Straits of Tiran to Israeli ships, an act of war according to international law. He also established a joint military command with Jordan. When all its attempts to resolve the crisis peacefully failed, Israel, on June 5, launched a preemptive strike against Egypt, Syria, and Jordan, destroying most of their military aircraft within the first few hours. In a lightning campaign over the next five days, Israel was victorious on all fronts. By June 11, when all the parties agreed to a cease-fire, Israel had occupied the Gaza Strip and all of the Sinai Peninsula, the Golan Heights, and the West Bank territories, including the historic Old City of Jerusalem. UN observers were posted between the opposing forces along the Suez Canal and on the Golan Heights. The combined Arab forces, which also included Iraq, suffered. more than 15,000 casualties and lost more than 70 percent of their heavy equipment, including over 400 planes and over 500 tanks. Israeli casualties were 777 dead and 2,856 wounded.

SKULLCAP

Headpiece. The custom of covering the head, though not based on Biblical or Talmudic law, is observed by traditional Jews. It developed in medieval times. The skullcap is called "Kippah" in Hebrew and "Yarmulka" in Yiddish.

SLAVERY

The Bible recognizes two types of slavery as legal. An Israelite may sell himself into slavery to another Israelite for a period of seven years, or he may be sold by a court if he is a convicted thief and cannot raise the funds he must repay. Upon the expiration of the seven-year period the slave can extend his term of service until the Jubilee year if he wishes. The Jewish slave was regarded by the Talmud as the equal of his master; indeed, he was considered by them more a laborer, hired for seven years, than a slave. The Bible also stated that Jews could hold heathen slaves, provided that they circumcise the males and have them observe part of Judaism. Jews of the Middle Ages held slaves, though the Catholic Church tried to prevent their holding Christian slaves. In more recent times, Jews were active in the abolitionist struggle against slavery in the United States: Judah Touro was one of the first men to free his slaves, while such men as Michael Heilprin and Rabbi Benjamin Szold (Henrietta Szold's father) were supporters of the abolitionist cause.

SMILANSKY, YIZHAR

(1916-   )—Israeli writer. Born in Rehovot, Smilansky, using the pseudonym S. Yizhar, is one of Israel's best-known authors and a recipient of the Israel Prize. Trained as a teacher, he fought in the War of Independence and was a member of the Knesset from 1949 to 1967. He is most famed for his panoramic war novel *Days of Ziklag*, considered the finest literary work of the "Palmach generation" of Israeli writers. In it he movingly poses the moral problems and challenges that confronted Israelis during their 1948 conflict with the Arabs.

SMOLENSKIN, PERETZ

(1842-1885)—Hebrew author. After a youth of hardship and wandering, Smolenskin settled in Odessa in 1862. There he became acquainted with the movement of Enlightenment which was stirring many Jews. In 1868 he moved to Vienna, there founding and editing *Ha-Shachar* (Hebrew for "The Dawn"), which became the main spokesman for the new Jewish nationalism, and to which Smolenskin contributed many articles. He may be called the creator of the journalistic style in modern Hebrew literature. Among his works are an autobiographical novel modeled on David Copperfield and called "The Wanderer in Life's Paths," and *Am Olam* (Eternal People), which called for a Jewish national revival.

SODOM AND GOMORRAH

The two most important of the five Cities of the Plain; destroyed for their wickedness and inhospitality. Only the household of Lot, who lived in Sodom, was saved—except for his wife who was turned into a pillar of salt because she looked back at the destroyed cities. The ruins of Sodom and Gomorrah lie at the bottom of the Dead Sea.

See also Cities of the Plains.

SOFER

A scribe, the man who writes by hand the sacred Torah scrolls in accordance with prescribed rules. He is traditionally a very pious man.

A sofer, or scribe, writing in the traditional way in which scrolls of the Torah and other holy works have been set down since the days of the Second Temple.

SOFERIM

A group of teachers under the leadership of Ezra. *Soferim*, somewhat erroneously translated as "scribes," comes from *sefer* ("book"): they should be called bookmen or Bible interpreters. Under Ezra, the Torah was adopted as the basic law of Judaism; and men were sought who would expound the laws to the people. Most of the *Soferim* were priests, since they were closest to Jewish law and observance. Their group, in fact, forms a link between Moses and the prophets, and all later teachers. In the second century B.C.E., many laymen also became *Soferim*. In later years the *Soferim* were replaced by men called sages and these were followed by the rabbis — *rabbi* meaning "my teacher" or "my master." Today the term *Sofer* is applied to the man who laboriously writes out the Torah on parchment to make the scrolls used in the synagogue. Other parts of the Bible, the Prophets, Esther, Lamentations, are also written on small scrolls by these learned and expert copyists. *Soferim* is also the name of a minor tractate of the Talmud which contains statements about liturgy and instructions on the writing of the scrolls of the Torah.

SOKOLOW, NAHUM

(1860-1936)—Zionist leader and Hebrew writer. As editor of *Hazfirah* (1884) in Warsaw, he is considered the creator of modern Hebrew journalism. Sokolow became a follower of Herzl after the first Zionist Congress, and served as general secretary of the Organiza-

Nahum Sokolow

tion from 1905 to 1909. He founded *Ha-Olam*, the Zionist Hebrew weekly, and edited *Die Welt*, the Zionist Organization's chief newspaper. From 1931 to 1935 Sokolow served as president of the World Zionist Organization. Among his works is a history of Zionism written in English.

SOLOMON

(961-920 B.C.E.)—Third king of Israel, the son of David and Bathsheba, he was the builder of the Temple and known as the wisest king in Biblical history. His name was first *Jedidiah* ("beloved of God") and became Solomon (*Shelomo*) from the word Shalom, "peace," referring to the peaceful time of his reign. Through his many marriages he formed alliances with neighboring kingdoms. But the people disapproved of his wives' pagan religions. For the building of the Temple, new fortifications, and many other public projects, he imposed heavy taxes and compulsory labor upon the Israelites; hardships paved the way for eventual revolt that, after his death, resulted in the division of the kingdom. He developed trade with many countries and sent ships to distant lands with his allies, the Phoenicians of Tyre, making his kingdom immensely wealthy. In his kingdom and far across its borders Solomon's great wisdom was famous. The Queen of Sheba, who heard about the wise king, visited Solomon to see for herself. She admired him and his statesmanship greatly. He is said to have written

Proverbs, the Song of Songs and Ecclesiastes. Countless legends have been woven around Solomon. In some he is described as the master of demons, even of their chief Ashmodai. Other legends tell that he knew the language of all living creatures and would converse and dispute with them. His legendary wealth inspired a Spanish navigator, who expected to find great riches in certain Pacific Islands, to call them "Solomon Islands."

SOLOVEICHIK FAMILY

Family of Talmudic scholars. Joseph Dov (1820-1892) served as rabbi of Volozin, Slutzk, and Brest-Litovsk. His main work is the three-volume *Bet Halevi*, which mainly deals with Talmudic and medieval law. His son, Chaim (1853-1918), originated a method of logical analysis of Talmudic law which strove to penetrate to the basic concepts involved. As a leading figure of the Volozin yeshivah from 1880-92, Rabbi Chaim was able to train a generation of Talmudists in his principles. In 1892 he succeeded his father as rabbi of Brest-Litovsk. Rabbi Chaim's grandson, Joseph Dov Soloveichik (b. 1903), received his doctorate from the University of Berlin in 1931 and settled in Boston in 1932. One of the foremost American halachic authorities, he has served as head of the Rabbi Isaac Elchanan Theological Seminary of Yeshiva University and as chairman of the Halachah Committee of the Rabbinical Council of America. Although he has not written extensively, except for a famous essay, *Ish Hahalachah* ("Halachic Man"), published in 1944, he is an important Orthodox thinker, and his teachings have had great influence through his disciples and students. Known to his admirers as "the Rav," Soloveichik is regarded as the leader of the progressive wing of North American Orthodoxy.

Rabbi Hayim Soloveichik.

SONCINO

Town in Lombardy, Italy, where the Soncino family founded a printing press in 1483 by issuing two tractates of the Talmud. The books that came from the press, such as the first printed prayerbook, and the first complete edition of the Bible are masterly achievements of early book printing. The name was adopted by a society of Jewish book lovers in Berlin (1925), and later by the Soncino Press in England (1929), which has produced many books of Jewish interest, including the English translation of the Babylonian Talmud.

Printer's mark of the Soncino family.

SONG OF SONGS

(Shir Hashirim) first of the Five Megillot of the Bible. This beautiful poem is considered to represent the love between God and Israel. It is ascribed to King Solomon. The poem is read in the synagogue on Passover.

SOUTH AFRICA

Jews settled in South Africa early in the 19th century; many were traders, industrialists and agriculturists who contributed greatly to the country's prosperity and growth. Jews were among the leaders in the development of the diamond industry and the gold mines, and were prominent in government and politics. South African Jewry (118,000) supports a vigorous Zionist movement.

SOUTH AMERICA

Large Jewish communities exist in Argentina (500,000 Jews) and Brazil (150,000 Jews), while the Jewish population of the other states is fairly small. Marranos were among the first settlers in South America, and though they were persecuted by the Inquisition, life was more comfortable for them in this region than in Spain. In the 19th century Baron de Hirsch established agricultural settlements in Argentina, and the 1930s saw an influx of European immigrants, as did the period immediately following World War II.

SPAIN

Jews had lived in Spain since Roman times. The Arab conquest of 711 restored their freedom, which had been restricted by Catholic rulers. Jews such as Hasdai Ibn Shaprut attained great influence in the state, and Hebrew literature and philosophy, represented by such men as Ibn Gabirol, Abraham and Moses Ibn Ezra, and Judah Halevi, flourished. Christian rule of the country, restored in the 12th-14th centuries, brought anti-Jewish regulations which culminated in the establishment of the Inquisition in 1478 and the expulsion of Jews from Spain in 1492. Most of the Marranos who remained were assimilated into the native population. There are now some 9,000 Jews in Spain, descendants of a 19th century immigration.

SPEKTOR, ISAAC ELCHANAN

(1817-1896)—Lithuanian rabbi. The founder and head of a major yeshivah in the city of Kovno in Lithuania, Spektor was the foremost rabbinical authority of his time. He was the author of numerous responsa on questions directed to him by Jews throughout Europe and the world. Many of his rulings were noted for their leniency and broad-mindedness.

SPICEBOX

(Besamim box) used in the Havdalah ceremony marking the end of the Sabbath and the festivals in the traditional synagogue and home. A prayer is recited over the spices which are inhaled as a remembrance of the beauty of the Sabbath (or festival).

SPINOZA, BARUCH

The great philosopher was born in Holland in 1632. Although he was excommunicated by the Jewish Community of Amsterdam for his heretic ideas, he is still thought of as a son of Israel. He received an excellent Jewish education and was impressed with the works of Maimonides. He was, supposedly, a great student of the mystical Kabbalah. He later studied science, mathe-

Drawing of Baruch Spinoza in a contemplative mood.

matics, Latin and philosophy. The works of the French philosopher Descartes influenced Spinoza to develop a philosophy which both the Jews and Christians of his time considered harmful to their faiths. Spinoza earned his living by grinding lenses, and refused calls to teach at the great universities of his time. He was a courageous and independent man, and he bore his loneliness among his contemporaries with great dignity. He wrote on politics, ethics, reason, Hebrew grammar and many other subjects. Spinoza's idea of God is called Pantheism, which means that God is found everywhere and in all things. Many have called him an atheist, but he taught what he called the "intellectual love of God." Spinoza died in 1677.

STRAUS, OSCAR S.

Eminent diplomat and philanthropist, he was born in Germany in 1850 and died in New York in 1926. The three distinguished Straus brothers, Isidor, Oscar and Nathan, have left a permanent impress on American life. Isidor, who served as congressman, died on the *Titanic*. Nathan's many philanthropies included the providing of pasteurized milk for New York's poor children. Oscar, among his many other distinctions, was the first Jew to hold a cabinet post in America. He had attracted attention with his brilliant legal book, still read today, *The Origin of the Republican Form of Government in the U. S.* He served as minister to Turkey under Presidents Cleveland and Harrison, and he helped to liberalize the Sultan's edicts against Christians and Jews. President Theodore Roosevelt made him Secretary of Commerce and Labor. Both Roosevelt and Wilson appointed him to The Hague Court. No other public figure in the United States can equal Straus' career in high official posts under five successive presidents—for McKinley and Taft had also called upon him. He also held other posts in the state and the city of New York. Despite his busy public life he continued his scholarly research and writing. Oscar Straus was active in many Jewish organizations and philanthropies, here and in Palestine. He was also one of the founders of the Young Men's Hebrew Association.

SUKKAH

A booth or hut made of branches and decorated with fruits and flowers, used during the holiday of Sukkot. These temporary huts are a reminder of the Israelites' wanderings in the wilderness, and serve as a place to thank God for His many blessings.

SUKKOT

This is the feast of Tabernacles ("booths"), the "Feast of Ingathering," of vintage, of harvest and of thanksgiving. It also commemorates the dwelling of the Israelites in the desert in temporary huts, partly open to the sky. Jews have observed the nine-day festival of Sukkot, which occurs shortly after Yom Kippur, by building such open huts. The *Sukkah* may not be too tall or too low; through the vegetation on its latticed roof more shade than sun must be seen. It is decorated with fruits and vegetables, showing God's bounties at this joyous time of harvest. As part of the religious service for Sukkot, four plant species are used. These are the *etrog*, (citron); *the lulav*, (palm branch), and these are bound together with *hadassim* (myrtles) and *aravot* (willows). The Midrash finds special meanings in these four plants: the etrog, which has good taste and odor, represents men with both learning and religious observance; the lulav, which has edible fruit but no fragrance, represents men learned but not observant; the myrtle, which has good odor but no taste, represents the pious who are without learning; and the willow, which lacks both food value and fragrance, represents men who are neither pious nor learned. Thus are men of all kinds bound together in Israel. The rites connected with Sukkot are most joyous and the festival is a fitting conclusion to the high holiday season.

See also Shemini Atzeret.

SUKKOT, FOUR PLANTS OF

Etrog (*citron*), Lulav (*palm*), Hadas (*myrtle*) and Aravah (*willow*); four plants used by the Jewish people since ancient times when they carried them in the joyous processions of the Pilgrimage festival of Sukkot to the Temple in Jerusalem. Lulav, Aravot and Hadassim, bound together, are held with the Etrog. These plants symbolize that God is everywhere and that, like the four plants, all Jews are bound together in brotherhood.

SURA

One of the three most famous Babylonian Talmudic academies, founded in the 3rd century, a foremost seat of Jewish learning. Saadia was Gaon of the Sura academy in the 10th century.

SURINAM

(Dutch Guiana) The Jewish settlement in this South American territory was established by Portuguese Marranos and European immigrants. Paramaribo, the capital, is the center of the Jewish community, which maintains a synagogue, a school, and a monthly periodical. The Jewish population numbers 1,000.

SYNAGOGUE

The Greek word for assembly or community. It was taken over by Judaism to describe its religious house of assembly. In Yiddish the traditional synagogue is called *shul*, from the German word for school, since the synagogue has always been a house of study as well as of assembly and prayer. The word "temple" is usually applied to a Reform house of worship. Before the Israelites were exiled to Babylonia (586 B.C.E.), there were no synagogues as such. In Babylon, Jews met at the home of a leader or prophet. But there were "meeting places of God in the land" in the days of the Maccabees. More than a century before that time Jews had adopted the lasting custom of building synagogues wherever they formed a community. These congregations were democratic. They were without a priesthood and without the awesome sanctity of the great Temple. Many old synagogues have been excavated, revealing that there has been a gradual development from a one-room prayer hall, with small anterooms, to tall and magnificent structures. Synagogues do not have to be built according to any set rules. The people of different lands followed the customs of their country in the selection of architectural styles. The splendor of many modern synagogues reflects the spirit of the verse: "This is my Lord, and I shall adorn Him."

SYNOD OF USHA

The first legally permitted gathering of *Tannaim* after the Hadrianic persecutions (c. 138 C.E.). The council, which was held at Usha, about ten miles from Haifa, was attended mostly by pupils of R. Akiba. Its purpose was the reconstruction of Jewish life, and with that end in mind the *Bet Din* was re-established in Galilee, schools were reopened and communal matters were discussed.

SYNODS

Conferences of rabbinical (and occasionally, lay) leaders. The council of Usha (c. 138 C.E.) which tried to revitalize Jewish life after the Hadrianic persecutions is one of the most important of the ancient synods. In the Middle Ages, Rabbenu Gershom convened a synod which prohibited polygamy, while synods dealing with other common problems were usual.

SYRIA

Originally ancient Aram, conquered and annexed to Assyria in the 8th century B.C.E., Syria was conquered successively by the Babylonians, the Persians, and Alexander the Great (333 B.C.E.). After Alexander's death, the Seleucid kings ruled over Syria from Antioch, their capital. Judea then was their vassal. The Maccabees led the Judean revolt against the Syrian King, Antiochus IV. The modern republic of Syria, northern neighbor of the State of Israel, was established in 1942.

SWOPE, GERARD

(1872-1957)—American industrialist. Long associated with the General Electric Company (as president, 1922-39 and 1942-4), Swope created the "Swope Plan" to aid industry at the start of the Depression (1931). He served his country as a member of the general staff of the United States army during World War I, and as assistant to the Secretary of the Treasury in 1942.

SZOLD, HENRIETTA

The founder of Hadassah was born in Baltimore in 1860. She was the daughter of Rabbi Benjamin Szold,

a scholar and prominent liberal associated with the movement for liberation of the American Negro. During the large wave of Jewish immigration, the Szold's home was a haven for the newcomers. Miss Szold, though teaching in a fashionable school, became interested in the education of the immigrants. She organized night classes in English and American history. Her project started with 30 students and soon expanded to an enrollment of 5000. Thereafter, similar classes were conducted in other cities. Miss Szold had become a pioneer in adult education. When her father died in 1902, she and her mother moved to New York, where she did volunteer work for the Jewish Publication Society of America. In 1892 she became the Secretary of its Literary Committee and served until 1916. She edited and translated, among other works, *Legends of the Jews* by Louis Ginzberg. Miss Szold's interest in Zionism grew at this time, and in 1912 she founded Hadassah, now an organization of over 300,000 women in the United States, which helps maintain hospitals and

Henrietta Szold.

other facilities in Israel serving Jews and Arabs alike. Miss Szold was commissioned by the Zionist organization to organize the American Medical Unit for Palestine and in 1918 staff and equipment for a 50-bed hospital left New York for Palestine. In 1919 the Henrietta Szold School for Nursing was opened, and that year Miss Szold went to Palestine. She was an active Zionist and held many distinguished posts in the organization. In 1933 the Rothschild-Hadassah University Hospital was built, one of her dearest projects. That year she became the leader and organizer of the Youth Aliyah (immigration of children under 16). In the dark years of World War II, Miss Szold was an active and inspiring figure. She died in Israel at the age of 85.

TAANIT BEHORIM

(Fast of the First-Born) a fast day on the 14th of Nisan, on the eve of Passover. The fast is observed in remembrance of the sparing of Israel's first-born, when the angel of death, who struck the first-born sons of the Egyptians, "passed over" the houses of the Israelites.

TAANIT ESTHER

(The Fast of Esther) a fast day commemorating the fast of the Jews of Persia, led by Esther and Mordecai, who were threatened with death by Haman. Taanit Esther occurs on the 13th of Adar, the day before Purim.

TABERNACLE

Called in Hebrew *Mishkan* or *Ohel Moed*. During the days of the children of Israel's wandering in the wilderness, they carried with them a sanctuary that could be taken apart and put together again. The Bible describes its construction and details fully— boards covered with gold, curtains, veils, hides, the gold-lined table for the showbread, the Menorah, the altar, the utensils. In the inner shrine stood the Ark of the Covenant, seen later only once a year, on Yom Kippur, by the High Priest. It took six months to build the Tabernacle, which accompanied the Israelites everywhere. Later the Temple of Solomon was erected as its successor.

A picture of the reconstruction of the Tabernacle.

TABLES OF THE LAW

The two stone tablets upon which were engraved the Ten Commandments, also called "Tablets of the Law," or "Tablets of the Covenant" (*Luchot HaB'rit*).

TABOR, MOUNT

Northeast of the Emek Jezreel, near the Kishon River, in ancient times a beautifully wooded mountain, often mentioned as a symbol of God's strength. Near Mount Tabor, Deborah and Barak defeated the army of Sisera and King Jabin.

TAKKANAH

(Hebrew, literally, "improvement") Any rabbinic regulation instituted to strengthen religious observance or to improve moral and social relations. The *Takkanah* of public reading of the Torah is said to go back to the time of Moses, while ten *Takkanot* are attributed to Ezra. During the Middle Ages the *Takkanah* became a powerful means in regulating the internal affairs of

Jewish communities, and affected every phase of communal, social, and home life—taxes, inheritance, marriage and divorce, and dress. A most famous *Takkanah*, still in effect today, prohibits polygamy.

TALLIT

The word *Tallit* (Tallis) which may possibly be derived from the Greek *stole*, a capelike covering, is used in the Talmud to mean a garment, a cloak thrown over the shoulder, a sheet of cloth or a bed sheet. But it is used today to refer only to the prayer shawl which Jews wear during worship, though not at every service. It is oblong in shape, usually with fringed ends, and with special fringes, *Tzitzit*, hanging from the corners of the shorter sides. The size ranges from the very small one used by little boys, to the large one that envelopes the head and the entire body. The larger *Talletim* are usually made of wool, but silk, rayon and other fabrics are acceptable. They may have blue or black stripes. The blessing spoken when the prayer shawl is put on signifies that the worshipper is now wrapping himself in holiness. Jews called to the reading of the Torah often kiss the fringes of their *Tallit* as they touch them to the Scroll in reverence for the Law; they are kissed when mention is made of *Tzitzit* in the reading of the Shema, and when the Scrolls are carried in procession and touched reverently with the *Tallit*.

TALMUD

The Talmud is the greatest and most impressive collection of religious-legal literature in history. It is composed of the *Mishnah* and the *Gemara*. The *Mishnah* was collected by Judah Hanasi about 200 C.E. It is a code of Jewish law containing the core of Oral Law as it had been transmitted since the Biblical period. The *Gemara* contains the commentary to the *Mishnah*. There are two Talmuds, the Babylonian Talmud and the Palestinian Talmud, each consisting of the same *Mishnah* but distinct, separate *Gemara*. The Babylonian Talmud is the larger and more important one. In the great academies the scholars discussed every paragraph of the *Mishnah*, and these arguments are recorded in the *Gemara* in the same order as the Mishnah itself, which consists of six *Sedarim*, or "orders," of the Jewish legal code. The *Sedarim* cover laws concerning agriculture and prayer; festivals and fasts and the Sabbath; civil and criminal procedure; the Temple service; and purity. Most of the *Gemara* is in Aramaic and "neo-Hebrew," not in classical Hebrew. For this was the language spoken by the sages and the common people in those days. The *Gemara* was completed about 550 C.E. and then was written and later printed in conjunction with the *Mishnah* under the single name Talmud, which comes from *lamod*, "to learn." The Talmud does not limit itself to dry disputes on law. It contains legends, tales, wise sayings and much related material. This latter text is known as *Aggadah* or *Haggadah* (narrative, story) while the legal portions are *Halachah* (directions, procedure, law). Thousands of pages of commentary have been written on the Talmud, one of the most important and widely used being that of Rashi.

See also Halachah.

TALMUD, BABYLONIAN

One of the two versions of the Talmud. It consists of the *Mishnah*, the *Tosefta* (supplement to the *Mishnah*) and the Babylonian *Gemara*. It was edited by Rabina and Rav Ashi and was completed by the *Saboraim* in the beginning of the 6th century C.E. It is longer and more complete than the Palestinian Talmud and is more frequently used. Its Hebrew name is *Talmud Bavli*.

TALMUD, PALESTINIAN

Consists of the *Mishnah* and the Palestinian *Gemara*, completed by the Palestinian *Amoraim* by the middle of the 4th century C.E. It is older and shorter than the Babylonian Talmud. Though not compiled in Jerusalem, its Hebrew name is *Talmud Yerushalmi*.

TALMUD TORAH

An afternoon school for the "teaching of the Torah," attended by students after their elementary school session.

TAM, JACOB BEN MEIR

(1100-1171)—French rabbinical authority, known as Rabbenu Tam ("Our Perfect Rabbi"). A grandson of Rashi, Rabbenu Tam was the greatest Talmudic scholar of his time and the most outstanding of the Tosafists (*see* Tosafot). He was a prolific author of responsa and *hiddushim* (also called *novellae*—analytic explanations and glosses on the Talmud), many of which are gathered in his best-known work, *Sefer ha-Yashar* ("Book of the Righteous"). He also wrote on Hebrew grammar and was the first French Jew to use rhyme in composing Hebrew poetry. In a famous dispute, Rabbenu Tam differed with Rashi about the arrangement of the four biblical verses inserted in the Tefillin. Rashi's opinion prevailed, but some very observant Jews wear two sets of Tefillin, one prepared according to Rashi, the other following Rabbenu Tam.

TAMMUZ

Fourth month in the Jewish calendar.

See also Calendar, Jewish; Months, Jewish.

TANACH

Hebrew for the Bible. The word is composed of the first letters of the following words: *Torah* (Pentateuch), *Nevi'im* (Prophets), *Ketubim* (Holy Writings, or Hagiographa). The *Tanach* is made up of 24 books, beginning with Genesis and ending with Chronicles.

TANNAIM

("Teachers" in Aramaic) teachers and scholars whose discussions and commentaries on Jewish law are recorded in the Mishnah. The period of the Tannaim (1st to 3rd centuries C.E.) started with the death of Hillel and ended with the death of Judah Hanasi.

TARGUM

In every complete Hebrew Pentateuch (Torah, Humash), next to the Hebrew text there is an Aramaic version called Targum, meaning translation. At an early time, when Aramaic was spoken by most Jews, a *meturgeman* ("translator") read the Torah portion verse for verse and translated it literally into Aramaic, often with comments. After Jews were scattered and spoke other languages, the function of the *meturgeman* was ended. But several versions of these translations have been preserved; they were set down in the time of the Talmud in both Babylonia and Palestine. The best known Targum is called Targum Onkelos, which covers the Five Books of Moses. This Targum sometimes adds Talmudic legal interpretations to the laws of the Torah. It also contains Aggadic (legendary, fanciful) additions. After long use the Targum Onkelos became so respected that it was the custom to read it weekly even in countries where Aramaic was not spoken, and it is retained in our Pentateuchs today. The Aramaic translation of the Prophets is known as Targum Jonathan.

TAV

The twenty-second letter of the Hebrew alphabet, has the numerical value of 400.

See also Aleph Bet.

TCHERNICHOVSKY, SAUL

(1875-1943)—Russian-born Hebrew poet. A physician by profession, Tchernichovsky arrived in Palestine in 1931. He is considered by some as great a poet as Bialik, though his work has a different emphasis. Tchernichovsky demanded that the newly reawakened Jewish nation abandon its traditional spiritual heritage, and become a people bound to the earth and alive to its beauty. Many of his ideas had a great influence on the generation which created the State of Israel. In addition to his original Hebrew poems and stories, Tchernichovsky did many translations from the Greek, among them the *Iliad* and the *Odyssey*.

TECHNION

The "Israel Institute of Technology," called the Technion in Hebrew, is located in Haifa, and was founded in 1912. This technological university has achieved a world-wide reputation for its high standards. It offers degrees of Bachelor of Science, Ingenieur, Master of Science, and Ph.D. Some 2,000 students are enrolled at the school which began, some years ago, to build a modern 300-acre campus on Mount Carmel.

or thanksgiving, applied specifically to Shemoneh Esreh. Today the word is used to describe any prayer.

TEFILLIN

Small leather boxes which contain four handwritten sections of the Torah and to which leather straps are attached. Traditionally, men and boys over 13 place these on the head and left arm during daily morning prayers except on Sabbaths and holidays. The tradition of putting on of *Tefillin* (phylacteries) is derived from the Biblical commandment, "And thou shalt bind them for a sign upon thy hand, and they shall be for frontlets between thine eyes."

Tefillin are two black leather boxes, fastened to leather straps, containing four portions of the Bible written on parchment (Ex. 13:1-10; 11-16; Deut. 6:4-9; 11:13-21).

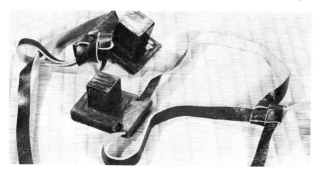

Tefillim with leather straps (retuzot).

TEL AVIV

("Hill of Spring")—The largest city in Israel, founded in 1909 on the sandy shores north of Jaffa. Tel Aviv is Israel's business and entertainment center, with important museums, theaters, a university, and the offices of many government agencies and other institutions. In 1971 its inhabitants numbered 383,200. The Tel Aviv metropolitan area, including such towns as Ramat Gan, Petach Tikvah, Holon, and Bat Yam, includes 42% of Israel's total population. *See also* Jaffa.

The First Temple according to the vision of Ezekiel.

TEMPLE

King Solomon built the first Temple about 950 B.C.E. on Mount Zion in Jerusalem, to replace the Tabernacle and other temporary shrines of the Ark. The Bible describes in full detail how the Temple was constructed and from this description artists have reconstructed models. The first Temple was destroyed by the soldiers of Nebuchadnezzar of Babylonia, on the 9th of Av, 586 B.C.E. All of its golden ornaments and vessels were taken away, and the people of Israel were carried into exile. The second Temple was built by the returning exiles in the days of Darius I, after Persia had conquered Babylonia. This Temple lacked the magnificence of Solomon's structure. It was desecrated by Antiochus of Syria and rescued by the Maccabees in 165 B.C.E. Later it was again attacked and plundered and had deteriorated so badly that Herod the Great, about 20 B.C.E., razed it in order to rebuild it. Herod's new Temple was of great splendor, admired and loved by the Jews of that time. It consisted of a great cluster of halls, surrounded by walls, and contained many parts, some of them for purposes other than religious. The Great Sanhedrin met in one of its splendid halls. The Temple of Herod never was completed and was burned to the ground in 70 C.E. Today only the Wailing Wall is left. This was not a part of the building itself and most likely consists of parts of the walls of all three Temples. Many prayers refer to the rebuilding of Israel's great Temple in the future.

TEN COMMANDMENTS

The ten rules for conduct toward God and man that form the basis of Jewish religious and moral law. According to the Bible, these laws were given by God to Moses at Mount Sinai, and engraved upon the two Tablets of the Law.

1. I am the Lord thy God who brought thee out of the land of Egypt, out of the house of bondage.
2. Thou shalt have no other gods before me.
3. Thou shalt not take the name of the Lord thy God in vain.
4. Remember the Sabbath day to keep it holy.
5. Honor thy father and mother.
6. Thou shalt not murder.
7. Thou shalt not commit adultery.
8. Thou shalt not steal.
9. Thou shalt not bear false witness.
10. Thou shalt not covet.

TEN DAYS OF PENITENCE

The days from Rosh Hashanah to Yom Kippur, inclusive. These days are devoted to repentance. Penitential prayers *(Selihot)* are said during this time. These days are also called Days of Awe *(Yamim Noraim)*.

TERAH

Father of Abraham, Nahor and Haran. Terah and his family left their home in Ur of the Chaldees and moved to the city of Haran, where they settled. Abraham left his family to live in Canaan, the land God had promised him.

TEREFAH

("Forbidden") foods that are forbidden according to traditional Jewish dietary laws.

See also Dietary Laws; Kosher.

TET

The ninth letter of the Hebrew alphabet, has the numerical value of 9.

See also Aleph Bet.

TEVET

Tenth month in the Jewish calendar.

See also Calendar, Jewish; Months, Jewish.

TIBERIAS

City on the Sea of Galilee founded by King Antipas and named in honor of the Roman Emperor Tiberius. In the Jewish War, the fortress Tiberias was a center of Jewish revolt. In the 3rd century it became the seat of the Patriarchate *(Nasi)* and the home of an important Talmudic academy.

Tiberias, Israel, and the tomb of Rabbi Meir Baal Ha-Nes, second-century scholar, member of the Sanhedrin, and pupil of Rabbi Akiba. In the background: the Sea of Galilee.

TIKKUNÉ SOFERIM

(Hebrew for "corrections of the Soferim")—The *Soferim*, or Scribes, introduced 18 changes into the text of the Five Books of Moses to avoid uncomplimentary references to God, particularly where the original wording seemed to imply that God could be thought of as having a body. These changes are listed in *Midrash Tanhuma, Beshallah* 16.

TISHAH B'AV

(The Ninth Day of the Month of Av) a day of fasting and prayer in commemoration of the destruction of the First and the Second Temples in Jerusalem and the fall of the fortress of Betar at the end of Bar Kochba's revolt.

TISHRI

Seventh month in the Jewish calendar.

See also Calendar, Jewish; Months, Jewish.

TITHE

(Heb. *Maaser*, lit., "tenth") The tithe was a tenth of the produce. There are three categories of tithes: (1) First tithe, given to the Levites; (2) Second tithe, eaten by the owner himself in Jerusalem, during the 1st, 2nd, 4th and 5th years of the Sabbatical cycle; (3) Tithe of the poor, given in the 3rd and 6th years of the cycle. Animals were also tithed but according to a different system. Levites, too, were taxed, their tithe going to the priests.

TOBIT, BOOK OF

Book of the Apocrypha. It relates the story of Tobit, the pious Israelite who compassionately buried the Israelites slain in Assyrian Exile.

TOLA

A judge of Israel, of the tribe of Issachar. Tola judged 23 years.

TOMBSTONES

The custom of placing monuments on graves dates back at least to the time of Jacob who is said to have erected a pillar to mark the tomb of Rachel. Tombstones may be erected thirty days after the time of burial. A special service is held at the unveiling.

TORAH

The original Torah contains the fundamental law Moses received for Israel at Mount Sinai. It consists of the five books of Moses: Genesis, Exodus, Leviticus, Numbers and Deuteronomy. It is also called the Pentateuch, the Greek word for Five Books. Torah is often translated as "law," but it also means "religious instruction and learning." Judaism is based on Torah, God and Israel. And Israel's world, according to the rabbis, rests upon three pillars: Torah, worship and benevolence. But Torah is the chief pillar, from which the others derive their strength. When in post-Biblical times events required specific laws not directly provided for in the "written" Torah, new laws were derived from it by the rabbis. These later decisions became known as the "oral" Torah (a term now applied to the Talmud) which has been collected in the Talmud. The Talmudic scholars have always found the basis for their new legal needs in the words of the Torah and they have always believed that everything yet to be decided or learned is already inherent in the Torah. Torah is constant and unchangeable; it lives and is constantly read, studied and loved by Jews all over the world. The love of the Torah is also expressed in the beautiful ornamentation of the Scrolls, their finely tooled silver breastplates, crowns and pointers (in the shape of a pointing hand, called *yad*, "hand"), and of the Ark in which they are placed. The Torah Scroll is hand-written on parchment by devout and pious men. A special spirit of devotion and consecration is required for this task which has to be executed with perfection, because no mistake should mar the holy Torah.

TORAH, READING OF

Portions (*Parshiyot*) of the Torah are read in the synagogue on every Sabbath of the year and on holidays and special days, such as Rosh Hodesh. The portions which are read on Sabbath are so arranged that over the year the entire Pentateuch (the Torah) is completed. On holidays and special days, selected portions chosen for their relevance to that particular day are read. Originally, each person called up to the reading of the Torah was expected to read a section by himself, but it has now become the custom for especially trained people to read the portion for those given an Aliyah. The weekly Sabbath portions are also called *Sidrot* (sing. *Sidra*).

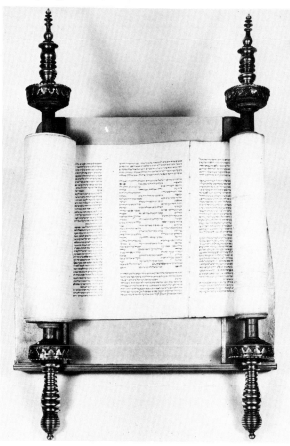

Torah Scroll, Germany, 1700. The Scroll is opened to the Song of the Red Sea, traditionally written in the form of interlocking bricks, symbolic of the walls of water into which the Lord divided the sea.

TORAH, SEFER

The Scroll of the Torah, handwritten on special parchment by the *Sofer*. The *Sefer Torah* is a large Scroll, mounted on two rollers: Each synagogue usually has several Scrolls, from which portions of the Torah are read at their prescribed times. If a Sefer Torah cannot be used any longer, it is buried or stored in a *Genizah*.

TOSAFOT

("Additions") commentaries on selected passages of the Talmud. They were written by the Talmudic scholars (Tosafists) of France and Western Germany in the 12th and 13th centuries. In editions of the Talmud, *Tosafot* are printed on the outer side of a page, while Rashi's continuous commentaries are printed on the inner side of the page. One of the important Tosafists was Rabbenu Tam (Jacob ben Meir), grandson of Rashi.

TOSEFTA

(Aramaic, "supplement") A supplement to the *Mishnah;* the exact relation between the two works is still debated by scholars. Individual paragraphs of the *Tosefta,* called *Baraitot,* are often quoted in the Talmud. R. Nehemiah, a pupil of R. Akiba, is considered one of the main editors of the *Tosefta,* though his work was probably supplemented by that of pupils of R. Judah Hanasi, the editor of the *Mishnah*.

TOURO, JUDAH

Soldier, merchant and philanthropist during America's early days. He was born in 1775 in Newport, Rhode Island, and died in 1854 in New Orleans. His father died when Judah was very young and he was reared by an uncle in Boston. He became a volunteer

Judah Touro.

in the War of 1812. Left for dead on a battlefield after carrying ammunition to an exposed battery, he was rescued by his friend, Rezin Shepherd, who remained his lifelong associate. Judah Touro, a devout Jew, gave much of his money to worthy causes. When Amos Lawrence of Boston pledged $10,000 for the building of the Bunker Hill Monument if another person contributed an equal amount, Touro at once offered the money. Later a banquet was held honoring these two public-spirited citizens—President Tyler was present and the eloquent Daniel Webster delivered the oration. At another time Touro purchased the mortgage of a Universalist church in New Orleans to prevent its sale and returned it to the church. Touro was a gentle and humble person. Though living in New Orleans in the first half of the 19th century, he disapproved of slavery. He once owned a slave but after training him for business and giving him a large sum of money he gave him his freedom. In 1850 he bought a church in his city and had it converted into a synagogue. One of his gifts, the Touro Infirmary, is still operating. He also founded one of the first free libraries in the world, the Touro Free Library in New Orleans. In Newport, a park and a street are named after him and in New Orleans a street and various institutions bear his name.

TOURO SYNAGOGUE

In Newport, R.I., the oldest existing synagogue building in the United States. It is the first Jewish house of worship to become a national historic shrine (1947).

Touro Synagogue in Newport, R.I.

TOWER OF BABEL

The high tower built by the descendants of Noah in the land of Shinar (Babylonia). In Genesis it is told that God punished the builders for trying to reach the heavens by making each of them speak a different language and scattering them all over the world.

TRIBES, LOST

The ten tribes which formed the Kingdom of Israel passed out of history with the destruction of the Kingdom by the Assyrians under Shalmanessar in 721-15 B.C.E. Since that time, however, various peoples have been identified with the tribes exiled by Shalmanessar, among them the English and the Japanese. Travellers of the Middle Ages claimed to have found the lost tribes in South America, Central Asia, and Arabia.

TROKI, ISAAC

(1533-1594)—Russian Karaite scholar, born in the city of Troki in Lithuania. A frequent participant in religious debates with Christians, Troki was a student of Christian theology. His *Hizzuk Emunah* ("Strengthening of the Faith"), a classic anti-Christian polemic, is the most comprehensive Jewish rebuttal of Christian teachings and beliefs. It is still widely used, and in its Latin translation had much influence on Christian anti-clericalists and freethinkers of the 17th and 18th centuries, including Voltaire.

TROPP

The ancient musical signs used to indicate to the reader of the Torah, the Haftarah and other parts of the Bible, the melodies in which they are to be chanted.

See also Accents.

TROTSKY, LEON

(born Bronstein; 1879-1940)—Russian revolutionary leader. In the Russian Bolshevik revolution which began in 1917 he directed the Bolshevik forces against both foreign and internal enemies and displayed his brilliant military genius. Trotsky was commissar for foreign affairs and negotiated the Treaty of Brest-Litovsk with Germany; later he served as war commissar. Differences with Stalin grew sharp after Lenin's death in 1924, and he was exiled in 1927. He found a refuge in Mexico City, where he was murdered in 1940. In addition to his practical abilities, Trotsky was a leading communist political theoretician and writer, and a stirring orator.

TRUMPELDOR, JOSEPH

A Zionist hero and the founder of the Hechalutz. Born in Russia in 1880, he fought as a volunteer in the Russo-Japanese War of 1904, and was decorated for valor several times. He lost his left arm in the siege of Port Arthur. When the fortress fell to the Japanese, he was captured and interned for a year. In prison he conceived the idea to go to Israel with a group of friends and found a communal settlement. After his return to Russia, though made an officer by the Czar, he resigned from the army and he and his friends went to Palestine to realize their plans. Their early settlement at Migdal lasted only a short time. He, like most Russians, was compelled to leave the country during World War I and he helped organize the famous Zion Mule Corps. He distinguished himself in action and was called by his commander "the bravest man I have ever seen." Trumpeldor returned to Russia to form

Trumpeldor monument in Tel-Chai.

a large Jewish army to take Palestine, but his venture was interrupted by the Bolshevik revolution. He gathered a band of young Jews, "Halutzim", to settle in Palestine but they were denied entry by the authorities. He returned to the land himself, with the plan of organizing Jewish laborers and bringing them to Palestine. When the Jewish colonists in Northern Galilee were left without protection from the French army and the British had not yet arrived, he organized a defense corps of about fifty men to resist the Arab border rebels. He died with five of his men in a treacherous attack at Tel Chai on March 1, 1920. Trumpeldor's last words were, "It doesn't matter—it's good to die for our country." Today the Trumpeldor monument stands in Tel Chai on the spot where he died. Shortly after his death his dream was realized and Hechalutz was founded.

TU BI-SHEVAT

See Hamishah Asar Bi-Shevat.

TUNISIA

Jews have lived in Tunisia since Roman times, and Kairouan was once a center of rabbinic learning. Until modern times (1881) Jews were forced to wear special clothing and pay heavy taxes. 75,000 Jews now live in Tunisia, most of whom are shopkeepers and merchants.

TURIM

1. The four rows (*Arba Turim*) of the twelve precious stones representing the twelve tribes of Israel in the High Priest's breastplate.
2. A code of Jewish law named after the *Turim*, compiled by Jacob ben Asher (also called *Baal Ha-Turim*, born in Germany, 1269, died in Spain, 1340). The *Turim* is a code of law designed for everyday use. It is arranged in four divisions and is also called *Tur*. It was used by Caro as the basis for the *Shulchan Aruch*.

TURKEY

For many centuries Jews were welcomed in Turkey during the period of the Ottoman Empire. Adrianople (modern Edirne) was a great center of Jewish learning, and Turkey became one of the principal lands of refuge for the fugitives from Spain and Portugal in the 15th and 16th centuries. Jews rose to high positions and were admitted into the army; Suleiman the Magnificent intervened on their behalf in foreign courts and appointed Joseph Nasi (1524-1579) one of his chief advisers and gave him permission to establish a Jewish settlement in Tiberias. But by the 18th century the position of the Jews in Turkey had deteriorated, and they have never recovered from this state of affairs. There are now 37,000 Jews in the country, living mostly in Istanbul.

TWELVE TRIBES

The divisions of the nation of Israel during the time of the Judges and the early kings. The Twelve Tribes were descendants of the 12 sons of Jacob-Israel. Each tribe received a portion of land when the Israelites entered Canaan after their Exodus from Egypt. The priestly tribe of Levi did not take a portion, but the division into 12 sections was maintained, since the portion of Joseph was divided between his two sons, Ephraim and Manasseh. The tribes slowly lost their distinct identities when Israel became a more consolidated nation.

Symbol of the twelve tribes.

TYRE

Royal city of the kings of ancient Phoenicia; great port and trade city of antiquity on the coast of the Mediterranean, now called Sur. King Hiram, ally of

David and Solomon, lived there. The prized city was taken by the Assyrians, Babylonians, Syrians and by Alexander the Great. Phoenicians of Tyre are said to have founded Carthage, the great rival of Rome.

TZADI

The eighteenth letter of the Hebrew alphabet, has the numerical value of 90.

See also Aleph Bet.

TZITZIT

The fringes on the prayer shawl *(Tallit)* and the "Arba Kanfot."

TZOM GEDALIAH

(The Fast of Gedaliah) a day of fasting and mourning commemorating the assassination of Gedaliah, the governor of Judea after the destruction of the First Temple.

See also Gedaliah.

UJA

The United Jewish Appeal is an American fund-raising organization founded in 1939. It has raised nearly $3 billion since 1948, most of which has gone to settling new immigrants in Israel and relieving Jewish war refugees; in all, some 900,000 were helped to settle in Israel, while some 2,500,000 Jewish war refugees were aided.

UNITED NATIONS

On November 29, 1947, the General Assembly of the United Nations voted for the partition of Palestine into Jewish and Arab states. On this legal foundation, the State of Israel was declared on May 14, 1948, one day before the end of the British Mandate. Israel was admitted to the United Nations on May 11, 1949, and its affairs have often been considered by this body. Following the Sinai Campaign of the fall of 1956, the United Nations sent a security force to patrol the Gaza Strip and other contested areas. The explusion of this UN Emergency Force in May 1967 by President Nasser of Egypt was one of the crucial events precipitating the outbreak of the Six-Day War. In the 1960s and 1970s the Arab states, backed by the Soviet bloc and many nonaligned nations of the Third World, have used their majority in the UN General Assembly to consistently condemn and harass Israel. They have repeatedly threatened to bring about Israel's expulsion from the world body, and in 1975 succeeded in having the General Assembly pass a resolution condemning Zionism as a form of racism.

UNITED STATES

Although individual Jews may have arrived in North America earlier, the first permanent Jewish settlement was established in 1654, when 23 Jewish refugees from Brazil arrived in New Amsterdam (later New York). By the time of the American Revolution (1776), there were about 2,500 Jews in the United States, mainly of Sephardic origin, with important communities in New York, Philadelphia, Newport, Savannah, and Charleston. America's Jews were guaranteed religious freedom by the U.S. Constitution (1789), although it was some years before all restrictions on the state level were eliminated. The American Jewish community remained small until the 1830s, when Jews from Germany and Central Europe began arriving in strength. By 1860 America had 150,000 Jews. An unprecedented mass immigration from Eastern Europe began in the 1880s, and by its conclusion, around 1925, the American Jewish community had leaped in size to around 4,500,000. German Jews fleeing Hitler began arriving in the 1930s, and other refugees came to the United States after World War II. In 1972 American Jewry included 6,115,000 members, the vast majority of whom were native-born and of Ashkenazic background—this constituted half of the total world Jewish population. There are important Jewish communities in all parts of the United States, but most Jews live in and around the big cities, especially New York, Chicago, Philadelphia, Cleveland, Boston, Los Angeles, and Miami. American Jews have fought in all of America's wars (550,000 in the service during World War II) and have made important contributions in all walks of life, including government, science and the arts, business, and industry. Although many American Jews were factory workers during the main period of mass immigration, most today are members of the middle class, clustered in such white-collar occupations as teaching, the professions, sales, and business. Reform and Conservative Judaism have both flourished in the United States, and American Orthodoxy has also experienced a major renewal. As the world's largest single Jewish community, surpassing even Israel in size, America plays an important role in all aspects of Jewish life and Jewish affairs, and is the home base of many major Jewish institutions and organizations. Primarily Zionist in sentiment, American Jewry has raised vast sums of money to aid Israel. Although assimilation and intermarriage have increased in recent years, most American Jews still retain a firm sense of Jewish identity.

UNTERMAN, ISSAR YEHUDA

(1886-   )—Israeli Chief Rabbi. Born in Belorussia, Unterman served as a rabbi in Lithuania and, from 1923 to 1946, in Liverpool, England. A staunch Zionist, he attended several Zionist congresses, was vice-president of the Jewish National Fund, and president of the Mizrachi Organization of Great Britain. In 1946 he was elected Chief Rabbi of Tel Aviv-Jaffa, and in 1964 he became Israel's Ashkenazic Chief Rabbi, serving in this post until 1972.

UNTERMEYER, LOUIS

(1885-   )—American poet and anthologist. Untermeyer is a noted translator of Heine, a poet (*Roast Leviathan*), a critic, and a compiler of many successful anthologies of poetry.

UR

The Bible tells that Ur, a Babylonian city, was Abra(ha)m's home before the family left for Haran. Scientific excavations have revealed that Ur was already a rich and well-developed city by 3500 B.C.E. In the Bible the city is called "Ur of the Chaldees."

Excavation site of a temple in the ancient city of Ur.

URIAH

Brave officer of King David's army, husband of Bath-sheba whom David later married. Uriah was sent into a raging battle where he died.

URIEL

Angel and messenger of God.

URIM AND TUMMIM

("Light and Truth") probably two sacred objects the High Priest carried under the Breastplate of Judgment. Some scholars today believe that the Urim and Tummim were really identical with the four rows of the twelve precious stones in the breastplate, representing the Twelve Tribes of Israel. The High Priest wore the Urim and Tummim upon his heart when he stood before God in prayer and in search of advice and judgment. The Latin form of Urim and Tummim (*lux et veritas*) is the motto of Yale University.

URIS, LEON

(1924-   )—One of America's most popular writers, Uris has written several best-selling novels on Jewish themes: *Exodus*, which deals with the establishment of the State of Israel; *Mila 18*, about the Warsaw Ghetto uprising in 1943; and *QB VII*, about Nazi war crimes.

URUGUAY

Most of this country's 50,000 Jews live in Montevideo, and are merchants. Many came in a 20th century immigration from Central and Eastern Europe. The Jewish community supports a school system and a number of daily and weekly newspapers.

USHA

City in Galilee, seat of the Sanhedrin (2nd century C.E.) and of an academy of Tannaim.

UZZIAH

Also called Azariah; son of Amaziah; father of Jotham; tenth king of Judah at the time of Jeroboam II of Israel. During his long reign (about 767-737 B.C.E.) he upheld the religion of the One God. He fortified Jerusalem, strengthened the army and held in check his country's foes. Judah flourished under the reign of Uzziah.

The grave of King Uzziah is marked by this engraved stone tablet.

VASHTI

Queen of Persia, wife of King Ahasuerus. She refused to appear before his guests and was cast out of the royal household. Esther succeeded her as Queen of Persia.

VAV

The sixth letter of the Hebrew alphabet, has the numerical value of 6.

See also Aleph Bet.

VENEZUELA

The first Jews arrived in Venezuela in 1850. Later Jewish immigrants from Germany and Eastern Europe played a large part in developing the nation's commerce and modernizing Caracas, the capital. 12,000 Jews now live in Venezuela.

VILNA

Lithuanian city, now in the Soviet Union. Jews first settled in Vilna in the 15th century. The Jews of Vilna suffered from discriminatory legislation, riots, and massacres, until 1747, when their legal rights were guaranteed; they were given the right of free residence only in 1861. Nevertheless, Vilna, called the "Jerusalem of Lithuania," had long been a center of Jewish piety and culture. From 1720-97 it was the home of Elijah, called the Gaon of Vilna, universally recognized as the greatest Talmudist of the day. In the 19th century the Haskalah movement grew influential in the city, but Vilna remained a fortress of traditional Judaism. The edition of the Talmud published there by the Romm family, familiarly called the "Vilna *Shass*," has remained the standard edition. At one time, as many as 140,000 Jews lived in Vilna; its present Jewish population is about 16,000. Under Soviet rule, the former center of Jewish culture now has only one small synagogue.

VITAL, HAYYIM

(1543-1620)—Talmudist and Kabbalist. Born in the town of Safed in Palestine, Vital studied under Moses Cordovero and Isaac Luria. His *Etz Hayyim* ("Tree of Life") is one of the most important expositions of the mystical thought of Luria. He was also the author of talmudical works and sermons.

VULGATE

A translation of the Bible into Latin made by Jerome towards the end of the 4th century C.E. The Vulgate was declared the official Bible of the Catholic Church in 1546 and was not superseded until 1940. Jerome's work follows the Masoretic text, on the whole, and shows the influence of the various *Targumim* and of rabbinical commentaries.

WAHL, SAUL

Legendary personage who is said to have been king of Poland for one day in the 16th century. According to the story, he was a son of Samuel Judah ben Abraham Katzenellenbogen, rabbi in Padua, and was found studying in a Yeshiva by Prince Radziwill, who took a liking to him. On the death of King Bathori, "Prince" Saul was chosen temporary king (hence his name Wahl, which means "choice" in German). In real life, Wahl was a financier who used his influence and money on behalf of his fellow-Jews in Poland and Lithuania.

WAILING WALL

The last part left of the ruins of Israel's great Temple in Jerusalem. The wall is 160 feet long and 60 feet high, and a large section of the stonework forms parts of inhabited houses. Experts have attempted to determine which parts of the wall are from Solomon's Temple, from the Second Temple and from Herod's. The Wailing Wall has been in Arab territory since 1948. Before that time as many as 50,000 Jews would visit the Wall to weep and pray for the old home of their faith on the 9th of Av (Tisha B'Av), and large crowds also assembled there on the special

At the Wailing Wall.

days before Passover and Yom Kippur. But every day of the year Jews gathered before the Wall to recite their daily prayers. On Sabbath and other special days an Ark and table would be brought to the Wailing Wall so that the Torah could be read there.

WAKSMAN, SELMAN A.

(1888-1973)—American scientist. Waksman arrived in the United States in 1910 from the Ukraine. In 1925 he joined the faculty of Rutgers University, and he became the head of its Institute of Microbiology in 1949. In 1944 he discovered the antibiotic called streptomycin, which is of great aid in fighting tuberculosis and other infectious diseases. Waksman was awarded a Nobel Prize in 1952 for his work in microbiology.

Dr. Selman Waksman.

WALD, LILLIAN D.

(1867-1940)—One of the most active and distinguished native American welfare workers. In 1908 she gave Congress the idea of the Federal Children's Bureau. The Henry Street Settlement in New York's lower East Side was her creation. More than these, she instituted the first non-sectarian public health nursing system; and the modern school nurse is the result of her planning. After her early education in Cincinnati, Miss Wald was graduated from the New York Training School for Nurses in 1891 and she then studied at

Lillian Wald .

the Women's Medical College. Her determination to devote her energies to social welfare was aroused by a visit to the crowded and unsanitary slums in which many thousands of immigrants were living before 1900. With another nurse, Mary Brewster, she founded the famed settlement house which bears her name. In 1893 she began the home nursing service that has made over twenty million calls at the homes of the ailing poor. Miss Wald received many honors during her lifetime, represented her country at international health conferences and authored many valuable writings on her activities.

WARBURG FAMILY

German-Jewish family with branches in America and England. Many Warburgs are financiers, while other have distinguished themselves in scholarly and cultural fields. Otto (1883-1970), a biochemist, received a Nobel Prize in 1931; James (1896-1969) was an American authority on economics and foreign policy; Felix (1871-1937) was a leader of the Jewish community and a noted philanthropist.

WAR OF INDEPENDENCE, ISRAEL

Despite the United Nations resolution to establish a Jewish State in part of Palestine (Nov. 29, 1947), Arab forces attacked the Jews early in 1948, the first point of attack being Tirat Zevi, a kibbutz in the Galil. Jerusalem was cut off, and ultimately, the Israeli forces surrendered the Old City. In April, the Haganah conquered large sections of Galilee; in May, following the establishment of the State of Israel, the armies of six Arab countries invaded the country. Despite the loss of the old city, New Jerusalem was saved by the heroic construction of the "Burma Road" which restored communication with other Jewish forces. Israeli victories mounted after the general truce of June 11—July 8. During the autumn Israeli forces took Beersheba and almost the entire Negev, as the Egyptian army retreated. Even the Sinai peninsula was penetrated by Israeli troops, who were forced to withdraw by British pressure. In February, 1949, Israel and Egypt signed agreements on the island of Rhodes ending the fighting; later, armistice papers were signed with Jordan, Lebanon, and Syria. Agreements were never reached with Iraq and Saudi Arabia.

WARSAW

The capital of Poland. Jews first settled in Warsaw in the 15th century, but they were expelled from the city in 1483. Small numbers of Jews were allowed to resettle there in the 18th century, and full rights were granted in 1862. Warsaw became a center of Jewish culture; besides the traditional institutions of learning the city also boasted many Jewish artistic ventures, such as a theater, a museum, etc. By 1939, there were some 360,000 Jews in Warsaw. In October 1940 the invading German forces established the notorious "Warsaw Ghetto," in which 85,000 died of starvation, and from which 300,000 were herded off to the Treblinka extermination center. In the spring of 1943 the remnants of the Ghetto staged an epic uprising, fighting German tanks and aircraft with home-made bombs and rifles. It took the fully equipped German army more than a month of house-to-house fighting to quell the revolt, in which 50,000 Jews perished. Some 8,000 Jews live in Warsaw at the present time, but most Jewish institutions ceased functioning in the outbreak of anti-Semitism that followed the Six-Day War (1967).

WASSERMANN, AUGUST VON

(1866-1925)—An eminent immunologist, he was born in Germany in 1866. After studying there and in Austria, he began his practice in Strasbourg. Later he devoted himself to his major interest—immunizing men against dread diseases—by becoming an assistant at the Robert Koch Institute for Infectious Diseases in Berlin. In 1906 he became director of the Department of Experimental Therapy and Serum Research and in 1913 was appointed director of the Kaiser Wilhelm Institute for Experimental Therapy. His task was to discover substances in the blood, or which might be created in the blood, which would prevent or overcome illnesses difficult to cure. August von Wassermann published works on the nature of infection, the transmission of disease to children, the uses of bacteria, and anti-toxins (fighters of poisons in the body). Certain dread diseases, such as syphilis, had proved almost impossible to fight. Dr. Wassermann discovered a test that could detect syphilis even before outward signs appeared on the skin. By rendering it possible to treat the early stages, he helped save innumerable patients. His discovery is called the Wassermann test and is known throughout the scientific world. This medical benefactor of mankind died in 1925.

WEIZMANN, CHAIM

The first President of Israel, was born in Poland in 1874. After early years of study in Hebrew and Talmud, he became interested in the sciences. He went to Switzerland to study chemistry. In 1904 he went to England to teach at the University of Manchester. It

Dr. Chaim Weizmann.

was not long before he gained international fame as a chemist. By developing acetone, needed for explosives during World War I, he gained the gratitude of the British Government. This was to serve him well in his later Zionist activities. Weizmann always strongly upheld and loved the ideals of Zion. At the Sixth Zionist Congress in 1903, he bitterly opposed Theodor Herzl because he considered Herzl undemocratic and too willing to substitute another territory (Uganda) for Palestine. His own Zionism combined an emphasis on Hebrew culture and political realism. Undoubtedly it was Weizmann's friendship for Lord Balfour that brought into being the Balfour Declaration which promised British help to the Jews in returning to their homeland. In 1918 Weizmann laid the cornerstone of the Hebrew University which he had helped create and of which he became president. He represented the Jews at international conferences. He served many years as president of the World Zionist Organization and he traveled throughout the world in behalf of the Zionist cause. When Britain tried to repudiate the Balfour Declaration, Weizmann resigned his presidency of the Jewish Agency in protest. He died in 1952 while President of Israel.

WEST INDIES

It is said that Louis de Torres, a Marrano who accompanied Columbus on his voyage in 1492, settled in Cuba and died there, making him the first Jewish settler in this region. The first sizeable group of Jews to settle in the West Indies were Marranos who came there in the 17th century; Barbados, a British colony, was the first of the islands in which professing Jews were allowed to settle. The largest Jewish communities in the area now are those of Puerto Rico, Curacao, and Cuba.

WIESEL, ELIE

(1928-   )—Novelist. Born in Sighet, Rumania, Wiesel was raised in a traditional Hasidic environment. He was sent to Auschwitz during World War II and was the only member of his family to survive the Holocaust. After the war he lived for a time in Paris and became a journalist. His first book, *Night*, de-

scribing his experiences in Auschwitz, was published in 1958 and won international acclaim. Since then he has published many other books, including *A Beggar in Jerusalem, Souls on Fire, The Town Beyond the Wall*, and *The Jews of Silence*. Regarded by many as a spokesman for the generation of the Holocaust, Wiesel is a compelling writer whose works have had a powerful, if upsetting, influence on many readers.

WIESENTHAL, SIMON

(1908-   )—Born in Poland, where he led a career as an architect, Wiesenthal was imprisoned in a Nazi concentration camp during World War II. After the war he helped the Allies track down Nazi war criminals. Later, supported by private donations, he founded and became the head of the Jewish Documentation Center in Vienna, a body devoted to amassing information on Nazi war crimes and bringing the perpetrators to justice. Over the years Wiesenthal has helped to locate hundreds of former Nazis, including the Gestapo officer who arrested Anne Frank in Amsterdam; Fritz Stangl, the commandant of Treblinka; and Hermine Braunsteiner Ryan, the first war criminal to be extradited from the United States. He also played a key role in determining the whereabout of Adolf Eichmann, who was then brought from Argentina to Israel to stand trial as a mass murderer.

WILLS

Jews dispose of their worldly goods in keeping with their religion. They do not only leave their possessions to their heirs, but often leave funds to charity and education, which have always been cornerstones of Jewish life. But many Jews willed more than their material possessions to their children. In the Bible, Jacob, Moses and David are among those who left words of spiritual counsel to those coming after them. In the Middle Ages the "ethical will" was customary and sought to hand over to the next generation the principles and practices which are the marks of a good Jew. Volumes of ethical wills of the Middle Ages have been published, urging children to be clean of body, garments and soul; they command the giving of alms, honorable dealing with men of every creed, speedy and proper justice, and that each heir serve as an example to those about him and to all the world. Often fathers would spend years preparing their ethical wills, adding and changing as new thoughts struck them. Some wills were book-length. The writers all tried to transmit the traditional Jewish ideal, that every member of the Jewish people must devote himself eternally to the service of God and man.

WISDOM OF SOLOMON

Book of the Apocrypha consisting of discourses and wise sayings.

WISE, ISAAC MAYER

(1819-1900)—Bohemian-born rabbi who did most to further the cause of Reform Judaism in America. Coming to the United States, for which he had already developed a strong affection, he served as a rabbi in Albany from 1846 to 1854. Although others had begun the Reform movement as early as 1824, it was Wise who became leader of the new form of Judaism. In 1854 he was called to Cincinnati. There, in twenty-six years of activity, he wrote extensively on religious subjects, founded two Jewish periodicals and organized the several groups and institutions that now comprise American Reform. These include the Union of American Hebrew Congregations, the Hebrew Union College and the Central Conference of American Rabbis. Although Wise's early labors were confined largely to Jews of German descent, today Jews of every origin are to be found in the temples that follow his teachings.

Isaac Mayer Wise.

WISE, STEPHEN S.

(1874-1949)—American rabbi and public figure. In 1907 he founded the Free Synagogue of New York, whose rabbi he was until his death, and in 1922 he organized the Jewish Institute of Religion to serve as a rabbinical seminary for Reform Judaism. An active Zionist, Wise was instrumental in the founding of the Zionist Organization of America whose President he was in 1917 and 1936-38, and the American Jewish Congress, whose President he was in 1925-9 and again in 1935-49.

WOLF, LUCIEN

(1857-1930)—English-Jewish statesman, journalist, historian and public worker. Wolf served as foreign editor of the *Daily Graphic* (1890) and pioneered in Anglo-Jewish history. Many international conferences, among them the Paris Peace Conference (1919), saw him as the representative of Jewry and he was active in the League of Nations.

WOLFSSOHN, DAVID

(1856-1914)—Zionist leader. A timber merchant in Cologne, Germany, he founded and directed the Jewish Colonial Trust, the first bank of the World Zionist Organization (1899). He was a good friend of Herzl and his confidante, and after Herzl's death became president of the World Zionist Organization. In contrast to those who demanded that the Organization spend its efforts in encouraging actual resettlement of the land, he felt that the political activities of Organization were most important.

YADIN, YIGAEL

(1917-   )—Israeli general, archaeologists, and politician. Yadin held high commands in the War of Independence and was chief of staff until 1952. As an archaeologist he excavated Herod's palace at Massada and is an expert on the Dead Sea Scrolls. In 1976 he founded the Democratic Movement for Change, a reformist political group that had a great impact on the 1977 Israeli election.

YAHRZEIT

The anniversary of the day of the death of a parent or other close relative. It is observed by the lighting of a Yahrzeit candle or light in the home, and the recital of Kaddish in the synagogue.

YEHOASH

(1872-1927)—Yiddish writer. Born in Lithuania, Yehoash (whose full name was Yehoash Solomon Bloomgarden), came to the United States in 1890. He is most famed for his masterly Yiddish translation of the Bible; in addition he wrote poems, fables, and stories and translated many works of Western literature into Yiddish.

YEMEN

In 1949-50 practically the entire Jewish population of Yemen, 46,000 strong, was transported to Israel by "Operation Magic Carpet." Until that date, the Jews of Yemen lived in a state of poverty. Most were craftsmen and some led a nomadic life very like the Arabs among whom they lived. The Jewish settlement in Yemen goes back to a very early period, and their tradition speaks of an immigration in the time of Solomon. Until the 5th century the Jews of Yemen were prosperous and there is even said to have been a king who adopted Judaism, Abu Karib Asad.

YESHIVA

("seat" or "session") A Talmudic academy where advanced students continue their Hebrew education and may be ordained as rabbis. When the Romans conquered Palestine, Rabbi Johanan ben Zakkai obtained permission to open a yeshiva in Javneh, which helped preserve the Jewish spirit and Jewish learning. The same goals have motivated all successors of this first yeshiva, from the Babylonian academies of Sura and Pumbeditha, through the Middle Ages, to modern times. The yeshiva of Volozin was the most noted of the many important academies in Russia; established in 1803, it continued until most of European Jewry was wiped out by the Nazis. Some famous academies of Eastern Europe have transferred their activities to the United States and other countries. Today a number of *yeshivot* (day schools) exist throughout America, where children receive an intensive Hebrew education in addition to their secular subjects. This school is often called *yeshiva ketanah*, "little yeshivah." The Yeshiva University in New York is the best known Jewish educational institution in the United States.

YESHIVA UNIVERSITY

Institution of higher learning in New York City operated under Orthodox auspices. Yeshiva University traces its origin to the Rabbi Isaac Elchanan Theological Seminary, a center for advanced Talmudic study and the training of Orthodox rabbis, which was founded in 1897. Secular studies were introduced in 1915, during the presidency of Bernard Revel, who guided Yeshiva College through its formative years. In 1945, during the presidency of Samuel Belkin, Yeshiva advanced from college to university status. The present university, which in 1972 had an enrollment of 7,057, includes the seminary, Yeshiva College, Stern College for Women, the Albert Einstein Medical School, and programs in the humanities, sciences, and social work.

Main building, Yeshiva University.

YIDDISH

A distinct language spoken by many Jews throughout the world. Most translations of the word Yiddish are misleading, implying that it is either a jargon or that it is spoken by all Jews. It has been the most important language spoken by Jews, with the exception of Hebrew, and it is almost one thousand years old. In its origin, it was a dialect of Middle High German. The Jews living in Germany adopted German as their vernacular but developed it in their own fashion as a separate language. When Ashkenazic Jewry migrated to Eastern Europe, Yiddish had its greatest de-

An ad for a Yiddish theatre performance at Providence, R. I., 1925.

velopment as a distinct language. The present form of Yiddish was reached by the eighteenth century. Elements from Hebrew and other languages have been incorporated into Yiddish. American Yiddish began to develop with mass immigration after the late nineteenth-century Russian pogroms. English words and terms were incorporated into Yiddish. A great literature and drama have been written in Yiddish; some of this has been recently translated into English.

See also Judeo Languages

YISHUV

The Jewish community of Palestine before the establishment of the State of Israel.

YIVO

(Yiddisher Vissenshaftlicher Institut—Institute for Jewish Research)—Yivo was founded in 1925 to carry on research in all fields of Jewish literature, language, history, and related fields. Its main office, library, and archives were located in Vilna, with branches in thirty countries. After World War II the main branch, with as much of its library as could be salvaged, was transferred to New York City. Yivo has many publications, and sponsors much valuable research.

YIZKOR

Memorial prayers for departed relatives, recited on Yom Kippur, Passover, Shavuot and Shemini Atzeret.

YOD

The tenth letter of the Hebrew alphabet, has the numerical value of 10.

See also Aleph Bet.

YOM HA-ATZMAUT

Israel Independence Day, 5th of Iyar.

YOM KIPPUR

The Day of Atonement is the holiest day of the Jewish year. It is the climax of the Ten Days of Penitence which, according to tradition, are a time for repentance, charity and prayer, in preparation for Yom Kippur. The day is observed by fasting and prayer for more than twenty-four hours. On Yom Kippur, Jews atone only for sins committed against God—"but for transgressions against a fellowman the Day of Atonement does not atone, unless and until man has conciliated his fellowman and redressed the wrong he has done him." Many Orthodox Jews wear white gowns (kittels) in the synagogue to represent their longing for purity, and they remove their shoes as was the custom of the priests when treading on holy ground. The best known prayer of Yom Kippur is *Kol Nidre* ("all vows"), the opening prayer chanted three times on the eve of Yom Kippur. *Ashamnu* and *Al Chet* are the two confessional prayers that are chanted several times during the day's services; all the sins are confessed by the whole congregation in unison. The ancient Yom Kippur service of the High Priest in the Temple in Jerusalem is described in the moving, poetic *Avodah*, which is recited during the *Musaf* (additional) service. The day ends with the *Neilah* (closing) prayer; before the "gates of Heaven" are closed, the worshippers pray that they may be "sealed" in the Book of Life. The Day of Atonement is devoted to earnest repentance and self-examination—to the renewal of the life of each individual and the ethical and religious life of the whole community of Israel.

YOM KIPPUR WAR

On October 6, 1973, which coincided with Yom Kippur, the most solemn day of the Jewish religious calendar, and an occasion when most Israelis were attending synagogue, the combined forces of Egypt, Syria, and Iraq carried out a surprise attack on Israel. Overrunning most of the thinly manned outposts of the Bar-Lev line, massive Egyptian armored and infantry units, equipped with the latest Soviet anti-tank and anti-aircraft missiles, crossed the Suez Canal and advanced inland. An equally powerful Syrian-Iraqi force pushed into the Golan Heights. During the next few days the outnumbered Israeli units held on, despite suffering many casualties and equipment losses, while waiting for the reserves to be mobilized. Once Israel's citizen army had reached the front in full strength, and with a U.S. emergency air-lift providing needed munitions and replacement equipment, the tide quickly turned. The Syrians were pushed out of the Golan Heights and the Israelis advanced to within 20 miles of Damascus. Israel then turned its attention to the Sinai. In an unexpected and tactically daring maneuver, Israeli forces broke through the Egyptian lines, crossed the Suez Canal under heavy fire, and encircled a major portion of the Egyptian army. On October 22, 1973 a cease-fire was imposed under United Nations auspices, saving the trapped Egyptians from total annihilation.

ZACUTO, ABRAHAM

(1450-1515)—Spanish astronomer and Hebrew writer. He served as professor of astronomy at the University of Salamanca and with the expulsion of the Jews from Spain in 1492 became court astronomer to King John II of Portugal. Zacuto promoted Vasco Da Gama's voyage to India in 1497-8, and provided the navigator with an astrolabe of his own invention. Columbus used Zacuto's maps as well. His chief literary work is the *Sefer Hayuchasin*, a history of Jewish rabbinic literature.

Abraham Zacuto.

ZADDIK

A completely righteous man. A Zaddik is just to his fellowmen and observes God's commandments. The leaders of the Hasidic movement often are called by the title Zaddik. According to Jewish legend, there are thirty-six Zaddikim in every generation, unrecognized and ignorant of their righteousness, to whose piety the world owes its existence.

ZADOK

With Abiathar, priest at the time of David. He helped David bring the Ark to Jerusalem. Zadok supported Solomon as David's successor and was made sole High Priest under Solomon. He was the ancestor of many high priests.

ZANGWILL, ISRAEL

(1864-1926)—An English writer who devoted his

caricature of Israel Zangwill.

talents to the depiction of the life of immigrant Jews in London. Working as a young teacher, he wrote sketches and stories for London periodicals; the best were about his Jewish neighbors. In 1893 the Jewish Publication Society of America published his *Children of the Ghetto*, an outstanding novel about the story of the new Jewish generation in London's East End, and their counterparts elsewhere. The collections *Ghetto Tragedies* and *Ghetto Comedies* portray similar characters. *The King of Schnorrers* consists mainly of humorous tales of an earlier period, and *Dreamers of the Ghetto* offers sketches of famous Jews. Zangwill is best known for his drama *The Melting Pot* — a term which has become a household phrase. He was not an exceptional poet but his translations of Solomon Ibn Gabirol and other Jewish poets are still read. Zangwill admired and furthered Theodor Herzl's early new Zionism. But after Herzl's death he broke with Zionism, in 1905, and helped organize the Jewish Territorial Association, which sought other lands for Jews to colonize. The organization disbanded in 1925 and Zangwill again expressed interest in the Zionist idea. He is best known for his books and some of them are still read today.

ZAYIN

The seventh letter of the Hebrew alphabet, has the numerical value of 7.

See also Aleph Bet

ZEBOIIM

One of the Cities of the Plain.

See also Cities of the Plain

ZEBULUN

Tenth son of Jacob, sixth son of Leah, ancestor of the tribe of Zebulun.

ZEBULUN, TRIBE OF

One of the tribes of Israel. Its territory was in the rich and fertile northern region of Israel. Zebulun became part of the northern Kingdom of Israel. The tribe's emblem was a ship; its banner was white. The stone representing Zebulun in the High Priest's breastplate was probably a diamond.

ZECHARIAH

1. Eleventh of the Books of Twelve (Minor) Prophets of the Bible. The prophet Zechariah was a contemporary of Zerubbabel, Haggai and the High Priest, Joshua. He helped in the building of the Second Temple. His writings contain visions and prophecies.

2. Fourteenth king of Israel, son of Jeroboam II. After a rule of six months, Zechariah was assassinated and succeeded by Shallum (about 741 B.C.E.).

ZEDAKAH

("Charity") righteousness, justice. The Jewish belief in Zedakah is based not simply on pity for the needy but also on the principle of justice and the belief that all men are brothers.

ZEDEKIAH

Also called Mattaniah, twentieth and last king of Judah (about 597-586 B.C.E., before the Babylonian Exile), son of King Josiah, renamed and appointed king by Nebuchadnezzar. Ignoring the warnings of the prophet Jeremiah, he revolted against mighty Babylonia and was defeated. Jerusalem and the beautiful Temple of Solomon were destroyed. Zedekiah was blinded and imprisoned, and, with his people, carried into Babylonian captivity.

ZEITLIN, HILLEL

(1871-1942)—Journalist and author. Born in Russia, Zeitlin lived in various places in Eastern Europe and was a prolific contributor to the Yiddish press of Poland and Lithuania. He wrote frequently on mysticism and regious philosophy, as well as on literary subjects and the social, economic, and political problems of East European Jewry. During World War II he was killed by the Nazis. His son, Aaron Zeitlin (1889-1973), was an important Hebrew and Yiddish poet. From 1939 until his death he taught Hebrew literature at the Jewish Theological Seminary.

ZEITLIN, SOLOMON

(1892-1976)—American scholar. Born in Russia, Zeitlin has for many years been professor of rabbinics at Dropsie University and editor of the *Jewish Quarterly Review*. One of the most prolific American Jewish scholars, he has written hundreds of articles, and numerous books as well (including the multivolume *Rise and Fall of the Judean State*), on the history of the Second Jewish Commonwealth and related subjects. Almost alone among scholars he maintains that the Dead Sea Scrolls date from the Middle Ages.

ZEMIROT ("Songs")

1. Term applied by the Sephardic and Yemenite Jews to the biblical verses in the morning service known as *Pesuke Dezimra* among the Ashkenazim.
2. Table songs and hymns sung by the Ashkenazim

during Sabbath meals and at the conclusion of the Sabbath (Havdalah). The tunes of many of these Zemirot were adapted from folk songs that were popular in areas where the Jews lived in Eastern Europe.

ZEPHANIAH

Ninth of the Books of Twelve (Minor) Prophets of the Bible. The prophet Zephaniah preached in the early years of the reign of King Josiah of Judah. He spoke bitterly against the corrupt conditions before Josiah's great reforms.

ZERUBBABEL

Governor of Judea, grandson of King Jehoiachin of Judah. At the time of King Cyrus of Persia, this prince of the House of David led the first Jews back from Babylon. With the help of the High Priest, Joshua, and the prophets Haggai and Zechariah, Zerubbabel started to build the Second Temple.

See also Sheshbazzar.

ZIKLAG

Philistine city near Gaza where David found refuge from King Saul. The Philistine king, Achish, gave Ziklag to David, who stayed there with his followers until the death of King Saul.

ZILPAH

Handmaid of Leah and concubine of Jacob. She was the mother of Gad and Asher, ancestors of tribes of Israel.

ZIMRI

Captain of the guard who assassinated King Elah and reigned as King of Israel for seven days (about 889 B.C.E.). When Omri attempted to dethrone him, Zimri burned the palace and killed himself in the flames.

ZIN

One of the four wildernesses of the Sinai Peninsula through which the Israelites wandered to Canaan, southwest of the Dead Sea region.

ZION, MOUNT

Mountain in Jerusalem, originally the site of the Jebusite fortress captured by David. David built his palace on Mount Zion and Solomon built the Temple there. The Second Temple was also built on Mount Zion. Later, Zion became a symbol for Jerusalem and Israel, as it is said: "For out of Zion shall go forth the Torah, and the word of the Lord from Jerusalem." At the time of Abraham, Mount Zion was known as Mount Moriah.

See also Moriah, Mount.

Pilgrims to Mt. Zion are greeted by the sound of the shofar as they ascend the mountain on an annual Passover pilgrimage. Note the curved ram's horn, typical in Oriental Jewish communities.

ZIONISM

A modern movement, the aim of which was to create a home in Zion for the Jewish people. Zion is the old, poetic name for the land of Israel, derived from Mount Zion in Jerusalem, where the Temples stood. The love of Zion and the hope for the return to Zion have been a great ideal and a driving force throughout the history of the Jewish people in Exile. Modern Zionism developed during the last part of the nineteenth century. In 1882 the *Hovevei Zion* (Lovers of Zion), one of its forerunners, was organized. In 1897, Theodor Herzl founded the Zionist movement and became its great leader. He united the many independent groups devoted to restoring Jewish life in Palestine and convened the First Zionist Congress in Basle, Switzerland. The organization grew, its various ideas were debated and crystallized, and a congress was called regularly, (the first five yearly, then every second year) to which all the membership sent its delegates. In 1917 the famous Balfour Declaration and in 1922 the Palestine Mandate promised aid in the establishment of a national Jewish home. In the twenties, and increasingly so in the thirties and forties, Zionism developed into a mass movement and many Jews came to Palestine. The situation between the Jews and Arabs, and the British mandatory rule, became more difficult. Jewish immigration was restricted more and more, despite the Jewish plight under Hitler's yoke. But Aliyah Bet, the "illegal immigration," never stopped, and many Jews came to Israel bravely facing the dangers of the voyage, British internment and sometimes the mortal risk of being returned to Hitler's camps. But in 1948, after the adoption of the United Nations Partition Plan, and after the War of Emancipation, the new State of Israel was born. Today the various Zionist organizations are helping in the rebuilding of the new Israel.

ZIONIST ARCHIVES AND LIBRARY

The Library was established in 1939 and serves as an information center for all phases of life in Israel and other Middle Eastern countries as well as for Zionism and Judaism. Today its collection numbers approximately 45,000 books and pamphlets; over 400 periodicals and newspapers in all languages received from all parts of the world; 25,000 photographs; 140 reels of microfilm which is steadily increasing through its own microfilming efforts on the premises; non-musical and musical recordings, Israeli symphonic scores, folk music, maps and historical films. It has an extensive archival collection rich in letters, documents, minutes of meetings, including material from the Herzl, Gottheil, Brandeis, De Haas and Friedenwald archives as well as from the National Archives in Washington, D.C. and the Roosevelt collection in Hyde Park. An intrinsic part of the services of the Library is furnishing special bibliographies for specific projects, implemented by lending material throughout the country on inter-library loan. Special exhibits are also set up and material is lent throughout the country for this purpose.

ZIONIST CONGRESS

Conferences of the Zionist movement. The first Zionist Congress was convened by Theodor Herzl in 1897, in Basle; the twenty-fifth met in Jerusalem in 1961. The Congress decides the budget of the organization, and fixes its policies. Memorable congresses were those of 1901, which established the Jewish National Fund; 1903 and 1905, which discussed the Uganda Plan; and 1921, which elected Dr. Chaim Weizmann president of the Zionist movement. Delegates to the congress are elected by the vote of *shekel* purchasers.

ZIPPORAH

Shepherdess, daughter of Jethro the Kenite priest of Midian. She became the wife of Moses when he found refuge with Jethro in Midian, after slaying an Egyptian taskmaster. Zipporah bore Moses two sons, Gershom and Eliezer.

ZOAR

The only one of the five Cities of the Plain, in the Dead Sea region, saved from destruction. It was saved for Lot's sake who found refuge there. Zoar was a town in Moab.

See also Cities of the Plain.

ZOHAR

("Bright light") major book of the Kabbalah, appeared first in Spain in the 13th century. Its author was probably Moses ben Shemtov de Leon, though it has been ascribed to Rabbi Simeon bar Yohai, famous Palestinian mystic scholar of the 2nd century C.E. The *Zohar* contains the central teachings of Jewish mysticism.

See also Kabbalah.

ZOLA, EMILE

(1840-1902)—French author. In literary history, Zola is famous as an early exponent of "naturalism." Alfred Dreyfus' conviction for treason, which Zola considered unjust, spurred him to the writing of *J'accuse* (I accuse) in Jan. 1898, in Dreyfus' defense. The pamphlet caused a furor throughout Europe, and Zola was forced to flee to England to escape imprisonment.

Emile Zola.

ZUGOT

("Pairs") the two scholarly religious leaders who presided over the Great Sanhedrin; the Nasi (who was head of the Sanhedrin and presided over its legislative sessions) and the Av Bet Din (who presided over its legal sessions). Five successive Zugot carried on the traditions of study and interpretation of the Torah from the period of the *Soferim* to that of the *Tannaim*. The last and best known of the Zugot were Hillel and Shammai. Some of their teachings came down through the Tannaim and were recorded in the Mishnah. After Hillel, the office of Av Bet Din was either dissolved or held by the Nasi himself.

See also Sanhedrin.

ZUNZ, LEOPOLD

(1794-1886)—German scholar. One of the founders of the Wissenschaft des Judentums, Zunz was the first scholar to apply the scientific and critical methods of modern historical, philological, and literary research to the study of Judaism. He made important contributions in many fields, including the study of the Mishnah, Hebrew poetry, the synagogue liturgy, and the development of the sermon. Religiously he believed that Judaism was constantly evolving and dynamic rather than static, and that genuine religious reformation must maintain the essential continuity and identity of historic Judaism.